INTERMEDIATE QUANTIFIERS

Intermediate quantifiers express logical quantities which fall between Aristotle's two quantities of categorical propositions - universal and particular. "Few", "many" and "most" express the most commonly referred to intermediate quantities, yet this book argues that an infinite number of additional quantities can be understood through a deeper examination of the logical nature of all intermediate quantifiers.

Presenting and analyzing the logical and linguistic features of intermediate quantifiers, in a fashion typical of traditional logic, Peterson presents the first account to integrate the logic and semantics of intermediate quantifiers with the two traditional quantities by traditional methods. Having introduced the basic idea of how to approach the task in Chapter 1, with heavy emphasis on the linguistic meanings and ordinary uses of English intermediate quantifier expressions, Peterson then undertakes the task of completely integrating the three basic intermediate quantities into traditional logic in Chapter 2. Drawing on the work of Robert Carnes and taking a critical look at James McCawley's grammatical analysis, the author then provides further revisions, extensions and explorations into logical inference, linguistic meaning, algebraic methods, rules of infinite-quantity syllogism to reach the conclusion that a new approach to foundations of mathematics, based on the syllogistic logic of quantifiers, is possible to produce a new explanation of classical distribution and an extension of "infinite-quantity" syllogistic to relations.

Considerable attention has been paid in recent decades to "generalized quantifiers", and this original completion of an explanation for extending traditional syllogistic logic to handle intermediate quantifiers offers invaluable insights for those studying across areas of logic, linguistics, and the philosophy or semantics of natural language.

This book is dedicated to Laura Anne

ASHGATE NEW CRITICAL THINKING IN PHILOSOPHY

The *Ashgate New Critical Thinking in Philosophy* series aims to bring high quality research monograph publishing back into focus for authors, the international library market, and student, academic and research readers. Headed by an international editorial advisory board of acclaimed scholars from across the philosophical spectrum, this new monograph series presents cutting-edge research from established as well as exciting new authors in the field; spans the breadth of philosophy and related disciplinary and interdisciplinary perspectives; and takes contemporary philosophical research into new directions and debate.

Intermediate Quantities

Logic, linguistics, and Aristotelian semantics

PHILIP L. PETERSON
Professor of Philosophy
Department of Philosophy, Syracuse University
New York, USA

Routledge
Taylor & Francis Group
LONDON AND NEW YORK

First published 2000 by Ashgate Publishing

Reissued 2018 by Routledge
2 Park Square, Milton Park, Abingdon, Oxon OX14 4RN
711 Third Avenue, New York, NY 10017, USA

Routledge is an imprint of the Taylor & Francis Group, an informa business

A Library of Congress record exists under LC control number: 99069528

ISBN 13: 978-1-138-70605-7 (hbk)
ISBN 13: 978-1-138-70604-0 (pbk)
ISBN 13: 978-1-315-20201-3 (ebk)

Contents

Preface

I did not begin to investigate the intermediate quantifiers with the aim of applying or defending the traditional syllogism of Aristotle and his medieval followers. Nothing was further from my mind. Rather, I began (over 25 years ago) by wondering about the *meanings* of the "other" quantifiers—those other than the universal and existential quantifiers of predicate logic—because of assumptions used in then current discussions in and about generative semantics. (For some early discussion about generative semantics, see my *Concepts and Language,* Mouton 1973.) It seemed to me that some of the arguments about examples depended on *mis*understanding the meanings of the natural language quantifiers—especially, in contrast to what use of those quantifiers *implied.* I return to this theme (basic meanings *versus* implications) in Chapter 3 herein. It seemed to me then that no one could be clear about what was meant by "many", for example, unless what was meant by its denial and/or negation were understood. And, of course, understanding that would require relating it to the uses of other quantifiers and to their negations and denials. I found nothing in my mind, or in the conversations and writings of others, about the meanings and logical roles of these natural language quantifiers until I began to think of them in the traditional manner—by examining appropriate affirmations, denials, contraries, contradictories, and entailments that contained the quantifiers.

The first results of the examination constitute Chapter 1 herein. So, some use of traditional concepts from the syllogism paid off with respect to getting the initial logical relations between some of these quantifiers correctly described. I might well have stopped there and used this achievement to re-examine the arguments about generative semantics that had stimulated me. However, I did not do that—and haven't done it yet. (And since generative semantics appears to be a moribund alternative in current research on generative-transformational grammars, I don't suppose I ever will re-examine those arguments.) Rather, what happened next was that I talked to Robert Carnes about these quantifiers. That conversation led to a full-scale syllogistic treatment of the three new quantities—quantities expressible in English with "few", "many", and "most", among other words and phrases. Again, what began as a curious exercise turned out to show that the traditional syllogism was very useful. For we quickly constructed a clear extension of the syllogism to cover the three new quantities—entirely within the traditional spirit. Distribution, for example, still plays a prominent role. We changed the traditional syllogism from being a two-quantity system (particular and universal) to being a five-quantity system (particular, universal, and three intermediate quantities). The complete account—*co-authored with Robert Carnes*—constitutes Chapter 2.

Speaking for myself (not for Carnes), I learned more about the basic Aristotelian syllogism while carrying out this extension than I knew about it before. I used to be a typical 20th century Anglo-American teacher of symbolic logic, the kind who gives a 20 minute lecture each semester on the syllogism—regarding it as, at best, an important achievement whose time has passed. Today, I have changed my mind. The syllogism is not merely of historical interest. For Carnes and I have shown, by *extending* it, that it has considerable value for current research. We have not defended the syllogism by answering various well-known objections to it (though I would be much more optimistic about that now). Rather, we have indirectly defended it by showing what *more* it can do —when extended in the right way. It can provide a rich foundation for our understanding of the logical nature of all intermediate quantifiers—not just "few", "many", and "most", but (as I show in Section 5 of Chapter 2, and in Chapter 4) an infinite number of additional quantities. Only a little imagination is required to see that a new approach to foundations of mathematics—based on the syllogistic logic of quantifiers (via "fractionals")—might well be possible as an alternative to the usual formal-system-with-set-theoretic-semantics foundations. As shown in Chapter 5, this defense-by-extension produces a new explanation of classical distribution (answering objections from Geach, for example). Finally, how to extend the "infinite-quantity" syllogistic to relations is treated in Chapter 6.

The challenge that results from the syllogistic treatment of intermediate quantifiers for *empirical* linguistic semantics is simply this: confirm (or disconfirm if you can) via empirical observations and analyses that sentences containing intermediate quantifiers do imply other sentences in exactly the way that the 81 intermediate syllogisms say they do (the 81 are the 105 valid 5-quantity syllogisms minus the 24 valid ones of the traditional 2-quantity syllogism). It does not appear that the meanings of natural language quantifiers *have* to be the way these syllogistic entailments predict they are. But I claim (as an empirical hypothesis) that they *are*—if all the relevant assumptions and presuppositions of the extended syllogism are honored. (Honoring these assumptions does not beg the empirical question, but only provides legitimate ground rules for testing natural language examples. One model for how to begin the empirical investigations occurs in my "Event", with Kashi Wali, in *Linguistic Analysis* 1985b, reprinted in Chapter 4 of my *Fact Proposition Event*, Kluwer 1997.) And the fact that these logical meanings *will* be confirmed for the intermediate quantifier words and phrases contributes to showing that the syllogistic framework is not only useful for characterizing the logical features of natural languages, but that the syllogism is the most (not the least) appropriate and fruitful approach to describing and explaining the "logic of natural language" today—a conclusion reached in an entirely different way by Fred Sommers in his *The Logic of Natural Language* (Oxford 1982).

Sommers defends the virtues of the traditional logic with ingenious new devices and relates it to several topics in contemporary logical research. We, on the other hand, do not defend the traditional doctrine directly (but rather presume it), nor do we make use of Sommers' innovations—not being aware of them until after we finished the basic components of Chapter 2, before his book was published. Although our account does not lean on Sommers' developments at all (and appears on the surface to be somewhat at odds with them), still the *separation* of our extension from Sommers' analysis also contributes support for the relevance of the syllogism today. For two entirely different and unrelated projects of natural language analysis hit upon the syllogism as exactly what was needed for their purposes. And they each worked—even if much is left to be done, such as combining the insights of both into a coherent super-syllogism for tomorrow.

I am very grateful to Robert Carnes for his major efforts in carrying out the research herein. I could not have devised and completed Chapter 2 alone. On the other five chapters, his advice, criticisms, encouragement, and hypotheses were also vital. I might have completed those parts alone, but not nearly so well. Mark Brown has also helped (see Chapter 2). Two linguists have been very helpful—Guy Carden in a brief conversation years ago, and more recently James McCawley. I am very pleased that McCawley could make use of Chapter 1 in his *Everything that Linguists have Always Wanted to Know about Logic* (University of Chicago Press, 1981). For it led to my thinking more clearly about meanings, propositions, and inferences (as detailed in Chapter 3)—as well as to certain criticisms of McCawley's transformational grammar rule for "there" insertion.

I am also grateful to Syracuse University for providing me with research leaves, and associated international travel grants, which were absolutely necessary for completing this research and some related investigations in epistemology and the philosophy of language. And I am grateful for permission to reprint portions of my articles to *Notre Dame Journal of Formal Logic* (in Chapter 1 and sections 5.2 and 5.4 of Chapter 2) and *Journal of Philosophical Logic* (in Chapters 4 and 5). I thank Bret Garwood, Julio Lora, and Anne Sullivan Peterson for help with the computer formatting of the text.

Some "modern logicians" have manifested an almost religious zeal in trying to quash anything in logic research which favors the traditional syllogism and/or departs from now orthodox methods of developing and analyzing formal axiomatic systems with set theoretic semantics. I have found their hostility—of *some* contemporary logicians, not all of them—truly remarkable, especially in its incompetence and irresponsibility about the actual facts of the syllogism. I do not expect this book to cure or destroy the hostility, but I do hope it will help future students to be both more open-minded logically (and philosophically too) and more competent in the history of logic as well as in contemporary linguistics. For additional details on my own, perhaps unorthodox (and rather linguistical) views on the philosophy of logic and mathematics, see my articles in *The Monist* (1986 and 1989) and *Philosophia Mathematica* (1991).

Introduction

This book presents and analyzes in a fashion typical of traditional logic, the logical and linguistic features of intermediate quantifiers. These quantifiers express logical quantities which fall in between Aristotle's two quantities of categorical propositions—universal and particular. "Few", "many", and "most" express three of these intermediate quantities in English. No previous account has integrated the logic and semantics of intermediate quantifiers with the two traditional quantities by traditional methods.

In Chapter 1, the basic idea for how to approach the task is introduced, with heavy emphasis on the linguistic meanings and ordinary uses of English intermediate quantifier expressions and on the traditional square of opposition. In Chapter 2, the task of completely integrating the three basic intermediate quantifiers into traditional logic is carried out in full. In Chapter 3, clearly differentiating logical inference from linguistic meaning (and also, propositions from sentence meanings) provides (i) a better understanding of semantic properties of some English quantifiers and (ii) some criticisms of James McCawley's grammatical analyses. In Chapter 4 , the algebraic methods for intermediate quantities, which were extended in Chapter 2 (Section 5) to fractional and proportional quantities, are further extended to modified quantifiers like "Much more than 1/2". In Chapter 5 , the rules of Chapter 2 are revised and extended to cover the infinite-quantity syllogism by relaxing the restrictions on "fractional" quantifiers and permitting any rational fraction (between zero and one) to be a quantifier. Then, the proportion expressed by rational fractions (as that is contained in the semantics of intermediate and traditional quantifiers) turns out to be what the traditional concept of distribution was aimed at (answering Geach's objections). Finally, in Chapter 6 how to extend all of intermediate quantity syllogistic systems to relations is explained.

An understanding of the traditional doctrine of the syllogism is presumed in Chapters 1 through 6. The aims adopted herein do not include fully describing and/or explaining the syllogism, nor defending it by treating its controversial features. This book is simply not a *basic* work on the syllogism. Rather, the syllogism is used in the investigations reported and, in the end, it is significantly extended. Since many logicians and linguists who might be interested in these results do not understand the syllogism very well, the following sketch is offered. It is a brief summary, then, of what is presupposed in Chapters 1-6.

After this introductory sketch of the syllogism, there is a more detailed summary of Chapters 1-6.

The Syllogism

The usual way to present the syllogism is to, first, define "categorical proposition", second, state the basic relations of negation and denial among categoricals via the "square of opposition", third, mention some other relationships of "immediate inference", and finally give some rules (e.g., the traditional six of distribution, quantity, and quality) and other tests (such as Venn Diagrams) for determining which of the 256 possible syllogistic argument forms (i.e., the well-formed argument structures) are actually valid (necessarily preserving truth from premises to conclusion). I myself prefer to present the syllogism somewhat differently—in reverse.[1]

Consider an absolutely simple sort of proposition that you might know or believe (or hope, fear, wish, or say) to be true—one with two "terms" in it. "Terms" are expressible by various "parts of speech"—nouns, verbs, adverbs, etc.—and by longer phrases as well. For the sake of initial discussion, just consider common nouns. (Many uses of verbs like "smokes", for example, can be regarded as replaceable, preserving enough sense, by verb phrases containing nouns or noun phrases that play the common noun term role—e.g., "smoker" or "one who smokes", and so "is a smoker" replaces "smokes".) For common nouns X and Y, the simplest thing to say (and, evidently, to believe, fear, hope, and/or want to know) is that X is Y—or else it is not. The idea is that you can't think or say anything (that could be or express a proposition that could be known to be true or be believed) with just one term. You combine at least two things in order to say (declare, or even believe) anything. The combining factor (to make the link, the propositional glue) is expressible with some form of the copula ("is", "are" in English).

So-called "modern logicians" might object here saying that a sentence like "Linguists exist" contains only one term, "linguists". The reply to this should be that "linguists exist" really does have two terms—"linguists" and "exists". For when we replace the verb with an appropriate noun phrase surrogate, the two terms are seen more clearly: "Linguists are existing things". Something else that modern logicians will certainly ask is whether singular terms like the proper noun "Socrates" in "Socrates is a philosopher" can equally well occur in the minimally simple two-term statements or thoughts. From Aristotle's point of view (as I understand it), the answer is no. For the purposes of this introductory sketch, I will ignore the issue of whether Aristotle's is a good answer. Also, it is not a topic addressed in this book.

Now consider that you want to defend the truth of such a declaration (or belief or knowledge claim)—one with only two terms in it, the minimal claim so to speak.[2] That is, you want to give evidence, reasons, or some justification for why it should be regarded as true. The simplest and easiest case of this is where you offer something else to be absolutely sufficient to force the initial proposition to be true. So, for

X is Y because ....

there might be some sort of filling of "......." which (i) absolutely forces "X is Y" to be true and (ii) does so in the simplest way. One way of thinking what this simplest way could be (without being too simple) was realized by Aristotle. His idea was that there could be a third thing which established the connection claimed or believed between X and Y. This third thing is what is referred to by the "middle term". So (perhaps), the simplest and easiest way to give absolutely sufficient evidence (absolutely good reasons) for X being Y is that some third thing, M, when properly understood, makes the connection (explains it, and is the reason why the X-Y connection obtains). Further, the simplest and easiest way this could occur (according to Aristotle, and I agree) is that we have exactly two other things to say or believe which are together the reason why X is Y. One of the things connects M to Y, and the other connects it to X. If these connections are really correct (this need not necessarily be obvious on the surface), then they force X to be Y.

This very strong relation between reasons and evidence and what they are reasons and evidence for (the 'forcing' of "X is Y" to be true) comes to be called, eventually, "deduction". That is, we define "deduction" so that it is the kind of relation exemplified by such reasons or evidence making "X is Y" true. The relation is one of deduction (and you can correctly "deduce" that X is Y from the two propositions containing the middle term) when and only when the supposition that the reasons are each true absolutely compels the proposition that X is Y to be true. (Classically expressed, truth is "preserved" from premises to conclusion.) And we also say we have a deductive structure which is the structure of an "argument". We then call the proposition that X is Y the "conclusion" of the argument, where the reasons or evidence, in two parts remember, are each called "premises". In the abstract, we speak of argument forms, when we are not considering any three particular terms to be filling the X, Y, and M positions. And we say that the argument (form) is "valid" if and only if the truth of the premises absolutely do require that the conclusion be true. So, the deduction of conclusion from premises is legitimate (not "fallacious") if and only if the argument is valid. Finally, we say a proposition "entails" another one if and only if the second is correctly deduced from the first.

So, we have one way to think about what the simplest and easiest way to give reasons or evidence for a simple two-term proposition (with "X" and "Y" in it) is; i.e., the reasons can be stated in exactly two other propositions, each of which contains the connection-making term "M". But this is still rather vague. For one never says or thinks (where actual common nouns do fill the "X" and "Y" slots) that X is Y without some specification of how many "X"s or how much "X" are in question. This is often tacit, of course; i.e., one says or thinks that politicians are liars, but (at least tacitly) a decision is made as to whether it is all politicians that are said or thought to be liars or whether it is some of them that are. And there are other alternatives for attaching quantity (or presuming it). For one might think that several politicians are liars, or few are, or almost-all of them are. Aristotle's decision, as I look at it, was to simplify. Don't consider all these possibilities, but rather select the smallest number which permits some interesting variations. Well, the smallest number which permits any variations at all is two. So, consider "all" and "some". In thinking or saying that X is Y, I might be thinking that all of the Xs (or all X, or every or each X) is or are Y, or I might be thinking that some X is, or some Xs are, Y. But if that is true for my conclusion, then the same holds for each premise (each participating reason for X being said or thought to be Y). It might be that some M is(are) X, and some M is(are) Y, so that these premises are absolutely sufficient (or thought to be) to make some X to be Y. Of course, these are not sufficient, as one can immediately see. But this is the kind of structure or pattern that Aristotle proposed we consider at the rock bottom of "arguing for" or justifying (with reasons or evidence) some case of X being Y in the simplest way.

Another possibility immediately arises. The pattern and/or order of the connections of the middle term to the others in the premises can vary. Perhaps all (or some) M are Y. But maybe vice versa: all (or some) Y are M. Similarly, for the second premise: all (or some) M are X, but maybe all (or some) X are M. Should we also permit such variation for the order of terms in the conclusion? In general, yes. However, it turns out that we can just ignore this variation in the conclusion because all the new cases it apparently allows do reduce, in the end, to exactly the patterns we can examine without reordering terms in the conclusion.

At this point, we have a widening range of simple argument forms (which I like to think of as forms of absolutely sufficient reasons, evidence, or justification for the truth of simple X-is-Y propositions)—as follows:

All (or some) M is Y......or......All (or some) Y is M
All (or some) M is X......or......All (or some) X is M

So, All (or some) X is Y

Any argument or deduction (or "reason-or-evidence-giving") that has one of these forms is called a "syllogism". Some of them will be valid syllogisms (the connection between premises and conclusions being deductively correct) and some not.

If you attend simply to the variations in premises due to order of terms in each, you will notice that there are only four possibilities. These possibilities are called "figures" traditionally (think of figures as "patterns" or matrices that the terms of the two premises exemplify), as follows:

M Y	Y M	M Y	Y M
X M	X M	M X	M X
Figure 1	Figure 2	Figure 3	Figure 4

All of the syllogisms so far presented (actually just syllogistic forms) contain only "affirmative" categorical propositions. No occurrence of negation or denial has yet been considered. So, this is the final source of variation beyond the first, quantity selection (universal and particular, "all" and "some" respectively), and the second, figure selection (patterns 1 through 4 just above). Again, the simplest way to do it (by all appearances) is chosen.[3] This choice is between affirmations and denials. I can affirm that X is Y, or I can deny it (ignoring quantity temporarily). It turns out that there are two basic ways I can deny X is Y. I can deny it flatly, from the "outside", so to speak—as in saying "No, it is not true that X is Y". Or, I can deny it "inside", so to speak, in saying "No, X is not Y". If the quantity in question is particular, I can claim (or think) that some (at least one) X is Y. But the two ways of denying it do not amount to the same thing—viz., "It's not the case that some X is Y", and "Some X is not Y". Similarly, for universal quantity, "It's not the case that all X is Y" (for short: "Not all X is Y") does not express the same thing (logically speaking) as "All X is not Y". (And worse, the latter in English is ambiguous—especially in written form.) Further, "Not all X is Y" seems not to be exactly the same thing (logically speaking) as "No X is Y". Aristotelians summed up all of these facts about denials and negatives in the following "square of opposition". (Hereafter, I substitute "S" for "X" and "P" for "Y" in order to use abbreviations that are both somewhat traditional and reminiscent of classical terminology—"S" for "subject term" and "P" for "predicate term".)

	affirmatives	negatives
universals	A: All S are P	E: No S are P
particulars	I: Some S are P	O: Some S are not P

This is a (so-called) square array of four propositional forms labeled A, E, I and O (by tradition), wherein the corners (A to O, I to E) contradict each other, the two members of the top row (A and E) are contraries, the two members of the bottom row (I and O) are sub-contraries, and the top of each column entails the member under it. Two propositions (or propositional forms) contradict each other if and only if the truth of one requires the falsity of the other and vice versa. A proposition p is contrary to a proposition q if and only if they cannot both be true, but they can both be false. So, "All politicians are liars" is contrary to "No politicians are liars" because they can't both be true (so that the truth of one does require the falsity of the other), but they can both be false. For it is possible, for example, that some politicians are liars (contradicting "No politicians are liars") and, at the same time, that some politicians are not liars (contradicting "All are"). (Contradictories, of course, can't both be false as well as can't both be true.) So, p is a sub-contrary to q if and only if they can both be true and they can't both be false.[4] The entailment down each column (often labeled "sub-alternation") introduces the most controversial element in the doctrine of the syllogism. In brief, it is simply the claim that if any proposition of the A form is true, then necessarily (by immediate deductive inference) one of the corresponding I form is true. Similarly, for E forms and corresponding O forms.

The controversy about the entailments rests on the question of "existential import" (for subject-terms of universals). That is, in A forms and E forms, is it presumed that some Ss exist? If it is so presumed, the entailments hold. If it is not so presumed, they don't. It is important to realize that the entailment of particular form by corresponding universal form does not require that "Some Ss exist" is entailed by "All S are P". For if the relation between the latter two propositions were entailment, then if "Some Ss exist" were to be false "All S are P" would also be false by *modus tollens*. (More strangely, in predicate logic if "Some Ss exist" is false, then "All S are P" is true!!??) Rather, the most that should be said is that if "Some Ss exist" is false, then "All S are P" is neither true nor false—an idea from Strawson (1957) which led to saying "All S are

P" presupposes, but does not entail, the truth of "Some Ss exist".[5] Thus, the entailment of "Some S are P" by "All S are P" is defended by holding that the latter presupposes (i.e., assumes but does not entail) that there are, in fact, some Ss.

Many of the syllogistic forms deemed valid in the syllogism are not valid if existential import is not honored. This is not a surprise. For existential import is a background assumption of great importance for the whole doctrine. Instead of thinking of the requirement as one of the existence of referents for the subject-terms in universal propositions, I prefer to think of existential import as the assumption, for any syllogism under evaluation, that each of its terms—the so-called subject and predicate terms (alternatively, "minor" and "major" terms) and the middle term—does in fact refer to something. In short, each term has reference (or denotes or applies to something). The terms "unicorn" and "ambrosia" do not have reference. For there exist no unicorns (and there never were any) for "unicorn" or "unicorns" to refer to. Similarly, there is no (and never has been) ambrosia for "ambrosia" to refer to (no stuff of that kind does, or ever did, exist). Existential import on those terms requires, however, that in evaluating syllogisms we pretend that each term does refer to some existing thing(s) or stuff. So, if "unicorns" or "ambrosia" occurs in a syllogism, we need to pretend there are (is) some. I do not see why this is any more difficult than pretending that some premises or other are true (in order to see if truth is preserved from premise to conclusion in evaluating an argument). But, contrary to my sanguinity, most logicians in recent times have felt very uneasy (to say the least) with the assumption of existential import.[6]

Using the traditional square to derive additional propositional alternatives *vis à vis* negation and/or denial produces more syllogistic forms. That is, each premise and the conclusion can either be affirmative or negative—where by "affirmative" is meant one of the forms of the first column in the square of opposition (A or I), and by "negative" is meant one of the forms from the second column of the square. Taking just the pattern of premise terms of Figure 1 (from above), we obtain these alternatives for syllogistic argument forms:

All (No, or Some) M are P......or......Some M are not P
All (No, or Some) S are M......or......Some S are not M

So, All (No, or Some) S are P.......or......Some S are not P

It may appear that I have left out some alternatives here; e.g., "All M are not P". Such omissions are already represented above via logically equivalent forms of them. For "All M are not P", we must first disambiguate between "All M are *not* P" and "*All* M *are* not P" (the Shakespearean pronunciation). (It is not clear that this ambiguity translates into any other language.) Then the former is not used in a syllogism as a completely legitimate categorical, but its logical equivalent, "No M are P", is. Similarly, for the latter (Shakespeareanly), which is represented by its logical equivalent, "Some M are not P". Analogously, though the same ambiguity does not arise, "No M are not P" is represented by its logical equivalence "All M are P". Obtaining these simpler equivalent forms from the slightly more complex ones is carried out by using the square of opposition judiciously and using certain rules for so-called "immediate inference" involve re-ordering and denying terms and propositions—rules of obversion and conversion. I won't go into them here. Finally, no proposition occurs in a syllogism (or is a "categorical proposition") if it has the form of a full sentence denial—e.g., "Not all S are P". However, the square of opposition can be used to substitute its logically equivalent form "Some S are not P'.

The Figure 1 alternatives for syllogisms just given amount to four alternatives for each proposition and, therefore, 64 (i.e., 4 x 4 x 4) alternatives altogether. Since there are three more figures, the total number of possibilities for syllogistic forms are 256 (4 x 64). Only a small sub-set, 24 in fact, are genuinely valid syllogisms—i.e., are cases in which the truth of the premises absolutely requires that the conclusion structure "be true" (i.e., be true when actual common nouns are inserted for subject, predicate, and middle terms place-markers). There are two very classical ways to show that any particular syllogistic form is in fact valid—and one rather classical way. (I ignore here the *Dictum de Omni*, but see Chapter 6, where it is required for relations.) The first way (very classical) to show that any particular syllogistic form is valid is to "reduce" it to one of the small number of forms that are taken to be valid intuitively or non-demonstratively (i.e., forms needing no justification)—to the so-called "perfect" syllogisms. (Aristotle says there are four of these, but as Lukasiewicz 1957 (p. 45) points out, the four can be reduced to two.) I won't go into the methods of reduction here. (See Section 4.1 of Part II herein for an illustration of reduction for the 5-quantity syllogism.) The second very classical way to determine whether a form is valid is to subject it to the following six rules (of which only four, distribution and quality, turn out to be absolutely necessary). If no rule is violated, the syllogism is valid (so the rules "filter" out the invalid syllogisms):

Rules of Distribution

R1. The middle term is distributed at least once.

R2. No term is distributed in the conclusion unless it is distributed in one premise.

Rules of Quality

R3. At least one premise is affirmative.
R4. The conclusion is negative if and only one premise is.

Rules of Quantity (dispensable)

R5. At least one premise is universal.
R6. If either premise is particular, the conclusion is particular.

To use these rules, you have to know what distribution is. But there have been continuing controversies about how to define it and whether it is a legitimate concept. Briefly, the subject-term of universal categoricals (A and E forms) and the predicate terms of negatives (E and O) are said to be "distributed". The other term positions are not distributed. In fact, we don't have to understand completely what distribution "really is" in order to use these rules to filter out invalid syllogisms. For we can consider it merely functionally; e.g., distribution is the "D-factor". Subjects of universal categorical propositions possess the D-factor, as do predicates of negative categoricals. Substitute "has the D-factor", then, for "is distributed" in Rules R1 and R2 and then that is all you need to know to use the rules, even if exactly what the "D-factor" is remains mysterious. Despite the controversies, I myself think that distribution is an interesting, and defensible, concept. I regard the basic concept to be indirectly supported (supported via the fruits of presuming it) by Carnes' extensions of it in Chapter 2, Section 2.2. In Chapter 5 , a new defense of distribution is explicitly presented—based on the achievements in Chapters 1 through 4.

The other classical (though not ancient) method of discovering which syllogistic forms are valid is to use Venn Diagrams. It is often said that Venn Diagrams do not validate all the traditionally labeled valid syllogisms, since the ones which depend upon the presumption of existential import turn out to be invalid on Venn Diagrams. Actually, they don't, if the diagrams are interpreted properly. To obtain the validation of all 24 valid forms via Venn Diagrams, it is only necessary to assume in reading a filled-in diagram (wherein the premises are already represented) that each circle actually contains a representation of some existing referent somewhere on it. So, at least one tacit "x" must be imagined to appear somewhere in each circle that does not already display an "x" via diagramming of the premises.

Summary of Chapters 1 through 6

In Chapter 1 ("On the Logic of 'Few', 'Many', and 'Most'"), the basic logic of intermediate quantifiers is shown to consist of the relationships displayable on an Aristotelian-like square of opposition—such as:

(A) Most S are P	(E) Most S are not P
(I) Many S are P	(O) Many S are not P

"Few" relates to these as follows:

(Most S are P) if and only if (Few S are not P)
(Most S are not-P) if and only if (Few S are P)

That is, "most" is interpreted (throughout Chapter 1) in the sense of "nearly all" rather than just "more-than-half". This analysis is presented and defended by describing the actual line of reasoning first used to reach these conclusions.

First, how negation works in Aristotle's approach to negation and denial is applied to English uses of "few" and "many" with a rudimentary square resulting. The senses of the English sentences and phrases are crucial to the explanation, so that it is the Aristotelian approach that is illuminated by (and illuminates) the natural language (i.e., non-stipulated) semantics of these quantifiers. "Most" (in the non-generic sense) is brought into the picture in Section 4. The crucial presupposition (parallel to Aristotle's on existential import) discussed in Section 5 is the so-called presupposition of a constant reference class. The new square for such quantifiers is integrated with Aristotle's in Section 6 (showing them to be genuinely intermediate between universal and particular), and the above developments are defended by recognizing the phenomenon of so-called quantifier-negation (a form of negation or denial previously untreated in traditional or contemporary logic).

In Chapter 2 ("The *Compleat* Syllogistic: Including Rules and Venn Diagrams for Five Quantifiers"), the traditional syllogistic is expanded to cover three more quantities (beyond universal and particular). The 105 valid forms of the 5-quantity syllogism are presented and explained in Section 1. New, but appropriately Aristotelian, rules are presented in Section 2. These rules still crucially depend on (and thereby further illuminate) distribution, and the Rules of Quantity are still demonstrably dispensable. New, but still appropriately traditional, methods for representing syllogisms on Venn Diagrams validate all 105 forms in Section 3, including those of the traditional 24 which unmodified Venn Diagrams do not validate.

The soundness and completeness of the Rules for the 5-quantity syllogistic are proved, in Section 4, in two ways—the first following the traditional method of reducing all valid forms to a subset of the traditional 24, and the second by emulating contemporary styles for demonstrating soundness and completeness of formal systems. Additional fractional quantities (starting with the contradictories of majority statements) are added to the 5-quantity system in Section 5, which leads to even higher-quantity syllogistic systems. For finite k quantities as high as you like, $s = 32k^3$ and $v = 3k(k + 2)$ where s is the number of syllogistic forms and v is the number of valid forms. Also, (i) the relationships of syllogistic (and fractional) quantifiers to integer quantifiers and straight-fraction quantifiers are specified and (ii) the relationships (and superiority) of the 5-quantity and higher-quantity syllogistic to Finch's (1957) proportionally quantified syllogism-analogues are described. As stated in Section 6, the 5-quantity and higher-quantity syllogistic is not antithetical to contemporary formal and mathematical methods, but is a propaedeutic for them and will provide indispensable data for devising empirical adequacy criteria needed for the evaluation of applications of formal systems for quantifiers to natural languages.

There are three sections to Chapter 3 ("Syllogistic Logic and the Grammar of Some English Quantifiers"). In the first section, it is shown how valid inferences between (non-linguistic) propositions are explanatorily linked to semantic properties of words, phrases, and sentences typically used to express them. Crucial to the analysis is the distinction between sentence meaning and proposition expressible in a use of a sentence. In the second section, it is explained how the many new inference patterns revealed by recent advances on intermediate quantifiers motivate hypotheses about semantic features of English quantifier expressions. The inference patterns provide new data for grammatical theory, but do not constitute a theory. The resulting semantics of "few", "many", and "most" based on the 5-quantity syllogistic shows that "few" does mean what "not many" does (following McCawley 1981, 14.1) but also shows (vs. McCawley) that "most" does not on any use or interpretation mean what "not many...not" means (even if they are logically equivalent on one reading of "most"). As a consequence, McCawley's argument (1981a, p. 428) for blocking "there" insertion in certain allegedly non-existential sentences fails.

Chapter 4 ("Complexly Fractionated Syllogistic Quantifiers") considers syllogism analogues which contain quantifiers that are modifications of straight fractions—such as "Almost 1/2 the S are P" and

"Much more than 1/2 the S are P". One attempt (Thompson 1986) to give rules for determining validity of such syllogism-analogues has failed; cf. Carnes & Peterson 1991 for proofs of its unsoundness and incompleteness. The correct way to comprehend these arguments within the approach developed in Chapter 2 involves rotating 90° the matrix of fractions embedded in squares of opposition containing modified fractional quantifiers. Some surprising results of the new algebra are: (i) the allegedly vague relation "very much greater than" (">>") can be made precise; and (ii) the strength of ">>" criterion varies inversely with "closeness" of "almost"-inferences (i.e., how close to X% of a quantity another quantity must be to be almost-X%).

In Chapter 5, the concept of distribution which Carnes developed in Chapter 2 to be at the heart of the Syllogistic Rules (of Quantity, Quality, and Distribution) is reconsidered. In the extension of the five-quantity syllogistic to systems with a specific number of quantities n (for finite n as large as you like), introduced in Chapter 2, Section 5, only the algebraic (semantical) methods were used. The same emphasis on algebraic methods continued in Chapter 4. In Chapter 5, Carnes' Rules are reformulated so that they apply to "fractional" quantity systems. After some illustrations, the new Rules (quintessentially Aristotelian in spirit) are extended to syllogisms with even more quantities (wherein restrictions over quantifier forms in "fractional" systems are relaxed) and to arguments with more than two premises and three terms. In a k-quantity syllogistic system, the "intermediate quantifiers" are any distinct ratios (between zero and one) modified with "more than" or "or more". The final system, the i-quantity system to which the reformulated Rules also apply, is produced by combining all possible k-quantity systems (where each k-quantity system contains a finite number of quantities k; e.g., for Aristotle, k = 2, for Chapter 2, k = 5). After applying these non-algebraic methods to sorites, syllogism-like inferences with quantifiers in the predicates (due to Finch, and earlier Hamilton) are analyzed. The climax of the Chapter is the discovery that the defensible concept of distribution (vs. Geach and others) just is the concept of proportion articulated in the i-quantity syllogistic.

The most efficient, accurate, and fruitful way to communicate reasonings is in natural languages. The proper way to approach the question of how human reasoning is expressed and communicated in natural languages is not via typical formal systems or analogous artificial languages, but with Aristotle's syllogistic. The syllogism is fundamental reasoning-wise via complex and complicated reasonings being broken down into syllogistic steps (as polysyllogisms, sorites, and enthymemes illustrate). A 5-quantity syllogistic gives the basic logic of "few", "many", and "most". Syllogistic systems for as many intermediate quantities as you like can be constructed, where the infinite-quantity (iQ) syllogistic is modeled on the finite higher-quantity fractional systems. To add relations to syllogistic systems, the *Dictum de Omni* (DDO) is reformulated in Chapter 6 first as DDO^P and then DDO^I is developed to cover iQ syllogisms. Finally, DDO* results from extending DDO^I to arguments wherein one or more iQ-categoricals is replaced by a (simple or complex) "basic relational categorical" (BRC). Challenges for further research on DDO* include iterations, embedded terms due to n-place relations (n>2), VP-modifiers, and other clausal NPs.

Notes

1 For an orthodox presentation of the traditional syllogism, please consult a typical logic textbook. I recommend, in particular, Angell 1964, but Copi (any edition) is satisfactory. Lemon 1971, though brief, is quite good. At bottom, I rely on Bird 1964 as absolutely authoritative. Also, see the entry "Logic, Traditional" in *The Encyclopedia of Philosophy* (P. Edwards, ed.), Lukasiewicz 1957, and Thom 1981.

2 Such a minimal two-termed proposition is called a "categorical" proposition. In the broad sense, any proposition is a categorical proposition (as is any sentence used to express it) if and only if it affirms or denies something about two categories of things (via the "glue" of the copula)—where (as explained below) the "quantity" is restricted to universal and particular (i.e., concerning all of the things or stuff or some of the things or stuff, respectively). In a narrower sense, however, categorical propositions are restricted to a subset of categorical propositions in the broad sense, the subset wherein each is in exactly the right form to occur in one of the 256 well-formed syllogistic argument patterns (as explained below). In the narrow sense, categorical propositions need to have one of the four forms which occur on the traditional "square of opposition" (about which see below). This means, among other things, that negative terms like "non-philosopher(s)" apparently can't occur. However, such negative terms can be analyzed syllogistically if we either replace the propositions they occur in with logically equivalent ones not containing the negative terms or else we completely disguise the negative term by never (in the same context) using the positive form of the term (i.e., if "non-philosopher" occurs in a particular syllogism, "philosopher" can't occur).

3 The general idea, of course, is that if we are successful in making a few variations as simple as possible, but complicated enough to obtain some non-obvious results, then

we can use this achievement as a basis for explaining anything that is still more complicated. Certainly Aristotle thought that way and it was believed for centuries that the syllogism could be used as the foundation for explaining all other possibly correct deductions or valid arguments. Aristotle turned out to be wrong, but he was close to being right. And there is some reason to suspect that if Aristotle's syllogism is understood in exactly the right way, with some new innovations, that he might be right after all; cf. Sommers 1982. (Also, see Englebretsen 1996 and Chapter 6 below.)

4 For a defense of propositional contrariety as basic (*versus* contrariety of terms), see Peterson 1995b.

5 For how this Strawsonian concept of presupposition fits together with the similarly named relationships that factives (in linguistic theorizing) stand in, see Peterson 1979b (especially, Section 2), reprinted as Chapter 3 of Peterson 1997b.

6 For details of my own views on reference to non-existing things, see Peterson 1996b.

1 “Few”, “Many”, and “Most”

1. Introduction

The traditional relations of contradictoriness, contrariness, and entailment (of universal to particular) hold for the square of opposition in (1), where (2) shows how “few” comes in.

(1)

	affirmatives	negatives
nearly universal	A Most S are P	E Most S are not P
more than particular	I Many S are P	O Many S are not P

(2) (Most S are P) if & only if (Few S are not-P)
(Most S are not-P) if & only if (Few S are P)

“Little” and “much” should be substituted for “few” and “many” respectively, when the S-term is a mass noun or abstract singular rather than a count noun. The relationships portrayed hold for “most” taken in the sense of “almost all” (i.e., the sense for which (2) does hold). The relationships do not hold for the generic sense of “most”, that wherein “Most S are P” means nothing more specific than that the number (or amount) of S that are (is) P is greater than the number (or amount) of S that are (is) not P.

These facts constitute the basic logic for “few”, “many”, and “most” in English. (I presume these facts will also obtain, with appropriate adjustments, in all other natural languages. It would be most surprising if they did not.) By ‘basic logic’ I mean the absolutely ground-level or baseline phenomena that any further logical or empirical account—such as an abstract formal system for these quantifiers with explicit (logical) semantics, or a method of natural language description incorporating semantic representations of these quantifiers—must build upon. The only purpose of this chapter is to explain and defend the claim that (1) and (2) do present the basic facts. I shall do this by describing the genesis of the claim (my actual line of reasoning that led to these results) and detailing the qualifications necessary to defend it. (The important qualification, beyond a reapplication of certain Aristotelian ones, is the presupposition of a constant reference class—i.e., no switching comparisons mid-stream, so to speak.) I shall offer, in conclusion, some comments on the relationships between these quantifiers and "all" and "some"—an integration of Aristotle's square with (1).

Realizing some of my motives should be helpful. Purely logical motives would certainly seem to be sufficient to arouse interest. For it is very unclear how the usual renditions of the first-order predicate calculus could be extended to explain the inferences expressible in English with "few", "many", and "most" in any way parallel to the way the calculus explains (in the qualified sense in which it does)[1] inferences expressible in English with "all" and "some" (and some similar expressions under specifiable conditions, viz., "every", "each", "any" "a few"). In addition, empirical motives must be recognized. The logical form of phrases containing "few", "many", and "most" is relevant to any approach to linguistic description (natural language description), but is particularly important for a transformational approach to semantic representation (generative semantics and/or 'abstract' syntax). Syntactically (in grammatical theory), "few", "many", and "most" often function in ways parallel to the functioning of quantifiers that we have a better (albeit not perfect) logical understanding. But semantically there are differences of course. What are they? How should we represent them? How far do parallels hold and how far not? Few answers to such questions are available today (at least to my knowledge).

2. Negation and Aristotle's Square

The place to begin the examination of the fundamental semantic properties of English expressions containing "few", "many", and "most" is the operation of these quantifier words with respect to simple negations—the kinds of negations that produce contradictions and contraries. Aristotle's square of opposition perspicuously introduces the fundamental (or baseline) concepts of contradiction and contrariety. There is doubtlessly more to explaining the negation and denial of expressions containing "few", "many", and "most" than merely describing the logical facts concerned with contradiction and contrariety (and closely related entailments). But these facts—what is summarized in (1) and (2)—are basic. In order to be very clear about the genesis of (1) and (2), I will review briefly what I take to be important about Aristotle's square of opposition. In English (and disregarding syntactical variations due to selection of subject and predicate term), Aristotle's four categorical proposition forms are:

(3) A: All S are P E: No S are P (All S are not P)

I: Some S are P O: Some S are not P

The A and E forms are deemed "universal" propositions and the I and O "particular". (In quantification theory, these translate into universal generalization and existential generalization, respectively.) The main point of the square format is that the corners contradict. Contradiction is the strongest "opposition" qua negation or denial that two propositions can stand in. A proposition p contradicts a proposition q if (and only if) they must have opposite truth values. If the one is true the other is false and vice versa. One alternate way of saying the same thing is that (i) they cannot both be true and (ii) they cannot both be false. In this way of looking at it, two propositions contradict each other if two conditions are met. If only one of the two conditions is met, the propositions do not contradict but they are contraries. If two of Aristotle's categoricals cannot both be true but can both be false, they are deemed contraries.[2] If two of them cannot both be false but can both be true, they are deemed sub-contraries. The A and E forms are contraries. The I and O forms are sub-contraries.

Two other features of Aristotle's square bear reviewing in order to be clear about my application of the ideas to "few", "many", and "most". First is existential import. It is necessary that the universal forms carry a *presupposition* of existential import for the entailments to their respective particular forms to hold. For example, "All Greeks are sailors" entails "Some Greeks are sailors" only if the truth of the first presupposes that there are Greeks. (In quantification theory, this presupposition of existential import is dropped and the entailments do not hold. For the kind of preliminary account of "few", "many", and "most" that seems required today it happens that following Aristotle is more fruitful than following quantification theory. This result may have some retroactive effect in serving to recommend Aristotle's approach *vis à vis* quantification theory. Of course, in other matters—e.g., relations—Aristotle's methods fail (apparently), a problem addressed in Chapter VI below.) Secondly, the entailments from universal to particular only hold if the quantifier of the particular forms is interpreted broadly or liberally. That is, "some" must be interpreted as "some or more". It carries that presupposition for the entailments to hold. (The recognition of this in quantification theory rests in the interpretation of the existential quantifier to mean "at least one, possibly more".) "All politicians are liars" does not entail "Some politicians are liars" when the latter proposition is interpreted to mean what "Some, but not more, politicians are liars" or "Only a few politicians are liars" do. But when "some" is interpreted liberally to mean "some (a few) or more", then the entailments from universal to particular hold.

To sum up, the relationships of Aristotle's square I am concerned with are the following[3]:

(4)

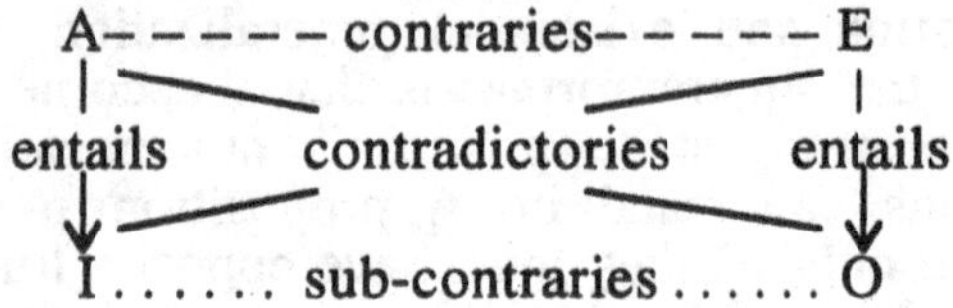

Finally, remember that the E form categorical (in English) is expressible by 'No S are P' (and close variants utilizing "no" and "none") and by "All S are not P", where the former is unambiguous and the latter ambiguous (at least in written form). Ordinary English intonations serve (or help) to disambiguate "All S is not P"—e.g., "All Greeks are not sailors" is not an English expression of an E form, but rather negation—negation *qua* contradiction—of the A form. Whereas, "All Greeks are not sailors" does express the E form (what "No Greeks are sailors" means). (The traditional logic-class example for the ambiguity is "All that glitters is not gold", which read with Shakespearean intonation is the denial of the A form—"*All* that glitters *is* not gold". To get the E form requires primary intonation on "not"—"All that glitters is *not* gold".) There is a lesson in this phenomenon. The disambiguation of a form like "All S is not P" clearly makes us aware of what the two forms of negation at issue—contradiction and contrariness—are. One is negation of the full sentence to yield contradiction. The other, contrariness, is predicate negation. In some forms (disregarding intonation clues), it is not necessarily clear which negation "not" is signifying. A corollary of this is that some useful equivalences of phrases—such as "not all" with "some...not"—may be misleading. The fact that "not all senators are honest" entails and is entailed by "some senators are not honest" does not mean that the application of "not" in the former sentence is primarily an application of it to the quantifier. For it is not. (In quantification theory one correlate of this—viz., "$\sim(x)Fx$" is logically equivalent to "$(\exists x)\sim Fx$"—can also be misleading in this regard. Taking a negation symbol 'through' a quantifier by changing it does not presuppose that full-sentence negation in fact reduces to negation of the quantifier. For it does not. Quantifier negation is another matter. I return to it below in Section 6.)

3. Negation, "Few", and "Many"

My reasoning, which led to the proposal of (1) and (2), began with simple sentences containing "few" and "many". I first treated "few" as exactly paralleling "all" in Aristotle's analysis. What is it to deny "Few S are P" in the sense of contradicting it? Particularly, contradicting it as "Some S are not P" contradicts "All S are P'. It seems obvious that "Many S are P" contradicts it. Or does it? Certainly "Few children are generous" opposes in some way "Many children are generous", but is it contradiction? Remembering that negation-*qua*-contrariness can be conceived of as predicate negation, we might retreat from seeking the contradictory of "Few S are P" and recall that the contraries in Aristotle's square derive from predicate negation. So, "Few S are not P" must (might) be the contrary of "Few S are P". (I will, hereafter, indicate predicate negation by explicitly eliding "not" with the predicate *term*—e.g., "not-P". When no such elision is indicated then the whole form may be ambiguous—though not always, e.g., "Some presidential assistant is not a liar" just does not seem ambiguous between "Some presidential assistant is a non-liar" and "It is not the case that some presidential assistant is a liar".) Then we could consider these to be parallel to the universal forms of Aristotle—A: Few S are P; and E: Few S are not-P—and the entailments to be the I and O forms. What does "Few S are P" entail? I would propose it entails "Many S are not-P", if only because that fits with the previously hypothesized contradictory of "Few S are P" to yield the following square of opposition:

(5) A: Few S are P E: Few S are not-P

I: Many S are not P O: Many S are P

The point of schematizing these forms in this way is just to construct something that might have all the relationships of (4)—contradiction, contraries, and entailments. (Note that this would probably mean that the "not" in the I form is to be taken as predicate negation.) An example does confirm (5) to some degree:

(6)
A
Few democrats are liberals
E
Few democrats are not liberals
↓ ↓
I
Many democrats are not liberals
O
Many democrats are liberals

In one particular sense of "few", the A and E sentences of (6) cannot both be true. If few democrats are liberals—not "a few", but "just a few", "only a few", or "not many"—then it cannot also be true that few are not. For if liberals and non-liberals are exhaustive categories (i.e., a democrat is either liberal or non-liberal (= not-liberal))—which I believe they are (in contrast, say, to liberal and conservative, which might not be exhaustive) then it cannot be the case (semantically speaking) that just a few (i.e., "few") democrats are liberals and just a few are not liberals. If that were the case it would permit lots of other democrats ("the rest", as we say) to be neither liberal nor not-liberal. And maybe it could be the case that few democrats are liberals and few democrats are conservative (because, say, most are something in between, called "moderates"), but that possibility does not carry over for genuine predicate negation which, I believe, is intended to express exhaustive classification.

Do the entailments hold—A to I, E to O? If few democrats are liberals, then are many (maybe most) not liberals? (Leave "most" aside, temporarily.) It seems so. Try other examples: if few politicians are honest, are many not-honest? If few citizens are well-informed, are many not well-informed? (Similarly, for the E-O entailments: if few republicans are not conservatives, are many of them conservatives; or, if few oranges are not yellow, are many oranges yellow?) To me, the answer is yes for all these cases. Could the I and O forms of (6) both be true, for that would suggest they are true sub-contraries? I believe they could. That is the point of disregarding "most". When "many" does not mean "most", then they could. If there are enough democrats (not a small number, like three or four, but a larger number, 100s or 1000s), then many could be liberals and many could not be without contradiction. What permits (5) and (6) to fully represent an application of the Aristotelian relations of (4) is that the corners be recognized to contradict—which was my initial hypothesis above. For if they do, then A and E are proper contraries (their denials could both be false) simply because their denials are the O and I forms, respectively. Similarly, for the I and O forms. They could both be true and they could not both be false, because their falsities are equivalent, respectively, to the E and A forms. Well, are these A and O forms (and E and I forms) really contradictory? I believe they are. Two observations help support the claim. First, "not many" (in English) means what, or functions like, "few" does. So, to attempt to form the contradictory of the O form by prefixing "not" to the whole proposition—exactly parallel, semantically, to doing so with an Aristotelian O form, "*NOT*-(Some Greeks are not sailors)" amounting to "It is not the case that some Greeks are not sailors" (= "All Greeks are sailors")—yields "Not many democrats are liberals". And "Not many democrats are liberals" means exactly what "Few democrats are liberals" does. Or, it does on one reading of the former, the one wherein full-sentence negation is intended. (I will return below to the possibility of such a sentence—or the denial of "Many S are (not) P", etc.—having a reading wherein the negation gravitates towards the quantifier itself.) Similarly, "Not many oranges are not-yellow" means what "Few oranges are not-yellow" means. Secondly, stripping the negation term "not" off of "not a few"—as in "Not a few democrats are liberals"—does *not* yield "a few", but merely "few". This is *very* important.[4] How does one *say* the result of applying full-sentence negation to "Few S are P", parallel to saying "Not many S are P" as a result of negating (denying) "Many S are P". "Not a few S are P" seems appropriate, so that some partial paraphrases of (6) can be

(7) A: Few democrats are liberals . . .

. . . O: Not a few democrats are liberals

just as (6), in the relevant part, can also be paraphrased:

(8) A: Not many democrats are liberals . . .

. . . O: Many democrats are liberals

The As and Os of (7) and (8) appear to contradict each other in closely analogous ways, close enough to suggest the semantic equivalences, respectively, of the As in (7) and (8) and the Os in (7) and (8).[5]

A final sort of evidence for the true contradictoriness of the corners of (5) and (6) rests in the prediction that "little" and "much" ought to function similarly, since intuitively they appear to be very close to "few" and "many". And they do. Consider:

(9) A: Little water is polluted E: Little water is not polluted

I: Much water is not polluted O: Much water is polluted

(10) A: Little humility is revealed in politics — E: Little humility is not revealed in politics

↓ (A to I) ✕ (diagonals) ↓ (E to O)

I: Much humility is not revealed in politics — O: Much humility is revealed in politics

The difference between pairs "few"-"many" and "little"-"much" seems to rest solely in the grammatical class of the S-term. If the term is a mass noun (as in (9)) or an abstract singular (as in (10)), then "little" and "much" must be used instead of "few" and "many". But the logical relationships of (4) all remain the same.[6]

Finally, with respect to (5) and its progeny, it should be realized that one of the reasons I place the two "few" sentence structures as A and E forms and the two "Many" structures as I and O forms, rather than vice versa, is the entailment relations. As represented in (5), (6), (9), and (10), the A forms entail, but are not entailed by, the I forms (and similarly for E and O). For if the entailments are ignored, *either* "Few S are P" *or* "Many S are P" might be taken as a starting point to which the two kinds of negation can be applied—analogous to two ways of negating "All S are P", one predicate-wise "All S are not-P" (= "No S are P") to get contraries and the other sentence-wise "Not all S are P" (= "Some S are not P") to get contradictories. In addition, whether the entailments held or not, the way the contraries turn out would also suggest the assignment chosen in (5) rather than its mirror-image (horizontally).

Two points, in concluding on "few" and "many". First, a mild objection can be answered—viz., why does not the square of (5) collapse in that the I and O forms *also* entail (as well as being entailed by) their respective A and E forms? The answer is simply an appeal to examples. Does "Many students are confused" entail "Few students are not confused"? They are certainly compatible, since the latter *does* entail the former. If few are not confused, many are. But if many *are* confused, then does not it follow that few are not? One answer (particularly if, at such a point, the reader feels a semantic saturation coming on) rests in remembering that *both* "Many students are confused" and "Many students are *not* confused" *could* be true together (though they do not have to be). But *when* they were, then "Many students are confused" could *not* entail "Few students are not confused", for the latter (E-form) is incompatible since contradictory to "Many students are not confused" (the I-form). Thus, there does exist a way in which "Many students are confused" *could be true* even though "Few students are not confused" *were false*. And the concept of entailment in use throughout is just that a proposition *p* entails a proposition *q* if and only if there is no possible way that (sense that, or possible world in which) *p* could be true and *q* false. But there is such a way for *p* = "Many students are confused" and *q* = "Few students are not confused".

Secondly, a consequence of (5) is that the phenomenon represented *contrasts* with the way negation operates with "all" and "some". Interpreting those quantifier words as is typical in the predicate logic amounts to bringing a negation 'through' a quantifier by changing it; viz.,

(11) "Not all ... " if and only if "Some ... not" .

or: $\sim(x)Fx \leftrightarrow (\exists x)\sim Fx$

or: $\sim(x)(Sx \rightarrow Px) \leftrightarrow (\exists x)\sim(Sx \rightarrow Px)$

$\leftrightarrow (\exists x)(Sx \;\&\; \sim Px)$

e.g., 'Not all politicians are liars" if and only if "Some politicians are not liars" (Similarly, for "Not some..." to "All...not.."; e.g., "It is false that some orators are intelligent" if and only if "All orators are not intelligent".) However, 'bringing a negation through' for "few" and "many" conceived as quantifiers analogous to "all" and "some" does not both change the quantifier to its complementary one and leave the negation to follow the changed quantifier. Rather, it only changes the quantifier. No negation is placed after the changed quantifier.

4. "Most"

Where does "most" come in? At first (even, perhaps, before proposing (5)), it might be thought that there is a square of opposition for "few" and "most" sentences, say:

(12)	A: Few S are P	E: Few S are not-P
	I: Most S are not-P	O: Most S are P

For "Few S are P" does seem to entail "Most S are not P" (similarly, "Few are not" entails "Most are") *and also* "Most S are P" seems to contradict "Few S are P" in a way that "Few S are not P" does not (i.e., maybe the distinction between contrary and contradiction is thereby captured for "few" and "most"). This is wrong. The clue to the mistake rests in noticing that the I and O forms of (12) *also entail*, respectively, the A and E forms. Thus, the distinction between contradictoriness and contrariety implied in (12) collapses! What we are left with, however, is significant. It is the *equivalence* between

"Few S are P" and "Most S are not P" and between "Few S are not P" and "Most S are not P"—for *one* sense (or use) of "most" (not the generic sense).[7] For example:

(13) "Few democrats are liberals" is equivalent to
"Most democrats are not liberals"
"Few democrats are not liberals" is equivalent to
"Most democrats are liberals"

A consequence of the equivalence of "few" and "most-not" (and "few-not" and "most") structures is that a new rendition of (5) is derivable, substituting "few" with "most" structures:

(14)

A: Most S are not P (from: Few S are P)	E: Most S are P (from: Few S are not P)
I: Many S are not P	O: Many S are P

Making this substitution provides a crucial prediction that is then confirmed—at least it is for my dialect and/or rational faculty. To me it was problematic what the negation-*qua*-contradiction of "Most S are P" (or "Most S are not P") was supposed to be. What is it to deny "Most Southerners are democrats", for example? In general, of course, it may be any number of things. One might deny it in order to assert that all Southerners are democrats. But what would denial amount to where exact contradiction is in mind? Intuitions failed me. (This is no surprise. They often do on logically interesting sentences—e.g., on whether or not "it must be necessary that 2 plus 2 is 4" intuitively follows from "2 plus 2 must be 4"). But the square of opposition of (14) predicts that "Most S are P" will have as its contradiction—what "~(Most S are P)" amounts to logically speaking—the sentence structure "Many S are not P". So test it with some examples. Could the contradictory sort of denial of "Most Southerners are democrats" be "Many Southerners are not democrats"? I believe now that it is. The 'flattest' sort of denial (negation-*qua*-contradiction) of "Most are" is "Many are not". Similarly, in the other direction. If it is false that many Southerners are not democrats, then most of them are democrats.

Now it is possible to bring in a missing elegance that Aristotle's square of opposition for "all" and "some" contains. (This detail is not nearly so important, I believe, as those discussed so far.) In Aristotle's square the members of the first column, A and I, were both affirmatives (no explicit negative present) and the members of the second column, E and O, were both negatives. And this regularity permitted the useful classification of the members of the square as universal affirmative, universal negative, particular affirmative, and particular negative. The same can be done now by interchanging the columns of (14)—which has no effect on the crucial relations displayed (contradictions, contraries, sub-contraries, and entailments). And, as a final bit of terminological simulation, I label the "Most" sentences "nearly universal and the "Many" sentences "more than particular:

(15)

	affirmatives	negatives
nearly universal	A Most S are P	E Most S are not P
more than particular	I Many S are P	O Many S are not P

(15) is preferable to both (5) and (14) for a number of reasons. First, it exactly emulates Aristotle's square for "all" and "some". Second, it permits the construction of a square like (5)—but with the columns reversed (an unimportant modification)—by recognition of the equivalences between "Few S are P" statements and "Most S are not P" statements (and, similarly, "Few are not" and "Most are"). Finally, it also permits a closer comparison of two of the three problematic quantifiers (viz., "most" and "many") with "all" and "some". For the way negation operates 'across' such quantifiers can be partially formalized in direct parallel to universal and existential quantification; viz.,

(16) (Most x) Øx <–> ~(Many x) ~Øx
(Many x) Øx <–> ~(Most x) ~Øx

(where, of course, restricted quantifiers must be introduced to defend these relationships).

5. Some Presuppositions

In addition to the train of thought that led to my claims in (1) and (2) (which I have just described above), there are two matters of immediate interest that ought to be dealt with in order to complete this account of the most basic logical features of "few", "many", and "most". First, there is the specification of some of the obvious presuppositions required to be in effect when statements are made that have the logical features I have indicated. Secondly, there is the question of the relationships of these quantifiers to others—particularly, "all" and "some". Two presuppositions from Aristotle's square carry over for (1). First is existential import. There can be some debate about Aristotle's assumption of existential import for universal categoricals just because there are two rather successful logical systems that work as well as they do precisely through dropping this presupposition. These are the method of Venn diagrams and, more importantly, first-order quantification theory (predicate logic). Remembering the Venn diagram techniques is particularly helpful, I believe, in making clear what is done in the predicate calculus. The representation of universal propositions on Venn diagrams is most easily grasped, I think, by conceiving of it as actually a representation of the denial of particular propositions (*with* existential import). One shades out a specific area to represent precisely that there is nothing 'in' it (no members of the class that the area can be taken to represent). But this is just representing a universal proposition by representing what is semantically equivalent to it—viz., the denial of the particular (particularly taken as an existential). "All S is P" represented on Venn diagrams is really a direct representation of "It is false some S is not P"—particularly when the latter is taken to be the same as "It is false there exists an S which is P". (Similarly, for the E and O forms.) This same (albeit slight) prejudice for the particular form (or existential) over the universal persists in quantification theory. The reason universal forms have no existential import is that we take them to be denials of the particular forms, particularly where the latter are interpreted to have existential import. The lack of existential import for universals, as should be well recognized, also turns on the connectives utilized (particularly, the material conditional).

But if Aristotle's A and E forms can be debated with respect to existential import, the 'nearly universal' forms of (1) and (15) do not seem to be open at all to the same discussions. For all forms appear to clearly carry existential import. "Most soldiers are (not) heroes" must presuppose or imply that *there exist* soldiers. The rather tenuous arguments that the ordinary usages of "All S are P" do not carry existential import do not apply.[8] For there is not any plausible paraphrase, subjunctive or not, of "Most S are (not) P" (or of "Few" sentences) which succeeds in even hinting at lack of presupposition of existential import. What would it be? "If there were any S, then most of them would be P"? But in such a structure, the whole matter is shifted to the consequent of the subjunctive conditional. This tends to confirm, rather than suggest an alternative to, the presupposition of existential import for "Most" sentences. (Similarly, an allegedly Belnap-inspired paraphrase, "Of the S, most of them are P", does not seem any better at loosening the obvious existential presupposition of the whole.) Indeed, both "Many" and "Most" propositions have as much (or the same) existential import as particular or existential propositions. For this reason, among others (such as confusing "few" with "a few"), there seems to have been a tendency to lump all of these quantifiers ("few", "many", and "most") with the existential quantifier "some". This is particularly true with regard to the second presumption that makes Aristotle's square work—which is as follows.

For "All S are P" to *entail* "Some S are P", the "some" must be interpreted liberally (or loosely, or 'inclusively')—to mean (approximately) "some or more", or "at least one, possibly more". If "some" is interpreted as "exactly some"—or, better (in English), "one, some, or a few, but no more"—then "All S are P" would *not* entail "Some are P". But in *one* sense it does. So, "some" must have a reading (or use, or role) distinct from meaning "exactly a few" or "some but no more". (Notice that it is the looseness of interpretation of "some" that makes Aristotle's square work out in another connection. A forms entail corresponding I forms, when "some" is loosely interpreted (similarly, E and O). But when sub-contrariness is in question, then the liberality of "some" cannot extend too far. For "some or more" might extend beyond "many" to "most" or "all"; i.e., "Some S are P" being true because "All S are P" is (because "some" permits "some or more") cannot be compatible with "Some S is not-P" (since that contradicts "All S is P"). So, the circumstances that do permit both "Some S are P" and "Some S are not-P" to both be true simply are not those that permit "All S is P" to be true.) Now the same holds for (1) with respect to "Most" forms entailing corresponding "Many"s. The latter quantifiers must be liberally (loosely, or 'inclusively') interpreted to permit the entailments. "Most democrats are liberals" entails "Many democrats are liberals" just in the sense in which "many" of the latter form is taken to mean "many or more". For if it is interpreted as 'many, but no more" (i.e., neither 'most' nor 'all'—for what is more than many except 'most' or 'all', short of counting or measuring?), then "Most S are P" cannot entail "Many S are P" (nor can the entailments hold for the negative versions). But the solution—or liberality—required is no more than what is required to defend Aristotle's entailments for "all" and "some". So, invoking the same presumption again is no departure (and what is useful and valuable for one—i.e., for Aristotle's square, which I believe is obviously useful and valuable—is useful and valuable for the other, (1)). (I return below to this topic of 'inclusiveness' of the entailed quantifier in relating Aristotle's quantifiers to those of (1) and (2).)

A final presumption that is required to support (1) and (2) is *new*—not found in Aristotle's square. It is most easily presented in answer to an objection—as follows. Take a particular example, say, "Most soldiers are abroad". Its contradictory is said to be "Many soldiers are not abroad". Well, let us test that. Imagine that we are talking of soldiers of the U.S. Army. Also, imagine that the total number of them is 1 million. To fit the example, let us stipulate that 900 thousand (give or take a few thousand, it does not matter) are abroad, and that that fact is what supports the claim expressed by "Most soldiers (of the U.S. Army) are abroad". (That is, nine out of ten are.) By (1), then, "Many soldiers (the U.S. ones) are not abroad" cannot also be true. because it is supposed to *contradict* "Most soldiers are abroad". But—and this is the objection—this is wrong! It certainly *can* be true, for it is in this case! For 100,000 soldiers are not abroad (according to the example) and even though 9 out of 10 of the soldiers are abroad, still 100 thousand are too many soldiers (viz., more than I have ever seen or can imagine viewing in a short time, say) to prohibit "Many soldiers are not abroad" from being true. For *many*—viz., 100 thousand—are not abroad. It might be that (1) holds for some collections (not too small and not too large, eggs in dozens for example), but it does not hold for large numbers. (E.g., if ten of the 12 eggs I bought today are rotten, then "Most of the eggs I bought are rotten" is true and prohibits the truth of "Many of the eggs I bought are not rotten". For ten are rotten, and that is most; but, only two are not rotten and that is *not* many.)

The objection can be answered, however. And, it is false that the objection shows that the square of (1) only holds for non-large numbers. What is required to defend (1) is the recognition of an as yet unmentioned presupposition. I shall call this ***the presupposition of a constant reference class***. It parallels in importance, I believe, the presupposition of existential import in Aristotle's square (to support the universal to particular entailments). Not only does any proposition of the form "Most S is P" presuppose that there do exist some S's—e.g., for "Most soldiers are abroad" to be true, there must *be* some existing soldiers—but further, the immediate inferences portrayed in (1) and (2) only hold if it is *presupposed* that the reference class remain the same and, thereby, *be* the size which any comparisons (tacit or not so tacit) refer to. For the example constructed it is the number of U.S. soldiers altogether—the class *with* 1 million members—that is the reference class. Nine out of ten are abroad. So, most of them are. But there are a *lot* of soldiers that are not abroad. (So, many are not?) The question is "A lot *compared to what*?" Compared to the number of U.S. soldiers that I have ever seen, 100 thousand *are* a lot. But that I submit, is evasion at best, and equivocation at worst. (Albeit a hidden equivocation, *not* perhaps ever noticed before by anybody *if* what I am presenting herein is unprecedented.) For the point of supporting a declaration of "Most soldiers are abroad" by citing the 900 thousand out of a million that are is that the sentence makes clear what the reference class is and the citation of the evidence gives us its size. Now compared to 1 million anythings (soldiers, pencils, or dollars), 100,000 *is not* many. So, if 1 million are abroad and 100 thousand are not, then it is simply not true that many of them are not abroad. For compared to the total, one-tenth of it is not many of the total. And this goes for *any* size class.

There is, of course, another sense in which "Many soldiers are not abroad" *is* true. This is when we *switch* reference classes—e.g., from all the soldiers there are, say, to the ones I have viewed in my life until now. Switching to that reference class does *support* the truth of "Many soldiers are not abroad", but in that case we are not considering exactly the same proposition, since we have changed a crucial presupposition. (That is, I will in the end maintain that propositions are distinct from sentence types and even from sentence meanings in that propositions 'contain' (*inter alia*) their presuppositions. We might have the same sentence type, with the same sentence meaning, but if presuppositions vary in the use of that sentence (*with* its meaning), then the same proposition is not necessarily expressed.) "Many soldiers—compared to all those I have ever seen—are not abroad" is simply not the same proposition as "Many soldiers—compared to all U.S. ones there are—are not abroad". And it is the latter, not the former which is at issue in (1) and (2). So, a crucial presupposition of the greatest importance for (1) has been revealed.

The easier way to defend against this objection would have been to move to (5) via (2). That is, in light of the arguments given previously "Most soldiers are abroad" is logically equivalent to "Few soldiers are not abroad" (as (2) represents). The drawback with this course is that it is too quick. It changes the issue, since it is less objectionable (it seems to me) that "Few soldiers are not abroad" contradicts (or, at least conflicts importantly with) "Many soldiers are not abroad". For either few are not or many are not, it cannot be both. But then the objection (if it is not, thereby, completely suppressed) *should* arise in the application of (2) here. Can it be true that few soldiers are not abroad (i.e., 100 thousand are not), if most *are* abroad (i.e., 900 thousand)? Well, by switching reference class—from all there are to, say, the number you have ever seen—one might well maintain (2) cannot apply. Since 100 thousand is very many more soldiers than you have ever seen (say), realizing that might cause one to balk at the truth of "Few soldiers are not abroad" (since 100 thousand is so many). But of course 100 thousand is not so many soldiers compared to all there are, so the application of (2) to "Most soldiers are abroad" is legitimate when the reference class is constant (not switched).[9]

6. Integration

How do the relationships in (1) relate to Aristotle's relationships portrayed in (3)? Can the two squares be integrated? In one way, the answer is easy. For the liberality of interpretation that permits the universal to particular entailments to hold in (3) and which carries over into (1), also permits the following entailments:

(17) "All S are P" entails "Most S are P" which entails "Many S are P" which entails "Some S are P"

(Similarly, for the negative forms of (3) and (1).) The "all" forms entail the "most" forms when "most" is taken as "most, or more". Similarly for from "Most" to "Many" (= "many or more") and "Many" to "Some" (= "some or more" or "a few or more").[10] This means that (1) and (3) can be combined as follows:

(18)

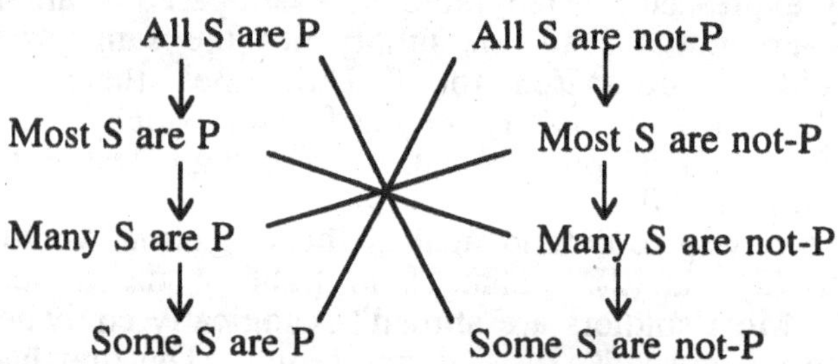

So, the square of opposition of (1) occurs 'inside of' Aristotle's. Or, Aristotle's universal forms occur 'above' the 'nearly universal' forms of (1) and his particular forms 'below' the 'more than particular' forms. None of this is surprising, especially in light of the entailments (as in (17)). What is troublesome is that (17) and (18) (or (1)) do *not* in any obvious way easily combine with what has been the traditional (or, 'logic-class') way of treating "many" and "most". Along with "a few" all of these quantifier words (except "all" and other genuine universal quantifiers) would have been grouped together and Aristotle's square would have merely been modified to appear:

(19)

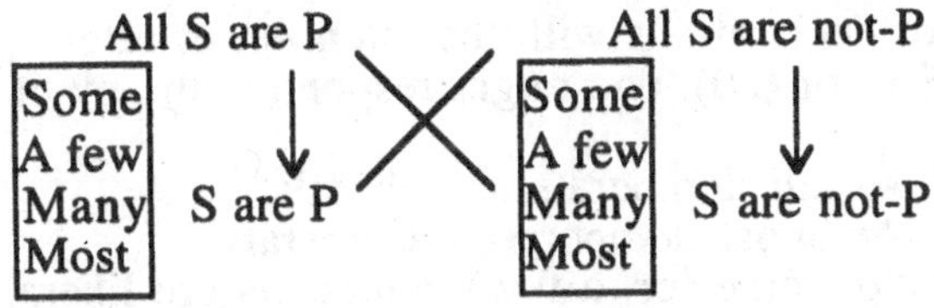

This rendition of the relationships would be particularly well supported by the liberal (or 'inclusive') interpretation of the existential (particular) quantifier "some". Universal forms entail their corresponding particulars just because "some" is taken as "some *or more*". And the latter liberality includes, thereby, other non-universal quantifiers like "a few", "many", and "most". And since that is the case, not only is "Some S are not-P" the contradictory of "All S are P", but so (e.g.) is "Most S are P".

How can the obvious incompatibilities of (18) and (19) be resolved? Can, for example, "Most atheists are not fools" contradict "All atheists are fools" (via (19)) and also contradict "Many atheists are fools" (via (1))? Before directly addressing this issue, a different source of perplexities should be noted. What can confuse the discussion at this point (and may have already above somewhere) is an application of negation or denial to quantified propositions that is neither full sentence negation (yielding contradiction) nor predicate negation (producing contraries). And an important case of this kind I have in mind I shall call "*quantifier* negation". The phenomenon is most easily revealed in considering negative replies to relevant declaration—e.g., "No!" said in response to any of the following:

(20) "Many democrats are liberals"
(21) "Most politicians are liars"
(22) "All citizens are well-informed"

One might, by disagreeing through saying "No" to the first, follow with the supporting declaration that is contradictory—viz., "Most democrats are not liberals" (or, equivalently, "Few democrats are liberals" or "Not many democrats are liberals"). Or, similarly one might follow it with a supporting contrary like "Many democrats are not liberals" (which, since it is a subcontrary is a rather weak denial, a weaker way of supporting "No"). But there is a *third* possibility. One *might* say "*All* democrats are liberals". Notice that in what I have said only the quantifier has been changed to "all" in supporting the denial. This is *quite* different from saying "All democrats are *not* liberals". Sometimes denial pertains to the *quantifier itself* (*not* to the whole sentence as when contradiction is at issue, nor to the predicate as when contrariness is raised). So, one might object negatively to these kinds of declarations with the intention of offering an alternative quantifier. So, for (20), one might respond with any of the following:

(23) "No, all democrats are liberals"
"No, most democrats are liberals"
"No, some (or, a few) democrats are liberals"

Analogously, for (21) and (22), one might respond (respectively):

(24) "No, all politicians are liars."
"No, some (a few) politicians are liars.
(25) "No, most citizens are well-informed.
"No, many citizens are well-informed."
"No, some (or, a few) citizens are well-informed."

So, in addition to negation *qua* contradiction and negation *qua* contrary, there is quantifier negation. The rule appears to be as follows. To negate (or deny), *qua* quantifier negation, a proposition of the form

(26)

$$\left|\begin{array}{l}\text{All}\\ \text{Most}\\ \text{Many}\\ \text{A few}\\ \text{Some}\end{array}\right| \text{ S are P}$$

replace its quantifier with a distinct one chosen from the set of quantifiers, ("all", "most", "many", "some", and "a few". In other words, there exist equivalences of the following sort (where "NOTq-" represents quantifier negation):

(27)

$$\text{NOTq-(All S are P)} \longleftrightarrow \left|\begin{array}{l}\text{Most}\\ \text{Many}\\ \text{A few}\\ \text{Some}\end{array}\right| \text{ S are P}$$

$$\text{NOTq-(Most S are P)} \longleftrightarrow \left|\begin{array}{l}\text{All}\\ \text{Many}\\ \text{A few}\\ \text{Some}\end{array}\right| \text{ S are P}$$

Etc.

One should have noted that "few" has been left out of the list of quantifiers available for quantifier negation. It does not belong. Not realizing this is probably the source of many confusions about these quantifiers. To see this, pretend that it did belong. Then, a 'quantifier negation' (or 'quantifier denial') of "Many politicians are liars" could be "Few politicians are liars". But the latter, via (2), is the same (semantically) as "Most politicians are *not* liars". But that is no mere quantifier negation. It is the contradictory (according to (1)). And remembering (2), we can see (suppose?) that the *reason* "few" cannot be in the list of available quantifiers for this kind of negation is that it amounts to "most are not". So, the replacement of "Many" by "few" is no mild mannered denial like quantifier-negation, but modification of more complicated structure. It is changing the form "Many S are p " into the form "Most S are not-P", the more complicated matter that (1) deals with.

Another way to make this clear is to recognize that quantifier negation (denial) is very *weak*. The quantifier-denial of p can be quite compatible with p (like sub-contraries), but so can their denials. For example, "All politicians are liars" and "Some politicians are liars". They conflict quantifier-wise, but they can both be true and they can both be false. This appears to be the case for all combinations of the quantifiers (pair-wise) of those mentioned in (26) and (27). But addition of "few" to that list destroys the weakness of the negations (denials) and introduces the stronger denials tantamount to contradictions and contraries.

It does not appear to me that all uses of "not" of the type found in Aristotle's square or (1) and (2) can permit interpretations that indicate quantifier negation. (That is., perhaps few of those structures are ambiguous between the previous forms and quantifier negation.) Certainly, one type of English expression for denial does express quantifier negation (beyond the discourse methods of (20)-(25)), viz., "it is not the case that". "It is not the case that all politicians are liars" can certainly be ambiguous between a flat denial of "All politicians are liars" (="Some politicians are not liars") and some quantifier negation—say, "Most politicians are liars". (Also, of course, it might be interpreted as the contrary of "All politicians are liars", so that "It is not the case that all politicians are liars" is at least three-ways ambiguous). However, it seems to me that there are at least a few (difficult to specify) intonations of sentences containing "not" that admit of a quantifier-negation interpretation—say, "*Many* politicians are not liars" (distinct from "*Many* politicians *are* not liars"), such as in "*Many* politicians are not liars, *all* of them are liars".[11] Now, with this interesting sidelight clarified, how can (18) be resolved with (19)? To shorten the discussion, I will just treat the question of "All S are P" in (19) contradicting (apparently) "Some (a few, many, or most) S are not-P" in light of the complexities of the

A to O sorts of contradictions portrayed in (18). (The relevant E to I contradictions will submit to exactly the same analysis.) Further, some abbreviations will be quite useful, since so many sentence structures are considered at one time. As follows:

(28)

ALL = All S are P	ALL-not = All S are not-P
MOST = Most S are P	MOST-not = Most S are not-P
MANY = Many S are P	MANY-not = Many S are not-P
SOME = Some S are P	SOME-not = Some S are not-P

(And I will presume that "a few", as distinct from "few", is close enough in function to "some" to not make any relevant difference.)

(19) appears to conflict with (1) and (18) because (19) says that the relevant denials of ALL forms entail any of the following—SOME-not (the obvious entailment), or MANY-not, or MOST-not.[12] And (18) does not represent such facts. Further, the reverse seems to hold—that the denial of any of those listed (SOME-not, MANY-not, MOST-not) entails ALL. In other words

(29)

$$\text{not-ALL} \longleftrightarrow \left|\begin{array}{c}\text{SOME}\\ \text{MANY}\\ \text{MOST}\end{array}\right| \text{ not}$$

(where "$\longleftrightarrow$" represents mutual entailments between noted forms and full sentence denial or negation is indicated by the prefix of "not-", a convention I will continue below.) There are four cases to be examined as a result:

(30)

$$\text{not-ALL} \longrightarrow \left|\begin{array}{c}\text{SOME}\\ \text{MANY}\\ \text{MOST}\end{array}\right| \text{ not}$$

(31)

$$\text{not} \left|\begin{array}{c}\text{SOME}\\ \text{MANY}\\ \text{MOST}\end{array}\right| \text{ not} \longrightarrow \text{ALL}$$

(32)

$$\text{ALL} \longrightarrow \text{not} \left|\begin{array}{c}\text{SOME}\\ \text{MANY}\\ \text{MOST}\end{array}\right| \text{ not}$$

(33)

$$\left|\begin{array}{c}\text{SOME}\\ \text{MANY}\\ \text{MOST}\end{array}\right| \text{ not} \longrightarrow \text{not-ALL}$$

(where (31) is the 'contrapositive' variant of (30) as is (33) of (32)).

Consider (30) with respect to the MOST alternative. The full-sentence denial of ALL is certainly *compatible* with MOST-not, for the denial of ALL forms entail SOME-not and the latter could be true because MOST-not is (remember (17)). However, it does not in fact *entail* it. For there could be circumstances in which a particular proposition of the form of a denial of ALL is true and the appropriate MOST-not is false. For example, consider the not-ALL form exemplified in "It is not the case that all politicians are liars" when that proposition is true only because there is only *one* lonely politician who is not a liar (say, the mayor of Tully, N.Y.—who is not, by the way, the mayor of Cicero, N.Y.). In these circumstances "It is not the case that all politicians are liars" (on the intended interpretation, not predicate negation nor quantifier negation) is true, but "Most politicians are not liars" would be false since no more than one is not a liar. So, not-ALL forms do not *entail* MOST-not forms. (The same example yields the same result substituting "MANY" for "MOST".)

Similarly for (31), using the same example. A not-MOST-not form can be true (viz., "It is not the case that most politicians are not-liars" true, which is equivalent to "Most politicians are not-liars" false—which presume) when the relevant ALL form is false (viz., "All politicians are liars", false because of the single exception in Tully). (And the same goes through substituting "MANY" for "MOST".) So, neither (30) nor (31) are entailments for the MANY and MOST forms. Only the SOME forms hold. But the latter are simple components of the Aristotelian square already incorporated in (18). (19) is misleading to the extent that the extractions from (30) and (31) utilizing MOST and MANY do not produce the indicated entailments.

What of (32) and (33)? Consider, for example, ALL forms entailing not-MOST-not forms—say, "All politicians are liars" entailing "It is not the case that most politicians are not liars". Is there any way circumstances permit such an ALL form to be true and the relevant not-MOST-not form to be false? For the not-MOST-not to be false, the MOST-not form would have to be true. So, could (32) be falsified via some circumstances in which ALL is true and MOST-not true? There are no such circumstances. If all my coffee is stale, then it can in no way be also true that most of it is not. Likewise, if all politicians are liars then it cannot be true that most of them are not. (And not even equivocating, by taking the first "not" of "not-MOST-not" as a predicate denial to produce the relevant contrary "MOST", is of any avail. For then not-MOST-not would be equivalent to MOST. And could ALL be true while MOST is false?

Not under the 'liberal' interpretation of quantifiers where "most" means "most or more", and where quantifier negation is excluded.)

Similarly for (33). MOST-not cannot be true where not-ALL is false—e.g., that most mushrooms are not-yellow while it is false that not all of them are yellow. That would require the joint truth of "Most mushrooms are not yellow" and "All of them are yellow", which is impossible if anything is. The same reasoning holds substituting "MANY" for "MOST" in both the analyses given for (32) and (33). Again, of course, substituting "SOME" (either "some is" or "some are") affirms (32) and (33). For that result is just a part of Aristotle's square—viz., ALL entail SOME-not, and SOME-not entail not-ALL.

Should (32) and (33), as extracted from (19), be at least partial support of (19) and evidence for some shortcoming of (18)? No, for (32) and (33)—and, therefore, analogues of these I did not consider (like ALL-not entailing not-MOST)—are already accounted for in (18). Consider, for example, ALL entailing not-MOST-not. By (18) ALL entails MANY (via the intermediate MOST). But also, via (18), MANY entails not-MOST-not. Thus, by transitivity of entailment, ALL entails not-MOST-not. (Similarly, ALL entails MOST which, via (18) still, entails not-MANY-not.) Finally, ALL entails not-SOME-not via the original Aristotelian square embedded in (18). So, at last, (19) should be completely dispensed with. It is mostly misleading and where it is correct the phenomena in question are adequately captured by (18).[13,14]

Notes

1 The first-order functional calculus is not, of course, an unqualified success, but it does explain some things to some degree of satisfactoriness. And, more importantly, it serves as both (i) the main model of how logical inquiry should proceed (resting as it does on the even more satisfactory propositional calculus) and (ii) the main starting point for investigating the same or related logical phenomena

2 Also note, then, that only contradiction satisfies the truth-functional concept of denial. Negation in the propositional calculus always signifies the contradictory (not the contrary) of what is negated (i.e., oppositeness in truth-value). The contrariness sort of oppositeness can be discovered in the propositional calculus, but it is not of much explanatory value—e.g., "p & q" is contrary to "~p" (they cannot both be true, though they can both be false).

3 The importance of utilizing the Aristotelian concepts of contradiction and

contrariety cannot be overemphasized. For example, the same phenomena are at the bottom of the initial definitions for modal logic-e.g., "NEC*p*" =df. "~POSS~*p*" even though it is not usually introduced this way. Consider necessity and possibility as operators on sentences (or, as 'higher predicates') expressible, respectively, "it is necessary that..." (as the form revealing what some other occurrences of "necessarily" express) and "it is possible that..." (the revealing form for some other occurrences of "possibly"). (These uses give rise to the *de dicto* alethic modalities. Other uses of "possibly" and "necessarily" can give rise to the de re forms. which are best thought of, I believe, as species of predicate modifiers.) For any proposition "p"

A: It is necessary that p   E: It is necessary that not-p

I: It is possible that p   O: It is possible that not-p

These A and E forms cannot both be true, but can both be false (because their falsities are the truths of I and O). The contradictions represented in the corners support the axioms (or definitions) "NECp = ~POSS~p" and "POSS*p* = ~NEC~*p*". The entailments support the axioms "NECp–> p" and "p –> POSSp". (See Peterson 1995b for discussion of complications.)

4 1 am indebted to Guy Carden for making this point clear to me. Without the distinction between "few" and "a few", it seems impossible to construct a cogent square of opposition. The nature of these quantifiers is not much discussed in the logical literature; e.g., Keynes (in his *Formal Logic*, Macmillan, 1887, pp. 61-62) correctly distinguishes "few" from "a few" and goes on to relate "few" to "most" as I do below, but he does not take the crucial step of relating them to "many".

5 This relatively simple point—that "Few S are P" is logically equivalent to (in a mutual entailment with) "Not many S are P" (and, similarly, that "Not a few S are P" is equivalent to "Many S are P")—is very basic. I claim that each of the following entails its partner:

Few democrats are liberals / Not many democrats are liberals
Few soldiers are not abroad / Not many soldiers are not abroad
Not a few democrats are liberals / Many democrats are liberals
Not a few soldiers are not abroad / Many soldiers are not abroad

In sum, applying "not" to "few" produces a quantifier equivalent to "many" and applying "not" to "many" produces a quantifier equivalent to "few". I emphasize this fact for two reasons. First, on the basis of this phenomenon, I propose further that the application of "not" to either "few" or "many" not be taken simply as some sort of modification of the quantifier (analogous, perhaps, to modification of head nouns by attributive adjectives)—which might easily and plausibly be thought to be the point. Rather, the square of opposition of (5) above results from taking the application of "not" to be a negation of the whole sentence. Taking it this way is what permits (indeed requires) the interpretation of the diagonal corners of (1) to *be* contradictories.

The second reason for emphasizing the equivalences of "not a few" and "many", and "not many" and "few", is that one can with troublesome cases (see below) fall back on this phenomenon as basic. If a troublesome example can be translated into terms simply with "few" and "many", then (often) this basic phenomenon can be used as indirect evidence to help decide the case. In fact, this will happen with respect to "most" and "many". A result will be that an important presupposition about such squares will be brought to light that is fairly submerged in (1).

6 As I mentioned, statements in English of the form "All S are not P" can sometimes be ambiguous between "No S is P" and "Not all S are P"; e.g., "All that glitters is not gold". It is not clear to me that either "Few S are not P" or "Many S are not P" can have usages that produce an analogous ambiguity. But even if they did, that would not serve to refute the analysis I offer, but rather to confirm it (since ways of specifying the ambiguities are herein provided). Try "*Much* that glitters *is* not gold". Does that differ from "Much that glitters is *not* gold"? Is the former equivalent to "Not much that glitters is gold" (= "Little that glitters is gold")? Maybe. Also, note that these sentences make it clear that the criterion for use of "little"-"much" needs expanding at least slightly, since "gold" (the mass noun) is *not* the S-term.

7 Another way of looking at this is that the use of "most" under consideration is just that which can be stipulated via (2) and illustrated via examples like (13). Label this use "most-f"—the "few-not" sense of "most". Label the more generic use (or sense) "most-g" —the 'generic' sense of "most". The generic sense in "Most-g S are P" is true under the interpretation whereby the quantity (number or amount) of S that are (is) P exceeds the quantity of S that are not-P. The few-not sense is more specific. "Most-f S are P" must be interpreted as:

> The quantity (number or amount) of S that are (is) P greatly exceeds the quantity of S that are (is) not-P.

Only in this way will "Many S are not-P" be a defensible contradictory of "Most-f S are P". Let 'Q(SP)" abbreviate "the quantity (number or amount) of S that are (is) P" and "Q(S~P)" abbreviate "the quantity of S that are not-P". Then, the denial of "Most-f S are P" requires one of the following conditions to be true:

(i) that Q(SP) = Q(S~P), or
(ii) that Q(SP) < Q(S~P), or
(iii) that Q(SP) > Q(S~P).

But (iii) can hold (as the condition for the relevant denial) only if Q(SP) is not very much greater than Q(S~P). If "Most-f democrats are liberals" is contradicted, then more democrats can be liberals than not liberals only so long as it is not *too* many more. Otherwise, where "Most S are P" is taken to be "Most-g S are P", a counter example to (1), (14), and (15) can be easily devised. Of the 5 million democrats (say), let one more than half of them (viz., 2,500,001) be liberals. This would not entail that it is false that many are not (what (1), (14), and (15) require). But if one more than half is not taken as enough to make "Most-f S are P" true, then this kind of counter example is avoided. (This point may be clearer in retrospect, after reading the following sections. See note 9 for additional discussion of the interplay between the two "most"s.)

8 Especially tenuous (to me) is the part of such arguments to the effect that indicatives like "All S are P" can express something common to statement with existential import and to others without it, because (would you believe?) what the subjunctive "If it (he, she, etc.) were S, then it (he, she, etc.) would be P" expresses is what the indicative "All S are P" can sometimes be used to express. So, I tend to side with Aristotle. This need not, however, be any criticism of quantification theory, for its defense comes mainly from another direction—viz., that of its abstract and theoretical utility. Its connection to English surface structures should not be taken to be direct, but to be quite indirect—such as furnishing abstract components which together with others combine to generate (not to be) surface structures. (Cf. my *Concepts and Language* (Mouton, 1973), Chapter 1 and the Appendix.)

9 For the solution to this objection I am indebted to Anne Sullivan Peterson who pointed out to me that switching reference classes was the source of the trouble. An objection somewhat analogous to this one occurs for the distinction between "most-f" and "most-g". First, adopt the following definitions (based on notations introduced in note 7 above):

(i) Most-f S are P if and only if Q(SP) >> Q(S~P)
(ii) Most-g S are P if and only if Q(SP) > Q(S~P)
(iii) Most-f S are P entails Most-g S are P
(iv) Most-g S are P does *not entail* Most-f S are P

Now notice that if Q(SP) > Q(S~P) *and if* the difference between Q(SP) and Q(S~P) is *not small* (i.e., there is not just a bare majority of S that are P), then that alone is sufficient to make "Most-f S are P"—or, Q(SP) >> Q(S~P)—plausible. The objection to (1) in this connection is that there are circumstances in which "Most S are P" could be true but that that would not entail that "Many S are not P" is false. For example, presume that there are 700 faculty members voting in an election for collective bargaining and suppose that 400 vote in favor of it and 300 against. The difference between those faculty members in favor of it and those not is not small, viz., 100. (Also, presume that no one abstains.) So, "Most-f of the faculty are in favor of collective bargaining" is plausible. So, if it is plausible, there is some sense to admitting its truth (or an interpretation, circumstance, or possible world in which it is true). But then its truth in those circumstances would not seem to entail the falsity of "Many members are not in favor". For it is true (not false) that many members are not in favor. 300 of them are not in favor.

The solution to this objection is not so striking as that which prompted the 'presupposition of a constant reference class'. The solution is simply an appeal to borderline cases. In the example given, the borderline between an application of "most-f" and an application of only "most-g" has just not quite been reached. Out of 700 voting, a greater difference than 100 is required before "most-f" applies. And the test is via (2). If it is not the case that few members are not in favor, then it is not the case that most-f members are in favor. If the vote were 550 in favor and 150 against, then relative to 700, 150 (by some) would be regarded as few. Then, in that case "Most-f of the faculty members are in favor" would be true and would entail the falsity of "Many faculty members are not in favor" (for only 150 of 700 are not in favor and, relatively speaking, that is not many). In other words, there are two ways borderline cases about "most-f" use can arise. The first is via (2). If the S that are P exceed the S that are not, then most-f S are P if and only if *few* S are *not*. But how few (or little) is few (little) enough? The second way of looking at it is that the S that are P must exceed the S that are not by more than a slight amount. Then the question is how much more than a slight amount is required. If *both* criteria are used, there results an appropriate continuum of borderline cases. For the lower end of the first criterion (when "Most-f S are P" is in question because there are enough, or almost enough, S that are not-P to make "Few S are not-P" doubtful) appears to merge with the upper end of the second (when S that are P exceed those that are non-P by somewhat more than a small amount). For example, consider 25 pencils of which 15 are new and 10 not. Then, are most-f of the pencils new? By (2), the test is that most-f of the pencils are new if 10 of 25 count as *few*. (I do not think it does; i.e., "Few of the pencils are not new" is not true if it is 10 of the 25 that are not new.) By the second test we can ask if 5 pencils—the difference between the new ones and the not-new—is 'small' relative to the whole set (25). That is, does that excess amount to only a 'bare majority', or is it somewhat larger than that? (I think it is small, or at least not clearly not-small—5, relative to 25, is less than a fourth of them.) Change the proportions. Let 16 be new and 9 not. Is 9 'few' compared to 25? (Still I think not, but this is closer to 'few'.) Now the difference between new and not-new pencils is 7. And 7 seems (to me) even more clearly not-small relative to 25 than 5 does. So, by the second test "most-f" might apply, but not by the first (9 is not 'few' enough). The clear case (for my intuitions) is reached when we change the proportions to 17 new and 8 not. By the second test, the difference is 9. And 9 is just not small relative to 15. The other test is via (2), that few are not-new—viz., 8. Is 8 'few' relative to 25? Well, it is less than one-third. By the second test (for my intuitions) the borderline has been crossed (9 is not small relative to 25). By the first, it is almost crossed. That is 8 is 'few' enough to (perhaps) count as few of 25. (So, "Few of the 25 pencils are not-new" is plausibly true because 8 are not-new.) Where the second test gives a clear answer (a not-small difference, or no longer a bare majority), the first very nearly gives a clear answer. Therefore, the combination of both tests gives an appropriate spread of borderline cases (with varying assessments possible, doubtless a function of other interests and purposes) which, to my intuitions, accurately represents the facts about the two uses of "most"—i.e., that there is a complex series of borderline cases between (i) "Most-g S are P" where "Few S are not-P" is false, and (ii) "Most-f S are P".

10 The difference between "some" and "a few" is very slight. My intuitions are that "some" indicates more than one when the subject term is plural and one when the subject term is singular. So it is hard in English to get a form that is generic for, *or* ambiguous between, "some" meaning one and "some" meaning more than one. You cannot leave it open in English. "Some men were late" means more than one was and "Some man was late" means one was. However, "a few" (to me) signifies three or more. If exactly two men were late, then though "Some men were late" is appropriate, "A few men were late" is not. But "a few" can permit more than three. To clearly limit the number requires "few", I believe (though some of the connotation of "few" certainly transfers to "a few"). This has clear ramifications for the analysis of "only" in English, since "few" seems to function like "only a few". But this issue is a larger one than might be supposed, I believe, since accounting for "only" ought to begin through examination of its contradictories and contraries. And examination of that raises interesting perplexities revealing that "only" is not quite like other quantifiers (if it is, indeed, one at all) due to its very clear relations to the connective "only if" (as in "if and only if"). (Also, see note 11.)

11 It should be noted that quantifier-negation added to the other sorts discussed probably does not exhaust the kinds of negation or denial that such propositions can be subject to. There are probably additional types—as many as there are semantic and pragmatic features of such sentences. The next thing I would look at is the possibility that implicit logical connectives might be the subject of negation; i.e., in addition to sentence negation, predicate negation, and quantifier negation, there might be 'connective negation'. I would begin the analysis by examining "only", which functions very much like the quantifiers under discussion but which also may not be one. (For the same reason cited above—its close relation to "only if" (="if-then").)

12 (19) could be thought of as the result of inferring (ii) from (i):

(i) (All S are P) if and only if not-(Some, or many, or most S are not-P)

(ii) [(All S are P) if and only if not-(Some S are not-P)] & [(All S are P) if and only if not-(Many S are not-P)] & [(All S are P) if and only if not-(Most S are not-P)]

When viewed this way, (19) certainly appears unpromising, since the inference is fallacious.

13 In the earlier stages of the inquiry reported herein I thought there might be something to the fact that (i) could be paraphrased by (ii), but (iii) could not be paraphrased by (iv)—since (iv) consists of ungrammatical forms:

(i) Some (one, few, a few, many, two, three, etc.) S are (is) P.
(ii) There are some (is one, few, a few, many, two, three, etc.) S that are (is) P.
(iii) All (Most, Every, Each, etc.) S are (is) P.
(iv) *There are all (most, every, each, etc.) S that are (is) P.

This grammatical fact makes it appear that "most" alone (of the non-universal quantifiers) gravitates towards "all" in some important ways (e.g.. as a modifier of it perhaps). And if so, maybe there is something logically or semantically important signified by it. If there is, I do not yet see it. For one thing, the ungrammaticality of (iv) may not be so striking as it first seems, since a very slight syntactical variation does permit paraphrases of (iii) that do contain "there is (are)"; e.g.,

(v) All (Most, Every, Each, etc.) S that there are (is) are (is) P.

So, maybe the ungrammaticality of (iv) is merely a superficial phenomenon with no particularly deep consequences semantically. Concerning these phenomena, Helen Cartwright has suggested to me that

(vi) Most soldiers are abroad, but there are not many of them.

could possibly be true. I take (vi) to be an only slightly elliptical version of (vii):

(vii) Most soldiers are abroad, but there are not many of them that are.

Taken in this way (about the shorter way, see the last paragraph of this note), (vi) would appear to be a counter example to (1) at least with respect to the universal-to-particular entailments. Worse yet, it suggests that

(viii) Most soldiers are abroad, but many of them are not.

might be non-contradictory (thereby, disconfirming (1) at its heart). (I speak here of "most" in the sense of "most-f", not in the sense of "most-g". (viii) could easily be seen to be non-contradictory for "most-g". See notes 7 and 9 above.) The way out (also suggested by H. Cartwright) is to note that sentence forms (ix) and (x) need not have all the same uses:

(ix) Most S are P
(x) Most *of the* S are P (or: Most S *that there are* are P)

The form illustrated in (x) is more to -the point of what is accounted for in (1) and (2). That is, the "of the" (like "that there are" of (v)) *expresses* what is a presumption on the shorter forms in (1) and (2) (the presupposition of existential import—which, together with the presumption that S-terms be 'distributed', permits the relationships of (1) to hold). But the shorter forms might also be the (surface) forms of some distinctly different kinds of sentences (ones not permitting synonymous "of the" paraphrases). And that kind of form is what must be involved when (vii) is deemed possibly true (non-contradictory).

One way of explaining this is to suppose that a non-contradictory use of (vii) would involve reference to the 'kind' soldiers. This reference would be similar to the way one sort of use of (xi) can (or might) involve reference to a 'kind'—in particular, when (xi) can be accurately paraphrased by (xii):

(xi) All soldiers are aggressive.
(xii) Soldiers (by nature, by definition) are aggressive.

(This proposal results from another idea of H. Cartwright, though the original context for it was slightly different from this one; cf. her "Some Remarks About Mass Nouns and Plurals", abstract in *Journal of Philosophy*, vol. *LXIX*(19) , 1972, p. 680.) (vii) might be plausible, self-consistent, and consistent with (1) in roughly the same way (xiii) might be possibly true (non-contradictory):

(xiii) All soldiers are aggressive, but there are not any of them who are.

(xiii) could be possible (non-contradictory) when it expresses exactly what (xiii)' does:

(xiii)' Soldiers (by nature) are aggressive, but there are not any of them who are.

(Try "Dinosaurs are the largest mammals, but there are not any of them that are" and "Cheetahs run faster than men, but there are not any of them who do (have)".)

In a similar fashion, "Most soldiers are aggressive" might also have a use wherein the subject term is not 'distributed' (and existential import not presumed)—roughly paraphrased (say) by "Soldiers (by nature, definition, etc.) are aggressive *for the most part*". Then (vii) could be true (and not in conflict with (1)), if taken as expressing the complex claim that

(a) Soldiers are the kind of things which by nature or definition are abroad (not in their home country) *for the most part* (i.e., a few may be at home, such as in training and in 'home' offices, but if most are home and are acting in typically soldierly ways then they aren't 'soldiers' but police, revolutionaries, or something else).

and

(b) *Not many* of the soldiers that *there are* are aggressive because (say) there do not exist many (or any) soldiers altogether.

That is, there is a superficial sense in which the contrariness relation of A and E forms in (1) can be disconfirmed by the 'counter example'

(xiv) Most soldiers are abroad & Most soldiers are not abroad (or: Not many soldiers are abroad)

when the conditions making it true are all and only those that would make true

(xv) Soldiers (by nature, etc.) are mostly abroad & Most of the soldiers that there are, are not abroad.

But that is no real disconfirmation, since it is based on an equivocation. Sentences that do not have 'distributed' subject terms (nor existential import)—those not permitting relevant "of the" paraphrases—do not disconfirm (1) since they are simply not the sentence forms (1) is intended to cover. (Whether or not those other forms, like (vii) or (xiii)', can be explained with some notion of reference to kinds, as I suggested, is not necessary to defending (1). I only mention the speculation in order to help convey the contrasts that the linguistic data seem to me to manifest.)

The other interpretation of (vi) is that shorter one in which the final clause merely asserts that not many soldiers—abroad or not—exist. On that interpretation (vi) is not even superficially at odds with (1); i.e., both "Most *of the* soldiers are abroad" and "Not many soldiers exist" could be true, for "Not many soldiers exist" is perfectly compatible with "Many of the soldiers are abroad". The 'many' and 'most' relations captured by (1) are all 'relative' quantifications. "Not many soldiers exist" is either 'absolute' or else 'relative' compared to some tacit standard—e.g., the number of presently existing humans. But if "not many soldiers exist" is true because the number is small relative to (say) the number of humans, then this proposition would be more revealingly expressed by "Not many (of the) humans (that there are) are soldiers".

14 I am grateful to *Notre Dame Journal of Philosophy* for permission to publish large portions of my 1979a in this chapter. That article was an extension and revision of an earlier paper of the same title, which was read to the Linguistic Society of America Summer Meetings, University of Michigan, Ann Arbor, August 5, 1973(!)

2 The *Compleat* Syllogistic: Including Rules and Venn Diagrams for Five Quantities (with Robert Carnes)

1. Intermediate Syllogisms[1]

In the traditional doctrine of the syllogism there are only two quantities involved—universal and particular. But additional quantifier *words* exist—"few", "many", and "most", etc.—over and above expressions for universal and particular quantity. We call these additional terms the *intermediate quantifiers* and the quantities they express the *intermediate quantities*. Further, we call certain propositions *intermediate categorical propositions*. To obtain such a proposition, simply take any traditional categorical and replace its universal or particular quantifier with an intermediate quantifier. Finally, we will call certain arguments *intermediate syllogisms*. To obtain such a syllogism, take any traditional syllogism (valid or not) and replace one or more of its categorical propositions with some intermediate categorical proposition.

Peterson (1979a)—the first published version of Chapter 1 above—showed how to begin the study of the intermediate quantifiers by defending the following square of opposition (one which occurs within the traditional square):

(1)

Almost-all S are P	Few S are P (Almost-all S are not-P)
Many S are P	Many S are not-P

Thompson (1982) extended the approach in the obvious way by (i) adding categoricals with "most" used in the generic sense (meaning merely "more than half", in contrast to Peterson who had used "most" in the non-generic sense synonymous here with "almost-all"), and (ii) devising some traditional-seeming rules for testing syllogistic validity. The complete square of opposition with contradictions, contraries, and subalternations noted, is as follows

(2)

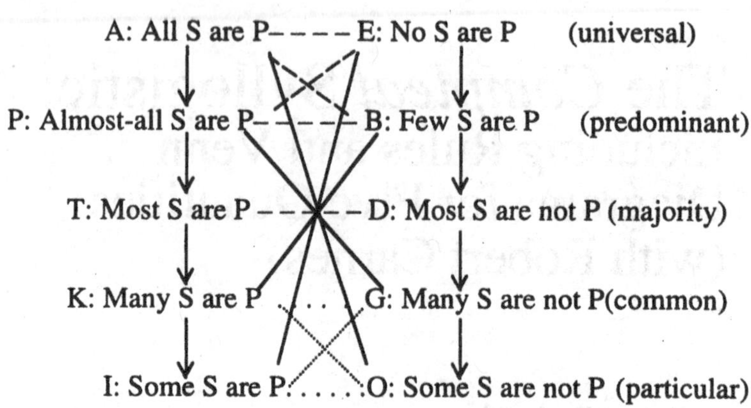

straight lines, ———, connect contradictories
dashes, – – – – – – – – – , connect contraries
dots, ... , connect sub-contraries
arrows,——>, indicate subalternations (immediate entailments)
(Cf. (18) of Chapter 1 above and Thompson 1982, Section 1.[2])

"Almost-all" and "few" statements are called *predominant* statements, "most" statements are called *majority* statements, and "many" statements are called *common* ones (*pace* Thompson, but see note 3). Each kind, of course, admits of both affirmatives and negatives (the left column and right column of (2), respectively).[3] The letters "P", "T", "K", etc. are introduced for their mnemonic value. The new letters are all consonant letters, contrasting with the vowels of the traditional square. Further, they are the simplest and most widespread consonantal stops of natural languages with point of articulation moving from front to back. The new letters for the negatives are merely the voiced counterparts of the letters for the affirmatives; i.e., B (the sound) is a voiced P sound, D (the sound) is a voiced T sound, and G (the sound, as in "go") is a voiced K sound.

The complete doctrine of the syllogism must consider, then, the 4,000 possible syllogistic arguments that result when the three intermediate quantities are added to the two traditional ones (rather than the 256 possibilities of the traditional syllogism). Thompson proposed that there are 93 valid forms—viz., the 24 traditional ones (cf. Bird 1964, 22-23) plus 69 valid intermediate syllogisms. We shall add 12 more, in Figure III. Aside from missing these 12 additional forms, Thompson's results suffered from at least three other defects—viz., his rules did not take full advantage of the traditional concept of distribution, his Rules of

Quantity were not dispensable, and there was no validation of his rules (except the sketchiest informal discussion of some examples). We shall remedy all of these defects in giving a new set of rules that adhere much more closely to the traditional model while encompassing the 12 new forms. Further, we give a new method for using Venn Diagrams to provide independent validation of the proposed 105 forms. Also, a number of other matters are cleared up along the way.

As an appropriate warm-up to these developments it is useful to take a brief look at the 69 new forms Thompson proposed to be valid (not including our 12 new forms). They are as follows, with the 24 traditional forms listed first (using Thompson's order of listing here):

(3) Valid Syllogisms:

Figure I	Figure II	Figure III	Figure IV
(The Traditional 24)			
AAA	EAE	AAI	AAI
EAE	AEE	IAI	AEE
AII	EIO	AII	IAI
EIO	AOO	EAO	EAO
AAI	EAO	OAO	EIO
EAO	AEO	EIO	AEO
(Intermediates containing majorities; i.e., "most" statements)			
AAT	AED	ATI	AED
ATT	ADD	ETO	ETO
ATI	ADO	TAI	TAI
EAD	EAD	DAO	
ETD	ETD		
ETO	ETO		
(Intermediates with majorities and commons; i.e., "most"s and "many"s)			
AAK	AEG	AKI	AEG
ATK	ADG	EKO	EKO
AKI	AGO	KAI	KAI
AKK	AGG	GAO	
EAG	EAG		
ETG	ETG		
EKO	EKO		
EKG	EKG		
(Intermediates with majorities, commons, and predominants; i.e, "most"s, "many"s, and "few"s)			
AAP	AEB	PAI	AEB
APP	ABB	EPO	PAI
APT	ABD	BAO	EPO

APK	ABG	API
API	ABO	
EAB	EAB	
EPB	EPB	
EPD	EPD	
EPG	EPG	
EPO	EPO	

The first thing to ask about the 69 intermediate forms proposed valid is: How surprising are they? What we would take to be surprising would be that intermediate syllogisms were not trivially constructed out of traditional valid forms. One way an intermediate syllogism could be considered to be trivially constructed would be that it 'reduced' to a valid traditional one—e.g., by simply identifying each intermediate quantifier with the particular one (since each is a non-universal quantifier), we could hold that substitution of the particular quantity for each occurrence of an intermediate quantity in a syllogism appropriately 'reduced' it to a traditional form. This gives us two questions: (i) Is substitution of the particular for any intermediate quantities to produce a valid traditional syllogism *necessary for* an intermediate syllogism to be valid? (ii) Is it *sufficient*? To us a surprising intermediate form would be one that did not 'reduce' to a valid traditional form, one that was thereby a counter-example to the necessity condition (i). There are no such cases on Thompson's list! A good way to get some comprehension of the whole of Thompson's list is to look for such cases.

First, define the rule for "resolving" an intermediate syllogism to a traditional one as follows:

(4) To resolve a syllogism XYZ-N, for each proposition in it,
  (i) if it is an intermediate affirmative (P, T, or K), replace it with the particular affirmative (leaving subject and predicate terms the same), and
  (ii) if it is an intermediate negative (B, D, or G), then replace it with a particular negative (leaving subject and predicate terms the same).

If we *resolve* via (4) every single intermediate form on Thompson's list, we will at most get 69 syllogisms that are all on the list of 256 possible traditional forms. Actually, what we do get—is a proper subset of the traditional 24 *valid* forms. In sum, *all* the 'resolved' versions of the 69 are valid traditional forms. This kind of resolution amounts to re-interpreting every occurrence of an intermediate quantifier as simply a particular quantifier—which is what the traditional doctrine would seem to imply ought to be done with these quantities.

What *is* interesting, however, is that there are also *invalid* intermediate syllogisms which resolve to valid traditionals. Consider Thompson's two main examples of *invalid* intermediate syllogisms (which we agree are invalid for the kind of reasons he gives—viz., models can be constructed in which the premises are true and the conclusions false):

Most M are P
<u>All M are S</u> ..... TAT-III
Most S are P

Most M are P
<u>All M are S</u> ..... TAK-III
Many S are P

Both of these 'resolve' to the same valid traditional syllogism; viz.,

Some M are P
<u>All M are S</u> ..... IAI-III
Some S are P

So, resolution to a valid traditional syllogism is *not a sufficient condition* for validity of an intermediate syllogism, though it is a necessary condition (for *Thompson's* list).

Finally, some of the intermediates seem to be quite trivial. Consider those *valid intermediate* syllogisms that have a traditional particular conclusion. (There is no valid intermediate syllogism with a *universal* conclusion.) The only difference, then, between these intermediate syllogisms and traditional ones is that one premise is an intermediate proposition. (For Thompson's list, only one premise can be intermediate, since at least one premise must be universal for the syllogism to *be* valid as in the traditional doctrine.) But given the basic relationships stated on (2) above, this single intermediate proposition does, in every such case, entail the proposition replacing it in the resolved form. That is, for some cases the only difference between unresolved and resolved forms is in one premise and in all such cases (where the intermediate *is* valid) the unresolved premise entails the resolved premise. These kinds of unresolved intermediate syllogisms might be regarded as 'constructed' by taking a valid traditional form and *just strengthening* one of its premises—e.g., "Most S are P" is logically stronger than "Some S are P". Then, of course, the constructed intermediate will also be valid, since what it was based on was valid to begin with. Roughly, the idea is that if you strengthen the premises of a valid argument, you will always get a valid argument. Where this is revealed in a resolution, we label the unresolved form *trivial.* The trivial intermediates (those with traditional conclusions and one premise that entails a premise of a corresponding valid resolved form) on Thompson's list are as follows.

(5)	Figure I	Figure II	Figure III	Figure IV
	ATI	ADO	ATI	ETO
	ETO	ETO	ETO	TAT
			TAI	
			DAO	
	AKI	AGO	AKI	EKO
	EKO	EKO	EKO	KAI
			KAI	
			GAO	
	API	ABO	PAI	PAI
	EPO	EPO	EPO	EPO
			BAO	
			API	

All of the Third Figure intermediates on Thompson's list are trivial. This leaves only 39 non-trivial intermediate syllogisms. Since none of the 39 are surprising (in the sense mentioned above), the upshot of the inquiry into intermediate syllogisms may seem rather tame. We believe the main significance of Thompson's list resides in the fact that some invalid intermediate syllogisms resolve to valid traditionals. Thus, to repeat, resolution to valid traditionals is only a necessary, not a sufficient, condition for the validity of intermediate syllogisms on Thompson's list.

This situation changes, however, when the 12 new valid forms for the Third Figure are added—namely;

(6) (Intermediates containing majorities; i.e. "most" statements)

TTI
DTO

(Intermediates with majorities, commons, and predominants; i.e., "most"s, "many"s, and "few"s)

PPI
TPI
KPI
PTI
PKI
BPO
DPO
GPO
BTO
BKO

The place to start in order to see why these 12 forms must be added is with TTI-III and PPI-III.[4] TTI-III is as follows:

(7)

Most M are P . . . . T		Figure III
Most M are S . . . . T		
So, Some S is P I		

Consider a set of Ms with 10 members, for example. If most of the Ms are P and also most are S, then at least 6 of the 10 Ms are P and 6 of the 10 Ms are S. Represent that on a Venn Diagram as follows (with each numeral appearing on a line serving to indicate that six Ms must be distributed so that that total is somehow divided among the two sub-classes represented by the areas on either side of the line):

(8)

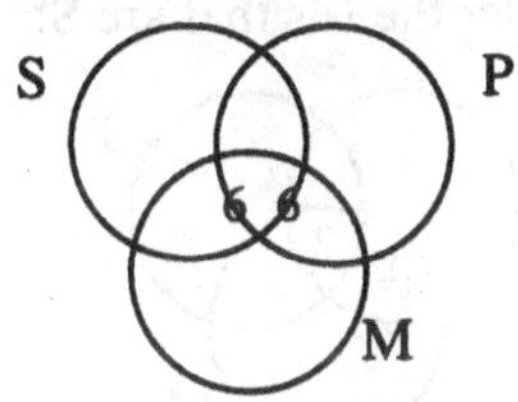

Now it is clear that the two six-membered sub-classes could not be distributed so that there are no Ms in the SPM class (the class the SPM overlap represents)—such as

(9)

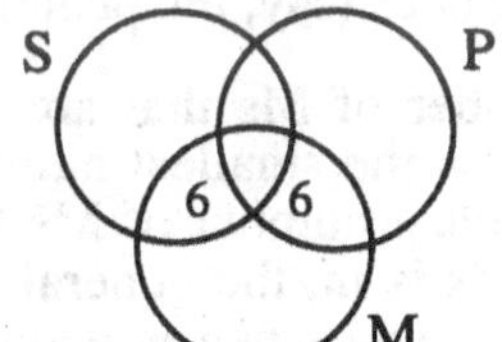

For on this distribution the total number of Ms is 12, not 10 as hypothesized. So, there is no choice but to place at least one M in the SPM class for example:

(10)

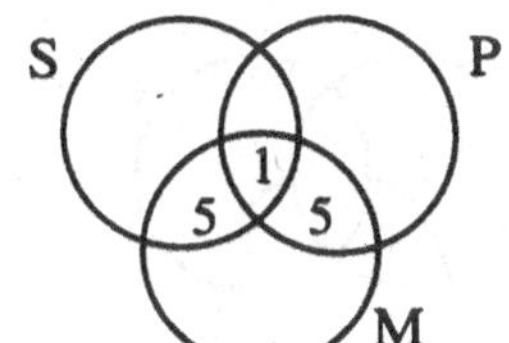

But, of course, this won't do either because according to (10) there are 11 Ms. In fact, the lowest number of Ms to be shared by the S class and the P class must be 2—i.e., the following is one proper distribution for 10 Ms satisfying the premises of (7):

(11)

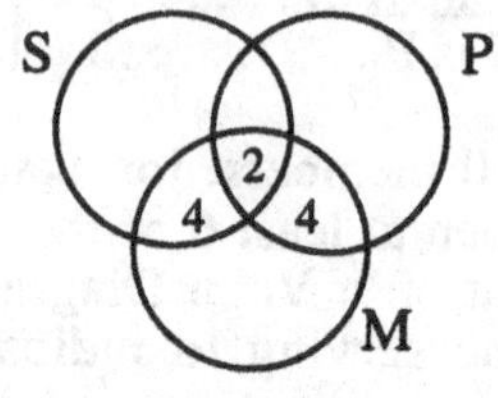

As the number of Ms are increased, the situation does not change—e.g., for 96 Ms the smallest number of Ms that are *both* S and P is still 2, *if* the Ms that are P equal in number the Ms that are S:

(12)

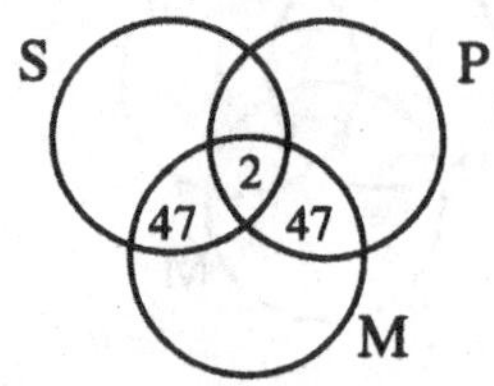

[From here on, ***underscoring***, rather than the traditional overscoring will be used to represent complementary classes or regions—e.g., "$\underline{\text{P}}$" (say, the non-poets) represents the complement of what "P" does (say, the poets).]

To obtain the smallest number of Ms that are S and P requires taking $\underline{\text{S}}\underline{\text{P}}$M to be empty. Where r = the smallest number of Ms that are P but not S which *also* is the smallest number of Ms that are S but not P, and where the total number of Ms is m, the general formula is r = (m – 2)/2 when m is even, and r = (m – 1)/2 when m is odd. If the stipulation that the size of MP equals the size of SM is dropped, then it is possible for SMP to contain only one member for all sizes of M greater than 2.

Considering smaller sets, the smallest set of Ms to which the locution "Most M are P" (or "Most M are S") can non-degeneratively apply contains only three Ms—e.g.,

(13)

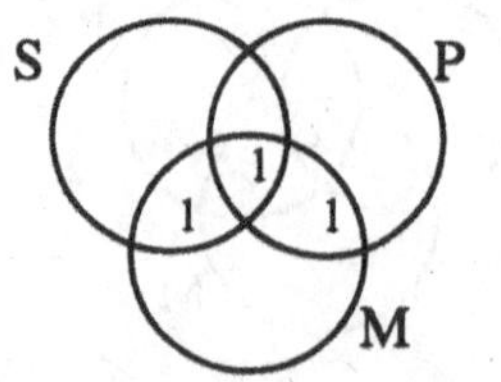

But even here there must be at least one M that is both S and P. If there are only two Ms, both premises cannot be true at the same time. Thus, sets of Ms that are smaller than three do not produce counter-examples to the claim that TTI-III is valid.

We conclude that no counter-examples of any sort to TTI-III will be found. Further, since PPI-III is just like TTI-III except that each of its premises is strengthened logically, PPI-III must be valid too. You can't turn a valid syllogism into an invalid one by simply strengthening its premises! Similarly, if only one premise in TTI-III is strengthened, the result will not be invalid either. So, PTI-III and TPI-III are valid too. Further, on the list of 12 new valid intermediates presented in (6) there are forms with particular negative conclusions and at least one intermediate negative premise. Each of these is a direct correlate of one of the other forms that consists entirely of affirmative premises and conclusion. The same sort of examples and arguments just rehearsed apply to all the negative cases, only the subclass that must share at least one member is switched from SPM to $S\underline{P}M$. Thus, in addition to the four valid intermediates with completely affirmative components on list (6), there are four more correlates of them that are valid by analogous argumentation. This leaves only four final cases to consider, the two affirmatives PKI-III and KPI-III, and the two negatives BKO-III and GPO-III. Before considering them, some consequences should be noted.

First, note that *none* of the 12 new forms on list (6) resolves to a valid traditional syllogism. Each of them resolves either to III-III or to OIO-III. So, we obtain from these 12 exactly what we originally thought would be a surprising result. That is, there do exist *invalid* traditional forms—viz., III-III and IOI-III—which can be changed into valid intermediate syllogisms (by substituting intermediate quantities for traditional ones, preserving quality). If either of these invalid forms is 'de-resolved' into one of the 12 on list (6), the result is a valid intermediate syllogism. So, it is not true that resolution to a valid traditional form is necessary (but not sufficient) for being a valid intermediate. *It is neither necessary nor sufficient!*

Second, if the 12 new forms are simply added to the lists when they are formulated in the order Thompson offers in (3), the result appears very peculiar. For all the new ones are added to his last group (intermediates with majorities, commons, and predominants). However, if we add up the numbers in each figure, we obtain a more satisfying result. The total number of valid traditional and intermediates for each of Figures I, II, and III is 30. Only 15 are valid in the Fourth Figure. Further, a much more informative style of displaying all the valid traditional and intermediate forms is as follows:

(14)

Figure I

AAA

AAP APP

AAT APT ATT

AAK APK ATK AKK

AAI API ATI AKI AII

EAE

EAB EPB

EAD EPD ETD

EAG EPG ETG EKG

EAO EPO ETO EKO EIO

Figure II

AEE

AEB ABB

AED ABD ADD

AEG ABG ADG AGG

AEO ABO ADO AGO AOO

EAE

EAB EPB

EAD EPD ETD

EAG EPG ETG EKG

EAO EPO ETO EKO EIO

Figure III

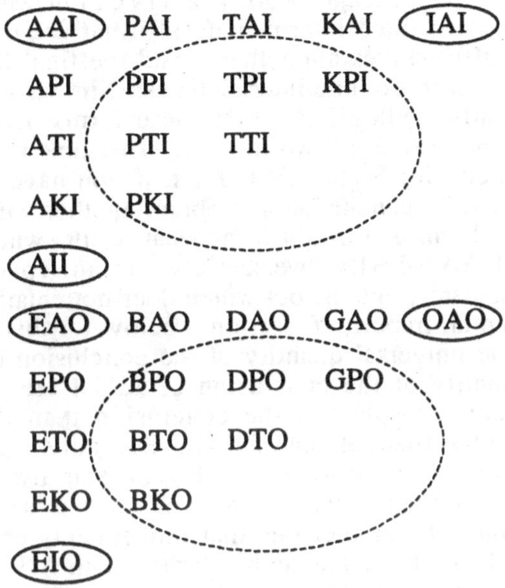

Figure IV

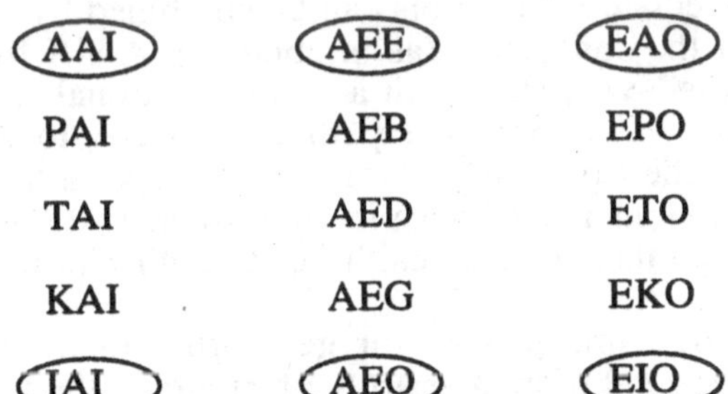

When all the valid syllogisms are arrayed in this way, the reasons why there are valid intermediate syllogisms are easily observed. First, for all figures, the intermediate valid syllogisms fall *in between* pairs of traditional 24 valid ones. In (14), each of the 24 traditional forms is circled. The valid forms in all four figures break down into forms which only have affirmative propositions in them (which we call affirmative syllogisms) and forms which do not (which we call negative syllogisms). Each of Figures I and III has three traditional affirmative syllogisms and three traditional negatives. All of Figure II are negatives, as are most of Figure IV. For each triangular array on (14), *in between* each pair of the three affirmatives, three intermediate affirmatives occur yielding nine intermediate affirmatives altogether. And the final three of each array occur in between those nine intermediates. Similarly, for the triangular arrays of negative syllogisms. *Why* these forms occur in between the others is for one or both of two reasons. (The same reasons hold, though less interestingly, for Figure IV.) First, if you have a valid syllogism, you can weaken its conclusion and obtain another valid syllogism. For example, AAI-I can be thought of as what results when you weaken the conclusion of AAA-I. (By "weaken", we mean replace it with another which it immediately entails, but which does not entail it. Of course, we assume existential import; cf. section 3 below for discussion.) However, *in between* the universal quantity of the conclusion of AAA-I and the particular quantity of the conclusion of AAI-I are three intermediate forms each being weaker in the conclusion than the preceding one (reading down the first column of (14)). Secondly, one can strengthen a *premise* (one or both) of a valid syllogism and always obtain thereby another valid syllogism. (By "strengthen", of course, we mean replace the proposition with another one that immediately entails it, but is not entailed by it.) So, for example, by starting with AII-I (in the first array of Figure 1 in (14)), we can strengthen the second premise and obtain successively valid forms (reading right to left along the bottom of the first triangular array in Figure 1). Now these *two* procedures for generating intermediate valid forms can be combined by reconceiving of the weakening of the conclusion (as in obtaining AAI-I from AAA-I) as the reverse process—viz., start with a valid traditional form and strengthen its conclusion. For then, the path from AII-I to AAA-I (along the hypotenuse of the first triangular array) can be seen to be a strengthening of both the conclusion of a valid traditional syllogism and one of its premises. (The other premise can't be strengthened because it is already universal.)

Exactly the same pattern for generating intermediate valid forms recurs in the second triangular array of Figure I (the negative forms) and in both arrays of Figure II. In Figure III the pattern is only changed slightly. First, there is no strengthening of conclusions in Figure III forms. (All such attempts turn out to be invalid.) However, there are strengthenings of one or another of the premises. First, if you start with AII-III and strengthen the second premise (working up the first column of the first array of Figure III), you reach AAI-III through three intermediate forms. If you start with IAI-III and strengthen its first premise then you reach the same form again, AAI-III, via three other intermediate forms, right-to-left across the top of the first row of the same array. However, at this point the interesting peculiarity of Figure III shows up. For it turns out that you can simultaneously increase the strength of one premise and decrease the strength of the other premise. Looked at this way, one generates AII-III from IAI-III by simultaneously increasing the strength of the first premise and decreasing the strength of the second, passing through KPI-III, TTI-III, and PKI-III. The same procedure (applied to previously generated intermediates) explains the other new affirmatives in the first array of Figure III—viz., TPI-III, PTI-III, and PPI-III. This simultaneous increase and decrease of premise strength serves to explain why all of the 12 new forms in Figure III occur. Six are affirmative forms and six are negative, those included in the dotted circles on Figure III in (14).

Figure IV does not have the interesting complexities of I-III. The first column of IV forms can be viewed simply as the successive strengthening of the first premise of IAI-IV. Similarly, the second column forms result from strengthening the conclusion of AEO-IV (or weakening AEE-IV's conclusion) and the third column results from strengthening the second premise of EIO-IV.

Now reconsider the four intermediate forms of Figure III that were not discussed above. Two of them are affirmatives—viz., PKI-III and KPI-III. And two are negatives—viz. BKO-III and GPO-III. Since the evidence is very clear that the other eight new forms of Figure III are valid, only these four remain. Our position is that, at worst, these are borderline cases.

Consider PKI-III. There are positive confirmations of this form in cases like the following. Let the class of Ms contain 50 members, of which 45 are Ps (so *almost all* of them are Ps) and 20 are Ss (so many of them are Ss, though clearly less than half are). How can we distribute these Ms with regard to the possibility of the conclusion of PKI-III being true—viz., that some S is P? To start with, then, we have:

(15)

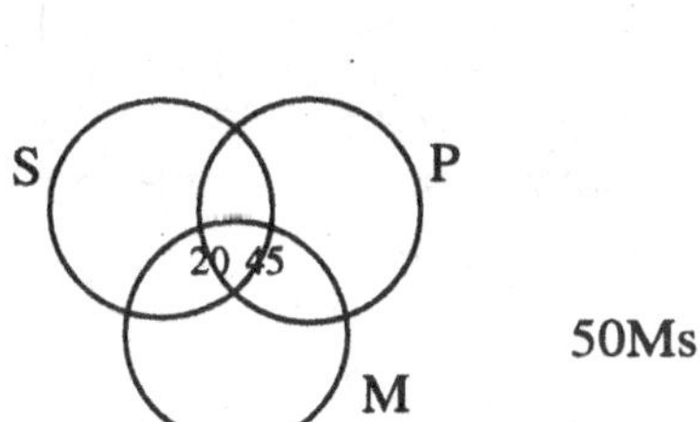

To get the smallest number of Ms that are both S and P, presume that there are no Ms that are both non-S and non-P. Then, the distribution of Ms is as follows:

(16)

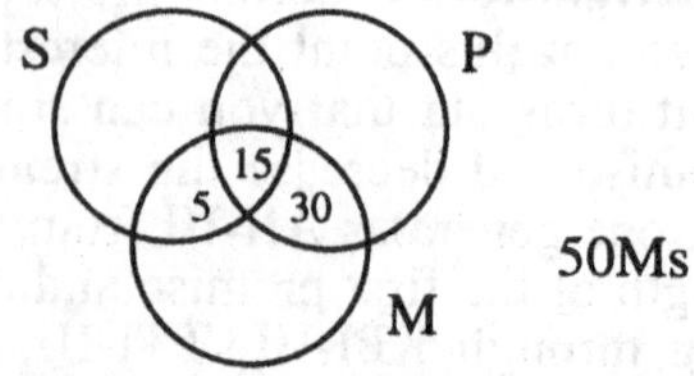

So, for 50 Ms where 45 are P and 20 are S, PKI-III is confirmed. Could we decrease the proportion that is required to make each premise true when there are 50 Ms so that SPM would be empty? If over 25% of the Ms are S (so many of them are S) and over 75% are Ps (so *almost-all* of them are P), we still get *some* Ms that are both S and P—e.g.,

(17)

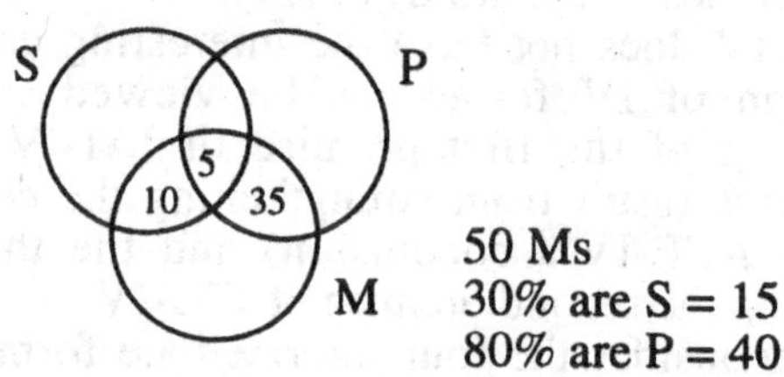

However, if we allow 20% of the Ms to count as *many* of them, then we need only 10 Ms to be S for "Many M are S" to be true. And if we maintain 80% of the Ms as Ps (viz., the previous 40 of them), then we can derive a counter-example of PKI-III with the following distribution:

(18)

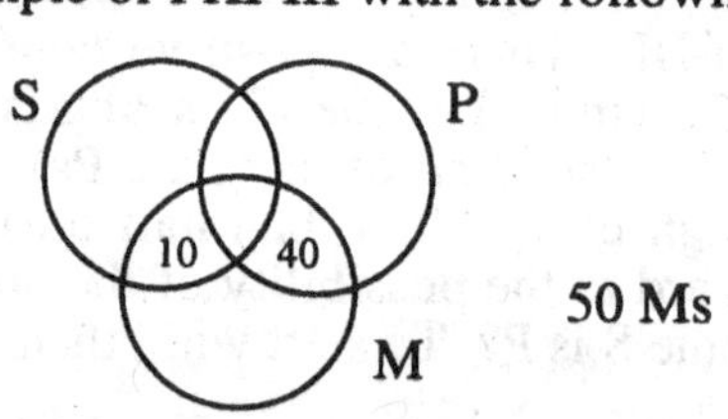

Similarly, if we keep the percentage of Ms that are S at 30%, but lower the percentage of Ms that are P to 70%i.e., 15 Ms are S and 35 Ms are P—then we obtain another counter-example to PKI-III.

(19)

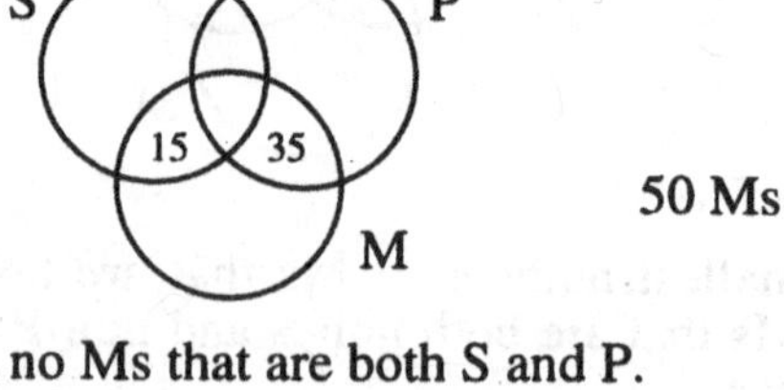

For in both (18) and (19), no Ms that are both S and P.

Doesn't this simply mean that PKI-III is invalid? We do not think so. For it is not clear that merely 70% of a set ought to count as almost-all of it, nor that 15% of a set ought to count as much of it (i.e., that many Ms are S because 15% of them are). One dividing line turns out to be exactly 25% and 75%; i.e., if (i) as few as 25% of the Ms that are S is to count as many of them and (ii) as few as 75% of the Ms that are P is to count as almost-all of them, then counter-examples to PKI-III can be obtained. We do not have strong intuitions that either of these sorts of proportions should not count as "many" cases, or "almost-all" cases respectively. But we do not have strong intuitions that they should either. Certainly some proportion equal to or less than 25% should fail to count as many. And some proportion equal to or less than 75% should fail to count as *almost-all*. But what percentages exactly? To that question we think an exact answer in isolation should be avoided. Rather, with such borderline examples, we recommend that they be allowed to remain simply borderline questions that *other* considerations can bear upon to resolve. Indeed, we think that the appropriate other consideration is which alternative—having this form, PKI-III, *in* the system (be counted as valid), *or* having it *out* of the system (be invalid)—fits into an overall method of accounting for all of the valid and invalid syllogisms. We conclude that having this form count as valid—making the decision to count this sort of borderline case as valid—fits the general account of all the traditional and intermediate syllogisms better than counting it as invalid. And this reasoning applies equally well (in exactly parallel fashion, in fact) to three other Figure III intermediate forms—viz., KPI-III, BKO-III, and GPO-III. For not only does it permit the pleasing display of the syllogisms of the first three figures given in (14)—*with* its accompanying explanation (given above) of how the intermediate forms fall *in between* pairs of traditional valid forms—but also the general syllogistic rules given in the next section (an extension of Aristotelian-style rules to intermediates) and the new method for using Venn Diagrams offered after that *both* include, rather than exclude, these forms (count them as valid rather than invalid.

Some developments inspired by Geach are useful for discussion and evaluation of all of these forms. Geach (1976) shows how to extend typical algebraic methods for evaluating syllogisms to arguments with majority propositions in them (which he calls "pluratives"). We extend his extension to cover all intermediate syllogisms. First, we adopt a Venn Diagram with sub-classes labeled as follows:

Venn Diagram Subsections:

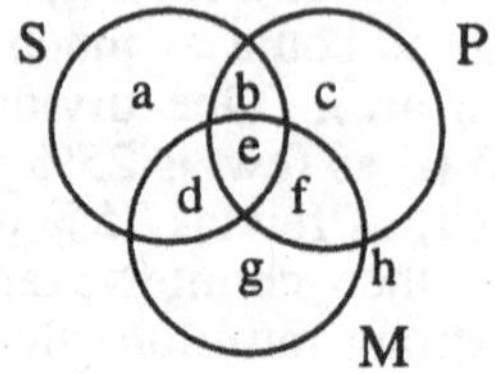

We will use this diagram for analyzing all syllogisms with the Geach-inspired algebraic method. (Geach uses rectangular diagrams, but they only amount to a notational variation of ours.) The heart of the algebraic method is to interpret each intermediate categorical as making a statement about the relative size of two sub-classes—e.g., "Most S are P" would be interpreted as claiming that $b + e > a + d$, where (since we assume existential import) $a \neq 0$ *or* $d \neq 0$. Going beyond Geach, we interpret "Almost-all S are P" as making the claim that $b + e >> a + d$ (read "b plus e is very much greater than a plus d"), where again $a \neq 0$ or $d \neq 0$. Introducing ">>" permits (via the squares of opposition relations) "Many S are P" to be interpreted as making the claim that it is *false* that $a + d >> b + e$ (where again the existential import clause is also added). We will give further examples of validating intermediate syllogisms with the algebraic method below, but now look at TTI-III and PPI-III to (i) see how the method works and (ii) thereby confirm the hypothesis that these forms should be added to Thompson's list. First TTI-III is interpreted as follows:

Most M are P . . . $e + f > d + g$	(we ignore existential
<u>Most M are S</u> . . . $d + e > g + f$	import temporarily)
So, Some S are P . . . $b \neq 0$ or $e \neq 0$	

To prove TTI-III valid, it is sufficient to show that (1), (2), and the denial of (3) lead to a contradiction:

(1)	$e + f > d + g$	premise
(2)	$d + e > g + f$	premise
(3)	$b = 0$ *and* $e = 0$ . .	denial of conclusion
(4)	$f > d + g$	from (1) and (3)
(5)	$d > g + f$	from (2) and (3)
(6)	$f > d$	from (4)
(7)	$d > f$	from (5)

contradiction

The interpretation of PPI-III looks exactly like that for TTI-III above, except that in each premise ">>" is substituted for ">". But it is axiomatic that if "X >> Y" is true then "X > Y" is also. So, the premises of TTI-III can be deduced from the premises of PPI-III and, then, the very same contradiction (as just given) can be derived.

To confirm list (6) for four of its six negative cases, via the algebraic method, consider DPO-III (using the Venn Diagram Subclasses notated as just above):

Most M are not-P . . . . $d + g > e + f$
<u>Almost-all M are S</u> . . . . . $d + e \gg g + f$
So, Some S are not-P . . . . $a \neq 0$ or $d \neq 0$

A contradiction is derived from these premises and the denial of the conclusion as follows:

(1) $d + g > e + f$ . . . . premise
(2) $d + e \gg g + f$ . . . . premise
(3) $a = 0$ and $d = 0$ . . . . denial of conclusion
(4) $g > e + f$ . . . . from (1) and (3)
(5) $e \gg g + f$ . . . . from (2) and (3)
(6) $e > g + f$ . . . . from (5)
(7) $g > e$ . . . . from (4)
(8) $e > g$ . . . . from (6)
contradiction

Finally, application of the algebraic method also supports the decision to count the four cases I called 'borderline' as valid. Consider PKI-III for example:

Almost-all M are P . . . . $e + f \gg d + g$
<u>Many M are S</u> . . . . $\sim(g + f \gg d + e)$
Some S are P . . . . $b \neq 0$ or $e \neq 0$

Proof: (1) $e + f \gg d + g$ . . . . premise
(2) $\sim(g + f \gg d + e)$ . . . . premise
(3) $b = 0$ and $e = 0$ . . . . denial of conclusion
(4) $f \gg d + g$ . . . . from (1) and (3)
(5) $\sim(g + f \gg d)$ . . . . from (2) and (3)
(6) $g + f \gg d + g$ . . . . from (4) via add g
(7) $g + f \gg d$ . . . . from (6)
contradiction

Peterson, in 1985a (p. 355), asserted that all that is needed to defend these Figure III syllogisms is the presumption that for some i and j such that $i < j$ and $i + j \geq 100$, "*Many* S are P" is true if and only if i percent (or more) of the S are P and "Almost-all S are P" is true if and only if more than j percent of the S are P. For $i + j$ can't be less than 100 on pain of PKI-III being invalid, and we have just given the algebraic *reductio* for PKI. So, $i + j \geq 100$? No, for it can*not* be that $i + j > 100$. For if $i + j > 100$, the basic square-of-opposition relations fail; e.g., no longer is "Almost-all S are not P" true if and only if "Many S are P" is false. For example, let $i = 20$ and $j = 90$ (so $i + j > 100$). Then, if only 18% of the Ss are Ps, "Many S are P" is false. But for $j = 90$ "Almost-all S are not P" is true only if more than 90% of the S are P. (Why "more than 90%" is required rather than just "90%" is discussed in Section 5.1 below.) But the condition that only 18% of the S are P requires (no more than) that 82% of the S are not-P. And this is *in*sufficient to make "Almost-all S are not-P" true (since the latter requires that more than 90% of the S are non-P). So, "($i + j > 100$)" has to be false because otherwise basic oppositions fail. And "($i + j < 100$)" has to be false because otherwise PKI-III fails (but we have proofs for it). *So*, it must be that $i + j = 100$ (exactly).

2. Rules

2.1 Distribution and Near Distribution

In the traditional doctrine, the notion of a distributed term was relative to the categorical in which the term occurred. If the O term occurred in a categorical which said something about every member of the term's extension, then the term was said to be distributed in the categorical. Otherwise, the term was said to be undistributed. So, the traditional notion of distribution is binary. There are only two choices—distributed or undistributed. Hence, subjects of universals and predicates of negatives were distributed, while all other term positions were undistributed.

We retain the traditional notion that a term T is distributed in a categorical C if and only if C says something about the entirety of T's extension. But we do not want the contrast with distribution to be merely 'undistributed. Instead, we introduce the notion of *'more nearly distributed'*. In so doing, we take the traditional notion of a distributed term as being absolute and then introduce the graduated concept of more nearly distributed to range through those positions that would traditionally have been labeled 'undistributed'.

To the traditionally distributed term, we assign the distribution index (DI) of 5. It will be the case, then, that the subjects of all universals and the predicates of all negatives will have a DI of 5. This means, in particular, that the subjects of A and E categoricals, and the predicates of E, O, B, D, and G categoricals all have a DI of 5. For the I and O categoricals, one normally assigns truth to them if at least one member of their subject term's extension belongs (does not belong, respectively) to the extension of its predicate. For this reason, we shall assign a DI of 1 to all the term positions which were traditionally labeled 'undistributed'. So, the subject of particular categoricals and the predicates of affirmatives are all assigned a DI of 1. Thus, the predicates of P, T, and K categoricals are all assigned a DI of 1. The remaining indices, 4, 3, and 2 are given to the subject terms of predominant (P, B), majority (T, D), and common (K, G) categoricals, respectively. To say that few S are P (or are not P) is to say that nearly all S are not P (are P). This gives the subject term of the P and B categoricals a very high DI—not quite all, but nearly all. Hence, the DI of 4. It seems that most S can be P (or not be P) without nearly all of them being so. Thus, the DI of the subject term for T and D categoricals must be lower than 4. But it seems, similarly, that the subject term of T and D categoricals is more nearly distributed than that of K and G categoricals. So, we assign a DI of 3 to the subject term of T and D categoricals. Finally, it seems that categoricals which begin 'many S...' more nearly distribute their subject term than do those that begin 'some S...'. Hence, we assign a DI of 2 to the subject term of K and G categoricals. There is some additional evidence for assigning the DIs in this way—namely, the whole notion of subalternation exhibits a relevant feature. If all S are P, then surely few S are not P (i.e., nearly all S are P). And if few S are not P, then surely most S are P. And so on for the rest. One seems to start out talking maximally of the subject term's extension (in universal statements) and, then, one *gradually reduces the extension of the subject to the minimum* (to reach particular statements). Hence, there is good reason to assign the DIs as summarized below.

DI=5: Subjects of universals and predicates of negatives
DI=4: Subjects of P and B
DI=3: Subjects of T and D
DI=2: Subjects of K and G
DI=l: Subjects of particulars and predicates of affirmatives

Note that the numerical indexes, 1 through 5, could easily be eliminated in favor of the relationship of more-distributed-than and the properties of distributed and undistributed; i.e., those terms with DI=5 are *distributed* and are *more distributed* than those terms with DI=4, those with DI=4 are *more distributed than* those with DI=3, those with DI=3 are *more distributed than* those with DI=2, those with DI=2 are *more distributed than* those with DI=l, and those with DI=l are undistributed.[5]

2.2 Rules of the Syllogism

Traditionally, the validity of a syllogism could be determined by the application of four rules: two involving distribution and two involving quality. For convenience, two additional rules of quantity were added, but these were derivable from the rules of distribution and quality mentioned earlier. To deal with the validity of intermediate syllogisms, we need a restatement of the rules of distribution in terms of the concept of 'near distribution' introduced in the preceding section. It will turn out that the revised rules entail the traditional rules. To see this, let us return to the beginning.

Distribution

The conclusion of every syllogism asserts a relation between S and P. These terms never occur together in the premises, hence, their relationship must be mediated by the middle term. From the traditional standpoint, in the major premise the Ms and Ps are related quantitatively (universal or particular) and qualitatively (affirmatively or negatively), and in the minor premise the Ms and Ss are so related. It should be clear that if the Ms related to the Ps are entirely distinct from those that are related to the Ss, there is no guarantee that the Ss and Ps will necessarily be related in any fashion. For example, if there are six Ms, and only the first four of them are related to P while only the remaining two are related to S, the premises do not furnish any grounds which deductively establish a relation between S and P.

It is for this reason that the rules involving validity for the traditional syllogism required the distribution of the middle term in at least one of its occurrences in the premises. For example, if M was distributed and related to P, then *all* the Ms were so related to P. In the remaining premise, the M could be distributed or not, but the Ms involved in that premise were related to S. Now since M was distributed in the first premise, *however* many Ms we talk about in the second premise, they are among those mentioned in the first premise, i.e., a redundancy has occurred. Since these latter Ms are related to S in some way and are among those related to P in some way, then S must be related to P in some way.

What we should notice here is that the premises of a valid syllogism require a redundant reference to some subclass of Ms. Again, if there are six Ms, and the term is distributed in one premise, we have talked about six Ms in that premise. Suppose M is undistributed in the remaining premise. It could be that we are talking about any number of Ms from one to six. (Being undistributed does not permit talking about *none* of the Ms, for in that case the premise would exclude the *entirety* of the M-extension. Hence, it would be saying something about all Ms, and the term would then be distributed.) If we total up the number of Ms talked about in *both* premises, we come up with more than six. But by hypothesis, there are only six Ms. The "overflow" must be those that are related both to P and to S. Hence, the relation between S and P is deductively established.

If we assigned values to distributed and undistributed terms in the classical syllogism, we could formulate an alternative but equivalent form of the rule that requires the distribution of the middle term in at least one premise which would make explicit the reliance of validity on redundancy. Say we let x be the value of a distributed term and y be the value of an undistributed term. Moreover, to achieve redundancy, $x>2y$, otherwise, two occurrences of an undistributed middle term in a syllogism could be wrongly calculated as saying something about all the Ms and as saying something about a subset of Ms as well. Using x and y as distribution indices, we could restate the traditional rule equivalently as follows:

> Rl': In a valid syllogism, the sum of the distribution indices for the middle term must exceed x.

Now this is, as we have said, equivalent to the traditional rule. For if the middle term is distributed at least once in the premises, it will have an index of x. Regardless of what index the other occurrence of M has (x or y), the sum of the indices will be greater than x. Conversely, given that $x>2y$, if the sum of the indices for M exceeds x, then at least one occurrence of M must have an index of x (=distributed). So the traditional rule and Rl' are equivalent.

What makes Rl' so insightful is its extension to distribution values *between* x and y—i.e., to values that are less than *fully* distributed, but more nearly distributed than terms traditionally labeled 'undistributed'. Such values were introduced in the preceding section of this paper. So we may now state the revised distribution rule for the middle term as follows:

> Rl: In a valid syllogism, the sum of distribution indices (DIs) for the middle term must exceed 5.

Since 5 is the maximum DI, Rl entails the traditional syllogistic rule. For traditionally, only DIs of 5 and 1 occurred. In order for the sum of the

DIs for M to exceed 5, M must have a DI of 5 (i.e., be distributed) in at least one premise of a traditional syllogism. The difference between Rl and the traditional rule is that Rl permits intermediate values, and hence, does not require that the middle term be maximally distributed in either premise, but only that redundancy occur with respect to the middle term. That is, at least some Ms mentioned in connection with S must be among those mentioned with respect to P.

The second traditional rule of distribution says that no term which is undistributed in the premises may be distributed in the conclusion of a valid syllogism. The force of the rule is to prevent one from arguing to a conclusion about the entire extension of a term based on information about only some members of that term's extension. In short, from a traditional standpoint you could not argue from some to all. With the presence of intermediate DIs, the rule may be revised as follows:

R2: No term may be more nearly distributed in the conclusion than it is in the premises (i.e., no term may bear a higher DI in the conclusion than it bears in the premises).

Our revised R2 does what the traditional rule does, plus it prevents our arguing from a statement about a given number of individuals in a class to a statement about a *greater number* of individuals in that class. In short, R2 does not permit us to argue from a set of objects "in hand", so to speak, to an extrapolated set. The extendibility of the traditional concept of distribution to the intermediate cases suggests that the ancients were correct in their conception of distribution.

Quality

The rules of quality remain unchanged:

R3: At least one premise must be affirmative.
R4: The conclusion is negative if and only if one of the premises is negative.

Quantity

We mentioned earlier that the traditional rules of quantity were only convenience rules—that they could be derived from the traditional rules of distribution and quality. The traditional rules are as follows:

QN1: At least one premise must be universal.
QN2: If one premise is particular, then the conclusion must be particular.

With intermediate quantities available, viz., those between all and some, these rules require revision. We propose the following:

R5: At least one premise must have a quantity of majority (T or D) or higher.
R6: If any premise is non-universal, then the conclusion must have a quantity that is less than or equal to that premise.

As in the case of the traditional rules of the syllogism, the revised rules of quantity can be derived from Rl-R4. Consider first the deduction of R5.

Suppose that neither premise is of majority or higher quantity. Then the premises must be some combination of K, I, G, and O. We may immediately rule out the negative combinations because of R3. We may also rule out the affirmative combinations. For by Rl, the combined DIs of the middle term must exceed 5. The highest combined DI for 'M' in two affirmative, less than majority premises is 4 (KK in the third figure). Hence, the premises must be a combination of affirmative and negative propositions. But by R4, the conclusion must also be negative. Hence, 'P' has a DI of 5 in the conclusion. By R2, 'P' must also have a DI of 5 in the premises. Given a combination of affirmative and negative premises of common or less quantity, this requires that 'P' be the predicate of the negative. But under these circumstances, the maximum combined DI of 'M' is again 4 (GK in the third figure). So, if neither premise is of majority or higher quantity, one of Rl-R4 must be violated. Hence, R5 follows from Rl-R4.

It should be noted that R5 reduces to the traditional rule of quantity when we consider the traditional syllogism. For in the traditional syllogism, the only way for a premise to be of majority or higher quantity is for it to be universal (since there are only two traditional quantities). Hence, Rl-R4 also entail the traditional QN1.

Let us turn now to a deduction of R6. Suppose that the conclusion of a syllogism XYZ has a quantity greater than that of the least non-universal premise (LNUP). We then have the following argument against that hypothesis.

1. Z cannot be I or O, for the particular quantity is the least possible quantity.
2. The DI of 'S' must be greater than 1 in Z. For the DI of the subject of any statement of common or greater quantity is greater than or equal to 2. (See section 2.1 above.)
3. Let Z be affirmative.
3.1 Both premises (X and Y) must be affirmative by R4.

3.2 S cannot be the predicate of Y (the minor premise). For the predicate of an affirmative proposition has a DI of 1. Given 2 above, if 'S' were the predicate of Y, R2 would be violated.
3.3 Thus, Y must be of the form 'YSM'.
3.4 Y cannot be the LNUP, since by 3.3, 'S' is the subject of both Y and Z. But by hypothesis, the quantity of Z is greater than that of the LNUP. So, the DI of 'S' would be greater in Z than in Y—a violation of R2.
3.5 Thus, X must be the LNUP.
3.6 Since Y is affirmative, the DI of 'M' in Y is 1. To avoid a violation of Rl, the DI of 'M' in X must be 5.
3.7 But X can only have one of the forms (a) 'XMP' or (b) 'XPM'.
3.8 The only way for 'M' to have a DI of 5 in 3.7a is for X to be universal. But it cannot be, for by 3.5, X is the LNUP.
3.9 The only way for 'M' to have a DI of 5 in 3.7b is for X to be negative. But it cannot be by 3.1 above.
3.10 Thus, Z cannot be affirmative, as against 3.
4. Let Z be negative.
4.1 By R4, at least one premise must be negative.
4.2 The predicate term 'P' in Z must have a DI of 5, since Z is negative.
4.3 By R2, 'P' must then have a DI of 5 in X (the major premise).
4.4 This can only happen in one of two ways: (a) 'P' is the subject of a universal premise; or (b) 'P' is the predicate of a negative premise. In case (a), X is universal and has the form 'XPM'. In case (b), X is negative and has the form 'XMP'.
4.5 Since X is universal in 4.4a, it follows that Y is the LNUP.
4.6 'S' cannot be the subject of Y. For by hypothesis, Z is greater in quantity than the LNUP, and hence, 'S' has a higher DI in Z than in Y, thus violating R2. So, Y has the form 'YMS'.
4.7 But then Y must be negative. For otherwise, 'S' would have a DI of 1 in Y. But since the DI of 'S' in Z is greater than 1 (by 2 above), this would again violate R2.
4.8 But if Y is negative, X must be affirmative, otherwise, R3 would be violated.
4.9 But there is no way that 'XPM' (universal affirmative by 4.5 and 4.8) and 'YMS' (non-universal negative by 4.5 and 4.7) can produce a combined DI for 'm' which is greater than 5. Thus, Rl would be violated.
4.10 So, if Z is negative, 'P' cannot be the subject of a universal X premise, as against 4.4a.
4.11 Then 'P' must be the predicate of a negative 'XMP', by 4.4b.
4.12 But by R3, Y must be affirmative.

4.13 Then 'S' cannot be the predicate of Y. For the predicate of an affirmative proposition has a DI of 1, and since 'S' has a DI in Z greater than 1 (by 2 above), this would violate R2. So, Y has the form 'YSM', where Y is affirmative (by 4.12).

4.14 But now Y cannot be the LNUP. For by hypothesis, Z has a greater quantity than the LNUP. Thus, 'S' would have a higher DI in Z than in Y, violating R2.

4.15 So, X is the LNUP.

4.16 But given that X has the form 'XMP' (by 4.11 above), M' has a DI in X of less than 5.

4.17 But since Y is affirmative and has the form 'YSM' (by 4.13 above), 'M' has a DI of 1 in Y.

4.18 By 4.16 and 4.17, the combined DI of 'M' cannot exceed 5, thus violating Rl.

4.19 So, Z cannot be negative, as against 4.

5. But now, if Z is greater in quantity than the LNUP (our original hypothesis), Z can be neither affirmative (3.1O above) nor negative (4.19 above). But Z must have one or the other of these qualities.

6. Hence, Z cannot be greater in quantity than the LNUP without violating one or more of Rl-R4.

7. Hence, R6 follows from Rl-R4.

2.3 Relation Between Systems

In section 2.2 above, we showed that our revised rule Rl entailed the traditional rule that the middle term of a valid traditional syllogism must be distributed (maximally) in at least one premise. Moreover, from the discussion concerning our revised rule R2 in section 2.2, it is apparent that R2 entails the traditional rule that no term which is distributed in the conclusion of a valid traditional syllogism may be undistributed in the premises. Since R3 and R4 are the same as the traditional rules, it follows that Rl-R4 entail all the traditional rules of distribution and quality.[6] Hence, all twenty-four syllogisms valid on traditional syllogistic theory, remain valid on the revised theory. Moreover, no invalid syllogism expressible in the traditional theory can be valid on the revised theory. For any such syllogism XYZ-N which is invalid on the traditional theory violates one of the traditional rules. Since those rules are entailed by the revised rules, XYZ-N violates one of the revised rules, and hence, is invalid on the revised theory.

Given ten functors, there are one thousand moods, each in one of the four figures. Hence, there are four thousand forms of the syllogism in the extended theory. As mentioned above, all twenty-four valid forms of the traditional theory show up valid in the revised theory-those circled in

(14). In addition, eighty-one other syllogisms turn up valid in the revised theory, each of which contains one or more of the intermediate functors—those not circled in (14).

The rules presented are very close to the rules of the traditional theory. As such, they are less *ad hoc* than Thompson's rules and also do less violence to the notion of distribution. Moreover, we use fewer rules than Thompson, and show (parallel to the traditional theory) that our two rules of quantity are consequences of our rules for distribution and quality

3. Venn Diagrams

3.1 Traditional Syllogism

We now introduce some modifications of the traditional Venn Diagram methods. To start with, consider just the traditional categoricals (universals and particulars). We represent them as follows:

(20)

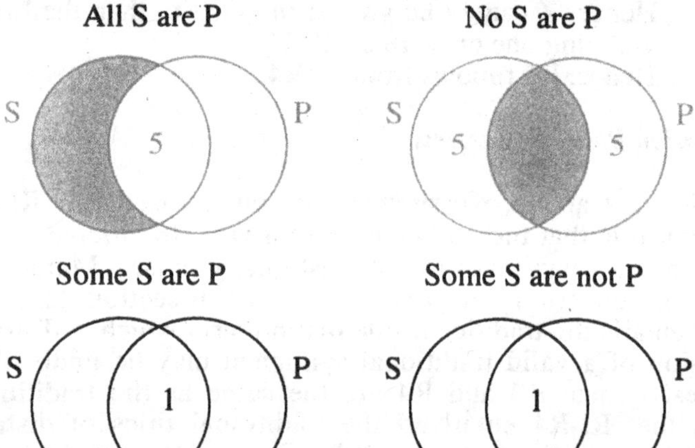

We interpret a labeled circle, and its subdivisions due to overlapping, to represent classes and sub-classes in the usual way. However, we are not committed to set or class *theory*. The regions of the Venn Diagrams can also represent numbers of individuals or portions of stuff of various types and qualities (indicated by the terms). (The overlap of two S- and P-circles could represent all the relevant soup(S) that is poisoned(P).) Thus, classes and sub-classes (and/or platoons and sub-platoons, portions and sub-portions) of Ss and Ps are represented in (20) as being empty or having at least one member (component or Cartwright-quantity), where no markings in a bounded region represent no commitment to either membership or nullity (presence or absence). On the new method, shadings indicate exactly the same thing as before, that the sub-class indicated by the shaded region has no members (e.g., the class SP is empty with respect to the diagram for "All S are P"). (We shall drop now the constant reminder of non-class alternative interpretations via constant repetitions of other groups and portions, and just speak loosely of classes and sub-classes for the sake of easier reading.) The role that the numerals play—the numerals "5" and "1"—is *not* to designate numbers. Rather, numerals represent exactly what "x"s do on the traditional Venn Diagrams—viz., the presence of at least one member in the sub-class in question. (Additional roles for numerals will be added below, such as their relation to DIs.) For example, the numeral "1" in the diagram for "Some S are P" represents the claim that there is at least one individual in the class SP. We stipulate that whenever the numeral "5" occurs in a bounded region, then *ipso facto* a "1" does; i.e., "5" represents what "1" does (though not *vice* versa, as will be seen below).

Slight peculiarities appear, then, in the representations for universals. For the presence of "5" in the universal affirmative diagram indicates that there is at least one member (not 5 members) in the SP sub-class, and its presence twice in the universal negative diagram indicates that there is at least one member in $S\underline{P}$ and at least one in $\underline{S}P$. The method is only a notational variant of the traditional Venn Diagram so long as the "5" occurrences are ignored. But use of the traditional Venn Diagram did not validate all the traditionally valid syllogisms. None in which existential import was crucial were validated on Venn Diagrams—viz., Barbari (AAI-I), Celaront (EAO-I), Cesaro (EAO-II), Camestrop (AEO-II), Darapti (AAI-III), Felapton (EAO-III), Bramantip (AAI-IV), Fesapo (EAO-IV), and Camenop (AIO-IV). Merely adding a representation for existential import by the universal affirmatives takes care of all cases except Camestrop (AEO-II) and Camenop (AEO-IV). To validate Camestrop with Venn Diagrams it is sufficient to add a representation of existential import for the subject term of the universal negative—in the terminology above, placing a "5" in the unshaded part of the S-circle (for the second premise). (And such would be required to permit universals to entail corresponding particulars (when the same in quality), a requirement we intend to satisfy.) However, representing subject existential import will not suffice for Camenop. To validate Camenop(AEO-IV) on the Venn Diagram requires that both subject and predicate of the universal negative have existential import. This is what was contained in (20) above. And there is another reason as well for the representation of double (subject and predicate) existential import—viz., universal negatives preserve truth through simple conversion. Thus, representing something more than just subject existential import is required for universal negatives, since simple conversion switches grammatical subject and predicate. Happily, these two motives for the universal negative representation offered in (20) fit neatly together.[7]

Contradictory denials are represented by these modified Venn Diagrams just as they are in the traditional diagrams. To represent the contradictory opposite of a proposition already represented, simply replace the shaded area with a "1" or replace a "1" with shading (i.e., contradiction comes down, class-wise, to the contrast between something in a sub-class in contrast to nothing in it.) The adding, or subtracting, of "5"s is regarded as a matter of remembering to represent existential import for universals (where that is not needed for particulars, since existence is asserted by them—or so it is customarily assumed). If the statement to be diagramed is a universal, then add the "5"s appropriately. If it's a particular, delete them. Contraries and sub-contraries are obviously representable, since one cannot simultaneously diagram both the universal forms, though one can diagram both particulars together.

All shadings for both premises should be carried out before any "5"s or "1"s are inserted (a slight extension of the usual recommendation of diagramming universal premises before particulars). The usual rules of interpretation in determining if a conclusion is diagramed apply. For example, a numeral inserted *on* a line indicates exactly what the traditional "x" on a line does—viz., that there is an individual (at least one) in one or the other sub-class indicated by the regions on either side of the line. Here are some examples, with brief comments.[8]

(21) Barbara

All M are P
<u>All S are M</u>
All S are P

The "5" in the SPM region is required for the conclusion to be already represented.

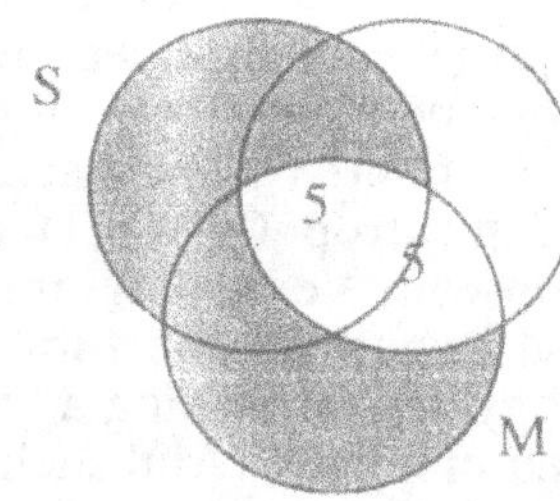

(22) Celaront

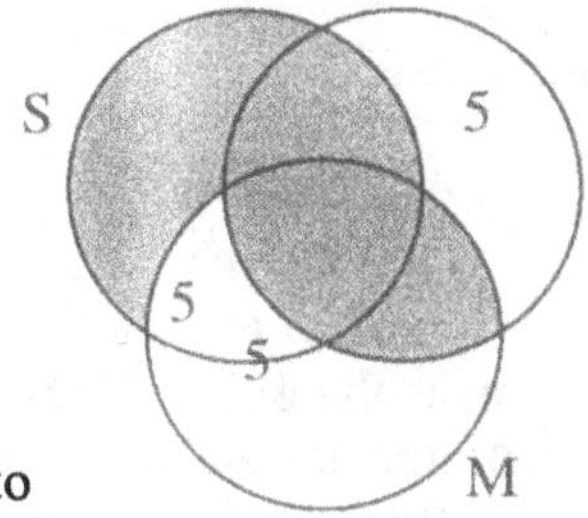

No M are P
All S are M
Some S are not P

The "5" of the second premise is required to permit the conclusion to be already diagrammed.

(23) Camestrop

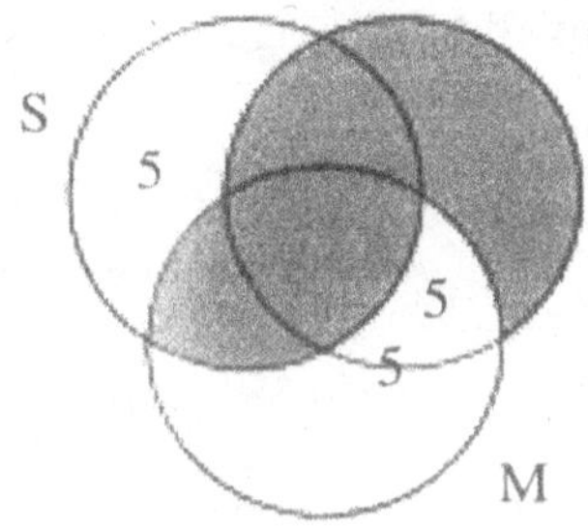

All P are M
No S are M
Some S are not P

Existential import of the subject the E-form premise is required!

(24) Felapton

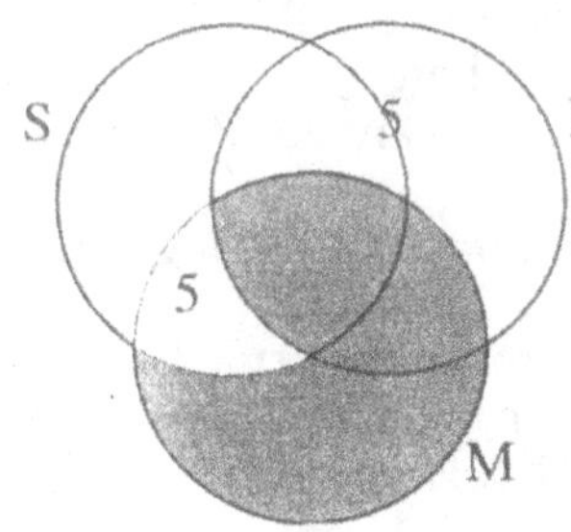

No M are P
All M are S
Some S are not P

The "5" in SMP is supplied by *both* premises.

(25) Camenes

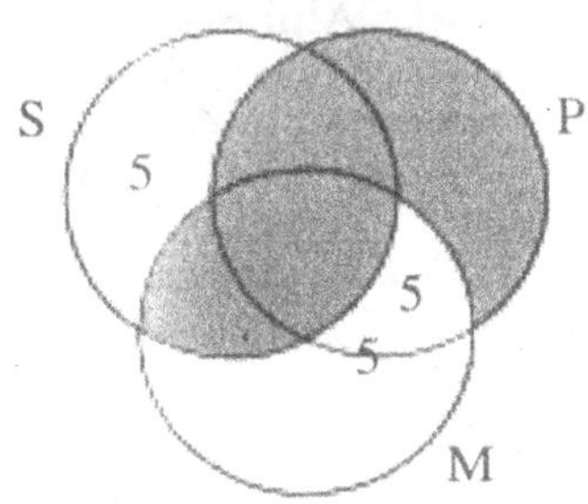

All P are M
No M are S
No S are P

The insertion of "5"s works out right even though the conclusion is universal.

(26) Camenop

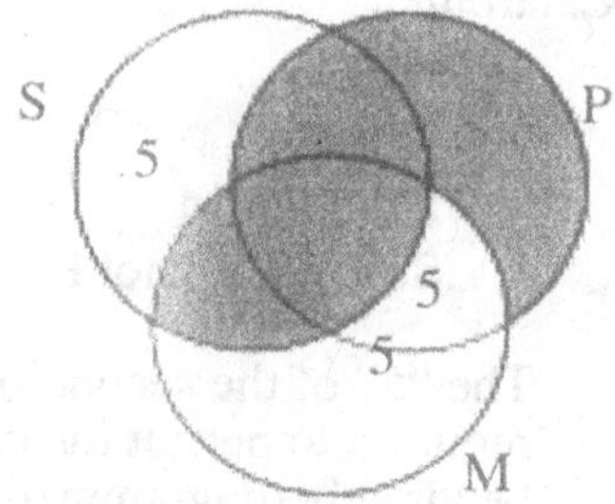

All P are M
<u>No M are S</u>
Some S are not P

This is the only syllogism that requires *double* existential import for E-form premise.

(27) Invalid Syllogisms[9]

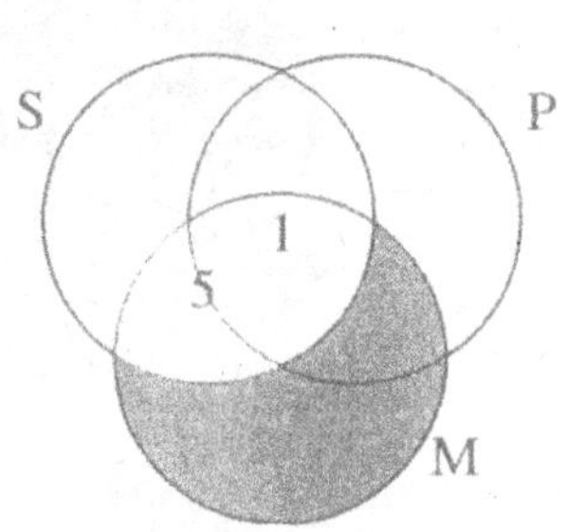

Some M are P
<u>All M are S</u>
Some S are not P

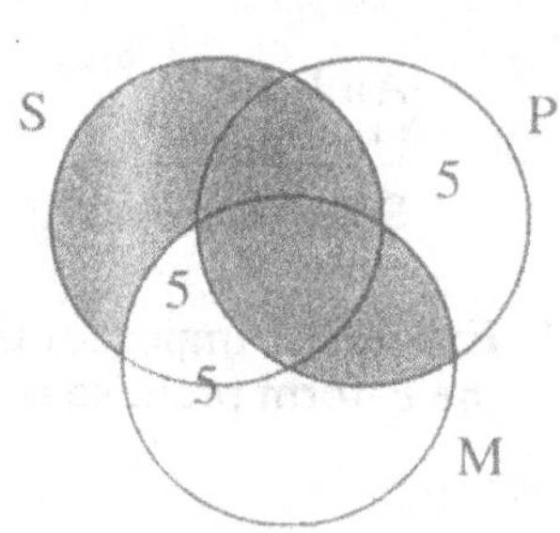

No P are M
<u>All S are M</u>
All S are P

3.2 Intermediate Syllogisms

To represent intermediate syllogisms on Venn Diagrams, we adopt the following basic (underived) representations for the six intermediate categoricals.

(28) Almost-all S are P

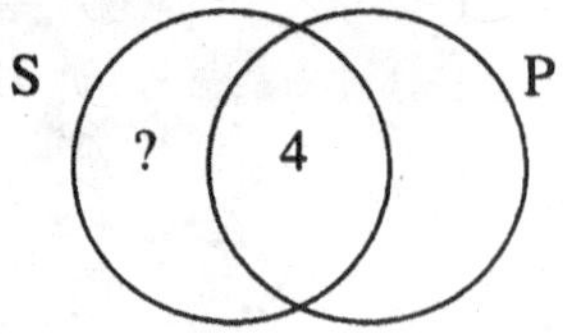

Few S are P

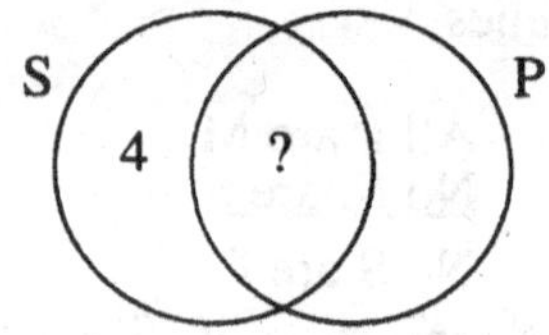

Most S are P

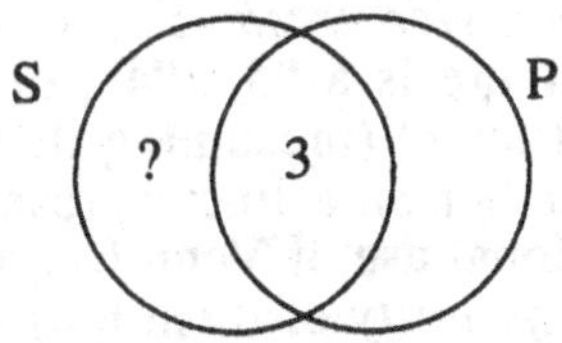

Most S are not P

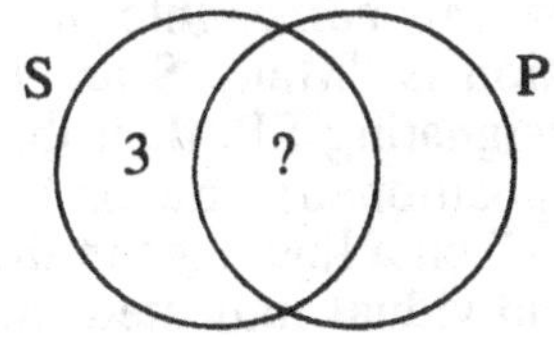

Many S are P

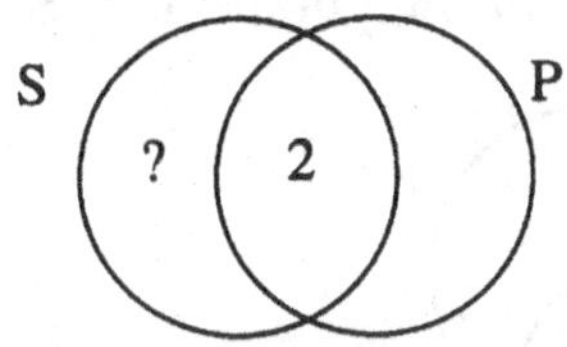

Many S are not P

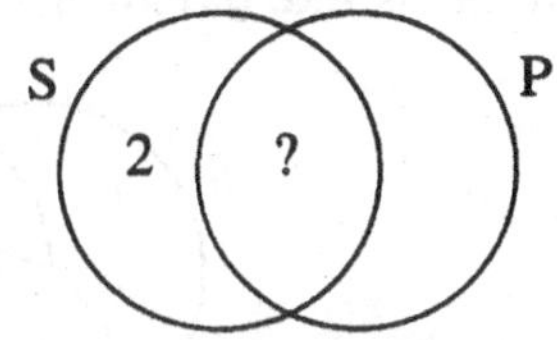

The numerals "4", "3", and "2" play the same roles that "5" and "1" did above—viz., *not referring to numbers*, but indicating that some member or members of the sub-class indicated by the region in which they appear *exists*. Now, however, the numerals play an additional role—viz., to indicate *relative size*. For example, "4" is to represent the claim that almost-all members of a class—a class, therefore, that has members—are in a certain sub-class. The general idea is that every numeral is paired (or pairable) with some "?". A "?" is analogous to shading. It is stipulated that the subclass(es) indicated by the region(s) the "?" appears in are *possibly* empty (possibly, though not necessarily). "?" is taken to be *explicit* information to that effect, something more committal than leaving a region completely unmarked (which in a weaker sense can be thought to represent that a sub-class is possibly empty—though it also leaves it open that a sub-class is possibly quite numerous which a "?" does not). Such possibly-empty sub-classes are always paired with a sub-class that, relative to the whole class (of which both sub-classes are parts), contains a *specified quantity* (or more) of the entire membership. So, the diagram for "Almost-all S are P" indicates that a high quantity (possibly all if the "?" sub-class *is* empty) of the Ss are Ps—the "almost-all" quantity of the Ss are Ps. This is "relative" in two ways: a high quantity relative to all the Ss; and a higher quantity relative to "most" (3) or "many" (2). The "3" in the diagram of "Most S are P" indicates that more than half (at least a bare majority) of the Ss are Ps and possibly almost all or even all are (e.g., all are if the "?" sub-class *is* empty). Finally, the "2" of the diagram for "Many S are P" indicates that at least a certain noticeable quantity (not simply few or possibly none) of the Ss are Ps (and possibly most are, almost-all are, or all are).

How to use these basic representations to validate intermediate syllogisms is somewhat more complicated than the traditional method.

First, any higher numeral represents any lower one (that ordering feature of the numerals comes into play), but *not vice versa*. So, for example, if a conclusion is "Many S are P" and there is a "5", "4", or "3" in the region designating SP, then that is sufficient (presuming that the "?" is properly positioned). Second, any number *on* a line represents exactly what an "x" on a line does in the traditional use of Venn Diagrams—viz., that the individual indicated (now the *quantity* of them too) is in one or the other sub-class. However, a "?" on a line does *not* function this way. A "?" on a line is like having a "?" on *both* sides of the line. So in

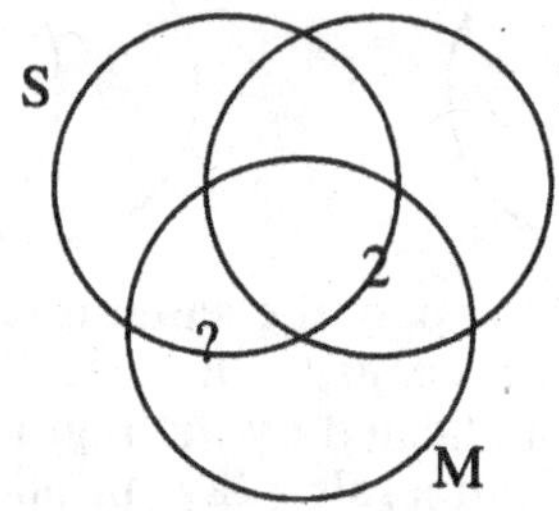

both $SM\underline{P}$ *and* $\underline{S}M\underline{P}$ are represented to be possibly empty—relative, that is, to MP wherein *at least many* of the Ms are represented to be. The conditions just represented would be satisfied by

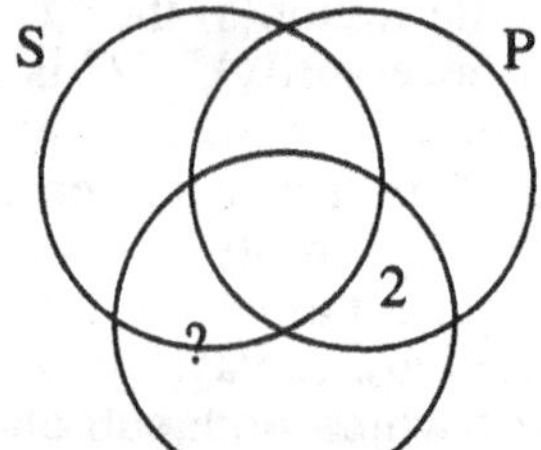

and by

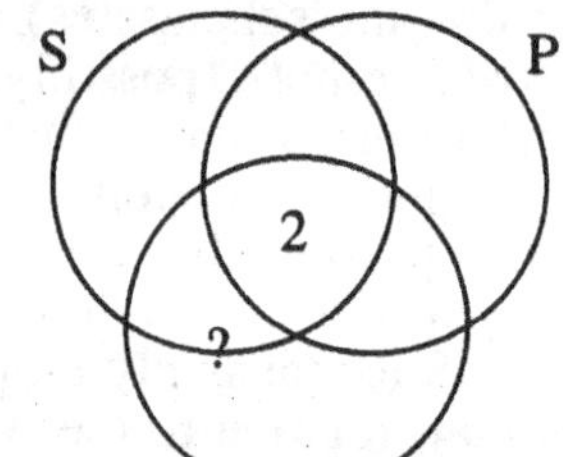

but *not* by

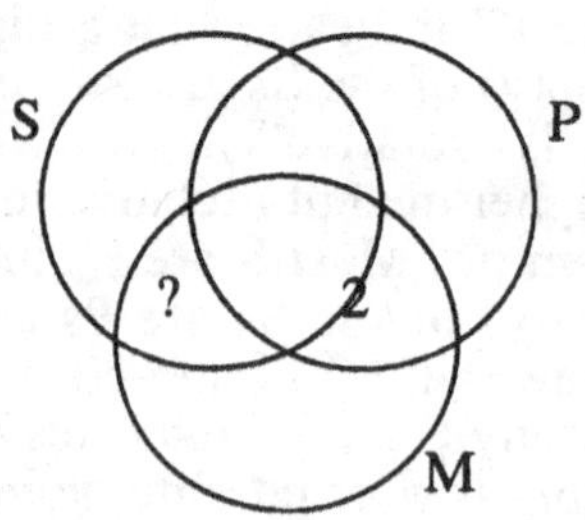

nor by

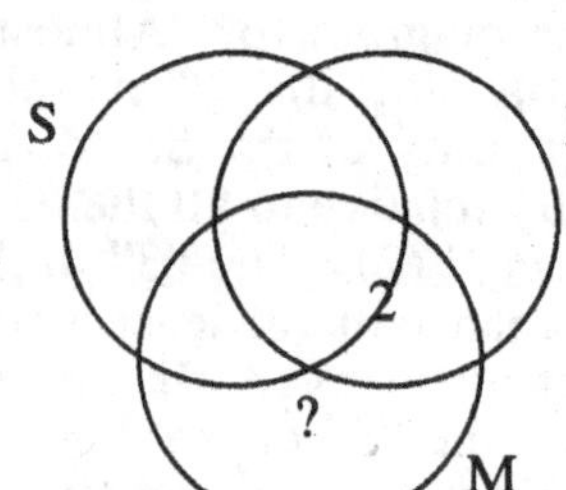

This will turn out to be crucial in filtering out invalid cases.

Third, any occurrence of shading in a bounded region can be interpreted as a "?", but *not vice* versa. If a sub-class is possibly empty (relative to some quantity—much, most, or almost-all—of it in another sub-class), then its actually being empty counts as an instance (since actuality entails possibility). This feature is required (together with larger numerals representing what smaller ones do) not only to validate many syllogisms, but also to permit higher quantity statements of the same quality to entail corresponding lower quantity ones—i.e., for affirmatives, universals entail predominants which entail majorities, which entail commons (similarly for negatives). (Of course, particulars are entailed by corresponding higher quantity propositions simply via the numeral interpretation convention.) Fourth, just as all shadings in premises should be carried out before numeral insertion, now also "?" insertion should come after shadings and before numeral insertion. (Also, insert all numerals, don't skimp.)[10]

Fifth, and finally, if there are two numerals on different borders of one undivided sub-area of the M circle (one of four, i.e., S$\underline{\text{P}}$M, '$\underline{\text{S}}$PM, SPM, or $\underline{\text{SP}}$M) where there are *no* marks (numerals, shadings, "?") out*side* the M circle, and if the numbers the numerals indicate add-up to a number greater than 5 (e.g., if they are "2" and "4" or "3" and "3"), then *interpret* the sub-area in question as *ipso facto* containing the numeral "1". That is, the sub-class in question has at least one member in it. This is a very special interpretation rule, without any counterpart we can see in the traditional methods. The rule is absolutely necessary, however, in order to encompass the 12 new valid forms of Figure III, those discussed in section 1 above.

3.3 Examples

Here are some examples of how the new system of Venn Diagrams works, beginning with the First Figure.

Figure I.

(a) Intermediate syllogisms with majority statements.

AAT-I All M are P
$\underline{\text{All S are M}}$
Most S are P

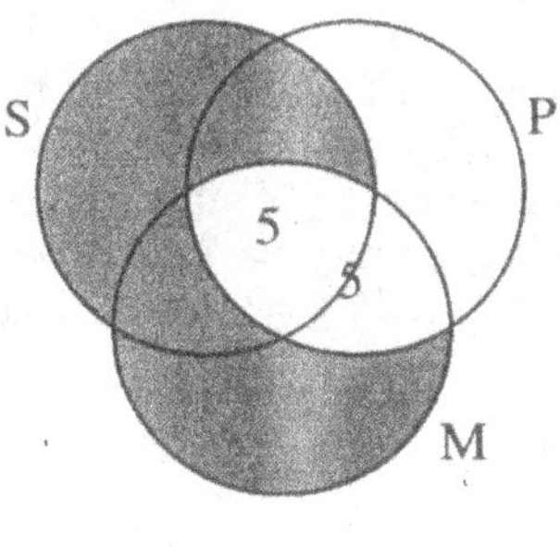

The conclusion would be diagramed as:[11]

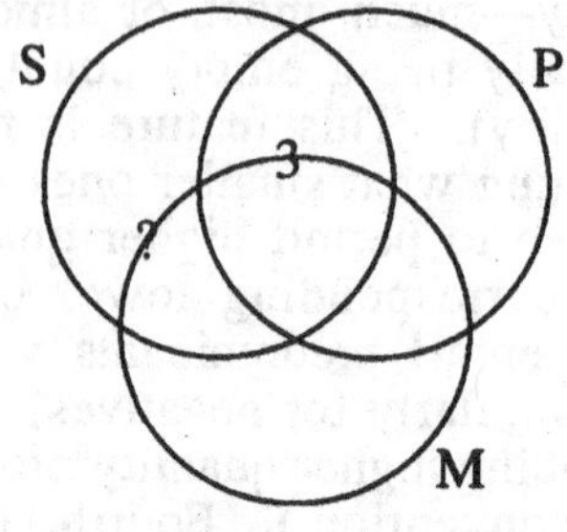

But this conclusion *is* already diagramed when the premises are because the shaded areas include those where "?" is needed and since there is a "5" in the SPM region that also represents a "3"; i.e., a "3" has to be represented in one or the other of the SPM region or the $SP\underline{M}$ region.

ETD-I No M are P
Most S are M
Most S are not P

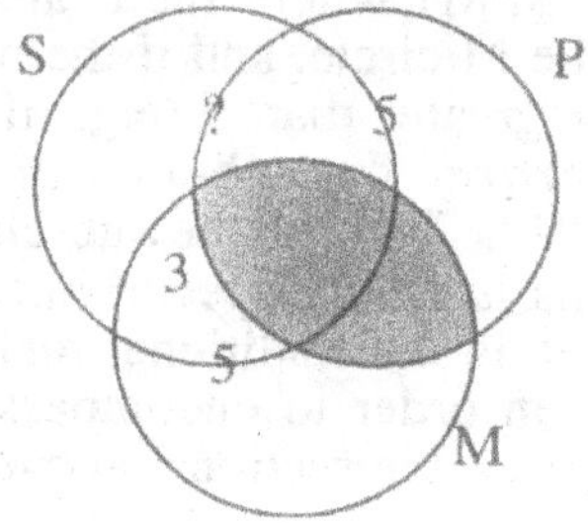

The conclusion would be diagramed:

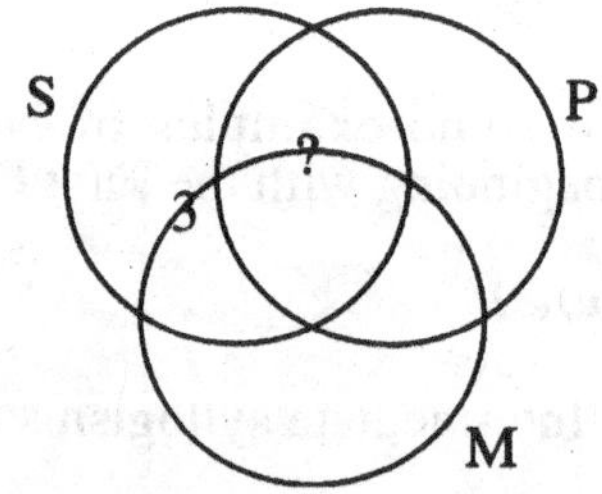

But this conclusion is captured by the preceding diagram, since (i) there is a "3" in the $S\underline{P}M$ region (which is sufficient to satisfy the diagram of it on the line between $S\underline{P}M$ and $S\underline{PM}$) and (ii) the SP region (both parts) must be possibly empty (= ?) and one part *is* empty (SPM) and the other *is* possibly empty ($SP\underline{M}$ =?) on the diagram of the premises.

(b) Intermediate syllogisms with majority *and* common statements.

ETG-I No M are P
<u>Most S are M</u>
Many S are not P

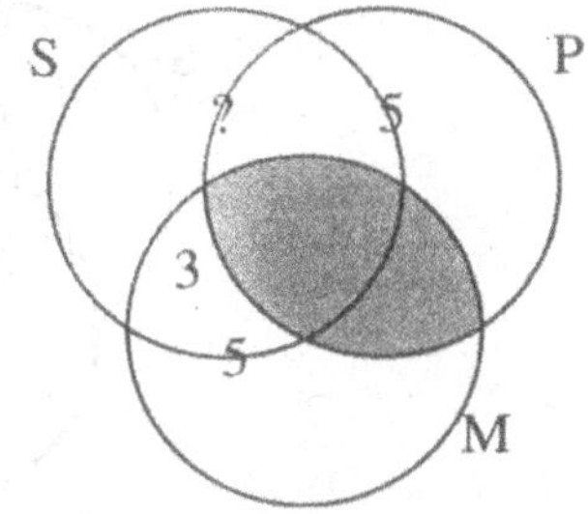

The conclusion would be diagramed:

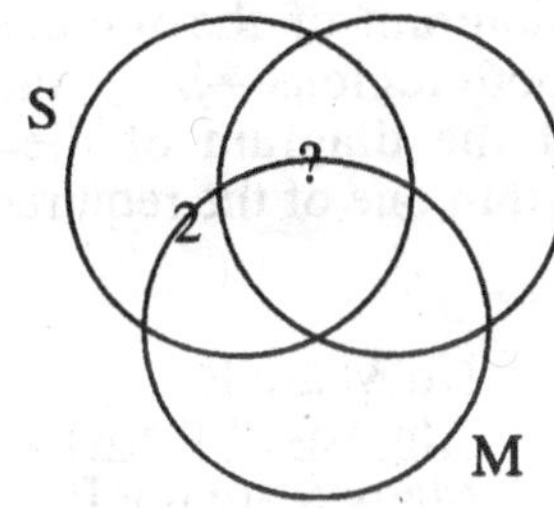

The "?" in the SP region *is* interpreted as diagramed when the premises are for exactly the same reasons stated for the previous example (ETD-I). The numeral "2" is interpreted to be diagramed, because "3" represents it (since any "3" represents a "2" also) and the "3" is in a region which is one of which must have a "2" in it if the conclusion is captured (which it is).

(c) Intermediate syllogisms with predominant, majority and/or common statements.

AAP-I All M are P
<u>All S are M</u>
Almost-all S are P

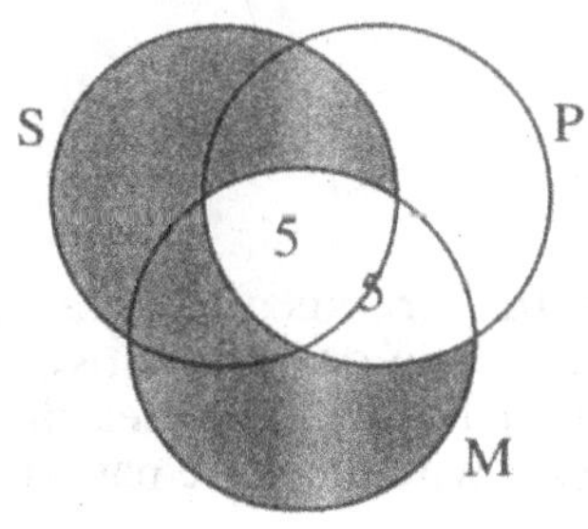

The conclusion would be diagramed as:

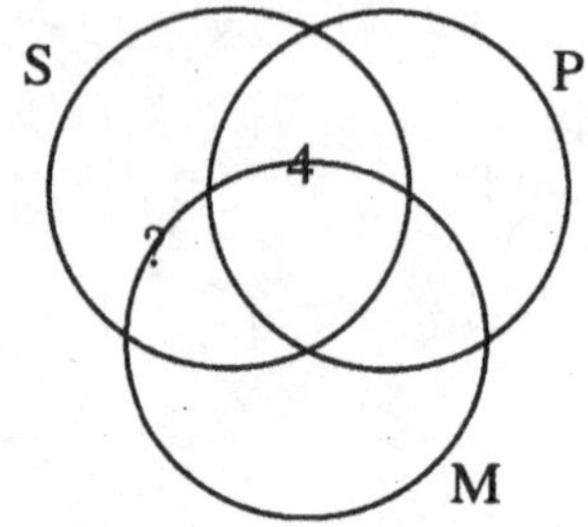

But the diagram of the premises does capture what the "?" represents because both regions—$S\underline{PM}$ and $S\underline{P}M$—are shaded. And "5" in the SPM region of the diagram of the premises represents "4" also and does represent it in one of the required alternative regions.

EPG-I No M are P
<u>Almost-all S are M</u>
Many S are not P

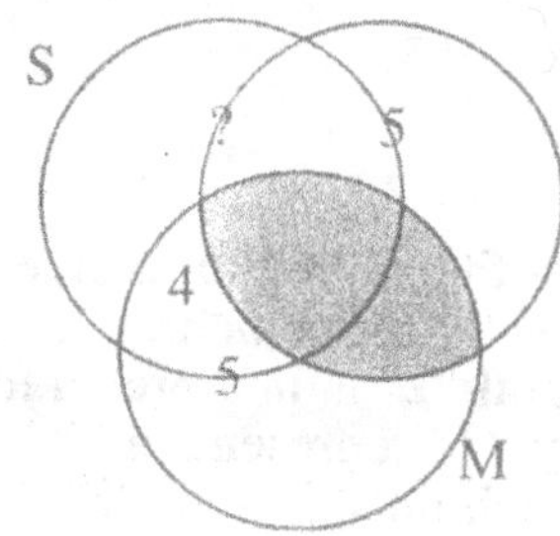

The conclusion would be diagramed:

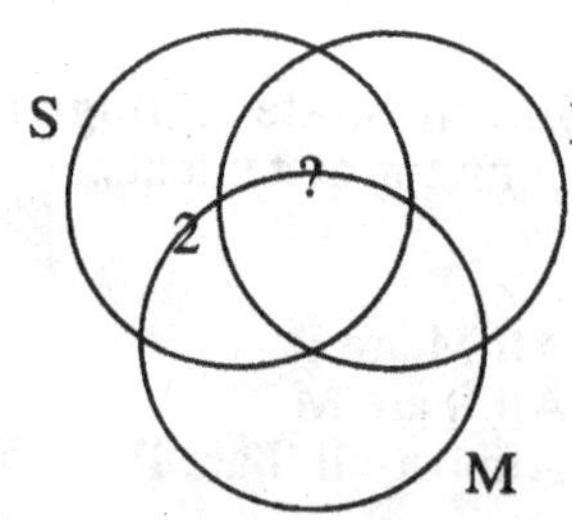

The "4" of the premises diagramed does represent "2" (a smaller numeral) and it is in one of the two sections required. That the required "?" *is* captured by the premises diagram has been shown in previous examples above with the same patterns.

Figures II-IV.

ADD-II All P are M
Most S are not M
Most S are not P

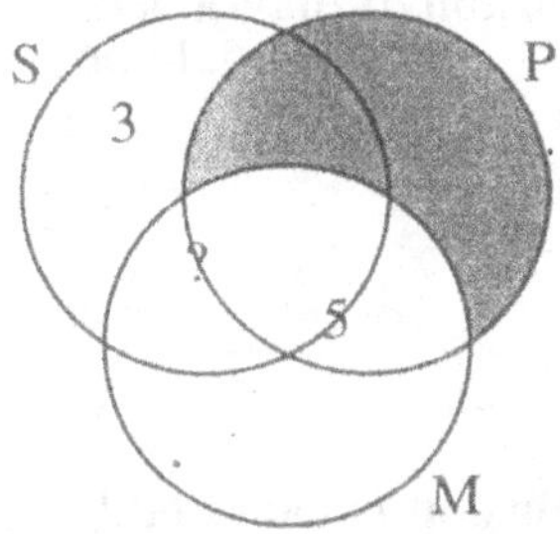

For the conclusion to be captured the S that are non-P must be "most" (=3) relative to those that are P (=?). But the premises *do* show the SP overlap to be possibly empty since part of it is empty and the other part is marked as possibly empty (=?).

EKG-II No P are M
Many S are M
Many S are not P

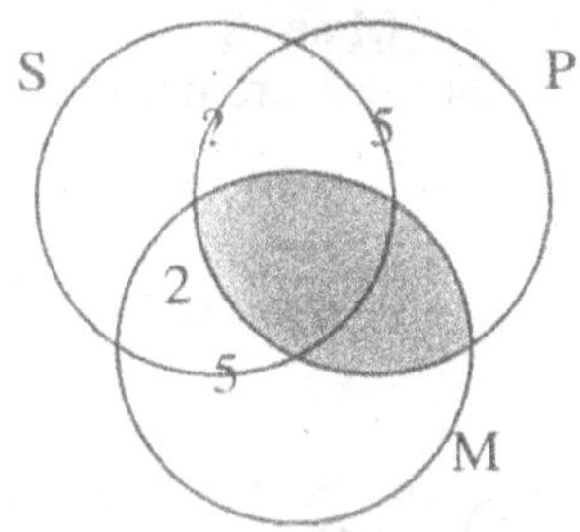

This has a pattern found in the above examples several times.[12]

EAB-II No P are M
All S are M
Few S are P

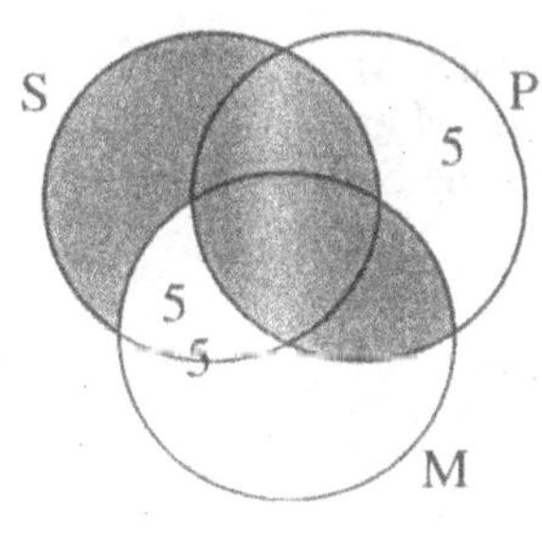

The conclusion, if diagramed, would be:

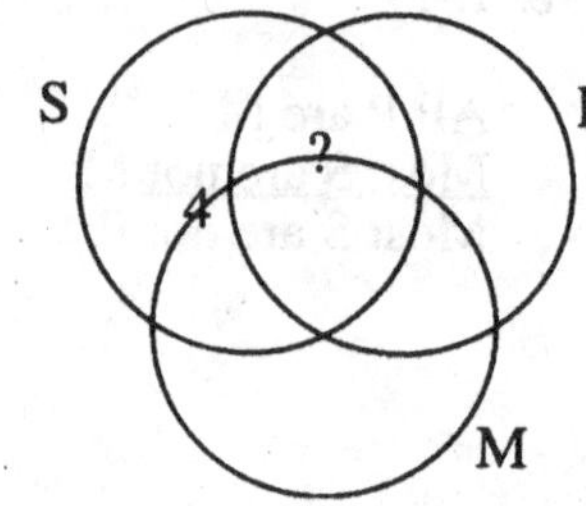

This conclusion *is* captured by the diagram of the premises, since the "5" in S$\underline{P}$M sufficiently represents the "4" required by the conclusion and the shading of the SP overlap in the diagram of the premises sufficiently represents the "?" (=possibly empty) required by the conclusion.

DAO-III Most M are not P
All M are S
Some S are not P

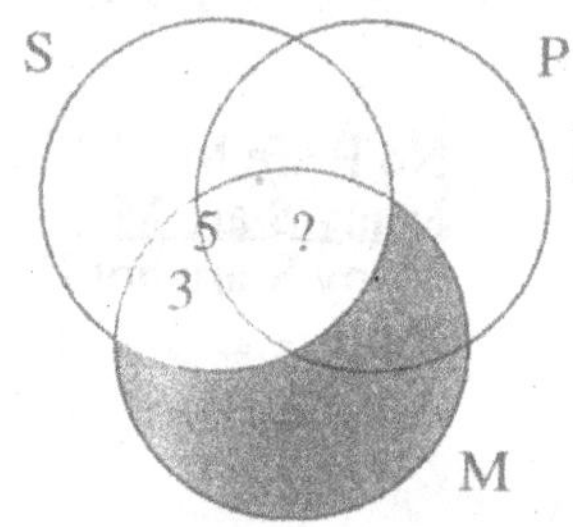

"3" is in one of the S$\underline{P}$ regions. But that is sufficient since "13" also represents what "1" would and only one of S$\underline{PM}$ or S$\underline{P}$M must have a member (some numeral or other) in it for the conclusion to be represented.

KAI-III Many M are P
All M are S
Some S are P

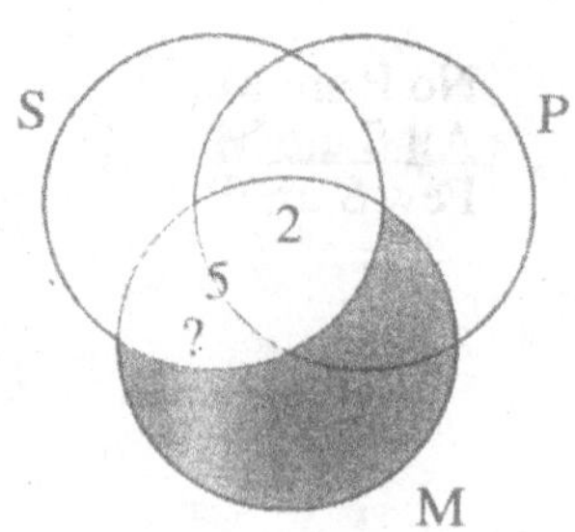

All that is required to capture the conclusion here is that there is a "1" in the SPM region. And there is a "2" there, which is sufficient.

Both of the next two examples require using the special interpretation rule mentioned at the end of section 3.2 above.

BKO-III Almost-all M are not P
Many M are S
Some S are not P

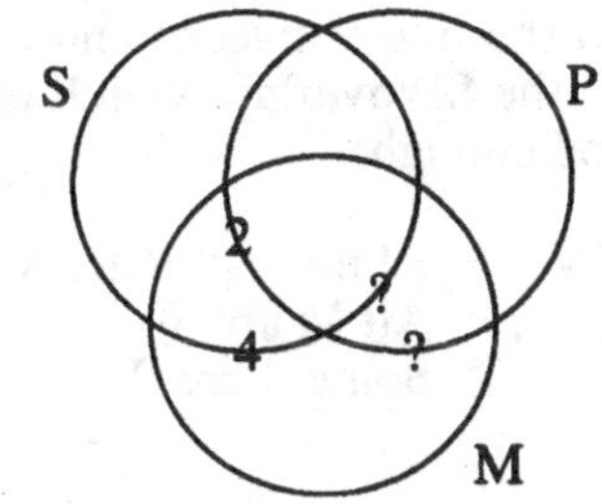

For the conclusion to be diagramed there would have to be a "1" in one of the two areas of the S$\underline{P}$ region. But a "1" does not appear there (nor any higher numeral). Still, if two numerals appear on borders of one undivided area and if the numbers they indicate add up to a number greater than 5, the diagram is interpreted as if there were a "1" within the area.

PKI-III Almost-all M are P
Many M are S
Some S are P

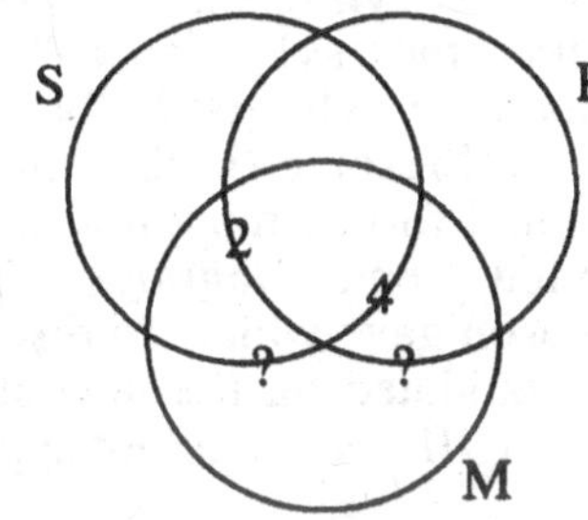

Again, the special interpretation rule applies. Thus, the diagram is interpreted as if there were a "1" within the SPM area.

AED-IV All P are M
No M are S
Most S are not-P

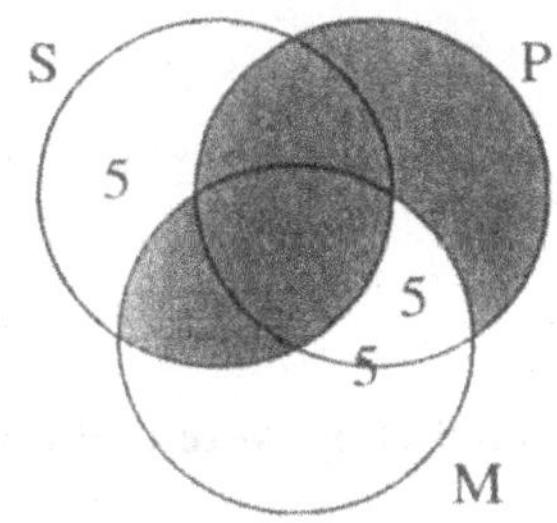

The conclusion *is* captured, for there needs to be a "3" in S$\underline{PM}$ or in S$\underline{P}$M (or on the line between) and there is a "5" in S$\underline{PM}$. There needs to be a "?" in the SP overlap, which there *is* since it's shaded out entirely (which is good enough).

PAI-IV   Almost-all P are M
    All M are S
    Some S are P

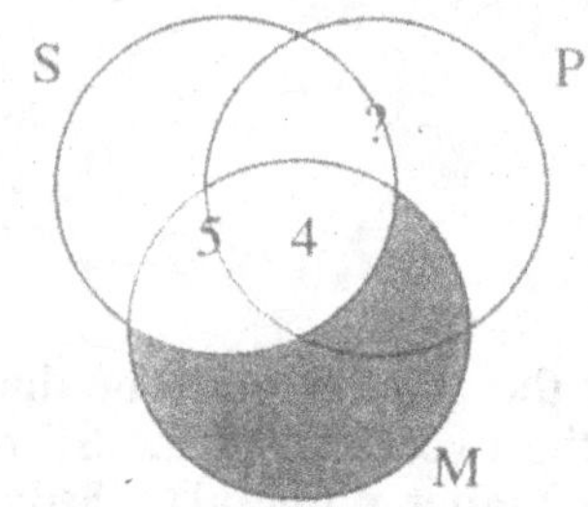

"4" in the SPM region is sufficient to represent a "1" somewhere in the SP overlap (which is what the conclusion requires).

All 105 syllogisms submit to this method! It is important, however, that *no* other syllogisms (beyond the 105) do. In particular, those intermediate syllogisms that are not valid according to the rules, but which still resolve (in the sense introduced above) to one of the valid 24 traditional forms, must not turn out to be validated on these new and/or extended Venn Diagrams. The two invalid intermediate syllogisms Thompson gave which *do* resolve to valid traditional forms *come close* to being validated on the new style Venn Diagrams. They were TAT-III and TAK-III (which do not appear on the list of 105). Consider TAT-III:

Most M are P
All M are S
Most S are P

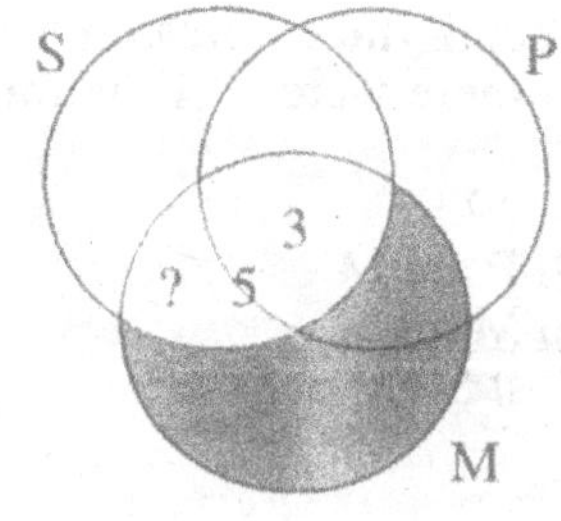

If the conclusion were diagramed, it would be:

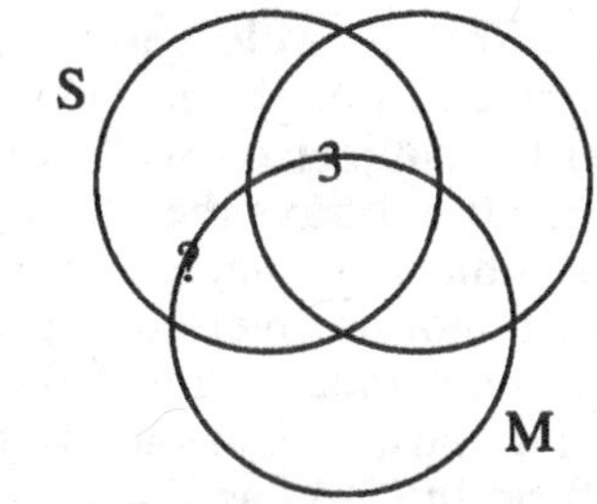

The diagram of the premises *is* sufficient for capturing what is needed for the "3" of the conclusion. What is *in*sufficient in the diagram of the premises is that the S<u>PM</u> region has *no* marking at all in it. To capture the conclusion, it must have a "?" or be shaded! Thus, the conclusion is not captured by the premises and, as desired, the syllogism is shown to be *invalid*.

The same pattern occurs in TAK-III:

Most M are P
<u>All M are S</u>
Many S are P

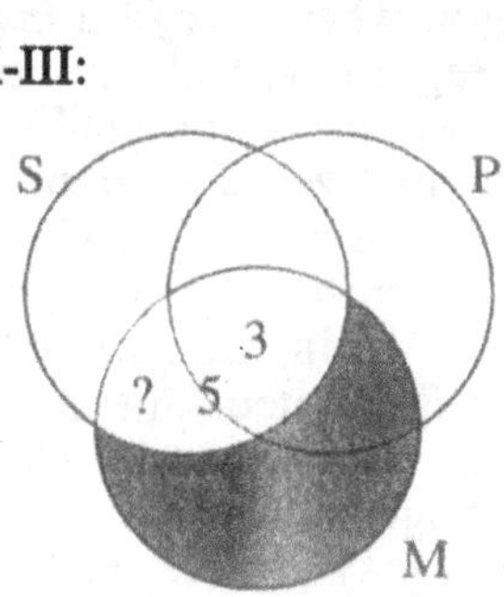

The numeral required by the conclusion is supplied ("3" representing "2"). The syllogism is *in*valid, however, because there is no required shading or "?" in the S<u>PM</u> region.[13]

We have not examined all 3895 (= 4000 – 105) invalid syllogisms with this new Venn Diagram method. We prove below (in section 4.2) that examination of each of the predicted 3895 invalid syllogisms will also fail to be valid when evaluated with the new method of Venn Diagrams. (We have, of course, confirmed all 105 valid forms with the method.)

3.4 Alternative Notation

The reader will doubtless have noted a correlation between the use of numerals in the new Venn Diagram method and the use of exactly the same numerals as distribution indices. Thus far on the diagrams, the numerals have been used only to represent existential import and relative size of sub-classes. But inspection of the diagrams reveals that the appearance of a numeral within a circle correctly portrays the *relative distribution* (from undistributed through the three stages of more-nearly-distributed to distributed) for subject terms.[14] Re-inspect (20) and (28) above. Each numeral correctly portrays the DI of the circle it is in. This is absolutely clear for the subjects of negatives, since the portion of the diagram the numeral is in is not an overlapping portion (so there is no ambiguity). For example the subject term of the universal negative E-form in (20) has DI = 5 (and, thus, is distributed) and the subject term for the common negative G-form in (28) has DI = 2 (and, therefore, is more nearly distributed than any term with DI = 1 but less distributed than any term with DI greater than 2). Ambiguity arises, however, with the affirmatives, for the numeral is in an overlapping region and, thus, is within two circles. Which circle is the numeral in for purposes of representing (or detecting) relative distribution? The answer is simple. Each numeral (greater than "1") in the above method is paired with a "?" or a shaded region when *it is first inserted.* The numeral with its paired "?" or shaded region will always both be in only one circle. Thus, checking to see which "?" or shading a numeral is paired with (to start with) in the affirmative cases completely determines which circle the numeral should be regarded as within for purposes of representing DI. (Since DI = 1 represents a term's being undistributed, the potential ambiguity of the "1" in the particular affirmative doesn't matter. For both terms are undistributed. Also, we ignore DIs for predicate terms.)

Recognizing how DIs can be accurately and unequivocally extracted from the basic diagrams of (20) and (28) suggests a notational variation that some readers may prefer. The basic idea is to replace the numerals in (20) and (28)—and in all their uses in applying (20) and (28)—with *subscripted* numerals, where the subscript indicates which term on the diagram the DI refers to. To carry out the replacement of subscripted numerals for numerals paired with "?" and shading on (20) and (28) (and by analogy on any applications of (20) and (28)), first detect which circle the numeral and "?" (or reshading) are both within. Then subscript the numeral with the letter ("S", "M", or "P") which is the label for that circle. Finally, *after* subscripting, erase the "?". Don't, however, erase any shadings. The alternative notation for (20) and (28) then, is as follows:

(20)'

All S are P

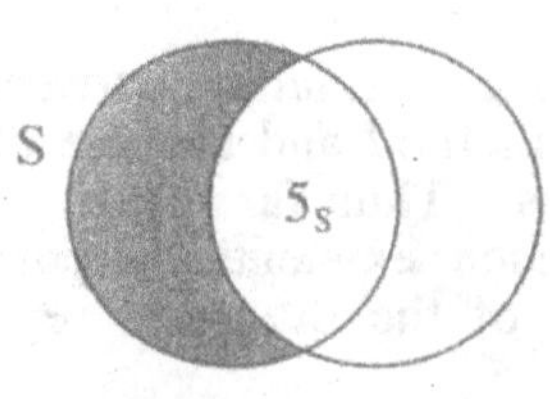

No S are P

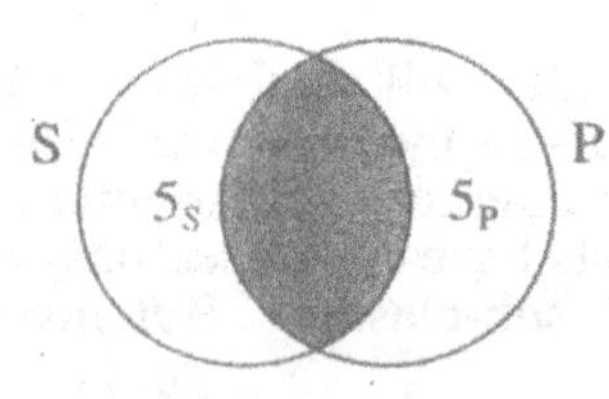

Some S are P

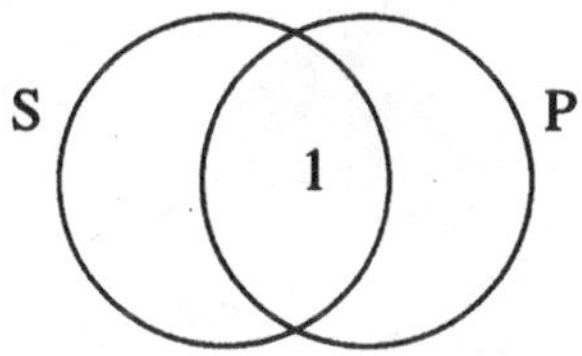

Some S are not P

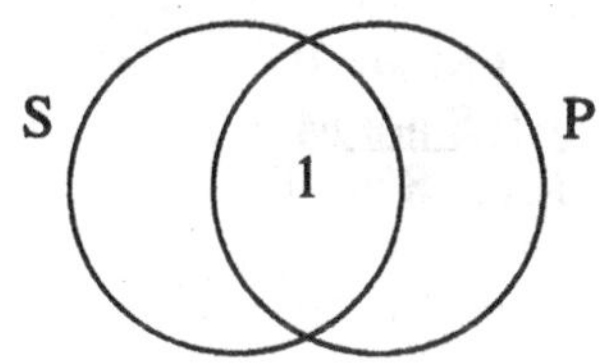

(28)'

Almost-all S are P

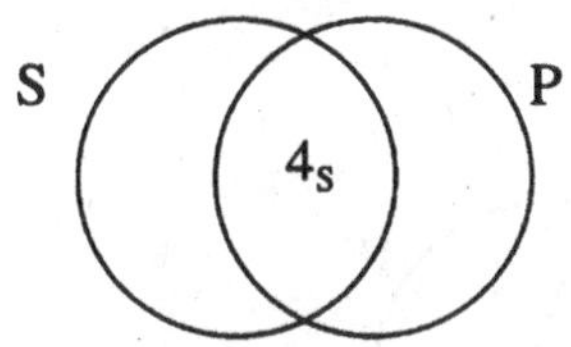

Few S are P

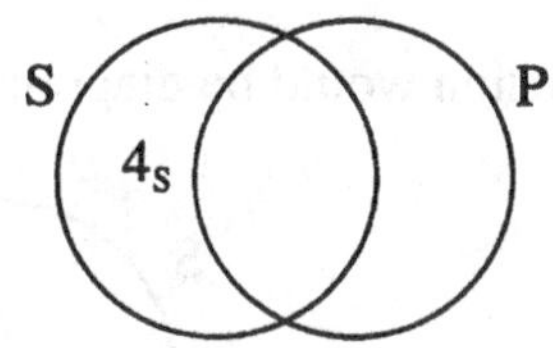

Most S are P

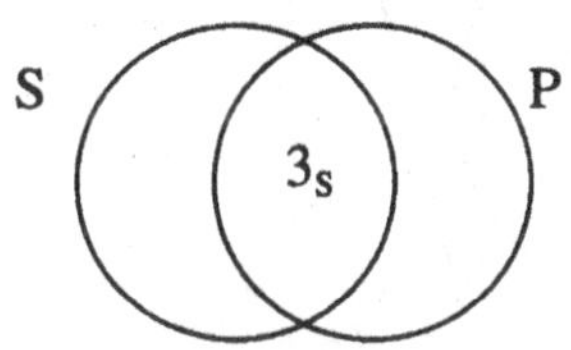

Most S are not P

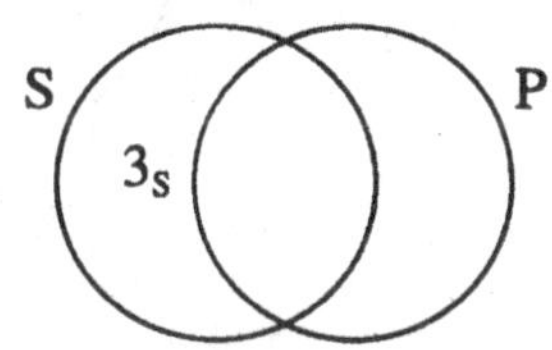

Many S are P

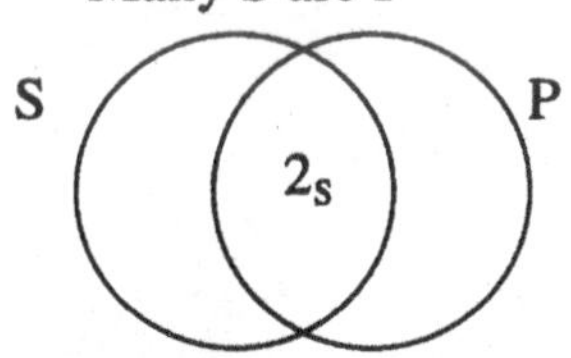

Many S are not P

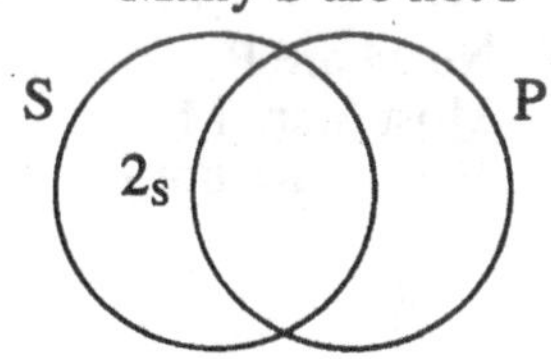

Here are some examples, illustrating the alternative notation. All of them are selected from those discussed above. No examples corresponding to (21) through (26) need to be given (those containing no intermediates), for the diagrams appear exactly the same except that subscripts are added to the numerals. The interpretation rules presented at the end of section 3.2 above still apply (except, of course, for those concerning "?"). The fifth 'special' interpretation rule applies exactly as formulated (concerning numerals appearing on the borders of one undivided region) except for the following addition. Now the numerals must each have the subscript "M" for the case to be interpreted as valid.

Figure I

AAT-I All M are P
<u>All S are M</u>
Most S are P

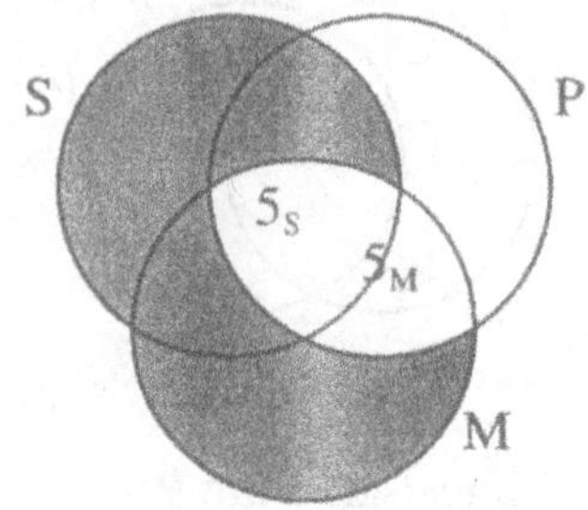

The conclusion would be diagramed as:

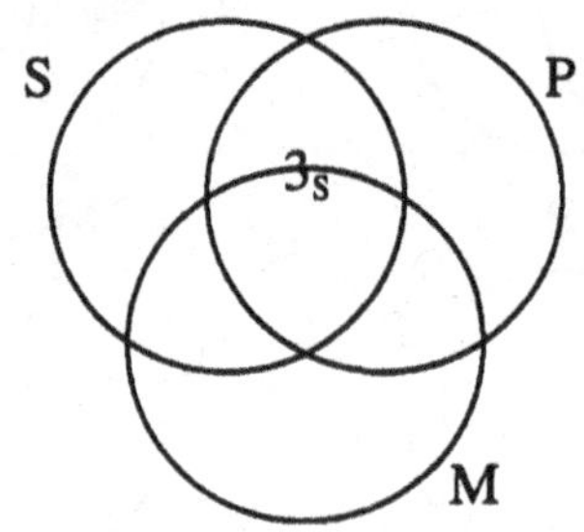

ETD-I No M are P
<u>Most S are M</u>
Most S are not P

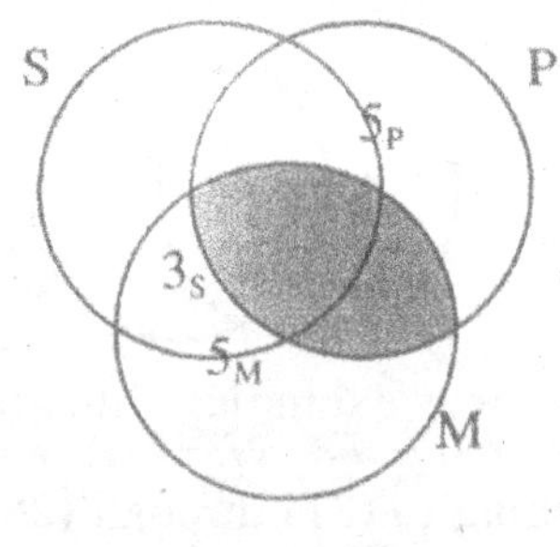

The conclusion would be diagramed:

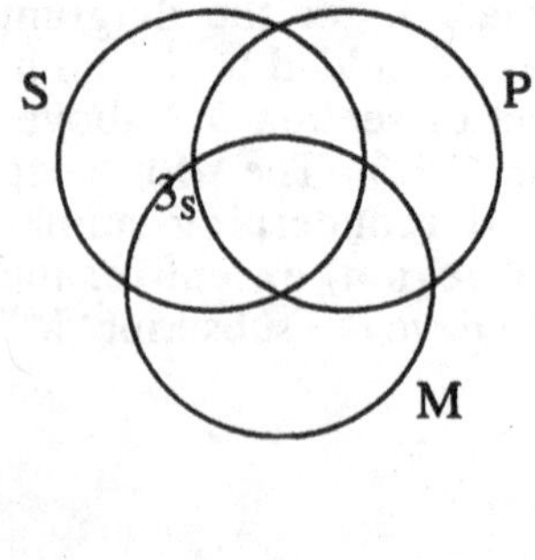

Figures II-IV

EKG-II No P are M
<u>Many S are M</u>
Many S are not P

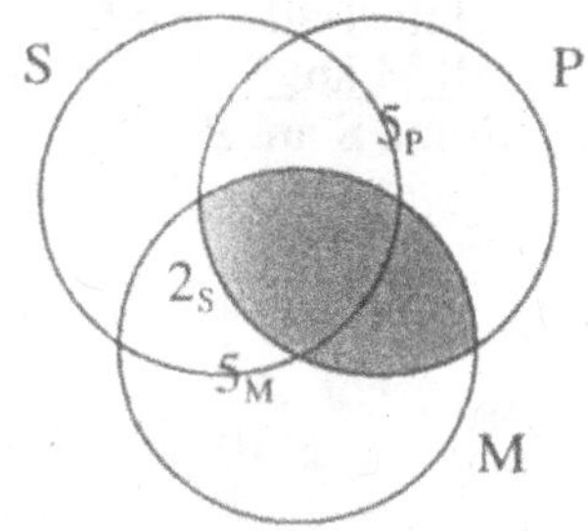

The conclusion would be diagramed:

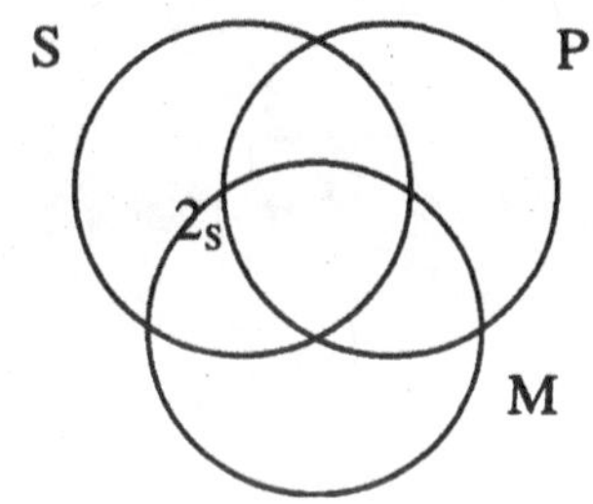

KAI-III Many M are P
<u>All M are S</u>
Some S are P

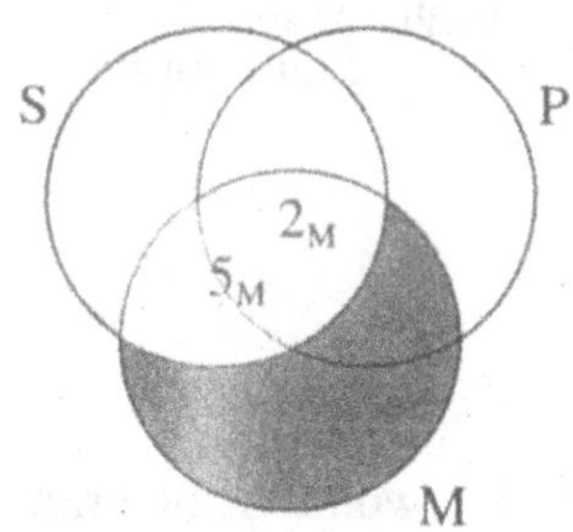

The conclusion would be diagramed:

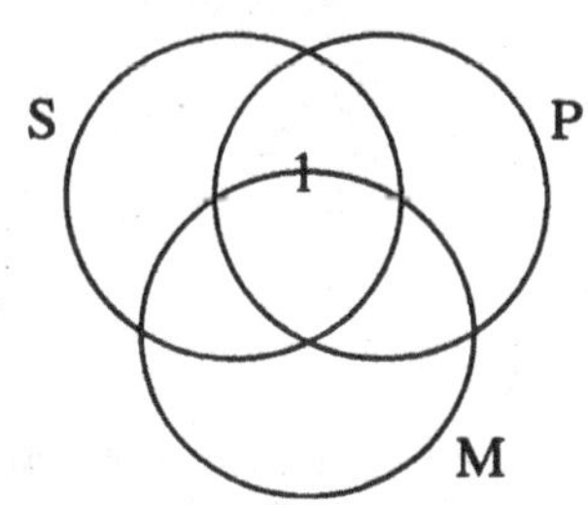

PAI-IV Almost-all P are M
All M are S
Some S are P

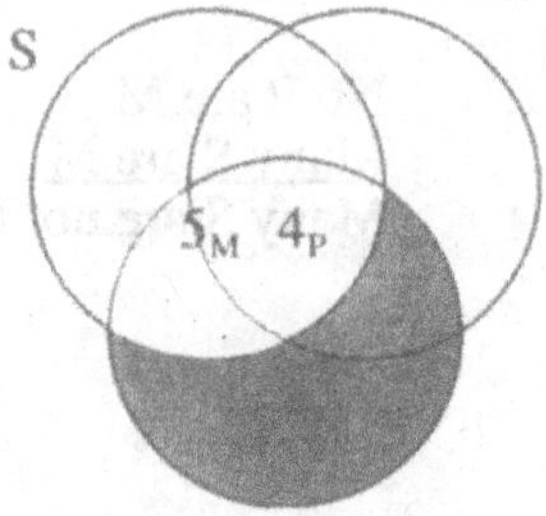

The conclusion would be diagramed:

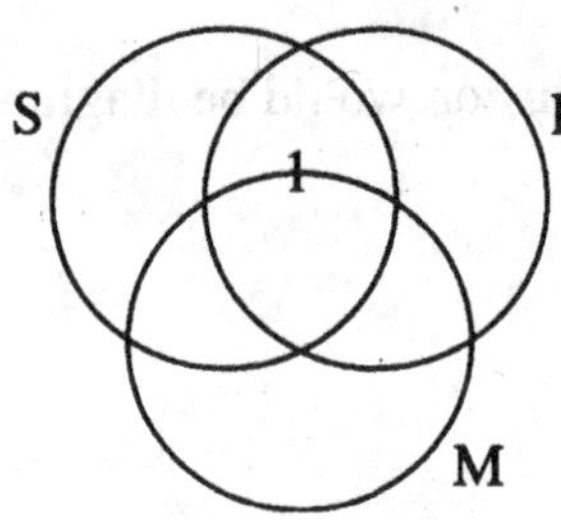

BKO-III Few M are P
Many M are S
Some S are not P

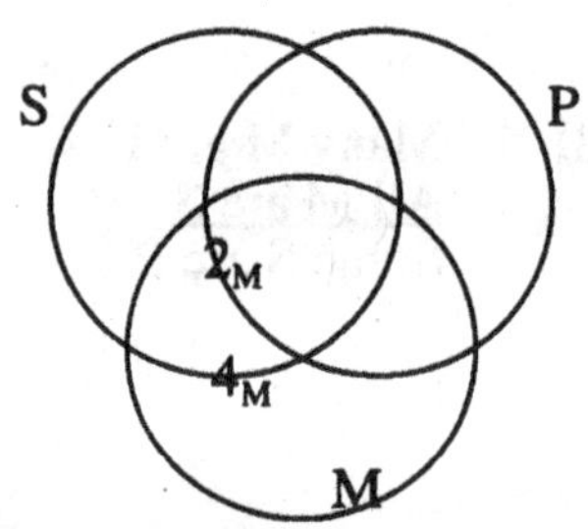

The conclusion would be diagramed:

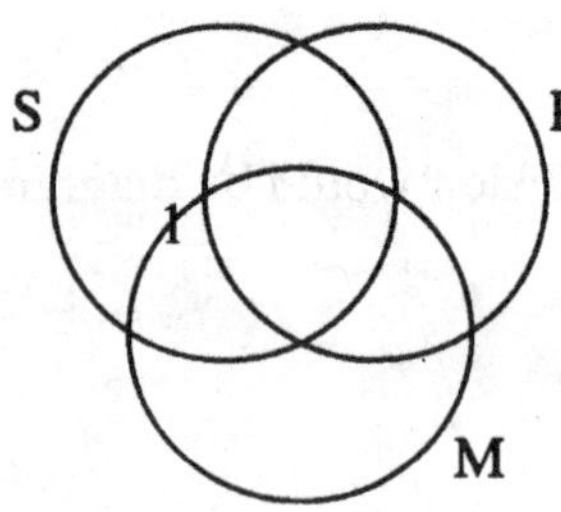

But the 'special' interpretation rule permits this diagramming to be already captured by the diagram of the premises, since the diagram of the premises is interpreted to have a "1" in the S$\underline{P}$M region.

Typical cases that must come out invalid, as discussed above, were:

TAT-III Most M are P
<u>All M are S</u>
Most S are P

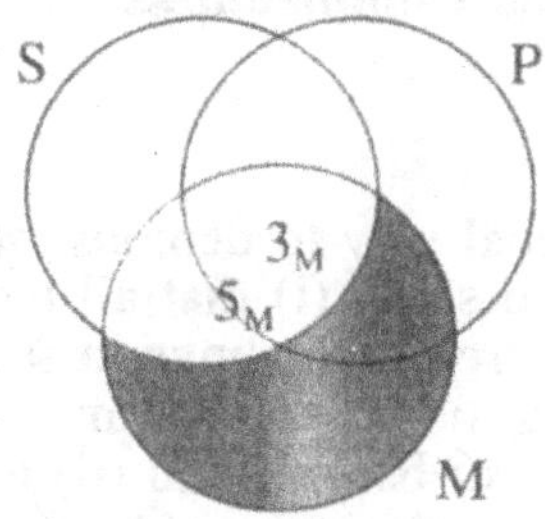

If the conclusion were diagramed, it would be:

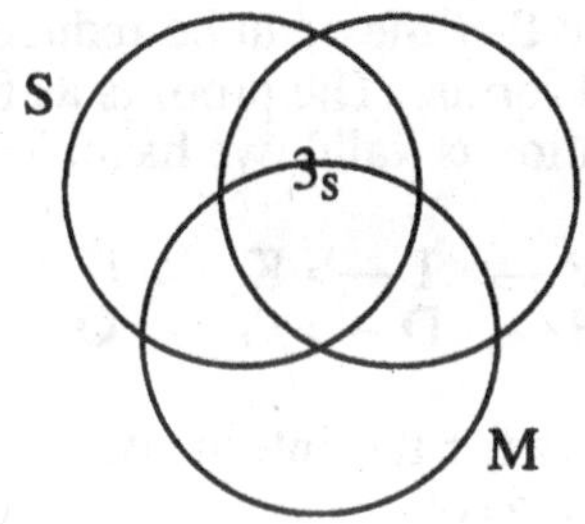

Note that the sub-scripts are wrong for the conclusion to be already diagrammed. Likewise for

TAK-III Most M are P
<u>All M are S</u>
Many S are P

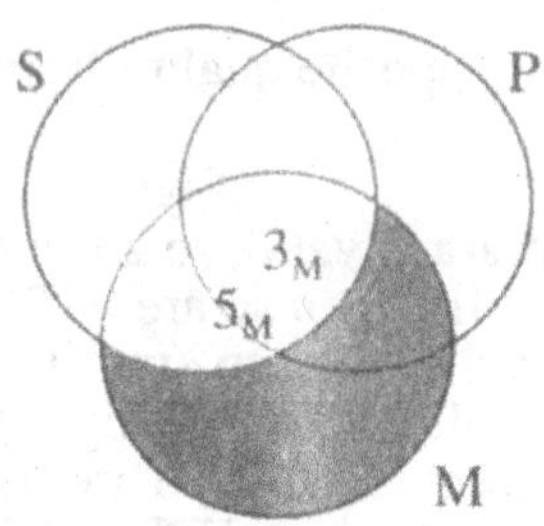

The conclusion would be diagrammed.

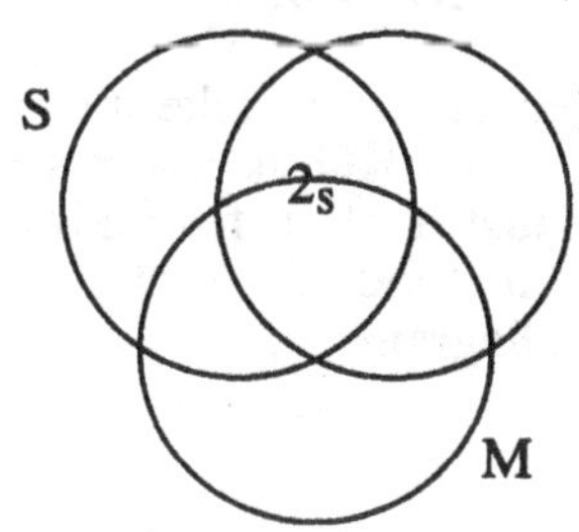

4. Soundness and Completeness

4.1 Traditional

The traditional way to demonstrate the soundness and completeness of the rules is to show (i) that all intermediate forms which satisfy the extended rules (presented above in section 2) can be reduced to a certain subset of the traditional valid forms (i.e., the rules as a whole are sound, if the traditional susbset is) and (ii) that all valid forms of the syllogism are recognized by the rules. (Applying the contemporary concepts of soundness and completeness is discussed below in section 4.2.)

The extended rules are sound, if all forms which meet the extended rules are valid in the sense that they can be reduced to an intuitively valid set of traditional rules and forms. The proof is as follows:

Given that subalternation is valid, we have:

SA1: A —> P —> T —> K —> I
SA2: E —> B —> D —> G —> O

Moreover, obversion holds for the intermediate forms as well as for the classical forms. Hence, we have:

OBV: Qxy <—> Q°xy*

where Q° has the opposite quality from Q, and y* is complement of y.

Figure 1

a. Since Barbara is valid, so are AAP, AAT, and AAK by SAl.
b. If APP is valid, then so are APT, APK, and API by SAl.
c. If ATT is valid, then so are ATK and ATI by SAl.
d. If AKK is valid, so is AKI by SAl.
e. Since Celarent is valid, so are EAB, EAD, and EAG by SA2.
f. If EPB is valid, so are EPD, EPG, and EPO by SA2.
g. If ETD is valid, so are ETG and ETO by SA2.
h. If EKG is valid, so is EKO by SA2.

In the spirit of classical reduction, we take the six additional forms APP, ATT, AKK, EPB, ETD, and EKG as axioms (on a par with Barbara, Celarent, etc.). Informal justification for taking these to be axioms can be found by applying the methods for sections 3.3 and 3.4 above. For example, APP-1 on Venn Diagrams is:

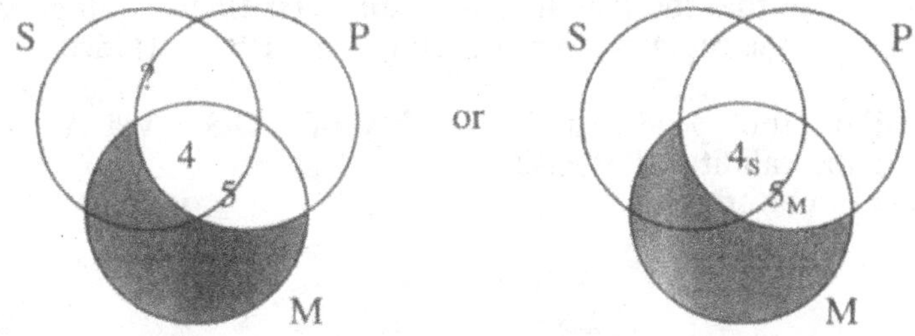

Notice that not only is the form obviously valid, but that whatever numeral is used ("4" above), the form is still valid (with "3", "2", or "1" instead of "4") thereby illustrating the validity of ATT-1, AKK-1, and AII-1. (Similarly, for EPB-1, ETD-1, and EKG-1 *vis à vis* the diagram for ETD-1 in Section 3.3 above.)

Figure 2

i. Since Camestres is valid, so are AEB, AED, and AEG, by SA2.
j. If ABB is valid, so are ABD, ABG, and ABO by SA2.
k. If ADD is valid, so are ADG and ADO by SA2.
1. If AGG is valid, so is AGO by SA2.
m. Since Cesare is valid, so are EAB, EAD, and EAG by SA2.
n. If EPB is valid, so are EPD, EPG, and EPO by SA2.
o. If ETD is valid, so are ETG and ETO by SA2.
p. If EKG is valid, so is EKO by SA2.

From j-1 and n-p it is sufficient to show the validity of ABB, ADD, AGG, EPB, ETD, and EKG. For ABB and AGG, we proceed by indirect reduction as follows. Given ABB,

Apm
<u>Bsm</u>
Bsp

Replace its minor premise with the contradictory of the conclusion and derive the following via AKK-1:

Apm
<u>Ksp</u>
Ksm

It is readily seen that the conclusion of this first figure syllogism is the contradictory of the replaced minor premise in ABB-2. Hence, ABB-2 is valid.

A similar proof produces the validity of AGG-2 via APP-1, thus establishing the validity of AGG-2.

ADD-2 is a bit trickier:

Apm
<u>Dsm</u>
Dsp

From the major premise we obtain Epm* by OBV. By simple conversion, we get Em*p, whose obverse is Am*p*. Taking the obverse of the minor premise yields Tsm*. So, if the premises of ADD-2 are true, so are Am*p* and Tsm*. But by ATT-1, they produce:

Am*p
<u>Tsm*</u>
Tsp*

But the obverse of its conclusion is just Dsp. Hence, if the premises of ADD-2 are true, so is its conclusion.

Next, consider EPB-2:

Epm
<u>Psm</u>
Bsp

By simple conversion of the major premise, we get Emp, which together with the minor premise yields Bsp via EPB-1. Exactly the same use of simple conversion on the major premise reduces ETD-2 to ETD-1, and reduces EKG-2 to EKG-1.

Figure 3

Suppose the following sets of premises are true.

(29)	Amp	Amp	Amp
	Pms	Tms	Kms

By SAl on each of the minor premises, Ims is true. Thus the following set of premises is true.

(29.1) Amp
Ims

But (29.1) entails Isp (Datisi). Hence, Isp follows from each pair of premises in (29). So the validity of API, ATI, and AKI in Figure 3 depends only on the validity of Datisi. (Note that each is the result of starting with Datisi and successively strengthening the minor premise.)

Similarly, the validity of PAI, TAI, and KAI in Figure 3 follows from the validity of Disamis by successively strengthening the major premise.

Exactly the same reasoning produces the validity of EPO, ETO, and EKO from the validity of Ferison, and the validity of BAO, DAO, and GAO from the validity of Bocardo.

Consider next, TTI-3:

(30)

Tmp
Tms
Isp

Replacing the major premise with the contradictory of the conclusion yields

(30.1)

Esp
Tms
Dmp

via ETD-1. But the conclusion, Dmp of (30.1), is the *contrary* of the major premise Tmp of (30). If Dmp is true, Tmp must be false. But Tmp and Tms were assumed to be true. Hence, if the premises of (30) are true, its conclusion must also be true.

With TTI-3 in hand, we may obtain (a) PTI-3, by strengthening the major premise, and (b) TPI-3 by strengthening the minor premise. We may obtain PPI-3 either by strengthening the minor premise of (a) or by strengthening the major premise of (b).

Suppose the premises of the following syllogism are true.

(31)

Pmp
Kms
Isp

Replacing the major premise with the contradictory of the conclusion yields the following set of premises.

(31.1)

Esp
Kms

So, if the premises of (31) are true, so are the ones in (31.1)—given the *reductio* assumption. But these latter yield Gmp via EKG-1. But Gmp contradicts the major premise of (31). Hence, if the premises of (31) are true, so is its conclusion. Thus, PKI-3 is valid.

Next, suppose that the following premises are true.

(32) Kmp
Pms

Then by reordering these premises, the following are true.

(32.1) Pms
Kmp

But since, PKI-3 has just been shown valid, Ips follows from the premises in (32.1). Then by simple conversion, Isp must also be true. Hence, if the premises of (32) are true, so is Isp. KPI-3 is thus valid.

Next consider DTO-3.

(33) Dmp
<u>Tms</u>
Osp

Replacing the major premise with the contradictory of the conclusion, we obtain

(33.1) Asp
Tms

which yields Tmp via ATT-1. But this latter is the contrary of Dmp, the major premise of (33). So, if Tmp is true, Dmp must be false. But Dmp was assumed true. Thus, if the premises of (33) are true, so is its conclusion, and DTO-3 is valid.

By strengthening the minor premise of DTO-3, we get DPO-3. By strengthening the major premise of DTO-3, we get BTO-3. And by strengthening the minor premise of BTO-3, we get BPO-3.

Only two syllogisms remain to be considered in the third figure, and both are justified by similar indirect reductions. First, consider that the premises of the following syllogism are both true.

(34) Bmp
<u>Kms</u>
Osp

Replacing the major premise with the contradictory of the conclusion renders

(34.1) Asp
Kms

But these premises yield Kmp via AKK-1. Since Kmp contradicts Bmp in (34), BKO-3 must be valid. The validity of GPO-3 proceeds similarly using APP-1.

Figure 4

a. Since Camenes is valid, so are AEB, AED, and AEG by SA1.
b. Given the validity of Dimaris, the validity of KAI, TAI, and PAI follows by successive strengthening of the major premise.
c. Given the validity of Fresison, the validity of EKO, ETO, and EPO follows by successive strengthening of the minor premise.

So, all 81 *intermediate* forms of the syllogism entered in (14) above and isolated by the extended rules are valid. Hence, the extended system is sound in the traditional sense. That is, if one accepts the six first-figure intermediates as additional axioms, the validity of the remaining 75 intermediate syllogisms depends only on subalternation, obversion, simple conversion, and on the validity of eleven of the traditionally valid syllogisms: (I) Barbara, Celarent; (II) Cesare, Camestres; (III) Disamis, Datisi, Ferison, Bocardo; (IV) Camenes, Dimaris, and Fresison. So the extended rules are sound if one accepts (a) the six first-figure intermediates as axioms, and (b) the eleven traditional syllogisms along with subalternation, obversion, and simple conversion.

The extended rules are also complete, if all valid forms of the syllogism are recognized by the extended rules. The proof is as follows.

We have just shown that only valid syllogisms are recognized by the extended rules. There are only (*sic*) 4000 syllogistic forms in the extended system. All but 105 of them broke at least one of the extended rules. If we can show that *no* syllogistic form which violates a rule can be valid, then we will have shown that all valid forms have been recognized by the extended rules. We proceed rule by rule to show that no syllogism which violates a rule can be valid.

In section 2.1 above, we mentioned why a violation of either of the distribution rules indicates an invalid syllogism. If the sum of the DIs for the middle term does not exceed maximal distribution in the premises, then each premise may be talking about totally distinct subclasses of M. Thus, the Ms related to P in one premise could be entirely different from those related to S in the other, thereby producing no relation between S and P. If a term is more nearly distributed in the conclusion than it is in the premises, then the syllogism has argued from the basis of a certain number of elements to a larger number of elements. It is always an invalid deductive procedure to assert something of a larger group on the basis of a smaller number of the same group.

In the case of quality, two negative premises make the terms in each premise totally disjoint. If the terms in each premise are unrelated, there is no way to relate S to P. In case one of the premises is negative, the following situation holds. One term (S or P) is affirmatively related to (i.e., coextensive with, included in, or overlapping with) the Ms, while the other term (P or S) is negatively related to the Ms (i.e., excluded from M in whole or in part). Hence, at least some Ss will be negatively related to P. Thus, a conclusion which stated a positive relation between S and P would be unwarranted. Conversely, if S is negatively related to P in the conclusion, but both premises are affirmative, then the relation between S and P must be affirmative. But this conflicts with the negative relation stated in the conclusion. So, if the conclusion is negative, then both premises cannot be affirmative. But as we saw above, they cannot both be negative either. So, a negative conclusion without a negative premise is unwarranted.

Thus, no syllogism which violates at least one of the extended rules is valid. At least one rule is violated by 3,895 syllogistic forms. So, the only valid syllogisms which exist must be in the remaining 105. Since none of them breaks a rule, they are all recognized as valid. Thus, all and only valid syllogisms meet all the extended rules.

4.2 Contemporary

To evaluate a set of inference rules in the contemporary manner requires encapsulating them in a formal system. Then the whole system is evaluated with respect to consistency, soundness, and completeness. Rather than presenting an appropriate formal system including the new rules (which, though possible, brings along many complications far beyond our purposes here), we will apply the contemporary concepts of consistency, soundness, and completeness *by analogy* to their application to explicit formal systems.

A formal system is inconsistent if its rules permit a formula *and* its denial to each be proved. Using syllogistic rules to produce valid syllogistic forms can be thought to *parallel* the way formulas are shown to be theorems in a formal system (by applying its rules of inference). To apply this (syntactic) concept of consistency to the syllogistic rules, then, would be to see if any syllogistic form and its denial were both deemed valid by the rules. But the denial of a syllogistic form doesn't make sense. An obvious modification is that the rules be said to be inconsistent if one and the same syllogistic form is deemed both valid and invalid by the rules. The rules Rl-R6, Section 2.2 above, are not inconsistent in this way. For their nature is such that a form is invalid if and only if it fails to be valid.

Another approach is to parallel the fact that a formal system is said to be inconsistent if there is a theorem in it which is false in every possible world (i.e., some provable statement that must be false like a contradiction is). Then we could say the syllogistic rules are inconsistent (semantically) if there is a form deemed valid by the rules which is non-truth-preserving in every possible world (for every uniform substitution of its terms). That there is no such form is obvious from the soundness proof below (for there is no valid form which is non-truth-preserving on even one of its interpretations).

Finally, if a formal system is inconsistent, then every formula of it can be proved. The analogy of that for the syllogistic rules would be that the rules are inconsistent if every syllogistic form can be deemed valid (by some application or other of the rules). But we have seen that that is not possible, since there are many examples mentioned above of syllogistic forms that do *not* satisfy the rules. Thus, since not every syllogistic form can be deemed valid, the rules are consistent in a *third* analogical sense of "consistent".

A formal system is sound, if all of its theorems are true on every interpretation. (A formula that is true on every interpretation is usually called "valid" in contemporary usage. To avoid specifying *two senses* of "valid", we will eschew the contemporary use of "valid" and speak rather of "true-on-every-interpretation".) What corresponds to true-on-every-interpretation with respect to analogically applying soundness to the rules? Evidently, it is truth-*preserving* on every interpretation. That is, if each syllogistic form that *is* deemed valid by the syllogistic rules is also such that there is no interpretation in which its premises are true and its conclusion false (i.e.., assignment of truth to premises in each interpretation also assigns truth to conclusion) , then the rules are sound. The interpretations that are relevant are, quite simply, the classes that can be assigned to the three *terms* tnat occur in a syllogistic term. That is, any *syllogism* is an argument that has specific terms assigned to the major, minor, and middle term positions; e.g., "All men are politicians, All sailors are men/ so, All sailors are politicians" is a syllogism which has the syllogistic form of Barbara, and has the terms "sailors", "men", and "politicians" for its minor, middle, and major terms (respectively). A syllogistic *form* (not a syllogism with specific terms, but one with markers—e.g., "S", "M", "P"—for its minor, middle, and major term *positions)* is a valid form, we say, if it satisfies the syllogistic rules. The rules themselves are sound, if they generate not one valid form such that there is an interpretation for it wherein truth is not preserved from premises to conclusion.

The rules are sound. This is shown via the new Venn Diagram procedure. First, a specific categorical such as "All sailors are politicians" is true, if the class of sailors that are non-politicians is empty and there is at least one member of the subclass of sailors who are politicians. This is *represented* on the revised Venn Diagrams as follows:

(39)

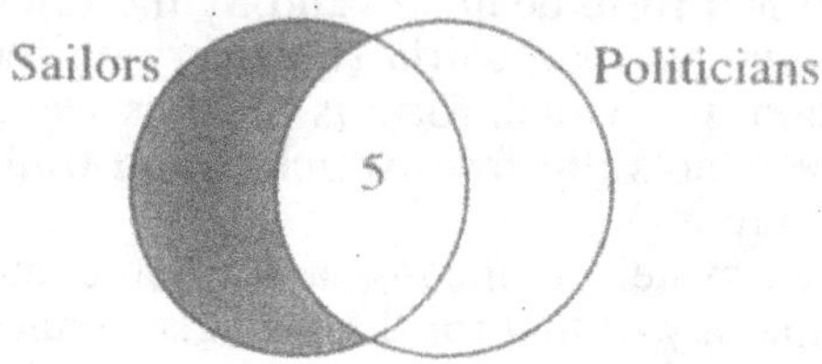

Then the conditions under which any sentence with the form "All S are P" is true is that the sub-class relationships for the two classes selected to be the interpretations of "S " and "P" are as follows:

(40)

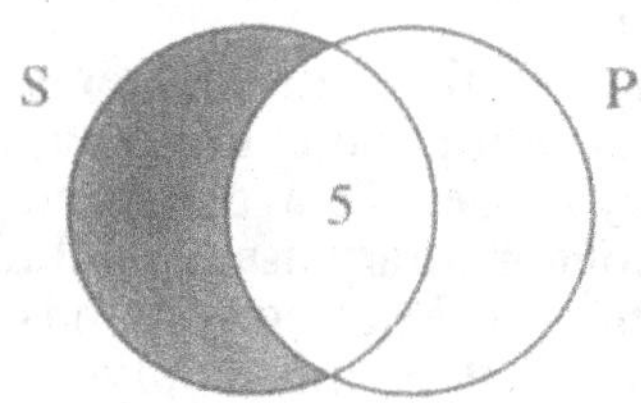

But, then, (40) can obviously be taken to represent all *possible* interpretations of "S" and "P" with respect to the form "All S are P". That is, for each pair of classes chosen, the characteristics and relations for them must be portrayed as in (40) for "All S are P" to be true.

Similarly, for the other categoricals (traditionals and intermediates). "Almost-all sailors are politicians" is true if the quantity of sailors that are politicians *greatly* exceeds the quantity that are not. This is, by stipulation in the new Venn Diagram procedure, represented by

(41)

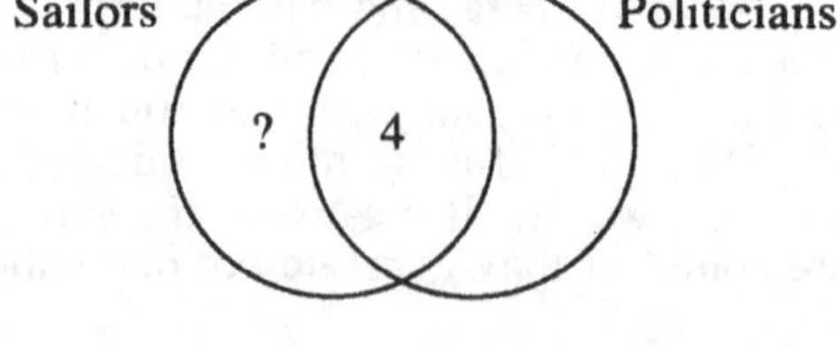

The more general diagram with the same form, therefore, represents the relationships and characteristics of sub-classes for any two classes designated by "S" and "P" in "Almost-all S are P". And so on, for the rest of the categoricals. We won't restate all the details, since they are easy to extrapolate.

Applying by the rules has shown the rules to be sound. (We have so applied the Venn Diagram procedure, though we don't show the results herein. Again, in order to conserve space, we leave the complete display as an exercise for the reader.) For each such application of the Venn Diagrams shows that for any interpretation of "S", "M", and "P" (= classes or portions assigned to each), the conclusion is already true (i.e., the required sub-class relationships are displayed), when the premises are true (the required sub-class relations are explicitly entered on the diagram).

A shorter method to use to demonstrate the rules' soundness in the contemporary sense (truth-preserving on all interpretations, i.e., all assignments of classes) is merely to examine the diagrams for the subalternations and the traditional forms cited above (in section 4.1), since the traditional soundness demonstration given above shows that only those syllogistic forms (and subalternations) need to be proved to preserve truth (in the contemporary sense), since the rest of the forms derive from them.

Are the rules "complete" in the contemporary sense? Well, the closest analog of contemporary completeness that applies to the rules is that the rules are incomplete if there is at least one syllogistic form deemed invalid by the rules such that for all its interpretations it preserves truth from premise to conclusion. That is, find at least one syllogistic form XYZ-N that is not on the list of 105, and show it to be such that for all assignments of classes to its terms, when the premises are true the conclusion is too. If you can show that, the rules are incomplete. The task amounts to finding one Venn Diagram of an invalid syllogism in which the diagramming of the premises already contains the diagramming of the conclusion (since diagramming in the correct way does represent assigning truth with respect to all interpretations, class-wide, of the syllogistic terms). You won't find such a diagram. The proof is as follows.

Proof

Rl-R4 select certain syllogistic forms and exclude others—the so-called valid ones and the invalid ones, respectively. Call the valid ones "theorems", since the use of Rl-R4 directly parallels the use of inference rules in a formal system to generate theorems. Since the Venn Diagram of the premises of a syllogistic form represents all possible ways those premise forms could be jointly true, if the diagramming also represents (without any addition) one of the possible ways the conclusion could be true, the form is a truth-preserving form (i.e., how the truth of the premises "contains" the truth of the conclusion is represented). If the diagramming does not already represent one of the ways the conclusion could be true, the form is non-truth-preserving. With this in mind, let us say that for any syllogistic form XYZ-N:

(42) "XYZ-N is truth-preserving under every interpretation" =df. "XYZ-N has a truth-preserving Venn Diagram (TP diagram)"

Then the completeness of R1-R4 will be shown if we can establish

(43) If XYZ-N has a TP diagram, then it is a theorem (for every syllogistic form XYZ-N).

We shall use the following labeled circles in our proof of (43):

(44)

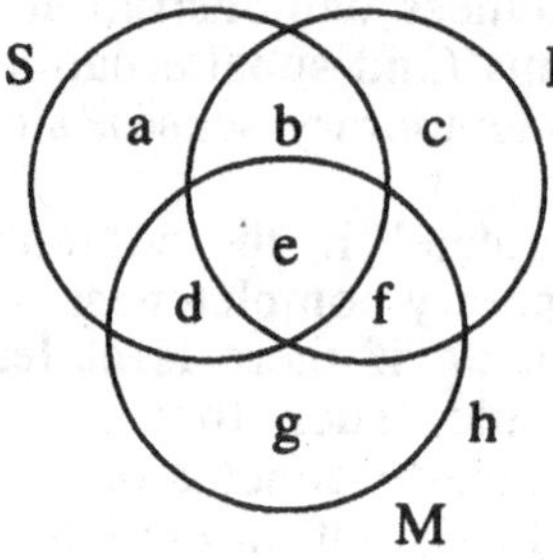

Our strategy is as follows. Since the conclusion of a syllogistic form must appear on every TP diagram, we look at the various ways each conclusion may be represented on (44) and then attempt to show that the only premise representations that could produce the conclusion (if any) are such that XYZ-N is a theorem, i.e., XYZ-N satisfies R1-R4. In other words, we work from the conclusion to the premises required to establish a TP diagram (if any) for that conclusion, and then show that the XYZ-N which has that TP diagram is a theorem by virtue of satisfying R1-R4. The conclusion representations appear below.

(45)

Asp:	$a + d = 0$	Esp: $b + e = 0$
Psp:	$b + e >> a + d$	Bsp: $a + d >> b + e$
Tsp:	$b + e > a + d$	Dsp: $a + d > b + e$
Ksp:	$\sim(a + d >> b + \mathit{b})$	Gsp: $-(b + e >> a + d)$
Isp:	$b + e \neq 0$	Osp: $a + d \neq 0$

Occasionally in the proof below, we use the following abbreviations.

(46) "U" = "universal" "U̲" = "non-universal"
"+" = "affirmative" "-" = "negative"

'U+', then, indicates universal affirmative, or A-forms. "U̲-" indicates non-universal negative, i.e., B, D, G, or 0-forms. And so on for the other possibilities. Also, Venn Diagrams are discussed in terms of the alternative notation of section 3.4 above.

Case 1: The conclusion of XYZ-N is Asp. Then a + d = 0. The only way to get a and d empty is to use two universal premises, and there is only one such pair.

(47) X: Amp d + g = 0
Y: Asm a + b = 0

Notice that in XYZ-N, (i) the middle term has a combined DI > 5, (ii) the DI(S) is not greater in Asp than it is in the minor premise, and similarly for DI(P) with respect to the conclusion and major premise, (iii) both premises are affirmative, and (iv) the conclusion is affirmative. Thus, XYZ-N satisfies Rl-R4 and is thus a theorem.

Case 2: The conclusion of XYZ-N is Esp. Then b + e = 0. To get b and e empty requires the use of two universal premises, and there are only two such pairs (the bracketed premises being diagrammatically equivalent):

(48) (i) X: Apm b + c = 0 (ii) X: | Emp / Epm | e + f = 0
Y: | Ems / Esm | d + e = 0 Y: Asm a + b = 0

Case 3: The conclusion of XYZ-N is Psp. Thus b + e >> a + d. This requires an existence marker (hereafter, 'EM') of the appropriate quantity in b or e. An existence marker can occur in a compartment (or compartments) in one of two ways: (A) by the use of two universal premises (which invokes the existential assumption), and (B) by the use of a non-universal premise.

A: We are here attempting to produce an appropriate EM in b or e by the use of two universal premises. Only three such pairs produce the desired result.

(49) X: (i) Amp d + g = 0 (ii) Amp d + g = 0 (iii) Apm b + c = 0
Y: Asm a + b = 0 Ams f + g = 0 Ams f + g = 0

Pair (i) of (49) produces 5_S in e, i.e., all the s's there are exist in e. Pair (ii) produces 5_M in e, i.e., all the m's there are exist m in e. Pair (iii) produces 5_P in e, i.e., all the p's there are exist in e. Only pair (i) adequately represents Psp. For the truth of pairs (ii) and (iii) is compatible with the interpretation that nearly all the s's are in a, and that interpretation falsifies Psp. So, only pair (i) of (49) can be involved in our present XYZ-N. But that form is readily seen to satisfy Rl-R4 and is thus a theorem.

B: We are here attempting to establish an appropriate EM in b or e by the use of a non-universal premise. Such premises, when diagrammed, produce EMs on lines between compartments unless aided, (in some cases) by a universal premise. In our present situation, the lines relevant to producing an EM in b or e via a non-universal premise are those between (1) a and b, (2) b and c, (3) d and e, and (4) e and f. But in the cases of (1) and (2), the only universals that could move the respective EMs into b are Asp and Aps, respectively. But neither of these is a premise and, hence, cannot be separately diagrammed. So, (1) and (2) won't do.

In the case of (3), the EM is produced by $\underline{U}$+sm or by $\underline{U}$+ms. The only universal premise which can move the EM into e is Amp. But unless the minor premise distributes 's' at least as much as the conclusion does, the truth of X and Y is compatible with the interpretation that nearly all the s's are in a, which would falsify Psp. Since $\underline{U}$+ms provides a DI(S) = 1, and Psp provides a DI(S) 4,

(50)
X: Amp
Y: $\underline{U}$+ms
Z: Psp

has no TP diagram. The only way that

(51)
X: Amp
Y: $\underline{U}$+sm
Z: Psp

will have a TP diagram is if $\underline{U}$ = P. But in this case Rl-R4 are again satisfied, and XYZ-N is a theorem.

Similar remarks hold in the case of (4), only here, the premise required to produce the EM is either $\underline{U}$+mp or $\underline{U}$+pm. The universal premise required to move the EM into e is Ams. This time, no TP diagram is produced. For Ams produces a DI(S) = 1, and the truth of the premises is again compatible with the interpretation that nearly all the s's are in a, which falsifies Psp. So, here we fail to satisfy R2, but also we fail to produce a TP diagram.

In the event that (3) and (4) are produced by some combination of $\underline{\text{U}}$+mp or $\underline{\text{U}}$+mp with either $\underline{\text{U}}$+sm or $\underline{\text{U}}$+ms, we obtain a similar result. All such combinations except possibly

(52) X: $\underline{\text{U}}$+mp
Y: $\underline{\text{U}}$+ms

fail to sufficiently distribute the middle term, in which case they do not force any EM into e and thus fail to produce a TP diagram. But in (52), DI(S) = 1 and in Psp, DI(S) = 4. So again we fail to satisfy R2, and we also fail to produce a TP diagram.

Cases 4-6: The conclusion of XYZ-N is Tsp, Ksp, and Isp, respectively. Exactly the same procedure used in Case 3 produces these three cases. So here, as before, when TP diagrams are produced, XYZ-N is a theorem, and when XYZ-N is not a theorem, no TP diagram is produced.

Case 7: The conclusion of XYZ-N is Bsp. Thus a + d >> b + e. This requires an EM of the appropriate quantity in a or d. As seen in Case 3, there are two ways in which EMs may appear in a compartment: (A) by the use of two universal premises (which invokes the existential assumption), and (B) by the use of a non-universal premise. The treatment of each part is similar to that in Case 3.

A: To produce an appropriate EM in a or d using two universal premises, only the pairs below suffice. (The bracketed premises are diagramatically equivalent.)

(53) (i) X: Apm b + c = 0
Y: |Ems| d + e = 0
|Esm|

(ii) X: |Emp| e + f = 0
|Epm|
Y: Asm a + b = 0

Pair (i) of (53) produces '5_S' in a, and pair (ii) produces '5_S' in d. Since each pair shows that all the s's are in a or all are in d, respectively, the conclusion Bsp may be read off the diagram for each pair. Thus, in each case, XYZ-N has a TP diagram. But it is readily seen that XYZ-N satisfies Rl-R4 in each case and is thus a theorem.

B: To produce an appropriate EM in a or d by means of a non-universal premise, we will again encounter the EMs on the lines between the relevant compartments. The lines in this case are those between (1) a and b, (2) d and e, and (3) d and g. In the case of (1), the EM could only be produced by $\underline{\text{U}}$-sm, and the only universal premise that could move the EM into a would be Apm. The two premises in question satisfy rules

R1, R3, and R4. To satisfy R2, U̲ must be B. But ABB-2 is a theorem. So again, if the syllogism satisfies the rules, it is valid.

In the case of (2), the EM is produced by U̲+sm or U̲+ms. The only universal premise that could move the EM into d is Epm (or Emp, which is diagramatically equivalent). But unless the minor premise distributes 's' at least as much as the conclusion does, the truth of X and Y is compatible with the interpretation that nearly all the s's are in b, which would falsify Bsp. Since U̲+ms provides a DI(S) = 1, and Bsp provides a DI(S) = 4,

(54) X: Epm (or Emp)
Y: U̲+ms
Z: Bsp

has no TP diagram. Moreover, the only way that

(55) X: Epm (or Emp)
Y: U̲+sm
Z: Bsp

will have a TP diagram is if 5 = P. But in this case, Rl-R4 are again satisfied, and XYZ-N is a theorem.

Similar remarks hold in the case of (3), only here, the premise required to produce the EM is U̲-mp. The universal premise required to move the EM into d is Ams. Here, however, no TP diagram is forthcoming. For Ams produces a DI(S) = 1, and the truth of the premises is again compatible with the interpretation that nearly all the s's are in b, which falisifies Bsp. Here we fail to satisfy R2, but we also fail to produce a TP diagram.

In the event that (2) and (3) are produced by a combination of U̲-mp with one of U̲+sm or U̲+ms, we obtain a similar result. All such combinations except possibly

(56) X: U̲-mp
Y: U̲+ms

fail to sufficiently distribute the middle term, in which case they do not force any EM in d and thus produce no TP diagram. If each premise in (56), however, is T or better in quantity, Rl is satisfied, and there will be members in d. But again, the truth of the premises is compatible with the interpretation that nearly all the s's are in b, which again falsifies Bsp. So, once more we fail to satisfy R2, but we also fail to produce a TP diagram.

Cases 8-10: The conclusion of XYZ-N is Dsp, Gsp, and Osp, respectively. Exactly the same procedure used in Case 7 produces these three cases. So here, as before, when TP diagrams are produced, XYZ-N is a theorem, and where XYZ-N is not a theorem, no TP diagram is produced.

This completes the proof of (43) above. We have considered every possible conclusion Z and investigated the premises (if any) which could produce it. In all cases where a TP diagram occurred, XYZ-N was a theorem, i.e., it satisfied Rl-R4. Thus, our rules are complete.

5. Other Quantities

5.1 Fractional Quantities

If we introduce a sixth quantity of the type suggested by Rescher and Gallagher (1965), it would be expressed by "Half-or-more". The following square results (with lines, dashes, dots, and arrows indicating the relations they do in (2) above):

(57)

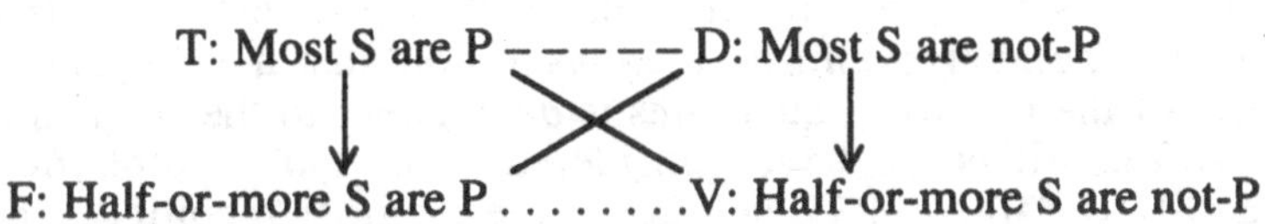

With six quantities, there would be 6912 syllogistic forms, some proper subset of which would be valid.

The "or more" in "Half-or-more" is superfluous. As discussed in Chapter 1 above, each of the non-universal quantifier expressions requires a tacit "or more" rider to make the relations of (2) work (which are the basis for developing the syllogism to encompass intermediate quantities). So, "some" means "(at least) one *or more*", "many" means "(at least) many *or more*", and "few" means "(at most) few *or less*" (since "few" is a negative quantifier word like "none", "or less" is substituted). Thus, if we were to introduce a new quantifier word for the sixth quantity, it would require the "or more" rider too. But that means "Half-or-more" in (57) is redundant. Using simply "Half" in the system already carries the rider "or more". So, we should revise (57) to obtain:

(58) T: Most S are P – – – – – D: Most S are not-P

F: Half the S are P . . . . V: Half the S are not-P

Then we could call the quantity "half" and call the categoricals containing this new quantifier "half statements" (corresponding to the universal, predominant, majority, common, and particular statements).

One of the virtues of the rules and methods offered above in sections 2 and 3 is that they are easily revised to include this additional intermediate quantity. An immediate challenge, however, is the question of how to interpolate even *further* such quantifiers. For if *half* categoricals are permitted, why not permit 'third categoricals', 'fourth categoricals', and so on? Even though they can be added, an important question immediately arises about 'third categoricals'. Should the DI for 'third categoricals'—those of the form "A third of the S are P"—be less, or else more, than 2. This is tantamount to the question of whether a statement of the form "Many S are P" should entail (but not be entailed by) a statement of the form "A third (or more) of the S are P" or *vice versa*. In sum, is a third *many*? Or is it less than many?

One conservative way to handle this problem with *fractional* quantities—i.e., halves, thirds, etc.—is to hold that the 'logical plane' (as it were) of the fractional quantities is *orthogonal* to the 'logical plane' of the five quantities we have considered. The *entry* point (or point of contact) to the fractional quantities is the majority quantity. So, even if the fractional quantities do not readily assimilate with the five we have considered (but 'pass through' as it were), there is a specifiable logic to the fractionals. To see this, first notice that majority statements can be re-phrased as follows:

(59) "Most S are P" =df. "More-than-half the S are P"
"Most S are not-P =df. "More-than-half the S are not-P"

Then, reformulate (58) as follows:

(60) T: More-than-half the S are P – – D: More-than-half the S are not-P

F: Half the S are P . . . .V: Half the S are not-P

Then, 'third categoricals' would appear in the following square:

(61) More-than-2/3rd the S are P – – More-than-2/3rd the S are not-P

↓ X ↓

A third the S are P . . . A third the S are not-P

(And, as previously raised, does a statement of the form "More than 2/3rd the S are not-P" entail one of the form "Few S are P", or is it rather entailed by it?) The general scheme of all future squares of opposition dictated by additional fractionals would be:

(62)

More-than-(n–m)/n the S are P – – More-than-(n–m)/n the S are not-P

↓ X ↓

m/n the S are P . . . m/n the S are not-P

for all pairs of integers n, m such that $1/2 \geq m/n$

Be careful to note that "more than" statements—such as "More than 2/3 S are P"—are *not* equivalent to "or more" statements—such as "2/3 or more S are P". For example, if 2/3 of 12 oranges are spoiled—viz., 8 of them—then that is enough to make "2/3 or more of the oranges are spoiled" true. However, if exactly 8 are spoiled, then though "2/3 or more of the oranges are spoiled" is true, still "More than 2/3 of the oranges are spoiled" is not true.

A schematic composite square of 'fractional' oppositions is:

(63)

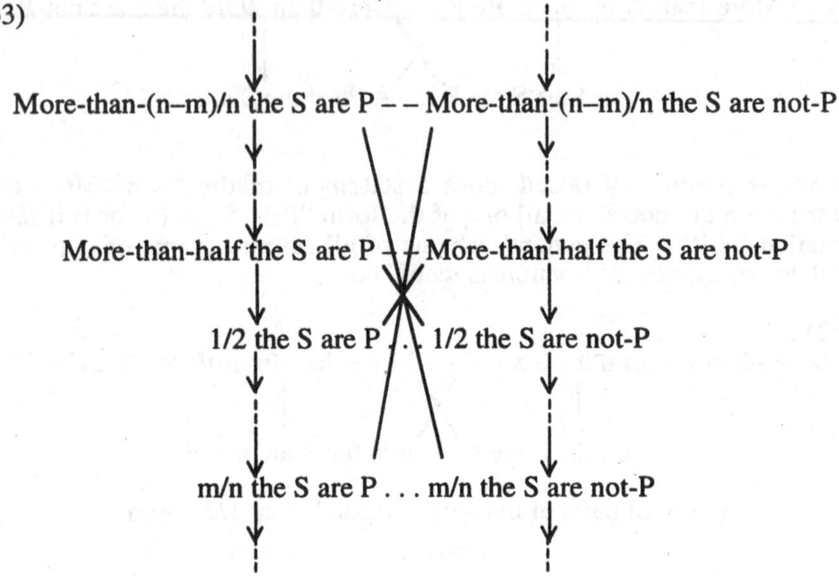

Fractional categoricals in the upper left-hand portion of (63), we will call "increasing fractional affirmative categoricals" (i.e., increasing from 1/2)—or "increasing affirmatives" for short. Categoricals in the lower left-hand portion of the square, we will call "decreasing fractional affirmative categoricals" (decreasing from 1/2) or "decreasing affirmatives" for short. Similarly, the upper and lower right-hand sides —'increasing negatives' above and 'decreasing negatives' below. Although this terminology has some further uses below, we need it here simply to express an important feature of the composite square of (63) —viz., the categoricals in each of the four 'corners' (increasing-affirmative, increasing-negative, decreasing-affirmative, and decreasing-negative) are conceived of as *ordered.* The ordering is according to size of fractional quantifier involved. The decreasing categoricals (affirmative and negative) are ordered from top to bottom with respect to the *decreasing* size of the fractional quantifiers in the statements—i.e., 1/2 ≥ m/n > 0 (=None) (e.g., "1/9" is *less than* "3/23" and so "1/9th the S are P" occurs below "3/23rds of the S are P" on the list of decreasing affirmatives). Similarly, the increasing categoricals (affirmative and negative) are ordered from bottom to top with respect to increasing quantity—i.e., 1(=All) > (n–m)/n ≥ 1/2.

5.2 Higher-Quantity Syllogistic Systems

In section 1, we pointed out that if the percentage of a class that is to count as "many" is as small as 25% and the percentage that is to count as "almost-all" is as small as 75%, then the counter-examples to syllogisms like PKI-III can be constructed. These aren't the only pairs of percentages that generate counter-examples. For any pair of percentages i and j (where i is the percentage that is enough to make a "many" statement true, j is enough to make an "almost-all" statement true, and so $j > i$), if $100 \geq i + j$, then counter-examples can be obtained (e.g., 20% and 80%, 10% and 90%, etc.) To maintain the soundness of the 5-quantity syllogistic—i.e.,for systems with "Almost-all" "Few" and "Many"—the following additional assumption is, therefore, required.

(64) For X as the percentage of members of a class of S's that are also members of a class of P's required to make "Many S are P" true, and
for Y as the percentage of members of a class of S's that are also members of a class of P's required to make "Almost-all S are P" true,
$X \geq i$ and $Y > j$, where $i + j = 100$.[15]

Consider $i = 25$ and $j = 75$ for example. By (64), it follows that

(65) (Many S are P) if and only if ($X \geq 25\%$)
(Almost-all S are P) if and only if ($Y > 75\%$)

Or consider $i = 20$ and $j = 80$, so that fewer are needed to count as "many", but consequently more are needed to count as "almost-all". Then, by (64), it follows that

(66) (Many S are P) if and only if ($X \geq 20\%$)
(Almost-all S are P) if and only if ($Y > 80\%$).

Thus, liberalizing what counts as "many" (i.e., allow fewer to count) results in constricting what counts as "almost-all", and *vice versa*.
Now it is not clear exactly what values of i and j to choose, but if the 5-quantity syllogism (as above in sections 1-4) is to be defended, some values or other must be selected. But then, for any particular values, the problem of integrating fractional quantities with the five intermediates is resolvable! For example, let $i = 25$ and $= 75$ so that "Many S are P" is true if and only if 25% or more of the S are P and "Almost-all S are P" is true if and only if more than 75% of the S are P. With this selection, the question of how much is "many" is answered. "1/4 the S are P" entails

(and is entailed by) "Many S are P" and for any fraction m/n, where m/n > 1/4, "m/n the S are P" also entails "Many S are P" since "m/n" like all the other quantifiers is interpreted as "at least m/n and possibly more". Of course, "Many S are P" does *not* entail "m/n the S are P" for m > 1/4, but "Many S are P" entails "m/n the S are P" if 1/4 > m/n. In sum, the decreasing-affirmatives portion of (63), for i = 25 is:

(67) 1/2 the S are P

↓

⋮

↓ for $m_1/n_1 > 1/4 > m_2/n_2$

m_1/n_1 the S are P

↓

⋮

↓

Many S are P (=1/4 the S are P)

↓

⋮

↓

m_2/n_2 the S are P

↓

⋮

Accepting (67) appears to be simply stipulating that "many", as in "Many S are P" *means* what "one-fourth" (or "1/4") does. At the very least, it *is* identifying "Many" with "one-fourth" in that "Many S are P", *given* that i = 25 (and so j = 75), functions exactly like "1/4 the S are P" does (logically speaking).[16]

Corresponding to (67) is the increasing-negative array, the denials (in reverse order) of (67), as follows:

(68)

↓

More than $(n_2-m_2)/n_2$ the S are not-P

↓

for $(n_2-m_2)/n_2 > 3/4 > (n_1-m_1)/n_1$

Almost-all the S are not-P

↓

More than $(n_1-m_1)/n_1$ the S are not-P

↓

Most S are not-P

Now the stage is set to extend the 5-quantity syllogism (developed in sections 1-4 above) to as many quantities as you like. For (i) majority propositions (positive and negative) are included among the fractional quantities (viz., they occur in denials of "half" propositions), (ii) predominant and common propositions are included among the fractionals by selecting values for i and j (which *must* be carried out in some satisfactory way in order to defend the 5-quantity syllogistic), and (iii) universal and particular propositions can be included among the fractionals by simply identifying them with limits of the series displayed in (67) and (68). To carry out these latter identifications, simply identify "Some S are P" with the last member of (67) and "All S are not-P" with the first member of (68). There must *be* such first and last members if we select a finite number of fractional quantifiers. Of course, we can choose the number as high as we like. For example, let the desired number of quantities be k (some finite whole number). Consider all the quantifiers m/n in the set of k quantifiers, where $1/2 \geq m/n$. The total number of quantities k will be *twice* the number of such quantifiers, when k is even. When k is odd, the total number will be twice that number plus one. One of the quantifiers m_i/n_i, where $1/2 > m_i/n_i$, will be identified with "Many" (e.g., perhaps "1/4" =df. "Many", when i = 25) and, consequentially, the quantifier "More than $(n_i-m_i)/n_i$" will be identified with "Almost-all". Since the set of quantifiers is finite (k in number), there will be a first quantifier in the set and a last one too, if the set is ordered in terms of decreasing size (a quantifier q_i is smaller-than another q_j if the fraction that q_i wholly or in part is is smaller than the fraction that q_j wholly or in part is.) Let the first such quantifier be identified with "All" (the universal quantifier) and the last such quantifier be identified with "Some" (the particular quantifier, meaning "at least one"). Then we can list the quantifiers for a syllogistic system of k quantities as follows—in the order from universal to particular—by listing the categoricals in which they appear:

(69)

More than $(n_A-m_A)/n_A$ the S are (not) P . . . . <=> All the S are (not) P

↓

More than $(n_X-m_X)/n_X$ the S are (not) P —— includes Almost-all S are (not) P

↓

More than 1/2 the S are (not) P . . . . <=> Most S are (not) P

↓

1/2 the S are (not) P

↓

m_X/n_X the S are (not) P —— includes Many S are (not) P

↓

m_A/n_A the S are (not) P . . . . <=> Some S are (not) P

Exactly where "Many S are P" occurs is determined by choice of value for i: i.e., "i/100 S are P" = "Many S are P", so "Many" = "m_X/n_X", when m_X/n_X = i/100. Similarly, "Almost-all" = "More than $(n_X-m_X)/n_X$" when m_X/n_X = i/100.

For example, consider having a syllogistic system with 12 quantities rather than 2 or 5. Also, select a class of S's that has 12 members. (Having the number of members of the class the same as the number of quantities is merely a convenience in constructing a perspicuous example. Any number of quantities in a syllogistic system should apply to classes of S's, M's, and P's with any different number of members.) Here are 12 quantities that we might select (i.e., 12 easy-to-understand fractional quantifiers for expressing 12 quantities).

(70)

12 Affirmative Categoricals	5-Quantity Correlates	Truth-conditions for 12 membered S-class
More than 11/12 the S are P	All S are P.	12 S are P
More than 5/6 the S are P		11 S are P
More than 3/4 the S are P	Almost-all S are P.	10 S are P
More than 2/3 the S are P		9 S are P
More than 7/12 the S are P		8 S are P
More than 1/2 the S are P	Most S are P	7 S are P
1/2 the S are P		6 S are P
5/12 the S are P		5 S are P
1/3 the S are P		4 S are P
1/4 the S are P		3 S are P
1/6 the S are P		2 S are P
1/12 the S are P	Some S is P	1 S is P

The 5-quantity correlates in (70) hold if i = 25. And, as explained, these correlates can just be adopted as definitions of "all", "almost-all", "many" and "some" (where "most" is already defined as "more than 1/2") in the 12-quantity system. Finally, each truth-condition statement contains an integer quantifier (discussed in the next section) which is subject to the same so-called 'liberal' interpretation as used for all the other quantifiers above; e.g., "7 S are P" is interpreted as "at least 7, possible more, S are P".

(70) illustrates how a selection of fractional quantifiers can be arranged to produce the candidate forms for a 12-quantity syllogistic system. By analogy, for any number of quantities k (for finite k), we can formulate the candidate categoricals; i.e., some selection of k/2 fractions (when k is even), or (k–1)/2 fractions (when k is odd), can be arranged to form a list of candidate categoricals for a syllogistic system of k quantities (i.e., via k fractional quantifiers).[17] The test of whether the candidates succeed in providing a syllogistic system is whether such a system can be developed that is a sound and complete extension of the 5-quantity system given above. What such a correct extension would be can be seen by considering, first, how to expand the 5-quantity system to 6 and, then, how to add further fractionals by analogy.

First, the basic square of oppositions for 6-quantity categoricals would be:

(71)

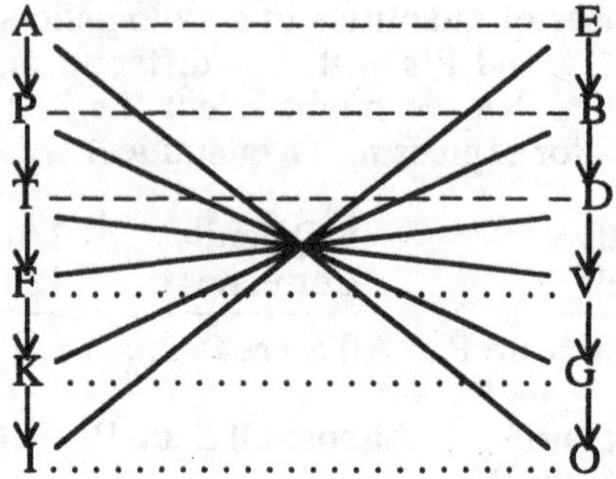

Consider a typical array from the table of valid syllogisms given in (14) above—e.g., the first triangular array of Figure I. If we were to add a sixth quantifier—viz., "Half" (as introduced in 5.1—the resulting additional categoricals (F and V statements) would occur within that array as follows (i.e., the new valid argument forms are those containing "F"s and "V"s, those enclosed in rectangular boundaries)

(73)

AAA					
AAP	APP				
AAT	APT	ATT			
AAF	APF	ATF	AFF		
AAK	APK	ATK	AFK	AKK	
AAI	API	ATI	AFI	AKI	AII

Similarly, the whole of a new table for Figure IV, with 6 quantities (via adding "half"-statements) would be:

(73)

AAI	AEE	EAO
PAI	AEB	EPO
TAI	AED	ETO
FAI	AEV	EFO
KAI	AEG	EKO
IAI	AEO	EIO

Now we have not given the rules for generating these valid forms (nor another new Venn Diagram method), nor any soundness and completeness proofs. Rather, we claim that sufficient study of the structure of the arrays in (14)—and of the reasons for those structures via the 'intermediate' nature of the new quantifiers (discussed in section 1)—will make it obvious that any extension of the 5-quantity rules (and of the Venn Diagram method of section 3) to 6 quantities will have to validate argument forms in the new positions given in (72) and (73)—as well as in analogous new positions for the other figures. For example, consider the new form FAI-IV alleged to be valid in (73). In (14), KAI-IV is listed as valid. The rules of section 2 (proved sound and complete in section 4) confirm it as valid. Now the new form FAI-IV is just like KAI-IV except that one premise is stronger. That is, "Half the P are M" replaces "Many P are M" in going from KAI-IV to FAI-IV. But this is simply taking a valid syllogistic form and strengthening one of its premises. But, then, the result must be valid too. For you can't make a valid form invalid by strengthening one of its premises. Arguments analogous to this one support the positions of all the new forms with "half" statements in them alleged to be valid in (72) and (73) as well as all the others for the rest of the array in (14) which we have not given here.

We believe it is quite evident how to construct syllogistic rules for a 6-quantity syllogistic system (and how to validate them via Venn Diagrams and other methods). The sensible way to revise the rules and Venn Diagrams for 6 quantities would appear to be re-numeralize—so that the DI of universals was 6 and the numeral used on Venn Diagrams for universals would be "6". Also, it would appear that the only rule needing to be changed from section 2 would be Rl—replacing "5" with "6". After re-numeralizing in the Venn Diagram method, and adjusting all the directions consequent on re-numeralizing, the only rule that must be adjusted is the last interpretation rule (at the end of section 3.2)—so that a "1" is interpreted to be present when the numbers the numerals indicate add-up to a number greater than 6 (rather than greater than 5). Finally, we claim that each additional quantifier to be added to increase the system from 6 to 7, from 7 to 8, and so on—must be introduced, supported, and defended in *exactly* the same way. New quantifiers occur in new valid forms that fall in between those already occurring—just as the valid forms proposed in (72) and (73) fall *in between* already existing forms. For example, if we add "third" categoricals (affirmative and negative) to incorporate a seventh quantity (after the sixth one in "half" statements), then the new valid forms are easy to interpolate. First, let affirmative "third" statements "1/3 the S are P", be abbreviated by "S" and negative ones, "1/3 the S are not-P", be abbreviated by "Z". Then revising the Fourth Figure again—adding this quantity to categoricals so that new valid forms can be added to (73) yields:

(74)

AAI	AEE	EAO
PAI	AEB	EPO
TAI	AED	ETO
FAI	AEV	EFO
SAI	AEZ	ESO
KAI	AEG	EKO
IAI	AEO	EIO

Again the new seventh quantity forms are enclosed in rectangular boundaries, their positions to be defended by arguments analogous to the arguments above for the sixth quantity forms (together with the reasonable assumption that whatever value is selected for i, such as i = 25, it will certainly be the case 33-1/3 > i).[18]

So, we have shown how to construct sound and complete syllogistic systems for k quantities, where finite k is as high as you like. You do this by selecting additional fractional quantifiers for insertion in new fractionally quantified categoricals and by inserting new intermediate (fractional) syllogisms in appropriate positions in the patterns for valid syllogisms—the patterns first introduced in (14). Some simple equations characterize the results. First, the number of syllogistic forms (valid and invalid), s, for k quantities is (as suspected):

(75) $$s = 32k^3$$

More importantly, the number of valid syllogistic forms, v, for k quantities is:

(76) $$v = 3k(k + 2)$$

The reasoning leading to (76) is as follows. First, the *patterns* of valid forms for all syllogistic systems (for k quantities) will look like those in (14), the 5-quantity system. For Figures I-III, there are six triangular arrays of valid forms. The number of forms in each array is $(k^2 + k)/2$. So, 6 times $((k^2 + k)/2)$ gives the number of valid forms for I-III. Figure IV contains 3k valid forms. So, the total for I-IV is

(77) $$v = 6(k^2 + k)/2) + 3k$$

The equation in (76) is an equivalent simplification of that in (77). Thus:

(78) For k = 2 (i.e., the traditional syllogism),
$s = 32k^3 = 32 \times 8 = 256$, and
$v = 3k(k + 2) = 6 \times 4 = 24$.
For k = 5 (i.e., sections 1-5 above),
$s = 32k3 = 32 \times 125 = 4{,}000$, and
$v = 3k(k + 2) = 15 \times 7 = 105$.
For k = 6 (as in (72) and (73) above),
$s = 32k3 = 32 \times 216 = 6912$, and
$v = 3k(k + 2) = 18 \times 8 = 144$.
For k = 12 (as in (71) above),
$s = 32k3 = 32 \times 1728 = 55{,}296$, and
$v = 3k(k + 2) = 36 \times 14 = 504$.

5.3 Other Numerical Quantifiers

In addition to the fractional quantifiers, there are at least two other kinds of quantifiers that can be considered for integration with the traditional and intermediate quantifiers—viz., the *integer* quantifiers (whole positive number expressions) and the *straight fraction* quantifiers. "Six" (and "6" too) in "Six men are asleep upstairs" is an integer quantifier. "19/23" (and "Nineteen twenty-thirds") in "19/23 of the students failed the entrance examination" is a straight fraction quantifier. "19/23" is not a fractional quantifier. Fractional quantifiers larger than one-half are written as "More-than" statements (except for one kind of case mentioned below, the "middle quantifier"). Thus, straight fraction quantifiers and fractional quantifiers only agree when they are less than or equal to one-half (= “Half”, often written “1/2”). Let “q” range over integer quantifiers, “m/n” range over straight fraction quantifiers, and “f” range over fractional quantifiers. Then the three forms of categorical propositions with numerical quantifiers in them are schematically represented:

(79) qS are (not) P . . . . e.g., “Two S are P”
m/n S are (not) P . . . . e.g., “3/13 the S are P”
fS are (not) P . . . . e.g., “More than 2/3 the S are P

Consider the *integer* quantifiers. The denial of “One S is P” (where the quantifier is still liberally interpreted, taken as “One or more” and/or “At least one”) is “Not one S is P”—which is synonymous (we hold) with “No S is P” and logically equivalent to “All S are not-P”. So, the denial of “One” quantified statements generates Aristotle’s square:

(80) All S are P - - - - - - All S are not-P
One S is P . . . . One S is not-P

But what do we get from “Two S are P”, “Three S are P”, etc.? The answer appears to be nothing, unless we introduce finite class size. Let t be the number of members of the class of S’s. Then the denial of “Two S are P”—relative to class size t of S’s—is equivalent to an interesting form:

(81) ~(Two S are P) <=> ((t + 1) – Two) S are not-P

For example, it’s false that at least 2 out of 10 forks (i.e., t = 10) are bent if and only if 9 (or more) of the forks are not bent. Generalizing for integer quantifiers q, where t is the number of members of the S-class:

(82) (t + 1 – q)S are P - - - - - - (t + 1 – q)S are not-P
qS are P. . . . . qS are not-P

(82) holds for t being an odd or even number, when $t/2 > q$. When t is odd and we let $q = (t + 1)/2$, the square collapses top to bottom. When t is even and $q > t/2$, *or* when t is odd and $q > (t + 1)/2$, the square of opposition in (82) flips from top-to-bottom.

(82) compares to (62). Each is a schematic representation for a set of Aristotelian-like oppositions. To finish the initial picture of numerical

quantities (prior to seeking equivalences), we need a similar schematic square of oppositions for straight fractions. Consider (where n > m):

(83) (n + 1 – m)/n S are P – – – – – – (n + 1 – m)/n S are not-P

m/n S are P. . . . . .m/n S are not-P

This schematic square does work if it is regarded simply as a translation of (82) for n = t. So, if the number of S's is t, and also n = t, then m = q. And the same restrictions mentioned at the end of the last paragraph for (82) also apply to (83). Note in particular, the second one—when it is odd and q = (t + 1)/2, the square collapses top-to-bottom. For example, let n = t = 7, and m = q = 4. This gives

(84) 4/7 S are P 4/7 S are not-P

4/7 S are P 4/7 S are not-P

wherein the square of opposition collapses. But now consider the case when t > n—say, let t = 14. Does the square hold? Applying (83) to n = 7 and m = 4, though now t = 14, would look exactly like (84). But (831, asserts, among other things,

(85) ~(4/7 (of 14) S are P) <=> 4/7 (of 14) S are not-P

But (85) is false! For it is false that 4/7 of 14 S are P if and only if it is false that 8/14 of 14 S are P. But it is false that 8/14 of 14 S are P if and only if it is true that 7/14 of 14 S are not-P. So, if there are 14 S's, the denial of (4/7 S are P) is equivalent to (1/2 the S are not-P) , since 7/14 = 1/2. Whereas, if there are only 7 S's, the very same denial is equivalent to (4/7 S are not-P). So (83) does not hold in general. It *only* holds for n = t and m = q.

The *only* way to get a general schematic representation for straight fraction quantifiers is to bring in explicitly the size of the class of S's—viz., t. The schematic square that works is (for n > m):

(86) (1 - m/n + 1/t) S are P – – – – – – (1 - m/n + 1/t)S are not-P

m/n S are P . . . . m/n S are not-P

In sum, you cannot obtain an unqualified answer to what is "~(4/7 S are P)" equivalent to (Aristotelianly)? The question is too indeterminate. The value for t must be brought in, as it is in (86). Notice that "4/7 (of t)

S arc P" for t = 14 via (86) is one of the flipped cases; i.e., the direction of entailments is reversed:

(87)

1/2 S are P		1/2 S are not-P
↑	╳	↑
4/7 S are P		4/7 S are not-P

So, something like the qualifications appended to (82) must also apply to (86). The first is that if n is odd or even, $n/2 > m$. When n is odd and also n = t, then $(n + 1)/2$ is permitted as a value for m. (The latter is the case like m/n = 4/7, when the square collapses, top-to-bottom.) When n = t, (86) still applies.

Many cases of (86) when $t > n$ give peculiar looking results. A little interpretation here is required, to save (86) from restriction to only very easy to compute cases. For example, consider m/n = 1/7 and t = 23. Then ~(1/7 S are P) <=> 145/161 S are not-P. But how could 145/161 of the 23 S be considered? Granted that 145/161 of 23 things is 20-and-5/7 of them, but we are not in a position to consider 5/7 of one thing. (The fractions we are considering herein are fractions of a set of things. Each member of the set we leave intact.) However, notice what "145/161 of the S are not-P" *says*. It says that *at least* that proportion of Ss are not-P. What is the greatest number of S's that would satisfy, without going beyond, that proportion? It's 20. But that is what the application of (86) has given us. It says that 20-and-5/7 of them, *at least* that many, are not-P. We cannot round that mixed number off to 21, because that exceeds the quantity (86) produces. Thus, we must round it to the next lowest whole number. So, for the purposes at issue here, 145/161 of the S is 20/23 of them—since there are only 23 altogether. In general, the interpretation rule is this: when $(1 - m/n + 1/t) = m'/n'$ such that $n' \neq t$ and $t/n' \neq u$ (for u being any positive integer), then substitute m^*/n^* for m'/n' where $n^* = t$ and $m^* = (t(m'/n') - x/y)$, where "t(m'/n')" has the form "W-x/y" for some positive integers W, x, and y (i.e., t(m'/n') reduces to a positive mixed number and m* is the next lowest whole number).

We believe that this strategy—rounding off the numerator of certain fractions to the next lowest integer—is the correct method of interpretation, not just an *ad hoc* device to save (86). Why should it be a surprise that some statements are not so easy to interpret when they contain straight fraction quantifiers that are ill-matched to the actual number of members of a set they are applied to (i.e., when m/n is ill-matched to t)? Similar technicalities in interpreting applications of (86) occur when $n > t$. We won't pursue them here.

To state some preliminary equivalences (and related entailments) between integer, straight fraction, and fractional quantifiers requires some rather strong simplifying restrictions.[19] Let k_1 be the number of integer quantifiers under consideration at some moment. To consider equivalences requires that $k_1 \geq t$, for t the number of S's (for a particular example). Let k_2 be the number of straight fraction quantifiers, and k_3 be the number of fractionals (both at some particular moment for some particular example). Also, let every set of integer quantifiers contain only consecutive integers (without gaps) beginning with "1"; i.e., each set of q's contains "1", "2", "3" and so on ending with "k_1" (skipping no integer q_i, where $k_1 \geq q_i \geq 1$). Similarly, let each set of straight fraction quantifiers contain consecutive rational fractions with one single numerator in their unreduced forms. Thus, a set of straight fraction quantifiers contains "l/n", "2/n", and so on ending with "k_2/n" (without gaps). (Since n = k_2, this makes it look like the last member will be m/n k_2/n = 1. Such will not be the case, since it will be stipulated that m,/n = All.) Similarly for each set of fractionals—let quantifiers of decreasing affirmatives and negatives (i.e., where 1/2 ≥ m/n) be consecutive, rational, and with a single denominator. Each set of fractionals, then, begins with "l/n", "2/n", and continues on to "m/n", where m/n = 1/2 (when n is even) or where m/n is as large as possible and still 1/2 > m/n (when n is odd). When k_3 is odd, and so n is too, there will be a so-called "middle quantifier", viz., ((n + 1)/2)/n. To achieve complete consecutiveness, it is hereby stipulated that for n odd and m = (n + 1)/2, m/n = Most.[20] For k_3 (=n) even, after m/n = 1/2, the increasing quantifiers begin—i.e., More than (n – m)/n for m/n = 1/2, and so on to More-than (n – 1)/n (=All). For k_3 (=n) odd, after the largest m/n, such that 1/2 > m/n, the first increasing fractional quantifier is not of the form "More than (n – m)/n", but is simply ((n + 1)/2) (the "middle quantifier", viz., "Most"). After that, the increasing quantifiers continue like those for k_3-even after m/n = 1/2.

Further, in all of the following the fractions within straight fraction quantifiers and within fractionals are assumed to be in 'highest' terms. To get m/n into highest terms, find the number of quantifiers in question (find k_2 or k_3). (For example, we might have a class of S's with 12 members, t = 12, but only have six straightfraction quantifiers—viz., 1/6, 1/3, 1/2, 2/3, 5/6, and All. Then k_2 = 6 (not 12).) Then replace m/n with (k_2(m/n))/k_2, where the "k" of the denominator remains *unreduced* while the numerator *is* reduced. (For example, consider "m/n" being "2/3", when k_2 = 6. Then "2/3" in highest terms is "(6(2/3))/6" or "4/6".)

(88) and (89) state some relevant equivalences and entailments between statements with integer, fractional, and straight-fraction quantifiers under the just-stated restrictions. (90) and (91) illustrate these relationships. ("<=>" represents logical equivalence and "—>" represents logical entailment.)

(88) Integer/Straight-Fraction Relationships
(a) For $t = n$, (qS are P) <=> (m/n S are p)
if-and-only-if m/n = All, when $q = t = m = n$, *or*
if-and-only-if $n = t$ and $m = q$, when $t > q$.
(b) For $t \neq n$, (qS are P) –> (m/n S are P)
if-and-only-if $q/t \geq m/n$, *and*
(m/n S are P) –> (qS are P)
if-and-only-if $m/n \geq q/t$

(89) Integer/Fractional Relationships (where $k_3 = n$)
(a) For $k_3 = t$,
when k3 is even, (qS are P) <=> (fS are P)
if-and-only-if f = More-than $(q - 1)/t$, when $(q - 1)/t \geq 1/2$, *or*
if-and-only-if $f = q/t$, when $1/2 \geq q/t$.
when k_3 is odd, (qS are P) <=> (fS are P)
if-and-only-if f = More-than $(q - 1)/t$, when $q - 1 \geq (t = 1)/2$, *or*
if-and-only-if $f = q/t$ (=Most), when $q = (t + 1)/2$, *or*
if-and-only-if $f = q/t$, when $1/2 > q/t$.
(b) For $k_3 \neq t$,
(qS are P) <=> (fS are P)
if-and-only-if f = More-than $(k_3 - m)/k_3$, when $1 > q/t > 1/2$ and $(k_3 - m)/k_3 = (q - 1)/t$, *or*
if-and-only-if $f = m/k_3 = q/t$ when $1/2 \geq q/t$ or when k_3 is odd and $m = (k_3 + 1)/2$ (the 'middle quantifier').

To relate straight fraction quantifiers to fractionals use *both* of (88) and (89)—i.e., posit some appropriate integer quantifiers to use to connect straight fractions in (88) to fractionals in (89). This is not a perverse method, since straight fractions cannot *be* related to fractionals without positing a value for t (since there won't be any contradictories of straight fractions without t). But with t specified, integer quantifiers are ready to hand (viz., $k_1 \geq q_i$, for $k_1 = t$ and integers q_i).

(89)(b) requires further explanation. Clearcut answers when using (89)(b) do not always result. First, t must be specified for any example (and, as always, presuming $k_1 \geq t$). Second, k_3, determining the set of fractionals in question, is assumed too. Then (89)(b) is used to calculate f given q, or to calculate q given f. Clearcut answers result when given f, q is a whole number (a positive integer), and given q, f is one of the acceptable fractionals (More-than $(k_3 - 1)/k_3 \geq f \geq 1/k_3$). Many such clearcut answers result. However, frequently, given q, an acceptable f does not result because the calculated m is not a whole number (but is a mixed number). Similarly, given f, an acceptable q often does not result because q itself is not a whole number (and, thus, is not an integer quantifier at all). There are two strategies to adopt when, given q, an unequivocal f is not obtained (because m is a mixed number) or when given f, an unequivocal q is not obtained (because q is a mixed number).

The first strategy is to choose another q or f, as the case may be, in order to achieve sufficient clearcut solutions to calculate all the desired entailments. What ought all the desired entailments be? If you are seeking equivalences and related entailments between members of two different sets of quantified statements about the same subject matter (a set of S's at least), and the statements from each are 'comparable' (i.e., each from one set has to do with counting the set, the integer quantified statements, and each from the other set has to do with fractionating it, the fractionally quantified statements), then each statement from one set is either equivalent to, or entails, or is entailed by, each statement from the other. So, the 'desired' entailments are many. On the first strategy, one tries for sufficient clearcut results from (89)(b) so as to calculate on their basis all other equivalences or entailments.

The first strategy does not always work, since some integer quantifiers and fractional quantifiers are entirely ill-matched (e.g., $t = 15 = k_1$ and $k_3 = 7 = n$). For these sorts of cases, given q, for $1/2 \geq q/t$, calculate m. When m is a mixed number (which it will be if it is not a clearcut example), drop the fraction component of m and label the result m'. (That is, m will have the form "W-x/y" for positive integers W, x and y. So, subtract x/y.) Then (qS are P) –> (f'S are P) where $f' = m'/k_3$ for $m/k_3 = q/t$. (The relation is entailment only, not equivalence.) For $q/t > 1/2$ either $q = (t + 1)/2$ or it does not. If it does, then q is analogous to a middle quantifier. Thus, if the fractional quantifiers contain a middle quantifier, f*, then (qS are P) <=> (f*S are P) for $q = (t + 1)/2$. If q is not analogous to (or equivalent to) a middle quantifier, then again calculate f via (89)(b)—viz., via $(k_3 - m)/k_3 = (q - 1)/t$ —to yield a value for m. But this m will be a mixed number (since it is not a clearcut case). Then this time do not drop its fraction component to derive m', rather round the number off to the next largest whole. (So, m' > m this time). Then (qS are P) –> (f'S are P) where f' = More-than $(k_3 - m')/k$. (Also, to generate entailments for $q/t > 1/2$, they can be based on appropriate contrapositives and substitutions via (62) and (86) above—a useful double-check.) Similarly, given f, a clearcut q may not result—q being a mixed number. Then follow the procedures just given for getting f from q, but in the reverse. For $1/2 > m/n$, calculate q via $q/t = m/k_3$. This will yield q a mixed number. Replace it with q' (which is q minus its fraction component). Then (fS are P) –> (q'S are P). If f is a middle quantifier, treat it as if $1/2 > f$. Other f's will have the form More-than $(k_3 - m)/k_3$. Use $(q - 1)/t = (k_3 - m)/k_3$. Since you are given f, $(k_3 - m)/k_3$ will be a simple fraction and q can be calculated. Again it will be a mixed number, so drop its fractional component to obtain q'. Then for the given f, (fS are P) –> (q'S are P).

(90) and (91) are two sets of examples illustrating (88) and (89). (90) contains fairly simple examples, and (91) contains more difficult ones. In both, the arrows connecting quantifier expressions are abbreviations. For "x" and "y" two different quantifier expressions,
"z ⟶ y" abbreviates "(xS are P) ⟶ (yS are P)" (entailment) and
"x ⟷ y" abbreviates "(xS are P) ⟷ (yS are P)".

(90) $t = 12$, $k_2 = 12$, $k_3 = 12$, 4, and 3:

m/n		q		f, n=12		f, n=4		f, n=3
All	⟷	12	⟷	More-than 11/12				
11/12	⟷	11	⟷	More than 10/12				
10/12	⟷	10	⟷	More-than 9/12	⟷	More-than 3/4		
9/12	⟷	9	⟷	More-than 8/12	⟷		⟷	More-than 2/3
8/12	⟷	8	⟷	More-than 7/12	⟷		⟷	2/3
7/12	⟷	7	⟷	More-than 6/12	⟷	More-than 2/4		
6/12	⟷	6	⟷	6/12	⟷	2/4		
5/12	⟷	5	⟷	5/12				
4/12	⟷	4	⟷	4/12	⟷		⟷	1/3
3/12	⟷	3	⟷	3/12	⟷	1/4		
2/12	⟷	2	⟷	2/12				
1/12	⟷	1	⟷	1/12				

(91) $t = 15, k_2 = 6, k_3 = 7$:

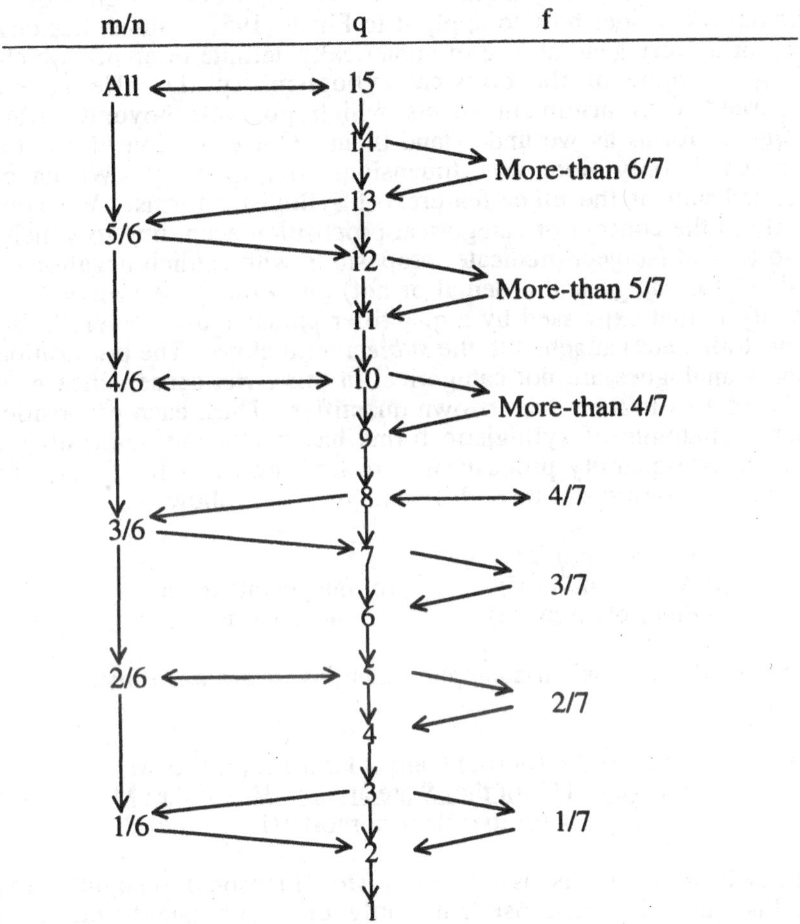

Obviously, less restricted equivalences and cntailments than (88) and (89) between forms with the three sorts of numerical quantifiers should be sought. Still, these preliminaries seem crucial to clearing up the nature of *simple* numerical quantifiers—ones explicitly related to purely logical quantifiers herein (albeit in a rather traditional framework)—so that mathematically and logically more interesting complex quantifiers can be properly integrated with (or related to) them.

5.4 Proportional Syllogisms

To demonstrate the *fruitfulness* of our approach higher-quantity syllogisms consider how to apply it to Finch (1957). Finch has devised rules for a "very general type of numerically definite inference which is a strong analogue of the classical syllogism" (p. 1). He is mainly concerned with argument forms which go well beyond orthodox syllogistic forms as we understand them. Our extension of Aristotle's syllogism is only along *one* dimension—viz., quantity. We have *not* extended any of the other features of syllogistic forms. We adhered strictly to the concept of categorical proposition according to which it is a two-termed (subject-predicate) proposition with explicit negation or not (making the categorical a denial or not) *and exactly one quantity.* The quantity is that expressed by a quantifier phrase ("all", "every", "some, "almost-all", etc.) attached to the *subject* term alone. The propositions in Finch's analogues are not categorical in this strict sense, since *each* of the two terms in them has its own quantifier. Thus, each proposition in Finch's analogue of syllogistic forms has two quantities (rather than one). Single-quantity propositions are limiting cases for Finch. Finch introduces quantifiers of three different types—as follows:

(92) (a) At least m/n (of)
(b) At most m/n (of) for integers m and n
(c) Precisely m/n (of) such that $n \geq m$

So, the kind of syllogism-analogue Finch investigates is illustrated in this example:

(93) At most 3/4 (of the) P are at least 1/2 (of the) M
<u>Precisely 1/3 (of the) S are at most 3/4 (of the) M</u>
So, At least 1/4 (of the) S are at most 1/10 (of the) P

But Finch limits his discussion (for *unstated* reasons) to slightly simpler conclusions—viz., to those with only one such quantifier, the one modifying the subject term. He gives (only!) three examples, the third of which is so simple as to not bear discussing further—viz., his analogue of Barbara (Precisely 100/100 M are P, Precisely 100/100 S are M; so 100/100 S are P). Here are the two others:

(94) At most 4/7 P are at most 2/3 not-M
<u>At least 3/5 S are precisely 7/8 M</u>
At most 1/3 S are P

(95) Precisely 1/3 M are P
Precisely 1/2 M are S
At most r of S are P . . . For finite size universe of discourse N, what is r?

Finch formulates six individually complex "rules of validity" for his multiple-quantity syllogisms. He "proves" these (i.e., deduces them) from four hypotheses, seven definitions, and six axioms. The proof amounts to demonstrating soundness at best, not completeness.

We shall now show that all that is needed to test validity or invalidity of multiply-quantitied syllogisms—Finch's "proportionally quantified syllogisms"—is already available in the algebraic methods introduced above for evaluating higher-quantity syllogisms. That is, we extend the algebra introduced in Section 1 above to the matters discussed in Section 5.2 above. (Also, see Peterson 1985a, Appendix II, especially (d).) Developing extensions of the 5-quantity syllogistic rules for the k-quantity syllogistic system (for some finite k) is not required. Neither is developing extensions of the 5-quantity Venn Diagram method required, though some use or other of Venn Diagrams seems irreplaceable.

The first thing to notice in approaching Finch's syllogism-analogues is that they are combinations of orthodox (one quantity per proposition) higher-quantity syllogisms. Take the first premise of (93). It is equivalent to

(96) At most 3/4 of the P are M *and* at least 1/2 of the M are P

Similarly, for the other propositions in (93). Listing the component propositions separately (except for the conclusion), (93) is a complex and particularly dense (or dense-appearing) version of

(97) At most 3/4 of the P are M
At least 1/2 of the M are P
Precisely 1/3 of the S are M
At most 3/4 of the M are S
So, At least 1/4 of the S are P & At most 1/10 of the P are

Evaluating (97) is like evaluating two or more higher-quantity syllogisms simultaneously. Before applying the appropriate higher-quantity algebraic methods, simplification of the quantifier *types* can be instituted. This is not necessary, but it helps in utilizing the algebra since certain assumptions are already in effect. Central among these is the assumption that every quantifier in a higher-quantity syllogism is *interpreted* (in context, for the sake of evaluating the argument in question) as having a tacit "or more" rider. (Cf. Peterson 1979a, p. 157 and Peterson 1985a, p.

351, as well as Chapter 1 above.) Notice that even an Aristotelian form like AAI-I wouldn't be valid without this assumption:

(98) All M are P
All S are M
Some S are P

For if "Some S are P" didn't mean (or wasn't interpreted so that it meant) "Some *or more* S are P", then the form wouldn't be valid. For the reason that the conclusion follows from the premises here (or one way of looking at it) is that the premises entail "All S are P" (via Barbara) and that proposition entails "Some S are P". But the only way that can be is if the latter is interpreted as "Some *or more* S are P"—which is the same thing as Finch's "At least some" (replacing his ratio with "some"). (If it were interpreted "At most some S are P" or "Exactly some (and no more) S are P", the inference would be invalid.) Since it is advisable (not just convenient, but very useful to comprehend the whole concept of an orthodox syllogistic system) to take every categorical proposition actually *in* a syllogistic argument (or form of argument) as automatically involving the "or more" rider (equivalent to an "at least" prefix), it is also advisable (at least convenient) to reduce Finch's three types of proportion quantifiers to one—where that one is the "at least" variety (equivalent to instituting the "or more" rider). So, any quantifier containing an "at least" remains as it is (even with "at least" dropped, since the "or more" is always tacitly in effect). "At most" quantifiers are reduced as follows:

(99) "At most m/n S are P" =df. "~(More than m/n S are P)"
=df. "(n-m)/n S are not-P"

"Precisely" quantifiers are reduced as follows:

(100) "Precisely m/n S are P" =df. "(m/n S are P) &
((n-m)/n S are not-P)"

Here is (97), an analysis of (93) remember, re-stated in reduced quantifier form:

(101) 1/4 of the P are not-M
1/2 of the M are P
1/3 S are M & 2/3 S are not-M
1/4 of the M are not-S
1/4 of the S are P & 9/10 of the P are not-S

To demonstrate the validity of (101) it is sufficient to show that the denial of the conclusion together with the premises produce a contradiction. To demonstrate the *in*validity of (101) it is sufficient to show that there is a possibility of assigning memberships to all the relevant sub-classes (including the classes of things that are non-S, non-P, and non-M) in such a way that the premises are true and the conclusion false.[21] Each line of the following table, (102), contains one proposition of the argument in (101) followed by two different versions of its truth conditions (the first being a notational variant useful for deriving the second—with some redundancy since either rendition of truth conditions could be used alone). (103) reveals how the relevant sub-classes are notated (as previously above).

(102)

Proposition	Truth conditions	Truth conditions
1/4 P are not M	$3(P\underline{M}) > 1(PM)$.	$3(b + c) \geq (e + f)$
1/2 M are P	$1(MP) \geq 1(M\underline{P})$.	$(e + f) \geq (d + g)$
1/3 S are M	$2(SM) \geq 1(S\underline{M})$	
& 2/3 are not M	& $1(SM) \geq 2(SM)$ . . .	$2(d + e) = (a + b)$
1/4 M are not S	$3(M\underline{S}) \geq 1(MS)$	$3(g + f) \geq (d + e)$
So, 1/4 S are P	$3(SP) \geq 1(S\underline{P})$	$3(b + e) \geq (a + d)$
& 9/10 P are not S . . .	& $1(P\underline{S}) \geq 9(PS)$	& $1(c + f \geq 9(b + e)$

where: for "X" and "Y" representing "S", "P", "M", "$\underline{S}$", "$\underline{P}$", "$\underline{M}$", let "(XY)" =df. "the quantity of X that are Y" or "the size of the subclass of Xs that are Ys", and read "m(XY)" as "m times the quantity of sub-class XY" (for any integer m); and the formula (rule) for producing truth conditions from these categoricals is:

$$m/n \text{ X are Y IFF } (n\text{-}m)XY \geq mX\underline{Y}$$

(103)

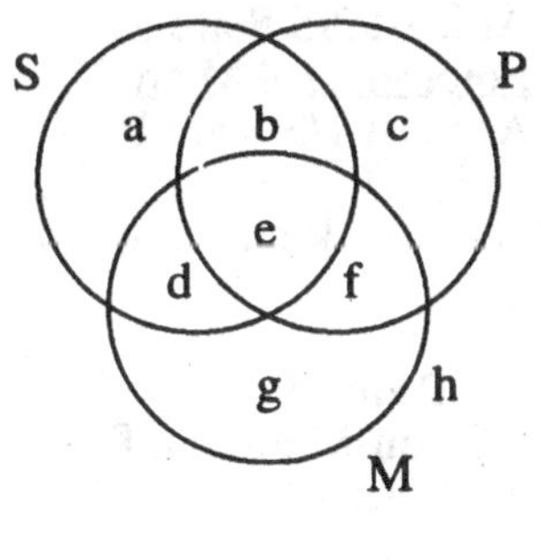

i.e., $S\underline{P} = (a + d)$,
$SP = (b + e)$,
etc.

The argument in (101), and thereby (97) and (93), is shown to be *invalid* by first assigning some sizes (amounts, quantities, measures) to the subclasses which make the conclusion false—e.g., b = c = e = 1, d = 3, f = 3, a = 7. (These values amount to overkill, since they make each conjunct of the conclusion false where only one needs to be false for the demonstration.) With these values the remaining four premises (right-hand column of (102)) amount to $6 \geq 4$, $4 \geq 3 + g$, $8 = 8$, and $3g + 9 \geq 4$ Then assigning g = 1 makes them all true. *So*, there *is* an interpretation of (93)—via (97), (101), and (102)—wherein the premises are true and the conclusion false. So, the argument is invalid. (One might consider whether simplifying the conclusion produces a valid argument, say dropping one of the conjuncts. It doesn't, due to the overkill already involved.) Here is a representation of the invalidity-making values for (101) which may help the reader check the demonstration:

(104)

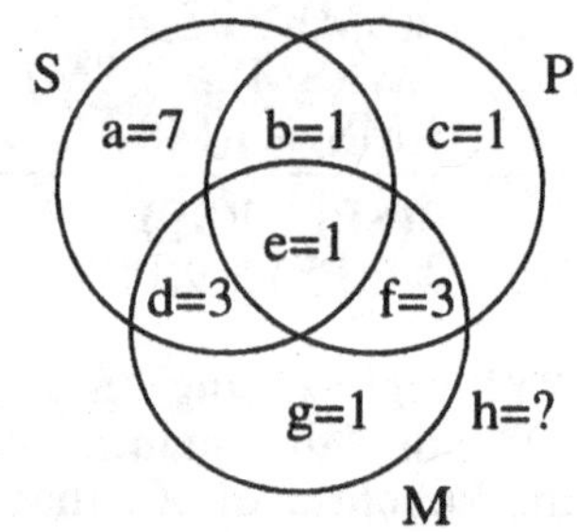

Finch's first example (Finch 1957, pp. 1 & 16) is (94) above. Here is an analysis of (94) paralleling the breakdown of (93) to (97):

(105)

At most 4/7 P are not M
At most 2/3 non-M are P
At least 3/5 S are M
<u>Precisely 7/8 M are S</u>
At most 1/3 S are P

Further reducing (105) to one kind of quantifier (rather than three) replaces (105) with (106):

(106)

3/7 P are M
1/3 non-M are not P
3/5 S are M
7/8 M are S
<u>1/8 M are not S</u>
2/3 S are not P

Here is a representation of the truth conditions for the components of (106)—in the style of (102), with two notational variants for each proposition:

(107)	3/7 P are M	$4(PM) \geq 3(P\underline{M})$	$4(e + f) \geq 3(b + c)$
	1/3 non-M are not P	$2(\underline{MP}) \geq 1(\underline{M}P)$	$2(a + h) \geq (b + c)$
	3/5 S are M	$2(SM) \geq 3(S\underline{M})$	$2(d + e) \geq 3(a + b)$
	7/8 M are S	$1(MS) \geq 7(M\underline{S})$	
	1/8 M are not S	$7(M\underline{S}) \geq 1(MS)$	$(d + e) = 7(g + f)$
	2/3 S are not P	$1(S\underline{P}) \geq 2(SP)$	$(a + d) \geq 2(b + e)$

In order to show that this syllogism-analogue is invalid it is sufficient to show that the conclusion can be false when the premises are true. To make the conclusion false, assign subclass sizes as follows: let a = d = 0 and b = 1 and e = 7. Then to make the premises all true, assign c = g = 0, b = h = f = 1, and e = 7. Here is a helpful representation of this assignment:

(108)

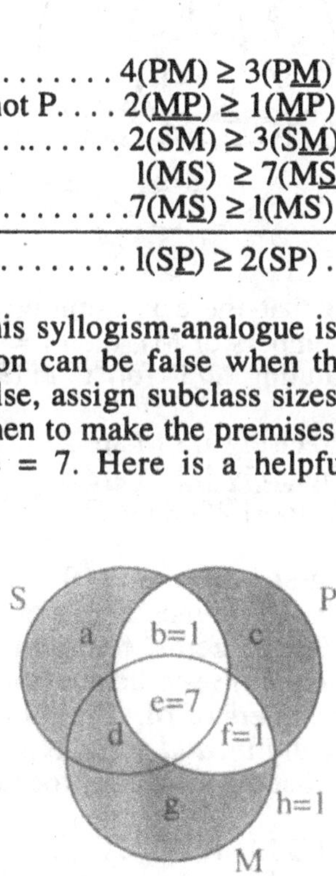

By inspecting (108) one can determine that it makes each premise of (106) true and the conclusion of (106) false. So, the argument *forms* in (106) and (105) are invalid and so, thereby, is (94)—Finch's example—invalid (as *he* also determines).

Finch's other non-trivial example (1957, p. 16) is (95) above. This isn't exactly a syllogism-analogue to test for (in)validity. Rather, it's an under-specified argument form of which Finch asks, what is the value of r—given some specific size of universe N. Finch derives the rule: $r = 1 - 1/(N - 3)$ (p. 17). Six members is the smallest number of members that M can have to make both premises of (95) true. This is most easily verified by inspecting a representation like

(109)

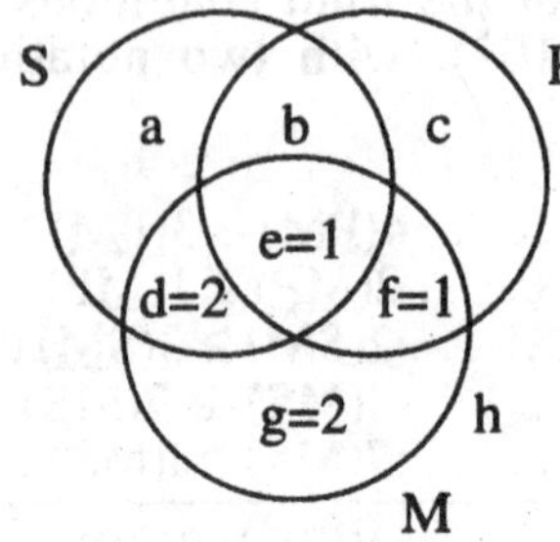

If we also set N = 6 (so that there is nothing else in the universe of discourse besides these members of M), then r = 2/3. Then the resulting syllogism-analogue (substituting "2/3" for "r" in (95)) is:

(110)

Precisely 1/3 M are 2
Precisely 1/2 M are S — given N = 6
At most 2/3 S are P

That is, if we deplete the assignments in (107) in any way, the premises of (110) can't both be true. Of course, N can be indefinitely larger; e.g., simply add the same number of zeros, for as many as you like, to each integer in (109) to preserve premise-to-conclusion entailment in (110) for N consisting entirely of members of M. From our perspective, what this means is that (110) is actually *invalid* when N is ignored. This is easily shown (shortcutting somewhat the leisurely procedure used above):

(111)

Precisely 1/3 M are P . . . . $2(e + f) = (d + g)$
Precisely 1/2 M are S . . . . $(d + e) = (g + f)$
At most 2/3 S are P. . . . . $2(a + d) \geq (b + e)$

Simply adding to (109) the assignment SP$\underline{M}$ = 32—i.e., b = 32 —assuming a = c = h = 0, produces a complete assignment wherein the premises of (111) are true and the conclusion false. (The first premise reduces to 2 x 2 = 2 + 2, the second to 2 + 1 = 2 + 1, but the conclusion to 4≥> 33—which is false.) But look at (109) again. If all the unmarked subclasses of S and P are empty (i.e., a = b = c = h = 0), then the premises and conclusion of (110) are all true. This does *not* show that (110) is, without restriction to N = 6, valid. For it is invalid (since just proved so). However, under certain conditions (e.g., N restricted to 6, distributed as in (109)), the premises and the conclusion are both true.

To *change* (111) into a correct entailment for the assignment just mentioned—b = 32, a = c = h = 0, d = g = 2, and e = f = 1 (i.e., (109) with b = 32 added)—use Finch's formula to derive a proposal for the value of r. Presuming no other objects in the universe of discourse, N = 38. Then r = 1 – 1/(38–3) = 34/35. So, the following premises entail the conclusion (for the assignment just given):

(112)	Precisely 1/3 M are P	for N = 38
	<u>Precisely 1/2 M are S</u>	
	At most 34/35 S are P . . . . . . .i.e., 1/35 S are not P	

That is, the first premise reduces again to $2 \times 2 = 2 + 2$ and the second to $2 + 1 = 2 + 1$, but the conclusion reduces to $34 \times 2 \geq 32 + 1$—which is also true.

Thus, any given value of N produces a restricted syllogism-analogue which *can* be tested for (in)validity by our methods. So, nothing in this kind of example (or "problem" as Finch calls it) outstrips, evidently, straightforward application of the algebraic methods associated with the higher-quantity syllogistic.

These developments do *not* disprove anything in Finch's rules (or associated discussion). However, it is now evident that it is unlikely there is anything in Finch's analysis which casts doubt on the nature and utility of the higher-quantity syllogistic systems (or the 5-quantity syllogistic). Especially with regard to determining validity and invalidity of Finch's syllogism-analogues—the multiply-quantitied, proportional syllogisms—it appears that Finch's rules are dispensable. In particular, although they do lead to quicker answers, they do not (it appears) lead to perspicuous or easy to comprehend demonstrations. On the other hand, analyzing such syllogism-analogues from our perspective (as we have just illustrated) *does* lead to absolutely convincing results. Further, we suspect that only by instituting *our* methods would anything like a completeness proof of Finch's rules be possible.

Our approach, in contrast to Finch's, has a more general advantage as well. A large part of the *philosophical* motive for investigating quantity, quantifiers, proportions, etc. in logic is to contribute to an eventual explanation of (i) how we humans reason (correctly!) and (ii) what we humans (*qua* philosophers) know about how we reason. The Aristotelian approach appears helpful in building this explanation—*very* helpful we would claim, even if others think it is only marginally helpful. Many investigators today would say that to explain the indefinite, vague, or general features of thought, language, and/or reality requires basing the explanation on something absolutely specific and definite. (For example, *vis à vis* ontological inquiry explain reasoning about *generalities* via a theory which at bottom only refers to, or presumes to exist, very *specific* particular objects and equally specific classes of them—the nominalistic tactic.) We conjecture that the reverse can sometimes produce the better explanation—e.g., in this case of explaining (especially epistemologically) allegedly vague or indefinite quantities (expressed by, say, "few", "many", and "most"). Finch, for one, *might* claim that the way to base a theory of such vague and/or general quantities on something secure epistemologically is to show how it is a departure from (or construction on) the very definite logic of proportions as *he* has begun investigating it. Well if he or someone else did claim so, then we would reply that the reverse might be a better possibility. That is, we have begun to provide (parts of) the explanation of how something quite definite, specific, and particular about our reasonings (such as concerned with *definite* proportions such as are expressed by "precisely 1/3 of") is actually explained in terms of more general and/or indefinite features of basic (orthodox) syllogistic reasoning (viz., the 2-quantity traditional syllogistic extended first to 5 quantities and, then, to k quantities). The virtue of the allegedly vague "few", "many", and "most" is that the "logic" of these quantities turns out to be *very systematic*—thereby revealing the real nature and wide explanatoriness (vs. its alleged idiosyncracy and limitations) of syllogistic reasoning. In the end, the *intermediate* quantity terms and concepts aren't vague at all, but merely generic. The final explanation of our reasoning (logically, mathematically, and otherwise) may well rest on the very exacting ways we can and do (correctly!) reason *with* these generic (non-vague) concepts.

6. Final Comment

In expanding the traditional syllogism from two to five (and finally to finite k) quantities, we do not by any means intend to reject or criticize contemporary styles of logical inquiry (via formulations of axiomatic systems with explicit semantics or via analogous attempts in formal pragmatics.)[22] However, to enlarge quantification theory to cover intermediate and any other quantifiers (beyond universal and existential quantifiers) in *multiply general* statements, in relational statements, and in various arguments with more than two premises (and three terms), it is first essential to have one's intuitions in good intellectual shape—one's *linguistic* intuitions and one's *logical* intuitions. Understanding the above extension of the traditional syllogism (changing it from two to five or more quantities) and understanding the previously published linguistical discussions (Peterson, 1979a; Chapter 1 above) are absolutely crucial, we think, to the recognition, labeling, ordering, and clarifying, of relevant linguistic and logical intuitions that is required. And it's not just in specifying and regularizing the relevant logical and linguistic intuitions that these syllogistic extensions are useful. Drawing from them criteria of logical and empirical adequacy that contemporary accounts must satisfy will be equally important.[23]

Notes

1 The first version of this chapter was circulated in manuscript in 1981. Responsibility for parts of this essay is as follows. Carnes devised the rules, proofs, and methods found in sections 2, 4.1, and 4.2.1, as well as writing both sections. Peterson dictated the overall order and style and provided the methods and discussion in sections 1, 3, 4.2 (except for 4.2.1), 5, and 6. The alternate notation in section 3.4 is due to Carnes, although Peterson wrote 3.4. Peterson 1985a is a brief summary of the whole, emphasizing Section 5. Some of the results herein have been presented and discussed in Denver (Peterson & Carnes, 1983), Montreal (Peterson 1983a), New York City (Peterson 1981), and Salzburg (Peterson 1983b, 1985c).

2 Not every contrary is portrayed in (2), nor is every contradictory—e.g., of T and D forms. The obvious sixth quantity (for contradictories of T and D) is Rescher & Gallagher's (1965) "half (or more)". This quantity is not included here because (i) Peterson (1979a) and Thompson (1982) did not consider it, (ii) "few", "many", and "most" seem to be the most prevalent English quantity terms (after universal and particular quantifier expressions), and (iii) "half" is the first of the "fractional" quantities (numerically specific ones), as discussed in 5.1 below.

3 Readers may notice that the earliest form of this chapter was circulated before Thompson 1982 appeared. The reason this was possible was that I (PLP) was a referee for NDJFL of his article, about which I provided him (anonymously then) with improvements of his categorical names, the consonants for mnemonic abbreviations, and other corrections and additions.

Thompson represents the predominant affirmative with "Few S are not P". Since "Few" is a negative quantifier word like "None", Thompson's choice amounts to representing the predominant affirmative with a double-negative—analogous to representing the universal affirmative with "No S are not-P". We prefer using the phrase "Almost-all" instead. Further, using positive quantifer words permits the column of negatives (the right-hand side of (2)) to be represented with negation uniformly attached to the predicate—i.e., "All S are not-P", "Almost-all S are not-P", "Most S are not-P", "Many S are not-P", and "Some S are not-P".

In light of this, we distinguish 'basic' from 'derived' quantifiers. There is one basic quantifier (a component of a proposition) for each quantity (a property of a proposition). (Different quantifier words may express the same quantifier—e.g., "every", "each", and "all" introduce, perhaps, the same quantifier.) Some quantifiers are not basic, but derived—e.g., what is expressed by "no" in "No S are P" and by "Few" in "Few S are P". There are (at least) two hypotheses for what the derivations are for "No" and "Few". One traditional-seeming proposal is that the "No" quantifier is derived from the basic universal quantifier and negation in that "No S are P" *means* what "All S are not-P" does (not just that propositions expressed by each are logically equivalent), and that the "few" quantifier is derived from the basic predominant quantifier and negation in that "Few S are P" *means* what "Almost-all S are not-P" does (not just that the propositions expressible by each are logically equivalent). Another proposal (which we prefer) is that the "No" quantifier derives from the particular quantifier and (whole-sentence) negation in that "No S are P" means what "Not-any S are P" means, which in turn means what the awkward "Not-some S are P" means (less awkwardly: "It's not the case that some S are P"). Similarly, the "Few" quantifier derives from the common quantifier and (whole-sentence) negation in that "Few S are P" means what "Not many S are P" does. So, we hold that E-forms and B-forms as expressed in (2) above are really propositional forms with derived quantifiers in them: i.e., "No S are P" is really synonymous with "It's not the case that some S are P" (on the second proposal), a sentence that can express a proposition that is only logically equivalent with the real E-form. The E-form is more perspiciously expressed by "All S are not-P". Similarly, "Few S are P" is synonymous with "Not many S are P" and is only logically equivalent with the *real* B-form—the latter more perspicuously expressed by "Almost-all S are not P".

4 We are grateful to Mark Brown for pointing out that PPI-III and TTI-III must be valid, an observation necessary to our discovering that the 12 new valid intermediates should be added to Thompson's list.

5 If the quantity expressed by "half-or-more" were interpolated (cf. note 2), subjects of F and V forms ("Half the S are P" and "Half the S are not-P", respectively; cf. Section 5 below) would be more distributed than subjects of K and G forms and T and D subjects would be more distributed than subjects of F and V forms. The easiest way to introduce a DI for F and V forms would be to assign them the index 2.5. Also, the Venn Diagram procedure introduced below could be expanded to include this new numeral. (Alternatively, we could renumeralize both DIs and the Venn Diagram numerals—from 1 to 6.) That this further quantity can be so easily interpolated, we take to be a definite virtue of our rules and Venn Diagrams.

6 Moreover, each of R5 and R6 entails the corresponding traditional rule of quantity. See section 2.2 regarding R5. For R6 simply note that traditionally the particular quantity is the only non-universal quantity. R6 and QN2 say the same thing when interpreted traditionally

7 The method adopted for representing existential import for universals can be regarded as a notational variation (or very close to that) of the following. Presume each class determined by the three terms has at least one member; i.e., at least one unshaded region of each circle would be presumed to represent a sub-class with at least one member whether or not there was a marker to that effect. In the crucial

cases mentioned, the existential import required to represent the conclusion always works out—e.g., Camestrop and Camenop ((23) and (26) below)—because three of the four sub-class regions of a circle will be shaded so that the only remaining region must be where the presumed individual is. Also, a comment on the diagram for particular negatives in (20): Since the diagram of the E-form has two existence indicators, it represents its convertibility. So, "No P are S" follows from "No S are P". But "Some P are not-S" follows from "No P are S" and, therefore, "No S are P" entails "Some P are not-S". And the latter is *not* represented in (20). To do so would require a "1" to be added in the $\underline{S}P$ region. The reason we don't add it is that, correct as this line of reasoning is, it does not pertain to devising a Venn Diagram method which validates *all* the traditionally 'valid' syllogisms (those deemed 'valid' by the traditional rules). A method with *only* those basic conventions given in (20) is sufficient to provide 'valid' Venn Diagrams for all the 'valid' forms. (Also, we claim this method or some notational variant is necessary as well as sufficient.) In sum, we do not put a "1" in $\underline{S}P$ for the reasons cited because we don't need to for *our* purposes.

8 Remember that the algebraic method (prior to Geach's extension) validates such syllogisms. For example, using the subclass labels from_the ends of Section 1 above, the deduction of Barbara's conclusion is as follows (ignoring existential import since it is not needed):

(1) $d = 0$ and $g = 0$ . . . premise
(2) $a = 0$ and $b = 0$ . . . premise
(3) $a = 0$ . . . . from (2)
(4) $d = 0$ . . . . from (1)
(5) $a = 0$ and $d = 0$ . . . .from (3) and (4)

Felapton (EAO-III), however, requires existential import. The addition of "where" clauses for certain premises (to indicate existential import) can help to illustrate validity. The proof of Felapton is as follows:

(1) ($e = 0$ and $f = 0$), where ($d \neq 0$ or $g \neq 0$)
and ($b \neq 0$ or $c \neq 0$) . . . . premise
(2) ($g = 0$ and $f = 0$), where ($d \neq 0$ or $e \neq 0$) . . . premise
(3) $e = 0$ . . . . from (1)
(4) $d \neq 0$ or $e \neq 0$ . . . . from (2)
(5) $d \neq 0$ . . . . from (3) & (4)
(6) $a \neq 0$ or $d \neq 0$ . . . . from (5)

The proof of the troublesome Camenop (AEO-IV) is similar:

(1) (b = 0 and c0), where ($e \neq 0$ or $f \neq 0$) . . . . premise
(2) (d = 0 and e = 0), where ($g \neq 0$ or $f \neq 0$) and ($a \neq 0$ or $b \neq 0$) . . . . premise
(3) b = 0 . . . . from (1)
(4) $a \neq 0$ or $b \neq 0$ . . . . from (2)
(5) $a \neq 0$ . . . . from (3) & (4)
(6) $a \neq 0$ or $d \neq 0$ . . . . from (5)

The "where" clauses in algebraic proofs (above and below) are not conjuncts (and "where" does not express conjunction). Rather, "where" clauses are mere reminders of existential import assumptions (analogous to Lemon's practice, 1965, p. 171)—which herein amount to presuming that each S-, P-, and M-class contains at least one member. When such relevant existential import assumptions are used in an algebraic proof herein, the line number referred to is that on which the appropriate reminder (in a "where" clauses of a premise) occurred. For a brief discussion of this method, see Appendix I of Peterson 1985a.

9 To show that a syllogism is invalid via the algebraic method it is sufficient to show that the denial of the conclusion is consistent with the premises. Thus, IAO-III is proved invalid as follows:

Some M are P . . . . $e \neq 0$ or $f \neq 0$
All M are S . . . . (g = 0 and f = 0), where($d \neq 0$ or $e \neq 0$)
~(Some S are not-P) . . . ~($a \neq 0$ or $d \neq 0$)
But a = 0, d = 0, $e \neq 0$, f = 0, and g = 0 permit all of these propositions (i.e., the premises and the denial of the conclusion) to be consistently true.

10 Rescher and Gallagher's Venn Diagram procedure can be seen to be a special case of that offered herein. To see this insert lines connecting pairs of "3"s and "?"s. Then change the "?" to an arrowhead (of their complex type) and the "3" to a 'vane' of their notation. Finally, their contracting and extending of vanes and heads can be seen to be a notational variant of the numerals and"?"s appearing on lines (together wwith the interpretation conventions just mentioned above). Rescher and Gallagher's method fails, however, to introduce any method for representing relation between quantities (as our numerals do).

11 Here and frequently below, we present a diagram for the conclusion for purposes of discussion. It is no part of the use of the new method to diagram conclusions separately. The procedure is the same as before -- (i) diagram the premises, (2) then inspect the diagram to see if the conclusion is already diagrammed, (3) if it is, the diagram is of a valid form (if not, it's invalid). Also, AAT-I is a typical syllogism

for which existential import is crucial. Thus, seeing how the extended algebraic method confirms its validity is interesting. The proof of its validity is as follows:

All M are P: (1) (d=O and g=O), where (e ≠ 0 or f ≠ 0) . . . premise
All S are M: (2) (a=O and b=O), where (d ≠ 0 or e ≠ 0) . . . premise
~(Most S are P):(3) ~(b+e > a+d) . . . . denial of conclusion
(4) ~(b+e > a) . . . . from (3) and (1)
(5) ~(e > a) . . . . from (4) and (2)
(6) ~(e > 0) . . . . from (5) and (2)
(7) e = 0 . . . . from (5) since there are no negative numbers of members of sets
(8) d ≠ 0 or e ≠ 0 . . . . from (2)
(9) d ≠ 0 . . . . from (7) and (8)
contradicting (10) d = 0 . . . . from (1)

12. To illustrate the algebraic method (for intermediates) for another example, consider EKG-II (clauses for existential import omitted since they are not crucial this time):

No P are M: (1) e = 0 and f = 0 . . . . premise
Many S are M: (2) ~(a + b >> d + e) . . . . premise
(Many S are not-P): (3) ~~((b + e >> a + d) . . . . denial of conclusion
(4) b >> a + d . . . . from (1) & (3)
(5) ~(a + b >> d) . . . . from (1) & (2)
(6) a + b >> a + d . . . . from (4)
(5) contradicting (7) a + b >> d . . . . from (6)

E. W. Adams has alerted me to a questionable inference principle in the examples of Appendix II, Peterson 1985a. The illicit principle is addition to both sides of a ">>" inequality; i.e. (W)(X >> Y -> X + W >> Y + W) is fallacious. So, in the proof of EKG-2 (Peterson 1985a, p. 358) replace line (6) with "a + b >> a + d" and change "a's" to "a", in the proof of PKI-3 (p. 359) replace line (6) with "g + f >> d + g", and in the proof of AFK-1 (p. 359) replace line (5) with "a + b >> b + e". To be more explicit about principles concerning ">>", I adopt (SUB) X >> Y -> (W)(X >> Y – W), (ADD) X >> Y -> (W)(X + W >> Y), (RED) X >> Y -> X > Y, and (NEG) ~(X >> Y) -> (Y > 0) (strange?). Double-subtraction—i.e. (DSUB) X >> Y -> (W)(X – W >> Y – W)—would only be correct in those cases where negative quantities are permitted (e.g., with respect to debit-and-credit accounts, but not for savings accounts). (The sets in question herein are like savings accounts: no negative quantities (debits) are allowed.)

13 The traditional algebraic demonstration of syllogistic *in*validity (as illustrated in footnote 9 above) applies in the Geachish extension. To show the invalidity of

TAT-III and TAK-III, it is sufficient to show that the premises and the denial of the conclusion are consistent (not inconsistent). For TAT-III:

Most M are P:	(1) $(e+f > d+g)$, where $(e \neq 0$ or $f \neq 0)$ . . . . . premise
All M are S:	(2) $(g=0$ and $f=0)$, where $(d \neq 0$ or $e \neq 0)$ . . premise
~(Most S are P)	(3) $\sim(b+e > a+d)$, where $(b \neq 0$ or $e \neq 0)$ . . denial of conclusion

To make each of (l)-(3) true together (to show they are not inconsistent), let $g = 0$, $f = 0$, and $e \neq 0$. Then (2) is true and (1) is true if $e > d$ and (3) is true if $\sim(b + e > a + d)$. To make these latter two formulae true, it is sufficient to let (e.g.) $e = 7$, $d = 5$, $a = 20$, and $b = 10$ (so that M has 12 members and S has 42). Then $\sim(b + e > a + d)$ is true since $\sim(17 > 25)$ and $e > d$ is true since $7 > 5$. To show TAK-III is invalid, follow the same pattern (with the denial of the conclusion being $(a + d >> b + e)$ where $(b \neq 0$ or $e \neq 0))$ and let (e.g.) $g = 0$, $f = 0$, $e = 7$, $d = 5$, $a = 93$, and $b = 3$.

14 This feature was an unplanned bonus. The order of discovery for us was, first, to use numerals simply as introduced on the diagrams above with no thought of distribution, second, to formulate the rules without distribution indices while only using the relation of more-nearly-distributed-than and, third, to introduce the DIs in order to connect distribution more closely to the new Venn Diagram procedure. We were not influenced in any of this by Rescher and Gallagher, since their article did not come to our attention until after all the methods and proofs herein were devised.

15 Alternatively, $X > i$ and $Y \geq j$. We ignore this alternative for the sake of smoother discussion. The alternative selected in (64) is particularly compatible with the use of "more than" of (62) and (63).

16 Maybe we should say, following Montague grammarians and some other formal semanticists, that the meaning of "many" is a function which has a value that is, in turn, a function—viz., the function which "1/4" denotes in such statements—when the argument for it (viz., some value of i) is supplied. For example, $\lambda x f(x) =$ "many", $f(i) = \lambda x g(x) = 1/4$, $f(S,P) = T$ if 1/4 the S are P, and F if ~(1/4 the S are P). (But maybe not.)

17 When k is odd, a minor peculiarity can result. Consider, e.g., $k = 7 = n$. Choose quantifiers so as to obtain "1/7 of the S are P" (<=> Some are), "2/7 the S are P", "3/7 the S are P", "More than 4/7 S are P", "More than 5/7 S are P", "More than 6/7 S are P" (<=> All are). This is an even number. We need one more, viz., "4/7 the S are P". But the denial of "4/7 the S are P" is "4/7 the S are not-P", *if* the number of Ss (for example) is 7. That is, "~(4/7 the S are P) <=> 4/7s the S are not-P" is a *collapsed* square paralleling the middle square when k is even (and the fractionals are consecutive). See the next section for a little more detail.

18 Also, be careful to note that adding "S" and "Z" statements—affirmative and negative "Third" statements—is not tantamount to adding their denials. Their denials would contradict the forms "More than 2/3 the S are (not) P". Just as "Half"

statements express the sixth quantity and are distinct from majority statements (equivalent to their denials) that express the fifth quantity, so "Third" statements express a seventh quantity and are distinct from statements (equivalent to their denials) expressing an eighth quantity.

19 Why would anyone want to know the equivalences between, or other relationships among, integer, straight-fraction, and fractional quantifiers? One motive is simply to expand the k-quantity syllogism as far as possible, and the numerical and straight-fraction quantifiers appear to be the next topic (or one of them) in any further investigations. (It is at least parallel in importance to the application of contemporary model theoretic techniques to these quantifiers. Incidentally, another step of perhaps equal importance as well is the application of all the analysis developed herein to mass-term subjects. We expect the general lines of the approach to carry through, but there will probably be many adjustments along the way—especially adjustments *away* from set theoretic concepts.) It will be more interesting, if the integer and straight-fraction quantifiers do not reduce in a simple fashion to constructions of intermediates and fractionals (which they appear not to, due to the modulus of class size). For then genuine new information about numerical quantification (i.e., about numbers, counting, etc.) might be discoverable. Further, certain enthusiasts may even hope that the relationship of the k-quantity syllogism to other numerical quantifiers is a key to a new method for grounding mathematics in something else (as has been attempted with logic, and then with logic and set theory together). It may be possible (according to these enthusiasts) to explain mathematics by way of the semantics of natural language mathematical sentences, where this task begins (*only begins*) by completing the semantics of natural language numerical quantifiers.

20 Thus, "most", like "many", is relative too. And, again, we might want to say that "most" denotes a function which takes arguments consisting of the parity of n (for "most" applied to sets of consecutive quantifiers) to give other functions—viz., More-than-1/2 (when n is even) and (n + 1)/2 (when n is odd)—which in turn take subject-terms, or subject-term/predicate-term pairs, as arguments.

21 "9/10 of the S" is not a higher-quantity quantifier, for it's not a fractional (since all fractionals greater than 1/2 have a "more-than" prefix). So, strictly speaking these arguments are not being reduced to higher-quantity syllogisms Indeed, they outstrip them. What is interesting is that the (semantically oriented) algebraic technique for higher-quantity syllogisms is completely applicable to Finch's analogues.

22 We find nothing to object to in Section 5 of Barwise and Cooper 1981, for example.

23 With respect to further linguistic features, cf. McCawley 1981, Chapter 14. With respect to using the material to formulate adequacy criteria, examine Barwise and Cooper 1981 to see if the clarified intuitions found above assist in evaluating their hypotheses. (Also, see Brown 1984.) Thompson (1986, p. 5) claims that the 5-quantity syllogistic system we have presented and defended is "included" in his so-called "statistical syllogistic". Maybe, but maybe not. For one thing, the

equivalences that he says "show how" (p. 95) are suspect and entirely undefended. Further, even if our 5-quantity system actually is included in his, it is only trivially included. For his system (as it stands) is provably inadequate, being neither sound nor complete—contrary to our system which we just proved to be both sound and complete. The systematic corrections needed to make his system approach adequacy reveal it to be *not* a syllogistic system at all, but rather rules for an unordered set of quantifiers. (It appears that Thompson tried to borrow Carnes' concept of distribution at the heart of the 5-quantity rules, but mangled the attempt. So, it is just as well he didn't acknowledge his debt.)

3 The Grammar of Some English Quantifiers

My aim in this chapter is to show how clear understanding and careful application of recent results in logical analysis—extending the traditional syllogism to cover intermediate quantifiers (as described above)—will (a) confirm one hypothesis in recent grammatical analysis (from McCawley) and (b) disconfirm two others (also from McCawley). The hypotheses in question concern the semantical nature of quantifier expressions—in particular the delicate difference between absolute synonymy of expressions and logical equivalence. The results, in sum, are as follows.

(i) Do "few" and "not many" mean the same thing? Yes, over and above logical equivalence, they are semantically identical.

(ii) Do "most" (non-generically, when synonymous with "almost-all") and "not-many...not" mean the same thing? No, though they are logically equivalent, they are semantically distinct.

(iii) Can the semantic relations between "most" (in non-generic sense) and "not many.....not" be used to block "there" insertion? No, merely logical equivalence is insufficient in the argument to block "there" insertion; and synonymy, though sufficient, doesn't exist.

1. Logical Inference and Natural Meaning

Propositions are the entities that possess truth-values, stand in logical relationships (such as entailment), and are the (so-called) objects of some central varieties of knowledge and belief relations (where the subjects of these relations are knowers and believers). Propositions are neither sentence-types, nor the meanings of sentence-types or sentence-tokens.[1] It is possible there is some particular sentence-type one of whose literal linguistic meanings alone completely determines what proposition is expressed when that sentence is used. (That is, on one semantic interpretation of it one and only one proposition can be expressed with it.) However, it is terribly hard to find that sentence (such an example) since matters of extralinguistic reference, conversational context and aims, the physical context, background knowledge, etc. seem always to provide information that is vital to understanding which proposition a particular use of a sentence-type is expressing. Seldom (perhaps never) is *purely* linguistic (syntactic, phonological, and semantic) knowledge sufficient to use to learn what proposition a sentence is expressing.

The simplest sort of examples concern use of proper names. "Tom is hungry" has a quite definite meaning aside from who is referred to (if anyone) by "Tom" when this sentence is (declaratively) uttered. But no proposition—as I shall use the word "proposition"—is understood unless who Tom is (in some sense or other of "who he is") *is* understood. For the proposition "contains" Tom in the sense that the proposition is what is true if Tom (the referent of a use of "Tom") has the expressed property. (Tom doesn't have to be hungry for the proposition that he is to exist, only must he be hungry for the proposition to be true. It would appear, however, that the proposition can't even exist if Tom doesn't or hasn't.) Further, some sentence types are nearly useless in isolation as a means for figuring out what proposition or propositions they might be used to express—e.g., "He did it." Yet, this does not mean that on a particular occasion, using such sentences does not quite perspicuously succeed in expressing a unique proposition without equivocation.

Some proponents of speech act theory (of the thesis that it is central and foundational with respect to linguistic meaning and cognitive competence) will say that such indeterminism of cognitive content in assertive uses of sentences (with subsequent problems for proposition specification) results from undue emphasis on *declarative* sentences (uses of them to assert or express truths). If one looks at other sorts of sentences, a different picture emerges (they say). Perhaps they are right. However, for the specific problem of proposition determination *vis à vis* linguistic meaning, emphasizing speech act descriptions does *not* improve the situation. Consider, for example, the imperative sentence "Cut the grass" used in some typical speech acts to issue commands. (I am indebted to John Searle for the example.) First, put aside obvious semantic ambiguities—e.g., that "cut" has a secondary meaning (not just a metaphorical use) in common with that of "dilute" and/or that "grass" can be used (again, non-metaphorically) to refer to marijuana rather than to typical lawn constituents. Then note that different actual physical and cognitive backgrounds (presuppositions) for the utterance of "Cut the grass" will necessitate different satisfaction conditions for the command. This suggests that there are different commands involved, different as a function of such satisfaction conditions even though sentence type used remains *exactly* the same—the same *semantically* as well as syntactically. Consider (i) that command given to John by his wife with respect to his overgrown lawn together with the lawnmower standing before them, in contrast to (ii) the same command (same syntactically and semantically, that is) given to John at the turf farm at which he works with respect to rolls of turf which need to be divided (by *literal* cutting) into manageable two-feet wide rolls. For John to satisfy the command in the first context is quite a different matter from his satisfying it in the second. Yet, the syntax and semantics of the command remain, the same. However, far from providing an anti-propositional picture of language and its use, these examples provide additional illumination of the proposition specification problem. For in the first case, the *proposition* which must be made true if John is to satisfy the command conditions is that he mow his own lawn with his (or something like his) own lawnmower (and also *not* use scissors to somehow divide his lawn). In contrast, the proposition to be made true in the second case is that John divide the turf rolls by cutting them in some appropriate way which clearly does not involve using any lawnmower (or anything like it) (nor is the cutting itself similar since in the latter case the average height of blades of the grass in question is *not* supposed to be shortened). So, even with non-declaratives like "Cut the grass", reference to various propositions is required (to specify which "understanding" of the command is involved as a function of cognitive and physical context). Finally, the declarative "John did cut the grass" can be used to assert either of the two propositions: first, that John mowed his lawn; or, second, that John divided the rolls of turf. Clearly, these propositions cannot be wholly determined by just the meanings (and/or disambiguations) of the constituents of the sentence "John did cut the grass". It is not *semantic ambiguity* (of the sentence or its components) which explains the propositional difference. Rather, it is physical and cognitive context of uses of the sentence.

Another problem concerns uniqueness. I am inclined to say and write things like the following about what proposition a given sentence-type might be used to express on a particular occasion.

> Consider the sentence-type given in (39).
>
> (39) All Greeks who can read love Plato's dialogues.
>
> The proposition that (39) would be typically used to express contains a universal quantifier—i.e., the proposition has the Aristotelian quantity 'universal'. Further it is an affirmative, though it is only limited to two Aristotelian terms if the first common noun and relative clause are considered to be one rather complex 'subject term'.

One trouble with talking or writing this way concerns the phrase "the proposition that (39) would be typically used to express". *Which* proposition is that? We know very well that most sentence types can be used to express all sorts of different propositions (not to mention the large variety of speech acts the utterances partially constitute). Is (39) different? If we examined all the uses of (39), would we find that in the vast majority of the cases the proposition expressed was the one I meant it to be? In spite of these difficulties with uniqueness, I will contend that there is still some use for the notion of the proposition a sentence "typically" expresses. It appears to be not a matter of counting or measuring utterances of the sentence type, however. For every use of (39) there has ever been might have been ironic or metaphorical. Alternatively, the only use ever of sentence-type (39) might be my inscription of it above. Even so, there is still something to the notion of a typical (or standard) use of it (or small list of them).

The short answer to all of these difficulties (context, reference, uniqueness, etc.) is just to admit that speakers of a language simply do have within their semantic—*and related*—competence in the language the capacity to readily apprehend (i) what proposition a sentence type might be said to "typically express" and (ii) what it does express on many (though surely not all) occasions. (I believe J. Katz once held, and perhaps still does, that this competence would be one of "semantic performance". Others might say it is a "pragmatic competence".) I do not know what the details of this competence are (though I am inclined to think they are rather semantical). Nor do I understand how it is applied so smoothly on most occasions. Yet, since we do (I contend) often zero-in on exactly the right proposition in using various identical and diverse sentence-types in conversation, there must be this ability to carry it out. Only *philosophical* skeptical arguments are to the point in objecting here—e.g., that we never really do understand each other (or, perhaps, even ourselves from time to time, as follows from Quine's philosophy of language), nor acquire or successfully convey information in conversations. I shall not address such purely skeptical objections herein, assuming this skepticism is false. (On Quine, see Peterson 1984.)

Since there is this ability, how much of it is relevant to semantic description and explanation? A lot, I think. The only way to begin to explain what this propositional competence is is, first, to assume that there is, for example, a unique proposition "typically expressed or expressible" by (39) (or else there is a small set of readily apprehensible candidates any one of which is easy to realize), and second, to try to say what the semantic features are of the words and phrases in (39) that permit this proposition to be zeroed-in on. One way to proceed is to work the two ends against the middle. On one end there are the linguistic-semantic aspects (concerning meanings, synonymies, paraphrases, translations, etc. of actual natural language segments) and on the other end there are logical-epistemological relations that are of interest. (Often, it is found that those working on the latter end use artificial symbolic languages to represent propositions. It is important not to confuse these artificial languages—their components, interpretations, and uses—with natural languages. It would be better to think of the artificial language as more like mathematical *notations* as in algebra or formal grammars, than like real natural languages.) In the following, I will be trying to get to the middle of some of these issues by working on both ends. On the one hand, I am concerned with quantities—which, in Aristotle's sense, are properties of propositions. But on the other, I am concerned with what quantifier *words and phrases*—like "all (of them)", "no(ne)", "some", "half", "nearly all", "many", "almost-all", "few", "a few", etc.—*mean* (or, if they don't have meanings like so-called 'content' words, then with what they do, or how they function, semantically).

The *validity* of some (though certainly not all) inferences—proposition to proposition—can be partially explained in terms of semantic properties of words, phrases, and sentences typically used to express them. Consider the following examples.

(1) Harry was seriously wounded, but he survived.
(2) Harry survived.

(3) Not all soldiers killed in Vietnam were eager to please.
(4) Some soldiers killed in Vietnam were not eager to please.

(5) All that glitters is not gold.
(6) Some non-gold glitters.

(7) The square that is twice the area of a given square has its side equal in length to the diagonal on the given square.
(8) Either the side of the given square or the side of the double area square has a length that is an irrational number (when both squares are measured with the same metric).

(1) entails (2), (3) entails (4), (5) entails (6), and (7) entails (8). That is, each of these pairs can express a valid inference from a proposition expressible by the first of the pair to a proposition expressible by the second. Crucial to understanding the validity of (l)-(2) is understanding that "but" has the role of logical conjunction with respect to validly inferring the proposition expressed by (2). It must be understood that the first proposition is a conjunction and the proposition expressed by (2) is one of the conjuncts of the first. Of course, this does not mean that "but" means (or does) all and only what "and" means (or does) in English. Yet, it is crucial to understand that "but" does express—among *other* things—*logical conjunction*. So, it is a crucial semantic property of "but" which helps to explain (in part) *why* (l)-(2) can express a valid inference.

Hereafter, I sometimes abbreviate "the proposition expressed by (n)" with "p(n)", where "n" is a numeral referring to a sample sentence or is a token of that sentence-type. Often though, I omit "p(....)" and "the proposition that" when it is perfectly obvious I am referring to propositions and not to sentence types or tokens.

The usual way of initially explaining why p(3) entails p(4) is by way of Aristotle's square of opposition. Full-sentence negation on a universal affirmative is equivalent to the corresponding particular negative. The point about English semantics with (3)-(4) is to compare (3) with (5). Full-sentence negation in English is not always expressed by placing "not" before the sentence to be negated. (In fact, it is often quite questionable—e.g., "*Not John is hungry", "*Not Mary was pleased because Harold left". *But* also see Peterson 1993b.) Typically, "not" occurs in close proximity to the main verb. (5) is ambiguous, though intonation can disambiguate it. The disambiguation (with the Shakespearean intonation) that makes (5)-(6) valid involves taking the "not" to indicate full-sentence negation—i.e., in asserting p(5) one is denying p("All that glitters is gold"). So, crucial semantic features of "not" (it's meanings and/or roles or uses) in English must be understood to see that (3)-(4) and (5)-(6) do express valid inferences. (7)-(8) also has such crucial semantic features involved in it. However, it goes beyond them. Understanding them is insufficient to understanding the validity of the inference expressed. What is needed is some *geometrical* knowledge. The reason the inference is valid is because of facts in plane geometry (principally the Pythagorean Theorem, but also "incomensurables").

Some will say that understanding such semantic features is not crucial to understanding why an inference is valid. Rather, it is only crucial to understanding which valid or invalid inference might be expressed or expressible with those words, phrases, and sentences. Well, maybe so. But is this all there is to it? It seems to me that Aristotle's square of opposition and resulting syllogistic would not have been discovered—the relevant propositions and inferences never have been apprehended—if ancient Greek did not have some of the semantic features it had, paralleling some in English (which helps to make his doctrine comprehensible to us English speakers). It is only by means of the semantic properties and structures that Greek and some other languages have that the contradictory and contrary oppositions found in his square can be expressed. It does *not* seem to be a logical requirement that quantifiers and negation in some natural languages work the way they do for the languages to exist. If all languages do permit Aristotle's logic to be explained in them, and to apply in them, then that would seem to be a *contingent* semantic universal (though maybe, of course, it is empirically necessary rather than contingent, cf. Peterson 1989, 1995c, and 1997b). Still, the objector will say that doesn't mean that the objective validity (*a priori* and necessary) of any inferences depends on contingent semantic features of some words and phrases. Yes, I agree! I would only add that the contingent semantic features just *partially* explain the validities. They partially explain them by making it clear what propositions, properties, relations, affirmations, denials, etc. various natural language segments can be used to express—what inferences and propositions, in particular, typical sentence-types (and pairs and n-tuples of them) can introduce for cognitive reflection and apprehension on particular occasions.

2. Intermediate Quantifiers in English

The advances in logical understanding of intermediate quantifiers presented in Chapters 1 and 2 above reveal many new inference patterns, patterns which in turn motivate hypotheses about semantic features of quantifier expressions like "few", "most", "almost-all", and "many". As shown in Chapter 2, there are 105 valid argument forms—forms that are generated by a new set of traditional-like rules, new Venn Diagram methods, and a new algebra. Peterson 1985a contains a useful summary and also sketches reasons (first stated in earlier versions of Chapter 2 above) why, for all syllogisms with two or more quantities, $s = 32k^3$ and $v = 3k(k + 2)$, for k the finite number of quantities in the system, s the number of forms, and v the number of valid forms.

The general point is that the traditional syllogism with two quantities—universal and particular—and 24 valid argument forms (out of 256 possibilities) can be correctly expanded to *five* quantities by inserting the three new ones—the *intermediate* quantities consisting of the predominant (expressible by "few", and "almost-all"), the majority (expressible by "most" in the generic sense, the sense *not* synonymous with "almost-all"), and the common (expressible by "many")—in between the universal and particular.[2] All the basic examples of categoricals with such additional quantities are represented schematically in the composite square of opposition that is the foundation of the 5-quantity syllogism:

(9)

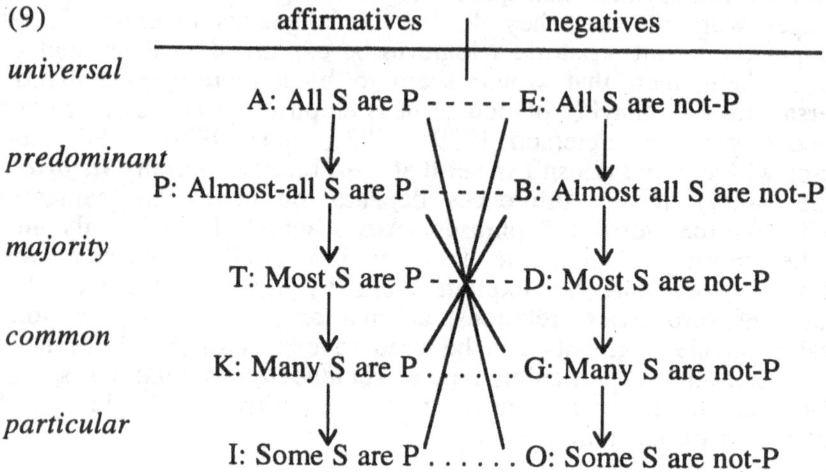

where: straight lines,——— , connect contradictories
dashes, - - - - - . connect contraries
dots, ... , connect sub-contraries
arrows, ⟶ , indicate subalternations
(certain immediate entailments)

There are 105 valid argument forms (out of 4000 possibilities) in the 5-quantity syllogisms. They are listed in (14) in Chapter 2 above. Each valid form represents a pattern of inference (for two-premise inferences, limited to two so-called terms in each proposition and three overall) which can be easily expressed in English (and all other languages, I suspect).[3] Just as "but" in English has to have the semantic features of expressing logical conjunction (under certain usage conditions, no doubt), so "few", "most", and "many" in English have to have certain features to express what they appear to express in explanations of the 5-quantity syllogistic in English.

As with the traditional two-quantity syllogism, existential import is required (for all subject terms) to defend the validity of all syllogisms claimed to be valid. Three plausible further assumptions are required to defend the five-quantity syllogism (as presented in Chapter 2). First, every quantifier must be read or interpreted as containing or implying a tacit "or more" rider. Thus, "Many S are P" is understood as synonymous with "Many, or more, S are P". This assumption is traditional (though seldom mentioned). Otherwise, if (e.g.) "Some S are P" were not interpreted as "Some, or more, S are P", it would have to be interpreted as "Some, but not (too many) more, S are P" and then "All S are P" would *not* entail it (as it does in the traditional doctrine). So, "Almost-all S are P" entails "Many S are P" because the latter "many" is understood as "Many *or more*". (For additional discussion, see Chapter 1 above.)

Secondly, standards of comparison must remain constant throughout a particular example syllogism—i.e., no switching comparisons in mid-inference. If comparisons were allowed to vary, then even "Almost-all poets are singers" would not contradict "Many poets are not singers" (which it does in the 5-quantity syllogistic). For example, we could take the first to be true because 90,000 of the 100,000 poets alive today are singers (i.e., 9 out of 10 are), where we take the second to be true because 10,000 poets are not singers—which is a lot of poets, so that "Many poets are not singers" is also true (and so we have lost the desired contradiction). The solution is *not* to switch reference classes, The reference class for the first sentence is the class of 100,000 poets. Compared to 100,000, the 10,000 poets which are non-singers are *not* so many (only 1 out of 10), though if you switch reference classes from the 100,000 poets to (say) the class of poets I have personally met, then "Many poets are not singers" is true. The solution is to *not to switch*—a background assumption, like existential import, which makes the system work, (For more discussion, Chapter 1 above.)

Thirdly, predominant and common categorical propositions (P and B, K and G) are always *linked* with respect to percentages sufficient to assign truth-values. We might just stipulate a percentage—say 85% of S's being P—which is sufficient to make "Almost-all S are P" true. And we might stipulate a percentage to make "Many S are P" true—say, at least 20%. A better alternative, since more general, is just to stipulate that (for each 5- or higher-quantity syllogistic system), there are some percentages or other i and j such that for "Many S are P" to be true at least i percent of the S must be P and for "Almost-all S are P" to be true more than j percent of the S must be P, where I < j and i + j = 100, (For more discussion, see Sections 1 and 5 of Chapter II and Peterson 1985a, pp. 345-355.)[4]

An objector could say that the 5-quantity syllogism is an algebraic construction based on the traditional 2-quantity syllogism. That is, one can postulate intermediate quantities and quantifiers as they are advanced in the 5-quantity syllogism, but (says this objector) it would be better to choose arbitrary symbols for them instead of using the English words mentioned. For the English words might not mean what the construction is attributing to them. For example, substitute the following for the left-hand column in (9) above (the affirmative categoricals):

(10)
A: All S are P
P: All* S are P
T: All** S are P
K: Some* S are P
I: Some S are P

This proposal amounts to asserting that the three new quantities are simply logico-mathematical analogues of the universal and particular quantity. The empirical question, the objector might go on, is whether there are any natural language expressions for "All*" (pronounced "all-star"), "All**" ("all-star-star"), and "Some*".

With this objector I agree. That *is* the empirical question. I claim that it is already answered by simple inspection of Chapter II. Although we did not use "all*", "all**", and "some*" in the presentation, we certainly could have—it would only be a mere notational difference. So, imagine we did adopt that notational variation. Then consider, sentence by sentence in the chapter, whether making the following substitution disrupts either ordinary English comprehension or the logical structures presented:

(11)
"all*" = "almost-all"
"all**" = "most"
some*" = "many"
where it would follow that p("all* S are not-P") is logically equivalent to p("Few S are P").

That is, making these substitutions would produce the actual typescript we authored. I conclude that absolutely no violence is done to English expressions like "few", "many", and "most" when this procedure is followed.

What this shows, I maintain, is that "few", "many", and "most" (and some other intermediate quantifier expressions) do possess the semantic features necessary to express the 5-quantity syllogistic inference patterns. Just as "but" possesses the semantic role of expressing logical conjunction (among other things), so "few" plays the role assigned to it in the exposition of the 5-quantity syllogistic system. For example, "few" means "not many" in that p("Not many S are P") is identical to, *not just logically equivalent to*, p("Few S are P")—rather like "No S is P" (or "None of the *S* is P") *means* what "It is not the case that some S is P" does and expresses a proposition (typically) that is *only* logically equivalent to P("All S is not-P"). That is, p("All S is not-P") is not identical to p("No S is P"), it is only logically equivalent to it. Similarly, "most" in English seems clearly to be ambiguous between "almost-all" in the 5-quantity system (i.e., "all*") and "most" in the "more-than-half" sense; ("All**")—i.e., sometimes the contradictory (in English) of the proposition expressed by "Most S are P" is the proposition expressed by "Many S are not P", but sometimes it is p("Half the S are not-P"). I shall return below to discuss, further and defend these conclusions. (Chapter 1 above is the crucial background.)

In sum, the semantic features of "few", "many", and "most" (and some other intermediate quantifier expressions) are the way the 5-quantity syllogism requires them to be (in the language we have written it). This is an empirical hypothesis, heavily confirmed by all our examples in Chapter 2 (Peterson 1985a summarizes). Quantifier words and phrases did not have to work the way we say they do—i.e., contribute to the expression of propositions that fit the 105 inference patterns. But they *do*. So, many new semantic features of these words and phrases have been discovered—even if they do not (yet) take the form of (i) dictionary entries stated in some standard form or (ii) semantic, syntactic, or lexical rules of some particular approach (or other) within current grammatical theory.

What is the status of these facts about some English quantifiers? Some might suggest that the inference patterns given in (14) of Chapter 2, as supported by (9) above, are a part of a theory of (or theoretical approach to) linguistic meaning. This theory might be labeled the "traditional", even "Aristotelian" (or, say, "*medieval!*"), theory of meaning. Then it could be maintained that this theory (or theoretical approach) has contemporary rivals in, for example, interpretive semantic theory, generative semantics, abstract syntax, applied formal semantics (model theory), speech act and communication theory, or some other current explanatory alternative. I do not accept this assessment. The inference patterns in (14) of Chapter 2 and the discursive framework in which they are presented do not constitute a theory, or theoretical approach, at all. Rather, the patterns provide additional semantic *data*. The framework in which these data are presented (so-called "Aristotelian") is no theory either. It is, rather, the slimmest skeleton of empirically based definitions that can be used to describe or present the data. Two points, then, arise (to defend the claim that (9) and (14) of Chapter 2 do not constitute any part of a theory, but present some data that any theory must account for). First, that expressible inferences do provide semantic data and, second, that the Aristotelian-like manner of presenting (9) and (14) of Chapter II contains no particular theoretical bias—i.e., they are inputs to an evaluation function (if such can be imagined) for which the other inputs are particular theories and the output an evaluation (of "best" or "better" theory). I will discuss only the first point herein.

Data for *semantic* analysis and theory (of natural languages and their uses) consists, to start with, of immediate intuitions on word, phrase, and sentence meanings. First, does a segment possess any meaning at all (significance, as *versus* nonsense or insignificance)? Second, if it does, what is it—to be reported by explanation or by giving a distinct expression that means the same thing (synonyms, paraphrases, and translations)? Intuitions about significance (meaning possession) and synonymies, paraphrases, and translations (shared meanings) are certainly the. basic data for all semantic analyses and theories—the data prompting analysis (such as when some of it seems to conflict, perhaps even paradoxically so), and the data against which any analysis and theory must be measured for empirical adequacy (i.e., adequacy to the facts, the "data-facts"). (Remember that all purported data need not be genuine. For often an apparent datum is a misperception, misapprehension, or outright phantom. Expressed another way, not all semantic intuitions are "veridical".)

But there is a further kind of data for semantics. This is the data provided by linguistically expressible *inferences* we make. How meanings of segments are revealed in inferences we express is not always immediately evident. In fact, that is what makes expressed or expressible inferences an interesting source for semantic facts—viz., they tend to reveal significances and synonymies indirectly (rather than directly, as in veridical semantic intuitions). Typically, one must demonstrate in an explanation how a certain expressed inference does reveal something about the meanings of segments. Yet, such first-level analysis is not theorizing, or explanation-building in semantics. Rather, it is simply *teasing out some more data*. Some examples will illustrate this point.

First, take simple examples wherein the citing of expressible inferences is not very *indirect* evidence at all for specifying meanings, but is nearly as direct as immediate semantic intuition. If I *say* (correctly let's pretend) that the proposition expressed by (12) can be inferred from the proposition expressed by (13),

(12) Oscar is a woman
(13) Oscar is human

then *that inferential connection can be evidence for semantic properties* of words or phrases in the whole sentences (12) and (13). Of course, the reasoning is usually in the other direction with such simple examples. That is, we *explain* (or propose to) the inference of p(13) from p(12) by citing the immediately intuitable semantic fact that the meaning of "human" is *part* of the meaning of "woman". (Such semantic intuitions about the language one knows and speaks are, of course, *not* "intuitions" in the *philosophical* sense of being instances of *a priori* knowledge which contrast with *a priori* demonstrations. For they *are* empirical, their similarity with *a priori* intuitions residing in their basicness.) Since that inclusion relation holds, the inference is correct (i.e., "valid" in the technical sense of logical inquiry). Fine, but if the inference in question is thereby *explained* by the semantic inclusion, then isn't *any* inference a candidate for being explained this way? That is, if p(i) is inferred from p(j), then might not the sentences (i) and (j) have in them words w1 and w2 such that, first, the meaning of w1 is contained in the meaning of w2 and, second, that meaning-inclusion relationship does *explain* the inference? Well, yes—maybe! But maybe not, too. Even though some inferences are explained via meaning inclusions of words and phrases contained in the sentences expressing the propositions standing in the inferential relationship, others do *not* submit to this sort of explanation. (Of course, when meaning-inclusion is not apparently relevant to explaining an inference, then we can still be wrong. Maybe there is a hidden or obscure meaning-inclusion which does explain the inference, but we just do not see it—i.e., "see" it with our immediate semantic intuition capability, or "hear" it with our "mind's ear".)

The notorious examples wherein meaning-inclusion is *not* explanatory concern words and phrases for so-called logical connectives. Consider "but", for example. What does "but" mean?

It is not nonsense or insignificant—as "fript" is. We can infer p(15) from p(14), because the latter entails the former.

(14) Harry was seriously wounded, but he will survive.
(15) Harry will survive (the wounding).

But no sort of meaning-inclusion about "but" *explains* the inference or entailment. Rather, we have to see (via an *explanation* this time, not via providing segments that share the same meaning with "but") that since the inference is correct (valid) it is a good semantic hypothesis that "but" is expressing (somehow) logical *conjunction* (= truth-functional conjunction such that the rule of natural deduction propositional logic called "simplification" applies.)

In sum, inferences expressed in a language are often good evidence for hypotheses about semantic properties. They do not provide absolute criteria for the presence of one sort of semantic property or relation rather than another. Yet, often they *do* (nearly always, as far as I can see) motivate some *first-level* descriptions of semantic facts (not higher-level, abstract descriptions of wide explanatory value such as might be claimed by some specific sort of analysis; e.g., from Montague semantics, or some rival). That is, what the correct expressible inferences are often provides significant data for semantics—not always unequivocally perspicuous and immediate, but still data that can be indirectly observed (as *vs.* the directness of veridical semantic intuition) in the expressions of inferences.

This semantic relevance of expressible inferences—relevance data-wise (as v*s*. higher-level hypotheses about general semantic principles, methods, or methodology)—for some quantifier words and phrases is fully illustrated in the English examples of valid and invalid inference forms for the 5-quantity syllogism. In particular, these examples show (following McCawley, 1981, p. 428) that "few" *does mean* what "not many" does the expressions are synonymous—although (*vs.* McCawley, p. 428) "Few" *does not mean* what "most....not" (nor "most" mean "not-many....not"), even though they are logically equivalent. My argument for these conclusions is as follows—based on (9) and (14) of Chapter 2.

"No S are P" (when suitable English NPs are substituted for " S " and "P" here, above, and below) means what "It's not (the case) that some S are P" does, in a manner that exactly parallels the way "Not all S are P" means exactly what "It's not (the case) that all S are P " does. Both forms beginning with the negative "no" or "not" express *denials* of certain propositions. Granted the denials are logically equivalent to, respectively. "All S are not-P" and "Some S are not-P". But what the Aristotelian treatment shows us is *not* that "Not all S are P" *means* what "Some S is not-P" means, nor that exactly the same proposition is expressed by each. Rather, a *mutual entailment* between distinct propositions is the relation between "Not all S are P" and "Some S is not-P". In short, I hold that (or am using the terminology in such a way that it is true that) for *any* distinct propositions p and q, *if* it is true that p if and only if it is true that not-q (i.e., "p if and only if not-q" is true, logically or contingently), then "p" and "not-q" *also express distinct propositions.* I call this the "negation principle"—to wit: propositions that are equivalent (i.e., logically equivalent) and are such that one is a widescope denial and the other is not are, thereby, distinct propositions. (This may result in a much narrower, finer-grained concept of proposition than many logicians prefer. That logical equivalence is necessary for, but *not* sufficient for, propositional identity is an epistemological requirement—not just a logical one. To explain the cognitive evaluation of beliefs and the acquisition of knowledge—especially for *a priori* justification and knowledge (such as in mathematics, and in logic itself)—a finer-grained-than-logical-equivalence criterion of propositional identity will be needed.)

But *why* do I think "No S are P" does directly express (not just entail and be entailed by) the denial of "Some S are P"? My reasoning, in sum, is (i) that the denial of "Some S are P" can be directly expressed using a sentence beginning with the English negative morpheme—just as "Not all S are P" more transparently can be used to directly express the denial of "All S are P"—and (ii) that "No S" in "No *S* are P" is (or is tantamount to) a *contraction* in English from "Not any S" (and/or "Not one S", "Not a S", etc.). Crucial to this argument is the status of "any". So, I shall display the details of my reasoning by discussing "any" in some detail.

The very standard and widely accepted thing to say about "any" in logical inquiry today (especially pedagogically) is that when it occurs in sentences which also contain negative expressions "any" always requires interpretation as a universal quantifier with widest scope (i.e., wider than the scope of negation). The kinds of examples which are typically produced to support this suggestion are the ones where a semantic contrast is obvious when "every" (or "all") is substituted for "any"—e.g., (16) *versus* (17):

(16) I didn't see any book (any of the books)
(17) I didn't see every book (all the books).

For the "wide-scope-to-'any'" rule (the "any-rule", for short) to apply, we interpret (16) as having the logical form:

(16)' $(\forall x\text{: Book } x)\sim(\text{I saw } x)$

That is, "any book" goes to wide scope *universal* quantifier "$(\forall x\text{: Book } x)$"—using restricted quantifiers for reasons McCawley (1981a) and Brown (1984) cite. Then the logical/propositional form of (17) is represented

(17)' $\sim(\forall x\text{: Book } x)\ (\text{I saw } x)$

My account of quantifiers herein may appear to conflict with this solution. Actually, it doesn't conflict *logically*. Rather, the any-rule is a logical *consequence* of what I take to be the basic truth in these matters. I claim that sensitivity to English grammatical facts leads to my analysis.

"Any" is a so-called negative polarity item: i.e., typically it occurs in the same sentential context with some kind of negation.[5] The sense that "any" contributes in such contexts can be seen by noticing the change of sense when "every" (for example) is substituted for it; e.g.,

(18) I didn't buy — { any/some book(s) | every book | all the books }

Notice that although (18) with "every" or "all" differs widely in sense from (18) with "any", the difference between the latter and (18) with "some" is very slight (if there at all).[6] This suggests that "any" might be represented logically with an existential quantifier in such contexts (leaving negation as it superficially appears to be, wide scope). If "any" is in the subject NP, the situation is similar, except that the use of "some" for "any" is ungrammatical:

(19) Not { any | *some | every } singer wrote a poem.

But notice that insofar as an ungrammatical sentence can be interpreted, (19) with "some" would have to be interpreted with an existential quantifer, where negation remained where it appears—wide scope.

Interestingly enough, it is not just negation that provides the context for "any"/"every" contrast. Modals and questions do too, so long as the modal or questioning element occurs in the sentence *before* the "any"/"every" position (as with negation); e.g.,

(20) (a) Did John buy any/every book?
(b) John might buy any/every book.

When negation, modals, and/or question-elements (including rising intonation) appear after the "any"/"every" position, the semantic contrast is somewhat less—or at least muddied:

(21) (a) *Any/Every singer didn't write a poem.
(b) *Any/Every book was not bought by John.
(c) Any/Every singer might write a poem.
(d) Any/Every singer wrote a poem?
(e) John bought any/every book?
(f) Any/every book might be bought by John.

At best, when "any" is grammatical in (21) cases, the contrast between "any" and "every" versions is less striking than those cases in which the negation-modal-or-question-element *precedes* the "any"/"every" position. (I find (21d) and (21e) very questionable with "any". Also, (21c)-(21e) seem to fit the any-rule best—i.e., expanding it to modals and questions.) I suggest that the cases in (20) be represented logical-form-wise as:

(20)'(a) QUES(∃x: Book x)(John bought x) ... with "any"
QUES(∀x: Book x)(John bought x) ... with "every"

(b) POSS(∃x: Book x)(John buys x) ... with "any"
POSS(∀x Book x)(John buys x) ... with "every"

However, I admit that there may be more to say about (20b) with "any". For even though (20b)' *does* institute a contrast between "any" and "every" for (20b), the "any" version of (20b)' might be better said to represent "John might buy a book" (so that what has been shown is the "a"/"every" contrast rather than the "any"/"every" contrast). A little reflection will reveal, however, that merely saying "any" takes wide scope universal quantifier in (20b)) and "every" takes narrow scope universal quantifer is incorrect (for the difference in (20b) is *not* simply *de re versus de dicto* interpretation of modal operators).

Sometimes "any" occurs without the negation (or modal, or questioning) context, and it is perfectly okay—e.g., "Any singer who writes poems is an artist". In all such cases I can think of, universal quantification seems to be expressed. I do *not* think, however, that such cases are most characteristic of the use and/or meaning of "any". Obviously, fans of the any-rule (viz., very many living logicians) do think these cases are the most characteristic.

My position, then, *vis à vis* the any-rule is that the English data best support interpreting the main use of "any" as an existential quantifier.[7] Roughly, the quantity concept typically expressed by "some" is expressed by (or pronounced to sound like) "any" *in* certain contexts (optionally in some, obligatorily in others). Interpreted this way, no special crossing of negation (or modal, or question) scopes is required. The only legitimate use of the any-rule are cases like (21c) and (21f)—and "Any singer who writes poems is *not* an artist" ("any" with negation, but before it). As I see it, these uses do not affect my arguments about "No", "None", and "Few" herein.

So, I conclude that the proper logical-form representation for (16) is not (16)', but rather

(16)'' $\sim(\exists x\text{: Book } x)(\text{I saw } x)$

where the proper form for (17) remains (17)'. In sum, "any" in a clause after negation expresses existential—not universal—quantification.[8] The difference, I claim, between (16) and (17) is simply the difference between existential quantification (*or* particular quantity) and universal quantification (*or* universal quantity). Now the any-rule fan (typical bourgeois philistine that he is) will reply that (16)' and (16)'' are logically equivalent, so that his rule is *not* refuted. Refuted? Perhaps that is more than I should (or did) claim. In any case, I do claim that my approach has the virtue of more carefully distinguishing entailments from one another. (16)'' illustrates what (16) means logically speaking (shows its relevant logical form), whereas (16)' illustrates not that but the form of a proposition which is only implied or entailed by p(16)—a proposition that might be *best expressed* by

(17)''' Each/Every book was unseen by me.

But could this be right?[9] (16)'' appears to be logically stronger than (17). That's not the difference between (16) and (17), is it? It is. p(16) entails but is not entailed by p(17)—a point that can be too easily unnoticed in this discussion. (I assume, of course, existential import for universal categoricals and their ilk.) But p(16)'' entails and is entailed by p(16).

Further reason for accepting my approach concerns (19). The real difference between "Not any S is P" and "Not every S is P" is simply the difference between particular and universal quantity. Thus, for (19) on the "any" alternative, (19)' represents (19)'s correct logical form (the form of p(19)), and (19)'' only represents the form of a different proposition that entails and is entailed by p(19):

(19)' $\sim(\exists x$: Singer $x)(x$ wrote a poem)
(19)'' $(\forall x$: Singer $x)\sim(x$ wrote a poem)

Someone will object here that distinguishing between such mutually entailed propositions (logically equivalent ones) is just too fine a distinction, and that nothing will go amiss logically speaking if we avoid it. I disagree. We do lose something important. The reason why the corners of an Aristotelean square of opposition contradict each other—according to some logicians—is the same reason any proposition p contradicts its denial ~p. For example, p("All S are P") contradicts p("Some S are not P") simply because the latter is *identical* to p("Not all S are P") which is simply the denial of p("All S are P"). However, as I see it, collapsing such distinct propositions (via logical equivalence) *destroys* what Aristotle's basic square of opposition shows—viz., that certain propositions p and q are genuinely contradictory *even though* one is *not the simple denial* of the other. This suggests to me that the best way to read the Aristotelian square of opposition is not top-down as is typical—where two universals, one affirmative the other negative, are noted as contradicting the propositions below them (though corner-to-corner). Rather, I think the original square is best introduced left-to-right. (I do *not* care that Aristotle himself did not quite see what I am getting at here—since he stuck to representing the universal negative with a format that is best thought of as the form of a proposition that is merely logically equivalent to it.)

So, first note the difference between universal affirmative and particular affirmative. Then, deny each via the simplest grammatical device of putting "not" in front of each. This produces propositions that are equivalent to the second column in the square (the negatives), corner-to-corner of course; i.e., "Not all S are P" and "Not some S are P". But look, something is wrong grammatically (though, notice, *not* wrong logically), "Not some S are P" is not the way you say it. To simply deny "Some S are P"—in parallel to denying (contradictionwise) "All S are P"—you *do* put a "Not" in front, but you also (for grammar's sake) must change "some" to "any". *Fine!!* It is only 20th century logicians that will get particularly perturbed with my approach here. For they think "any" is a universal quantifier. (This is due to their habit of taking universal quantity as universal quantification (without the dreaded existential import) where they are used to reading (and thinking of) a symbolic universal quantifier in quasi-English as "For *any* x".) But it simply is not. Or better: it isn't always, or even typically. And, to continue, "Not any S is P" and "Not all S are P" are *not* expressions of universal negative and particular negative—not *literally*, that is. Rather, they are expressions of propositions that are logically equivalent to the universal and particular negatives—viz., "All S are not P" and "Some S are not P". "All S are not P" contradicts "Some S are P" (and "Some S are not P" contradicts "All S are P") *not simply* (like p contradicting q because "q" *abbreviates* "~p"), but complicatedly! In sum, "Not-all" propositions (i.e., propositions expressed by denying universal affirmatives) are *equivalent* to—though interestingly distinct from—"Some-not" propositions. Similarly, "Not-some" propositions and "All-not" ones. This is the historical basis for the modern treatment of symbolic logic quantifiers (wherein it is sometimes said that to "bring a negation across a quantifier, replace it with its dual",).

It is useful here (or, at least, interesting) to define a quasi-transformational operation called "NEG". NEG, by definition, is an operation on sentence types (as arguments or inputs). The output (or value) of the operation is a different sentence type—one which most directly expresses the proposition that is the *contradictory* of the proposition expressed by the input sentence. For example, NEG("All S are P") = "Not all S are P" and NEG("Some S are P") = "Not any S are P" (i.e., NEGing includes changing "some" to "any" after a "Not" has been prefixed). To see that NEG might not be so simple an operation as it first appears, considers NEGing "Some student might buy some book". To start with "Not any student might buy some book" seems the likely output. But wait, why not "Some student might not buy some book"? Or "Some student might not buy any book"? In fact, all of these are candidates (and there may be more). Obviously, then, the moral is that you can only NEG a sentence which is disambiguated with respect to logical structure. So, NEGing isn't so innocent a task, nor so syntactical or merely surface-structural (as versus semantical and/or logical) a matter as it first appeared to be.

I suggest that NEGing "Some books have disappeared" to obtain "All books have not disappeared" is counter-intuitive. The latter is *not* at all the *simplest* denial of the former. "Not any books have disappeared" is—just as "Not all books have disappeared" is the *simplest* denial of "All books have disappeared". From here it is but a short step to my final conclusion—viz., that the form "No S are P" is a *poor* candidate for expressing the basic universal negative categorical (never mind that Aristotle and all traditional logicians prefer it and/or its cognates). For "No books" in "No books have disappeared" (for example) seems to be rather like a *contraction*! "Not a book has disappeared" is the NEG of "A book has disappeared". "Not one book has disappeared" is the NEG of "One book has disappeared". "Not any book has disappeared" is the NEG of "Some book has disappeared". Okay, now what is a *very* short way of *abbreviating* any and all of "Not a book", "Not one book", and "Not any book"? It's "No book"!! Thus, I conclude that "No books have disappeared" is an all-purpose output for NEG applied to a number of sentences that express particular affirmatives. But this means that the traditional "No S are P" is misleading. It is not a proper rendition of the universal negative categorical form (for English). What if we were to propose that the *particular* negative be displayed as "Not all S are P" or "Not every S is P"? Wouldn't that be misleading—misleading in that the square of opposition displayed as

(22) All S are P - - - - - - Not any S are P

Some S are P . . . . Not all S are P

would reveal somewhat less than what it was supposed to? Similarly, representing the universal negative "No S are P". I grant that it is traditionally represented so. This leads, however, to a very confusing result—viz., that there are negative quantifiers like "No" and "None", rather dense quantifers which somehow contain within one single component two distinctly different logical features (universality of quantity and negativity of quality).

I think that there exist no such quantifiers, *logically* speaking! There are such *expressions* of course—e.g., in English, and in French, German, Latin, Greek, Arabic, etc. (so seemingly it's a linguistic universal). But it is the *expressions* which are complex. They are not simple expressions for a complex logical entity—a quantity-*and*-quality, the alleged "negative quantifier". Rather, they are complex expressions for *two* simple logical entities (universal quality and negative quantity). And now we see, as I have sketched, why the traditional logicians (and many others) have been misled. They confused a *contraction* of a complex expression (contractions like "No" and "None" from complex expressions like "Not one", "No one", and "Not any") with a simple expression. "No S are P" expresses the *denial* of the particular affirmative form. It does *not* directly express the universal negative form. It only expresses a proposition that is equivalent to the universal negative proposition. (I admit that calling "No" a contraction might be novel, since it is not so simple a contraction as "wanna" or "isn't". But how better should I characterize it?)

Now it is very important to see how strongly—and how empirically motivated—I make the claim that "No" is not an expression for a special logical entity or concept (e.g., the negative quantifier). For I now argue *by analogy* to my generation of "No" with respect to "Few". And with "Few" I have no chance of claiming (even metaphorically?) that it is a contraction. Rather, it appears, that "few" is quite simply strictly synonymous with "not many". (And recall from 1979a (and Chapter 1 above) that the initial trick to making sense of the logic of "few", "many", and "most" was realizing the vast difference between "few" and "a few".) "Few singers are poets", "Not many singers are poets"—they mean the same thing. No logical inference is involved (via propositions they can express). It is simply word meaning. The synonymy parallels the the way in which "No" and "Not one" in some contexts are synonymous—e.g., "No book has disappeared" *vis à vis* "Not one book has disappeared". Again no logical reasoning is involved. It is a matter of word meanings (and/or word usages, if you prefer). But this means that saying "Few singers are poets" is an alternative way of saying exactly what "Not many singers are poets" can be used to say. What about "Almost-all singers are not poets"? Isn't that another way to say it? *No!!* That is an inference. Reasoning is involved.

An objection to this identification of "few" and "not many" semantically (pre-logically)—parallel to the (so-called) contraction "No S" being semantically identified with "Not an S" and "Not any S"—arises from reconsidering the "negation principle" I introduced above. The negation principle provides a sufficient, though not necessary, condition for the distinctness of propositions. For propositions p and q, according to the principle, *if* p is equivalent to q (say, the two have the same truth value in each possible world), *and* p has the (logical and/or propositional) form "not-X (i.e., it is a wide-scope denial of another proposition) and q does not have this form, *then* p and q are distinct propositions. On the surface, this principle makes p("Few S are P") *distinct* from p("Not many S are P") (for, say, "S" = "singers" and "P" = "poets"). For the latter *is* a wide-scope denial of another proposition—viz., p("Many S are P")—and the former is not. However, I want to hold that these two propositions are identical. So, it appears that I must hold that "Few S are P" can (or typically does) express a proposition which *is* a wide-scope denial (even though there seems to be no surface clue to that via the occurrence of some obviously negative morpheme—in English, typically, one beginning with "n"). But if I hold this, then I am simply begging the question that the negation principle is a test for. That is, I want to determine whether p("Few S are P") *is* identical to p("Not many S are P") and to get the result I want (viz., that it is) I must presume that "Few" really is a negative expression akin to "No", "None", and "Not any" (phrases which obviously contain negative morphemic elements). But presuming this just is the same thing as *stipulating* that the test result shows the two propositional forms to be identical,

I have to admit that this problem is *real*! My only answer to it is empirical; i.e., the empirical facts about how English quantifiers are used (and what they mean) is, roughly, as I have sketched it herein and the question is what is *the best explanation* for the empirical facts. I believe (to express the matter most briefly) that it comes down to a two-quantifier *versus* three-quantifier form of explanation. I opt for, a two-quantifier explanation because (i) it is simpler (i.e., fewer kinds of quantifiers in logical and/or propositional form—though some will doubtless *not* find this simpler) and (ii) it seems to me that the empirical evidence supports it (though "proves it" is out of the question since it is a genuine empirical question not to be replaced by *a priori* intuitions or demonstrations).[10] The choice between two and three quantifiers (*relative* to a set of them which stand in Aristotelian-square relationships—one set of which contains "every", "all", "none", "not-any", "some" and another set contains "most", "almost-all", "many", and "few") can be most easily explained by considering particular and universal quantifiers first. The two-quantifier explanation of universal and particular quantifiers is summed up as follows:

(23) All S are P - - - - - All S are not-P

Some S are P . . . . . . Some S are not-P

where "Not-any S are P", "No S are P" and "Not any of the S are P" are taken to be synonymous (or nearly so for the aims herein) with the full-sentence denial of "Some S are P" (what is often in logic class expressed by "It is not the case/true that some S are P")

On this account there are exactly two *logical* quantifiers (what English expressions, phrases, and sentences are used to express one way or another). (Remember that the components of (23) are components of propositions. I use English in the diagram because it is convenient. Some other natural language *or* some artificial notation could be used to represent *exactly* the same thing—*same* thing, not equivalent thing.) I am inclined to call this the "new" explanation of Aristotelian quantifiers (or, perhaps, the "neo-Aristotelian" explanation of them). The *orthodox* explanation (genuinely Aristotelian) is the three-quantifier account—viz.,

(24) All S are P - - - - - No S are P

Some S are P . . . . . . Some S are not-P

where universal negative quantifer combines both universality and negativity in one element

The point of (24) is *not* that one natural language expression combines two elements of logical or propositional form (universal quantity and negative quality), for that is the neo-Aristotelian view I advance. Rather, the point is that there is one quantifier in logical or propositional structure which is the source of the two features or properties of universality and negativity (the "No" quantifier). Thus, although there are only two quantities in my preferred approach (universal and particular), there are three quantifiers (universal, particular, and universal-negative) the orthodox explanation.

Incidentally, I doubt that cross-linguistic empirical study will produce evidence that will dictate which account (two-quantifier vs. three-quantifier) is correct. For just as ancient Greek and Latin seem similar to English in this regard (containing both positive and negative universal quantity *expressions)*, so very many other natural languages appear to contain exactly the same sorts of expressions—e.g., they all have expressions akin to our "few" (vs. just having "not-many" without a "few") and "not any" or "none" (vs. just having "not+some"). I would have been happier if some natural language were discovered which failed to have any expressions paralleling our "none", "not any", "few", "no"(used as a quantifier), etc. (My evidence, however, is all informal to date, gathered from some friends and some multi-lingual students in introductory logic classes—covering French, German, Spanish, Arabic, Japanese, Korean, Hindi, Marathi, and Hebrew.)

I conclude that "few" in English just happens to be one of the few words of English which is definitely negative in semantic content (while being quantitative), but which has no "n" sound in it. There are a few others—e.g ., "scarcely", "hardly"—even if so many negative expression in English do begin with the alveolar nasal stop ("nor", "neither", "not", "never",, "nearly", "nobody", "no one", etc.) . Parallel to the neo-Aristotelian preference proposed above, (23), I also prefer—and find explanatorily more illuminating—the following square for intermediates (the first two of them):

(25)

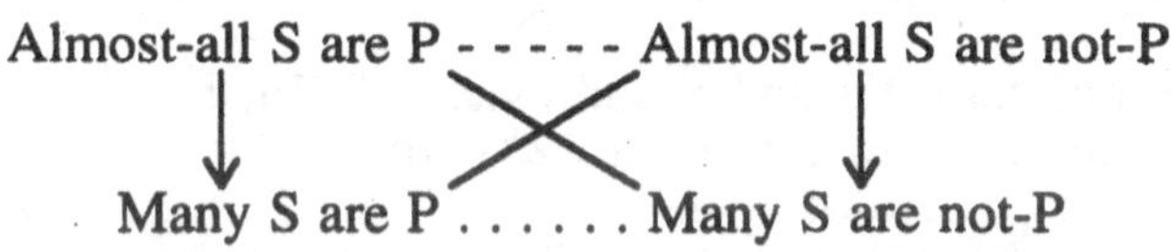

where "Few" *vis à vis* (24) is parallel to "No" or "Not-any" *vis à vis* (22), so that "Few S are P" is synonymous with "Not many S are P" (not just logically equivalent with it)

Thus, I reject the three quantifier correlate of (25)—as (24) stood to (23)—as being less simple as an explanation and not fully suitable for playing a role in the full semantic explanation (necessarily including the "logic") of English quantifiers; viz.,

(26)

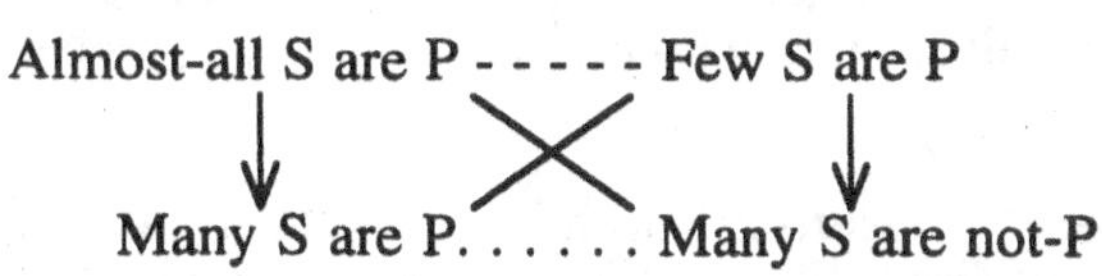

In sum, then, the traditional doctrine of the syllogism is not a theory or higher-level description or explanation of important semantic properties of natural language expressions for universal and particular

quantities. Rather, the traditional syllogism is low-level *description* of basic semantic relationships between universal and particular quantifier words and phrases for very simple subject-predicate sentences in light of the *simplest* basic alternatives for negation (whole-sentence negation, on the one hand yielding contradictories, and predicate-negation, on the other yielding contraries[11]). So, the traditional doctrine of the syllogism provides *empirical* data (albeit indirectly revealed) that any more complicated and explanatorily ambitious account of the quantifiers in natural languages must account for. For the traditional syllogism has been extended (above) to cover three important quantities—those expressible by "few", many", and "most" (among other English quantifier words and phrases). The extension provides further data for what such words *mean*. Among other things, the extension supports the hypothesis that "few" (in English) means what "not-many" does and that it does not mean what "most...not" means (even though propositions with the form expressible by the sentence types "Few S are P" and "Most S are not-P" *are* logically equivalent, when "most" is taken as synonymous with "almost-all").

3. "There" Insertion

One problem that McCawley addresses (1981a, 14.1) is why sentences like (27) are okay but those like (28) are not.

(27) (a) Some singer is in debt. Many poets are beneath contempt.
(b) There is a/some singer in debt. There are many poets beneath contempt.
(c) There is a/some singer who is beneath contempt. There are many poets who are beneath contempt.

(28) *There | is every singer / are all singers | in debt. *There are most poets beneath contempt.

*There | is every singer who is / are all singers who are | in debt *There are most poets who are beneath contempt.

Why is "there" insertion prohibited with universal and "near" universal quantifiers like "all", "every", and "most", but not prohibited with others like "some" and "many". McCawley's proposed solution is that in deeper syntactic (semantic and/or logical) structure an existential quantifier (represented herein by "∃") can occur and that when "∃" is "immediately above" (directly commands, evidently) a clause, then "there" can be inserted in the clause (if not first, then later obligatory transformations render it first in the sentence or clause) Of course, no "∃" is associated by McCawley with the universal quantifer.

Consider,. to start with, McCawley's introductory examples—sentences like:

(29) Bertrand thinks some singers are beneath contempt.
(30) Bertrand thinks there are some singers beneath contempt.

McCawley says that sentences like (29) are ambiguous with regard to existential quantifier scope; i.e., (29) is generated (somehow) from either (31) or (32), but (30) is only generated from (31).[12]

(31)

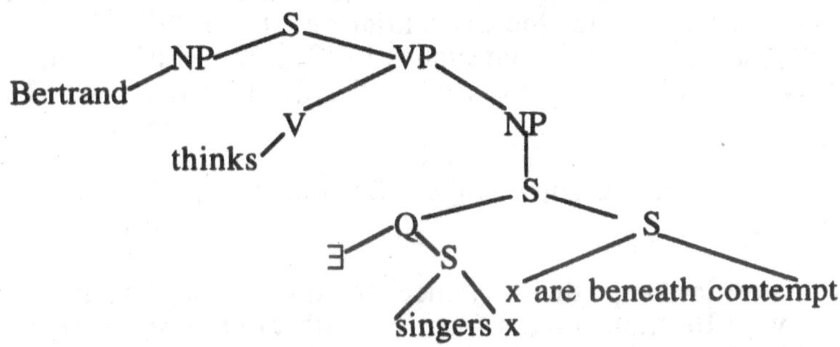

(32)

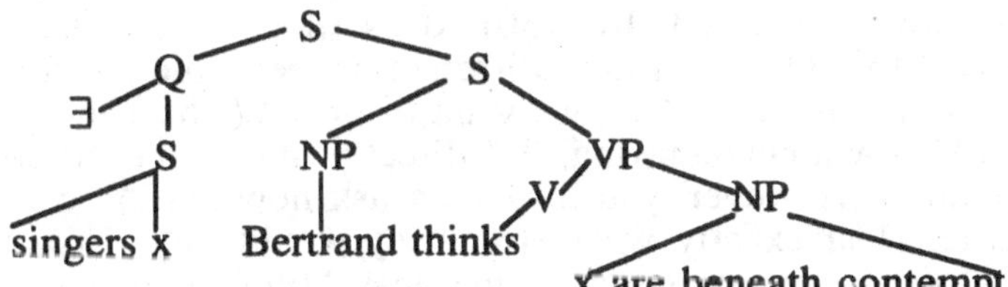

With regard to "there" insertion, McCawley's analysis is that "there" is inserted in the (supposedly) lowest clause in (31)—viz., "x are beneath contempt"—and then "∃(some) singers x" (the whole restricted-quantifier-phrase) is "lowered" into the clause with "there"; i.e., so-called "quantifier-lowering" (cf. 1981b, p. 126) follows "there" insertion to produce:

(33)

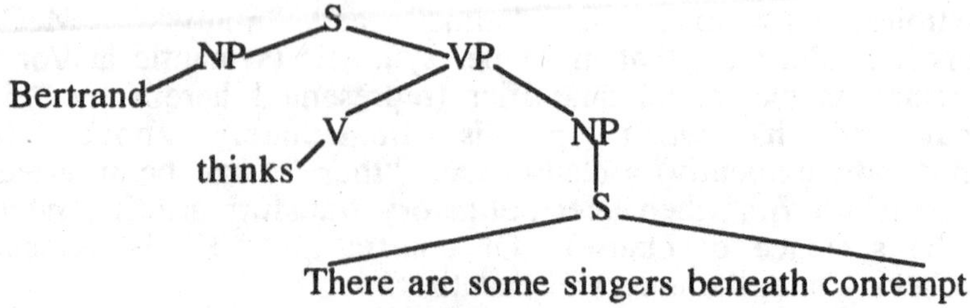

(There would appear to be some problem about moving the copula next to "there", or perhaps inserting it appropriately assuming it does not occur in underlying structures like (31). However, I don't think how this is effected influences my aim herein, so I will not pursue the details and just assume McCawley's proposals elsewhere take account of the problem.) McCawley's proposal is that such "there" insertion cannot apply to (32)—with, say, subsequent quantifier-lowering—because the clause into which "there" would be inserted does *not* contain "directly above it" (i.e., is not directly commanded by a clause containing) the existential quantifier "∃". That is, "∃" is "directly above" the relevant clause in (31), but is not so in (32).

What about "there" inserted at the front of sentences like (29)? Say:

(34) There are some singers Bertrand thinks (are) beneath contempt.

(Take care to keep this sentence separate from "There are some singers who Bertrand thinks (are) beneath contempt". This variation fits with cases like (27c), to which I return below.) Since the proposition expressed by (30) does not entail the proposition expressed by (34), we need a different deeper structure for (30). This is what (31) supplies. And, we want to prevent the generation of (30) from (32)—which requiring "E" directly above the "there"-inserted clause does. However, you may then ask how *is* (34) generated? It is not at all clear exactly what McCawley would say. However, the gist of his discussion suggests to me that "there" would have to be inserted in the clause "Bertrand thinks x are beneath contempt" of (32), but then something else must be effected before or instead of (so-called) quantifier-lowering so that "there are singers" appears at the front of the sentence (and something like "There Bertrand thinks

E(some) singers are beneath contempt" is *not* generated—nor is (30)).

Now with cases like (27b), we could simply place existential quantifer in the right place in the deeper structure e.g., letting (36) parallel (35):

(35)

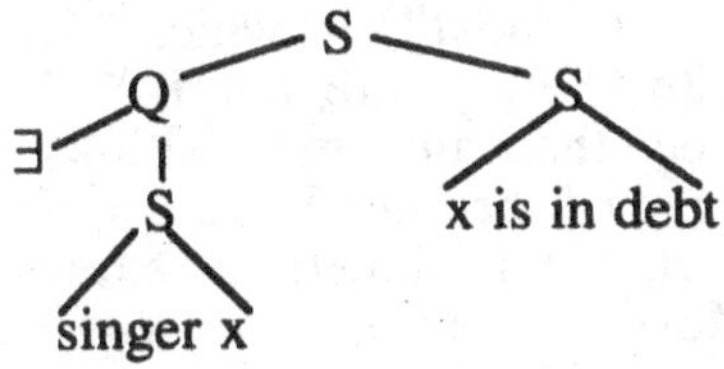

(36)

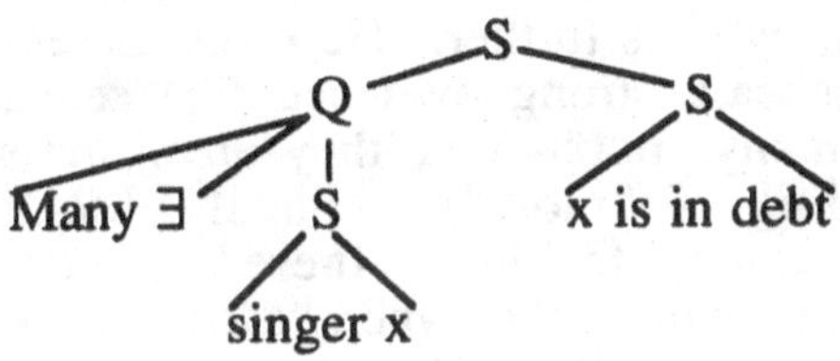

Then *just as* (35) can generate the structure for "There is some/a singer in debt"—via "there" insertion in (35) followed by quantifier lowering—*so* the same thing happens to (36) to generate "There are many singers in debt". (That is, "many" is an ∃-type quantifier.[13] Then, finally, we could simply say that underlying structures for cases like (28) simply do not contain the required "∃" to permit "there" insertion—e.g., (37) contains no "∃" in its Q-phrase:

(37)

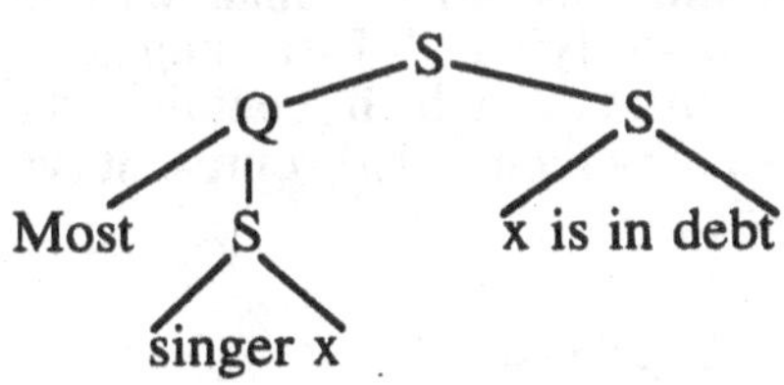

For then (37) could underlie "Most singers are in debt", but not "*There are most singers in debt" (since "there" insertion would be blocked). But this is *not* McCawley's proposal. (Perhaps it would be the proposal of a McCawleyish grammarian who also advanced the criticism I discussed concerning (10) and (11) of section 2 above.) Rather, McCawley introduces the semantic relations between "many" and "most" which were contained in the first basic square of opposition for intermediates—viz.,

(38)

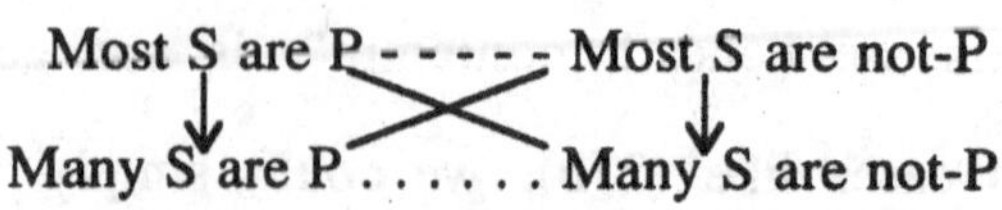

where, in particular, the interpretation of "most" is, not that synonymous with "more than half", but rather is that synonymous with "Few-not" (i.e., the use of "most" in which "Most S are P" is taken to be synonymous with "Few S are not P").[14] In particular, these relationships guarantee that any propositions of the forms "Most S are P" and "Not many S are not P" are logically equivalent (mutually entailed). For short, this is sometimes expressed (by me as well as McCawley) as "Most..." is logically equivalent to "Not many...not". But to *use* this logical equivalence (even semantic equivalence), McCawley goes further. He takes the equivalence to be tantamount to (or, at least, strong evidence for) semantic *identity* of "Most" and "Not many...not"—i.e., they *mean* the same thing (on the appropriate reading of "most"). Finally, McCawley uses this alleged identity of meaning to block "there" insertion in "most"-sentences. The idea, in sum, is that when "Most" occurs in quantifier position, it is the result of lexical insertion on a more complex structure—viz., a "Not many...not" structure. (So, the analysis involves a lexical decomposition claim and an interpolation of lexical insertion among syntactic-semantic transformations. Both of these claims can be expected to face objections concerning the adequacy of *any* generative-semantic-type of proposal of this sort. I am not, however, concerned to make such objections—or defend against them—herein. My own objection will apply prior to, and/or independent of, these anti-generative-semantics complaints.) Thus, the appropriate structure underlying "Most singers are in debt" is not (37), but rather the structure which contains the necessary "Not-many-not" components (which I will represent via ordinary English orthography here)—viz.,

(39)

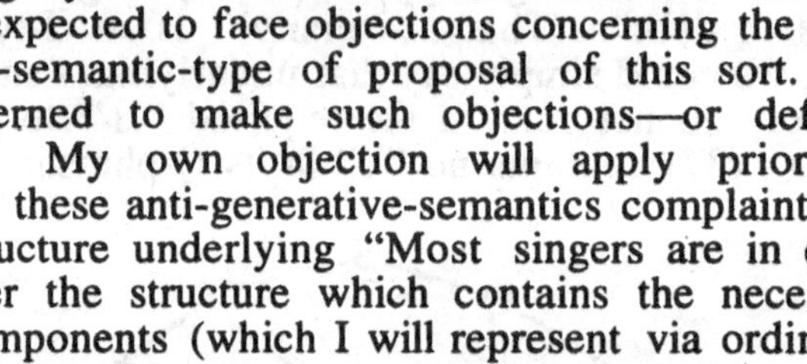

Since this is the underlying structure for "Most singers are in debt"[15] and, evidently, insertion of "most" will *precede* negation-lowering (wnich would produce the clause "x are not in debt") and quantifier lowering (to produce "Not(Many singers are not in debt)"), no intermediate structure will satisfy the conditions for inserting "there" when "most" is present (since, I take it, "most"-insertion will obliterate not only the neg(Q(neg))-structure of (39), but also will erase "∃").

What if "most" is not inserted in structures derived from (39)? Can "there" be inserted? Yes—in at least two ways. First, consider a structure just like (39), but without the topmost negation. Such a structure would be appropriate for underlying "Many singers are not in debt". What if "there" were inserted? If so, it would have to be *after* negation-lowering; i.e., on (40) to get (41):

(40)

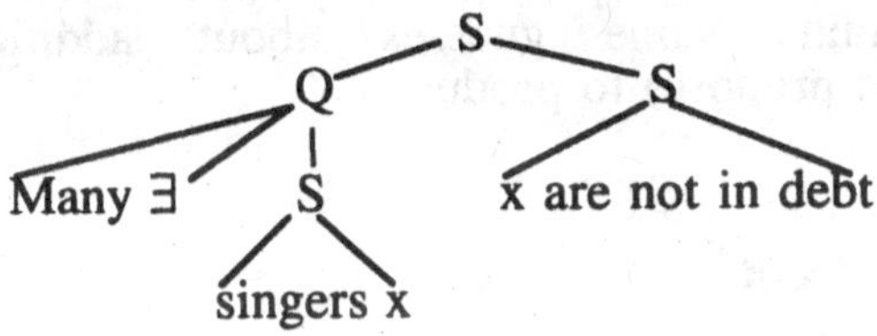

(41)

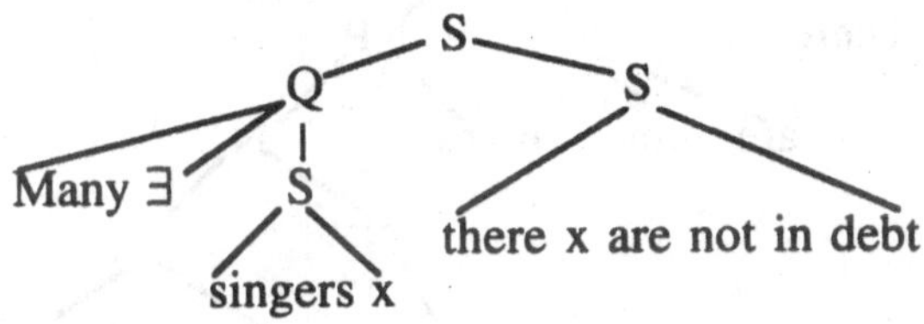

Then quantifier-lowering will produce a surface-like structure appropriate for "There are many singers not in debt". What of the same sort of operations that give (40) and (41), but when there is a higher negation, as in (39)? It seems to me (extrapolating on McCawley's approach) that there are two possibilities: first, when a highest "Not" is present something must block the production of "Not there are many singers not in debt"; or second, when a higher "not" is present negation lowering applies again to

(42)

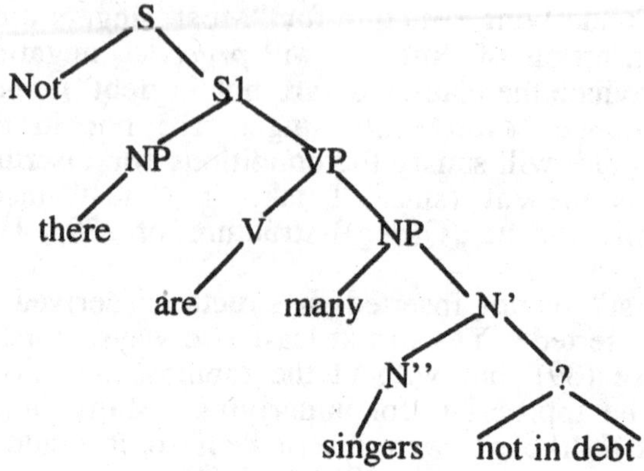

(where S1 is identical to the product of quantifier lowering applied to (41)—and contains some guesses about additional structure McCawley would propose) to produce

(43)

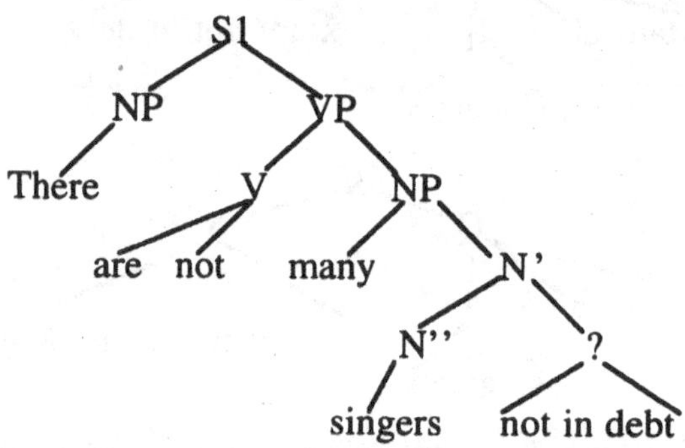

I prefer this second alternative (to produce (43) from basic (39)) as my best guess of what McCawley had in mind (or would have produced if pressed). For one thing the (39) + (41)-to-(43) sort of derivation clearly hints at how "There are some singers Bertrand thinks beneath contempt" *and* "There are not any singers Bertrand thinks beneath contempt" might be generated (though details are unclear to me).

Two small matters I've left hanging can be cleared up now, before proceeding to my objection to McCawley's "there" insertion rule. The first concerns my interpretation of what McCawley means by "immediately above" in saying "...*there*-insertion requires that the existential quantifier be immediately above the clause into which *there* is inserted..." (p. 428, 1981a). An objector might say that I have misinterpreted McCawley; i.e., where I assume "there" should be inserted in (36), for example, to produce (44) (the input to quantifier-lowering), is wrong. McCawley really meant for "there" to be inserted as in (45).

(44)

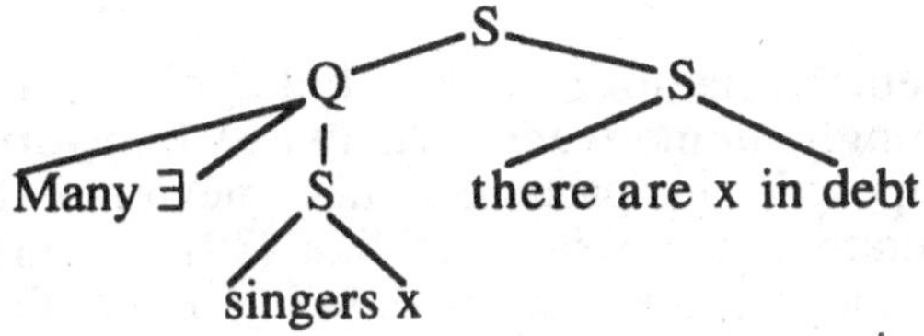

(45)

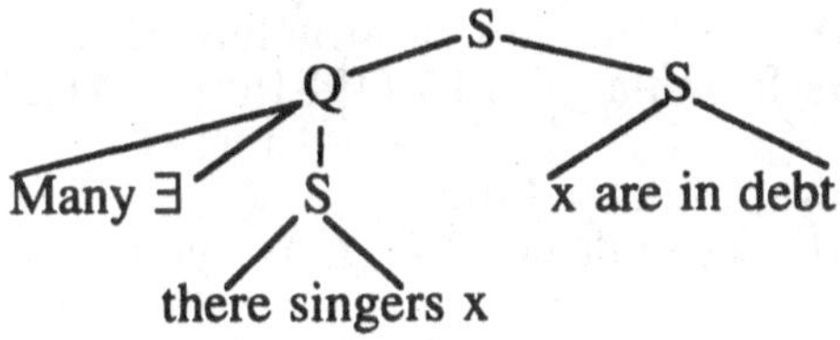

A particular virtue of this interpretation of McCawley is that there is absolutely no question about what he means by "immediately above". It does mean "directly command" and there is no question about whether "∃" in (45) directly commands "singers x" But this objector can't in the end be right, for if he were then the explanation McCawley goes on to offer wouldn't work, In particular, this interpretation would *permit* "there" insertion in (39)—since "Many ∃" would be immediately above "singers x" (with "not" above and below the Q-phrase)—which is exactly what McCawley was trying to block. That is, the Not-many-not structure represented in (39) is appropriate for lexical insertion of "most" on McCawley's analysis), and when it is inserted no "there" is supposed to be present (at all). So, (45) does *not* represent what McCawley had in mind for where "there" could be inserted.

A parting shot the objector might produce is that I have also misinterpreted where the two negations should appear in a "Not-many-not" structure so that "there" insertion is blocked. Along with his idea that "there" insertion should be conceived of along the lines of (45), he might say the flanking "not"s would appear under "Q"—for example:

(46)

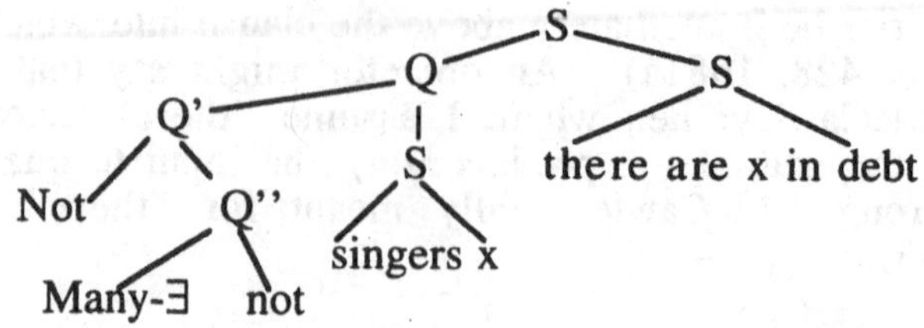

This proposal seems to me to have very little going for it, since many additional (seemingly unmotivated otherwise) transformations would have to be proposed (in particular new negation lowerings and raisings) to generate either structures like (39) or surface structures for "Not many singers are not in debt". Even though "there" insertion would be blocked by McCawley's strictures for (46), it is also pretty clear (46) is not the sort of structure he had in mind. For example, observe his formula 14.2.15 (1981a, p. 441):

(47) (a) Most gold is yellow.
(b) $\sim(\exists E\text{: }\&(\text{gold}(E), \text{large}(E)))\ \sim\text{yellow}(E)))$

The flanking negations (around "∃" and "large" underlying "many" are not *directly* surrounding "∃" (as in (46)), but are more remote (as in (39)). (Remember that (47b) is McCawley's fuller account of how a "not-many-not" structure underlies the quantifier "most"—containing not only the reduction of a superficially non-negative quantifier to an existential one with flanking negations, but also McCawley's further proposals about the *meaning* of "many" analyzed in terms of his predicate "large" (together with various set and/or ensemble interpolations). Herein, I am not discussing (neither adopting nor arguing against) this last semantic analysis (that which prompts his proposal of the transformation called "aggregation")—though I can say I am not at all inclined to these proposals. It appears that incorporation of the 5-quantity (and higher-quantity) syllogistic into the basic logical facility necessarily associated with (or contained in) natural language semantic competence will provide all that McCawley's "large" supplies semantically.)

The second matter concerns so-called pseudo-relative clauses, such as in (27c). All "there"-inserted revisions of categorical sentences *without* prepositional phrase predicates would have to contain pseudo-relatives—simply because all forms like the following are ungrammatical:

(48) (a) *There is some singer a poet
(b) *There are some singers happy
(c) *There are many poets sing madrigals

While some sentences for categorical propositions can't take "there" in any way (e.g., "*There is every singer (who is) a poet", "*There are most singers (who are) poets"), still those sentences behind (48) can be "there"-inserted if pseudo-relative clauses are used—e.g.,

(49) (a) There is some singer who is a poet
(b) There are some singers who are happy
(c) There are many poets who sing madrigals

What are the underlying forms for sentences like (49a-c) and (27c). According to McCawley, (i) there are crucial changes in deeper syntactic-semantic structures (revising structures like (35) and (36)), and (ii) there are fine semantic differences between what genuine restrictive relatives contribute to a sentence and what pseudo-relatives contribute (cf. McCawley 1981b, pp. 114-115). McCawley's proposal is that pseudo-relatives result from a transformation that raises (as he says, 1981b, p. 115) the subject term clause (the "domain" expression in the quantifier-phrase), though not the quantifier, to "...a position as daughter of the next higher S-node, with concomitant reinterpretation of the original main clause...as a S-final adjunct..."(p. 115). For example, this unnamed transformation ((27), p.115) would produce (50) when applied to (36):

(50)

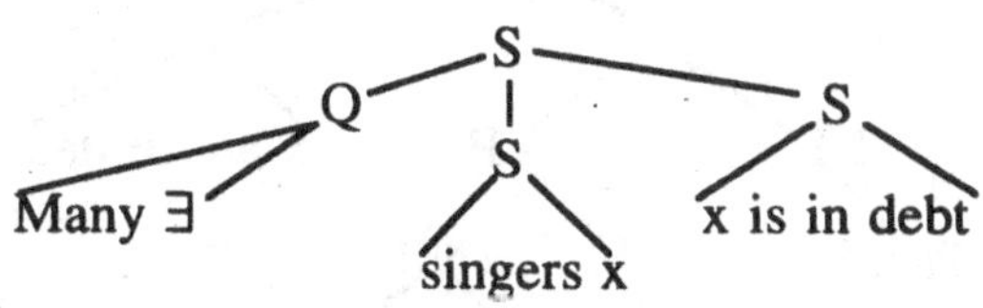

Such a structure is appropriate for expressing a proposition containing a "pure existential" quantifier (rather than the typical restricted quantifier). (That is, "There are many singers who are in debt" parallels "There are wingless insects" in that quantification is not over singers or wingless things, but rather over some unspecified general domain, where what is asserted with these sentences is that in that domain are found singers-in-debt and wingless insects.) When such structures actually underlie real sentences (in English), it would appear that "there" insertion is mandatory (contrary to its optionality in sentences discussed above) and pseudo-relative clause construction follows automatically. That is, (50) must surface, for example, in "There are many singers who are in debt". It appears to me that in addition to "there" insertion, the same transformations are needed as required for restrictive clause formation (cf. pp. 126-127) but the order is different—viz., quantifier-lowering before relative clause formation (similar to *restrictive* relative clause formation). For example (based on what McCawley has said in both 1981a and 1981b), the near-surface structure for "There are many singers who are in debt" would be generated from (50) (which, remember, was previously generated from (36)) by, first, inserting "there" to get (51), and then forming (52) by (a variant of?) quantifier lowering, finally obtaining (53) from (52) by relative clause formation (or pseudo-relative clause formation):

(51)

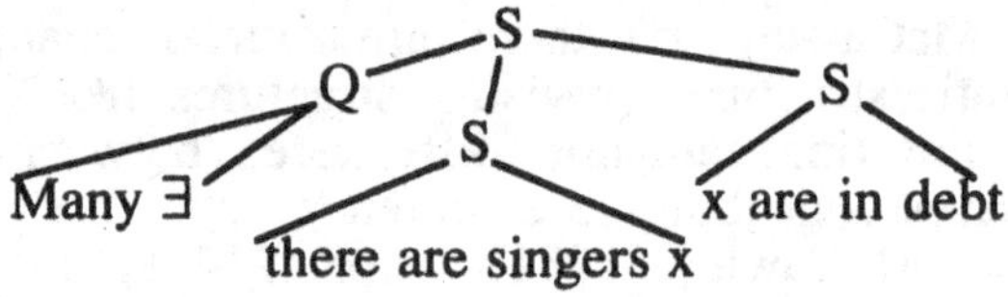

(52)

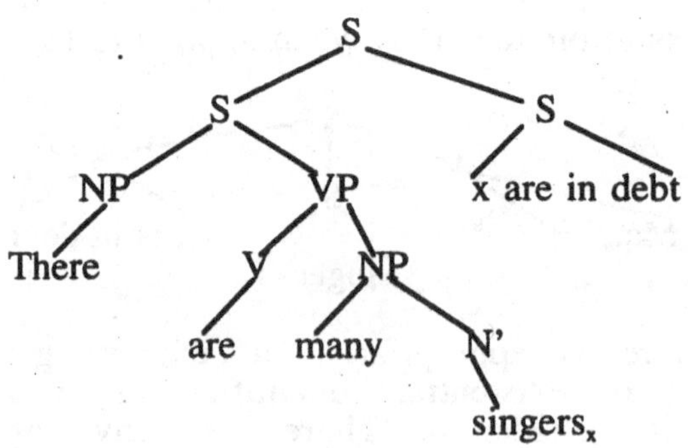

(53)

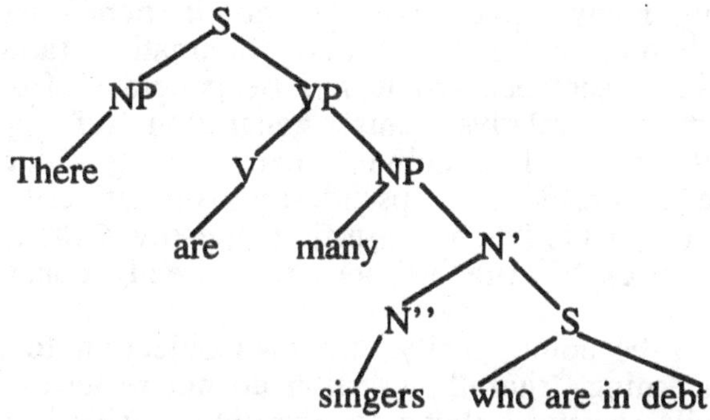

Simply because the derivation of pseudo-relative clause sentences (53), (49), and (27c) take different derivational routes from those without such clauses—such as "Many poets sing madrigals", "Some singer is a poet", or (27a), as well as previous "there"-inserted forms like (27b) and (43)—that does not mean that any variations exist for McCawley's "there"-insertion rule (especially, that it requires an "∃" immediately above the clause into which "there" is inserted). For if the transformation producing (50) from (36) were applied to (39) to obtain (54), "most" insertion on (54) would still be presumably blocked—since the precise "not-many-not" structure permitting it (viz., (55)) has been destroyed (i.e., doesn't appear in (54):

(54)

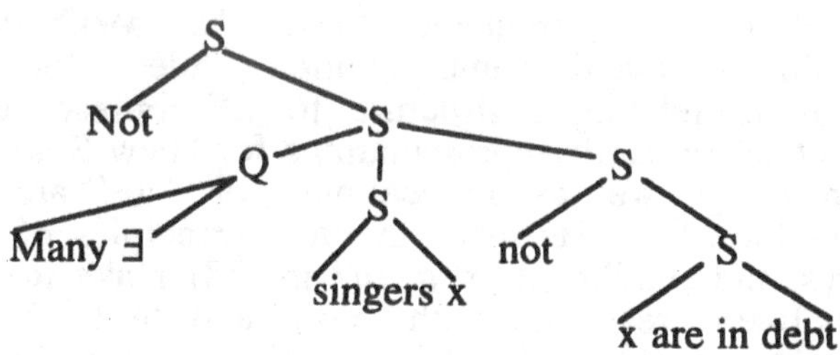

(55)

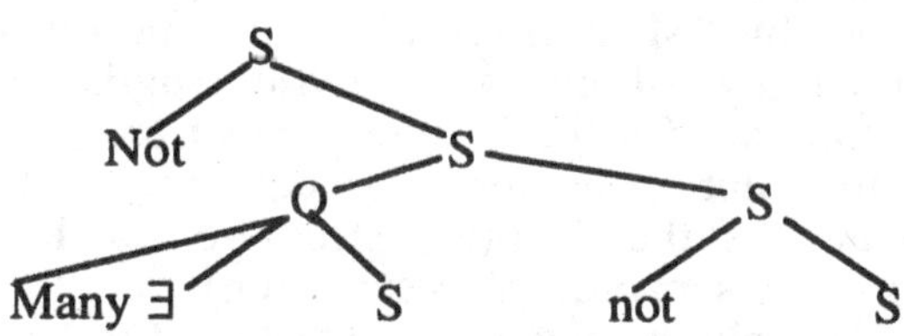

So, (54) will not lead to an illicit string—say "*There are most singers who are in debt". On the other hand, (54) can *only* surface if "there"-insertion *is* instituted—to yield the near-surface structure for

"There are not many singers who are not in debt"—since "*Not many singers who are not in debt" is ungrammatical (and if required for a NP in some sentence would *not* be generated from (54), but rather by restrictive relative clause generation (cf. pp. 125-126, McCawley 1981b)). I conclude that nothing concerned with variations due to presence of pseudo-relatives affects McCawley's basic arguments *for* his "there"-insertion rule (even though in 1981a where he introduces the rule he does not directly consider pseudo-relatives).[16]

To come to the point, finally, my own objection to McCawley's proposals concerning "there" insertion do not relate to most of the particular details reviewed above (concerning positions of "∃" and negation, or variations for pseudo-relatives), but concern McCawley's use of my results in Peterson 1979a to support the lexical insertion of "most" (in the appropriate non-generic sense) for "not-many...not". My objection is with McCawley's *assumption* that since the proposition expressed by sentences like "Not many singers are not poets" is logically equivalent to a proposition expressed by "Most singers are poets", it follows that (i) the two propositions are identical and (ii) "most" *ipso facto means* what "not many...not" means. Now I agree that sometimes this sort of reasoning has some force. For it is the sort of reasoning that supports the generation of "Few" and "No" (and "Not any" and "None of the") from, respectively, "Not many" and "Not some" structures; i.e., "None" *does* mean "not any", "few" *does* mean "Not many", so lexical insertion of the sort frequently used by McCawley, *or* some corresponding semantic interpretation rules (or even some transformations relating S-structure to LF representations) should permit identical semantic representations for "Few S are P" and "Not many S are P"—as well as identical ones for "No S are P" and "Not any/*some S are P".[17] However, the very principles of contradiction, contrariness, and entailment expressed in (38) make it *not possible* to follow this line of reasoning with "most" and "not-many-not". The proposition expressed by "Not many S are not P" is *not* identical with that expressed by "Most S are P". They are distinctly different propositions (assuming, of course, specific English terms such as "singers" and "poets" fill the S- and P-positions in the sentences) that happen to turn out to be logically equivalent. For this reason *alone*, (39) cannot be the deep(er) structure (or logical form, or propositional form, or semantic representation) for "Most singers are in debt". (39) can only be the deep structure (or LF, propositional form, and/or semantic representation) for a sentence that (typically) is used to express a proposition that is logically equivalent to that expressed by "Most singers are in debt".

So, I conclude that McCawley has not given a successful argument for blocking "there" insertion in "most" sentences (nor that he has provided the materials for constructing an analogous argument in interpretive semantics for *blocking* the derivation of a semantic interpretation (and/or LF) for "There are most..." strings in English). Now I don't expect McCawley to acquiesce at once, but before I consider what some of his replies might be (and how they should be assessed) I want to belabor even more my point about *not* using mere logical equivalence (even when very tight) as evidence for propositional identity which, in turn, is used to propose semantic identities and McCawleyish lexical insertion rules.

Consider various pairs of sentences such that each member of every pair expresses a proposition logically equivalent to its mate (as all such do in both (56) and (57)), *but* where some pairs consist of synonymous sentences—such as in (56)—and other pairs consist of non-synonymous sentences—such as in (57).

(56) Synonymous Sentences:
- (a) John read the poem. It was John that read the poem.
- (b) John is easy to please. It's easy to please John.
- (c) John doesn't want Mary to sing. John wants Mary not to sing.
- (d) Harry believes that John neither read the poem nor sang the song. Harry doesn't believe that John either read the poem or sang the song.
- (e) John gave the poem to Mary. John gave Mary the poem.

(57) Non-synonymous Sentences:
- (a) John didn't read the poem and didn't sing the song. John neither read the poem nor sang the song.
- (b) Harry doesn't believe John did not read the poem. Harry believes John read the poem.
- (c) John did or did not read the poem, and Mary sang the song. Mary sang the song.
- (d) Not all poets are singers. Some poets are not singers.
- (e) No more than half the singers are poets. Half the singers are not poets.

Many of these sentences (perhaps all) are ambiguous—have more than one semantic interpretation, or "reading". When I claim that each of (56) is *exactly synonymous* with its mate, I mean (of course) that on some reading or interpretation of each there is a reading or interpretation of its mate on which they are exactly synonymous (have the same reading, interpretation, meaning, or semantic representation).[18] The same goes for all sentences in (56) and (57) with respect to logical equivalence; i.e., each sentence of both (56) and (57) has a reading *and a use* (to express determinate propositions) which expresses a proposition that is logically equivalent to a proposition expressed by some reading *and use* of its mate. Of course in (56), all of these equivalences have the form "p if and only if p" (i.e., all (56) equivalences follow from the logical law that any proposition is logically equivalent to itself).

I claim that the fact that each member of each pair in (56) expresses (or can express) the same proposition as its mate is good evidence for proposing semantic identity (synonymy), on a reading, between members of each pair. (This is *not* necessary, it seems to me. But one way to *make* a connection between proposition-expressed by a sentence and the sentence's meaning is to *use* propositional features (identities, entailments, etc.) as very good evidence for semantic properties. I suppose it is *possible* that "John read the poem" and "It was John that read the poem" can be used to express one and the same proposition *without* being synonymous. But I think that is unlikely, and with such simple examples it will not probably turn out to be a fruitful direction of analysis to pursue.) I also claim that the same thing does *not* hold for (57)—i.e., (i) each sentence does not express exactly the same proposition, and so (ii) each does *not* mean what its mate does (even if, proposition-wise, they are logically equivalent). The non-synonymy of (57a) sentences is based on the contention that DeMorgan's Law—i.e., any proposition that is a conjunction (alternatively: denial of a conjunction) is logically equivalent to one which is the denial of a disjunction (alternatively: a disjunction) wherein the disjuncts are each denials of the original conjuncts—is a law that relates *distinct* propositions. My claim that (56d) sentences are synonymous is based on the proposal that "neither-nor" is a *grammatical* construction based on wide-scope negation over "either-or" being *pronounced* as "neither-nor". (Again, there are always dissenters. Some logic textbook writer or other will no doubt propose that "neither-nor" *means* what "not...*and*...not..." means.) The reason I embedded the two denied disjunctions of (56d) under the verb "believes" is to let the identity of "neither-nor" and "not(either-or)" *show* (since "*Not either John read the poem or sang the song" is ungrammatical in isolation). In contrast, (57a) expresses two propositions that are related logically by DeMorgan's Law. But for them to be so related they have to be sentences expressing distinct propositions. *For DeMorgan's Law is simply not the logical law that all propositions are self-equivalent!* And (57b) illustrates the law of double-negation (rather like "It's false John did not read the poem" is logically equivalent to, yet semantically distinct from, "John read the poem"). If anything is clear in this area, it must be that the (57c) sentences express different propositions. The surprise, if there is one about these sentences, can only be that they are equivalent. (Of course, some observers may agree with McCawley that pairs like (57c) *are* co-expressive proposition-wise; cf. 1981a, p. 461 (in note 2), where he says it's not clear that a proposition of the form "p and (q and p)" is a different proposition from "p and q".[19])

McCawley should *not* propose that structures underlying any members of a (57)-pair underlie structures of its mate (nor should any G&Ber propose that any near-surface structure for one of these sentences has a logical form, semantic representation, or propositional form which is identical with that for the other). The reason I think this should be a general rule (of grammatical/semantic methodology or theory) is based on examining simple cases like (57a-c). Associated with (57a) are the following structures:

(58)

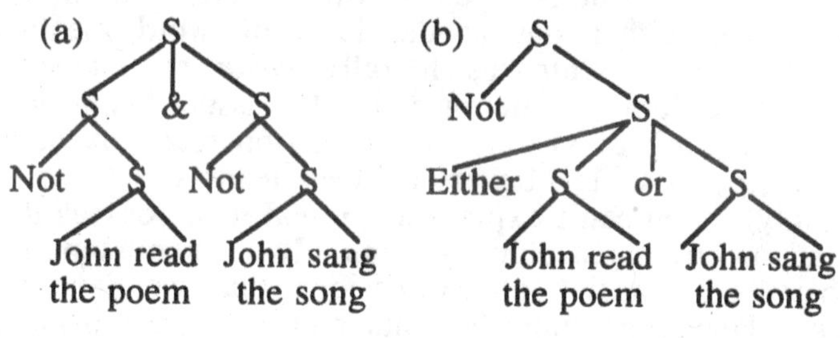

Should (58a) underlie, or be grammatically derived from, (58b)? Or *vice versa*? I propose that any evidence for proposing merely grammatical relations (e..g., McCawley's lexical insertion rules, as well as Logical-Form component "transformations" and even, perhaps, semantic component rules for semantic interpretation) between these structures (structures of syntax, semantics, or (even) pragmatics) must be seriously questioned. For the relationships seem to be preeminently *logical*; i.e., cases like these are the main simple cases used to get the inquiry into logic started. DeMorgan's Law relates propositions with different forms. If someone proposed that "neither-nor" *meant* what "(Both)...not...and ...not" means, then the onus should be very heavily on him(her) to argue for it. For it seems to be that conjunction and disjunction are different connections (sometimes operations) *logically speaking*. And we have (luckily?) distinct natural language expressions for these different logical operations. For anyone to propose (literally!) that the logical relation of conjunction was contained in the meaning of "neither-nor" (or, contrariwise, that the logical relation of disjunction was contained in the meaning of "(both)not-and-not")—where (McCawleyishly, for example) "neither-nor" was derived by lexical insertion, perhaps, into a structure like (58a) (or contrariwise, "(both)not-and-not"was derived from a structure like (58b) by lexical insertion)—is to incur a heavy debt of argument and evidence (logically as well as grammatically). For any such proposal to succeed would mean revising our very well-established understanding of what simple logic is (particularly that relating to DeMorgan's Law).

Similarly for the other sorts of cases in (57). Could Harry's belief that John read the poem be the very same belief that it's false that John did not read the poem? (Some metaphysicians will want to make such a claim in order to avoid unwelcome proposals about the nature of negation and negativity. Metaphysically, it does not seem to me at all likely that all the annoying epistemological and ontological aspects of negation and negativity can be explained away by simply claiming that negation and negativity arises because we have certain words—viz., "not", "non-", etc.—which when combined in pairs somehow cancel either out at the level of word meaning. For example, that (57b) sentences literally *mean* the same thing.) I strongly believe logical inference is the issue here—*not* merely linguistic paraphrase or synonymy. Negation really exists as a topic (relation, etc.) in logic—being at the heart of it (as I see it, Aristotelianly). You can't explain away real negation (as it occurs in correct and incorrect reasonings) as merely a phenomenon resulting totally from peculiarities of expressions that we have in natural languages. To express our thoughts and our reasonings, we don't need to have every word we find in English. If the word "None" did not exist in English, we could get along with various other substitutes. Similarly, if "kill" didn't exist, we could probably make do with "cause", "die", etc. and various constructions and explanations. (What if no expression for directly expressing causation or causality existed—like "cause", "make", etc.—could we express everything we wanted to? Could we express typical explanations we give today for complicated causatives?) *But* could we get along with no expressions for negativity and/or negation—except those introduced by definitions (such as a definition proposed by the "affirmativist" who believes (57b) sentences are synonymous: e.g., "Not-(not-p)" =df. "p"). I don't think so. (Also, see Peterson 1993b.)

Explaining away one or another quantifier expression should be viewed, as I see it, as on a par with trying to explain away negation (e.g., claiming that double-negation is no logical law, but merely a grammatical/semantical rule whereby two "not"s cancel either out word-wise). Consider (57d) and (57e). Should (59a) be the syntactic, semantic, or (even) logical structure which "underlies" expressions which have the structure of (59b)? Or, *Vice versa?*

(59)

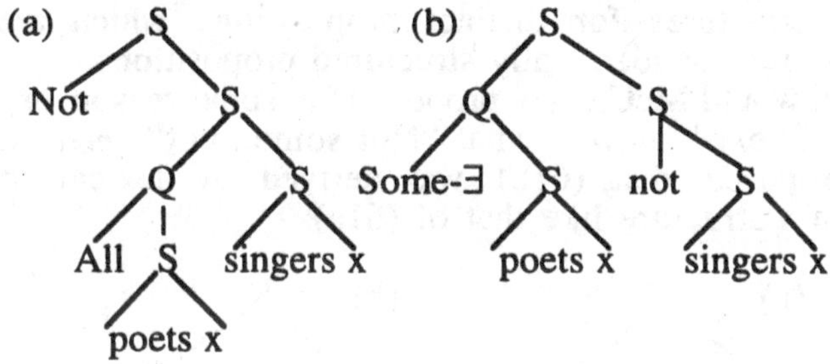

I say *neither*! The point (first discovered by Aristotle) is that these structures are typical of *different propositions* that are very interestingly related via immediate inference (one-step inferences, a batch of which provide the basis for the more interesting two-premise syllogisms, each with three "terms"). The way the system of syllogistic inferences works turns out to be not only the most historically important result for founding the inquiry of logic (the study of forms and characteristics of correct reasonings), but also still provides today one of the very best examples of what correct reasoning between distinct propositions or thoughts *is*. So, the grammatical reduction (elimination from real logic) of crucial items in the syllogistic—such as one of the quantifiers via taking (say) "some" as basic and introducing "all" as merely a defined term (and similarly for all other univeral quantifiers like "every", "each", etc.)—must only be undertaken (i.e., believed!) on the basis of overwhelmingly convincing evidence. (57e) is similar to (57d). Could "Half-not" *mean* what "no more than half" means (when the first "half" is interpreted liberally after the practice explained above, cf. the second paragraph following (9) above). I do *not* think it plausible to propose that (60b) "underlies" (syntactically, semantically, or pragmatically) (60a) , or *vice versa*:

(60)

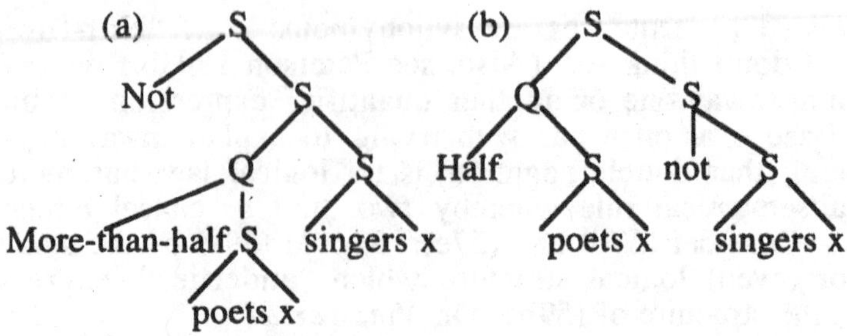

These are structures for distinct propositions which are logically equivalent—not for identically structured propositions.

Finally, would McCawley propose (for some reason or other) that the word "Every" *means* what "Not-some...not" *means*. Imagine that he proposed that (61b) was derived by lexical insertion of "Every" on a structure like that of (61a):

(61)

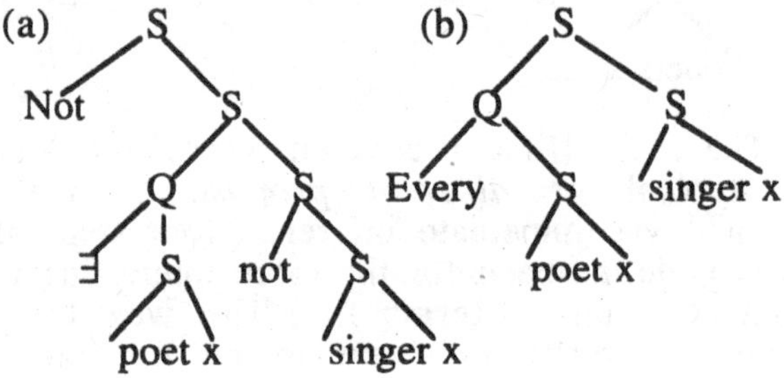

(This would parallel, even, the practice of using Venn Diagrams to analyze syllogisms. For the shading out of regions of a Venn Diagram does not literally represent categorical *universal* propositions (negative or affirmative), but rather directly represents the denial of particular propositions. This corresponds to a similar practice in some versions of the predicate calculus in which only one quantifier is basic and undefined.) In fact, maybe avoiding "there" insertion in sentences like (62) should be effected in just this way.

(62) *There is every poet in debt
*There is every poet who is a singer
*There are all poets who are singers
*There are all poets in debt

For "every" and "all" to occur in a sentence, there must be an underlying structure like (61a). This is a structure in which "there" cannot be inserted (following McCawley's rule) since a "not" intervenes between the clause in which "there" would be inserted (viz., "poets x") and the Q-phrase containing the necessary "E". So, if "every" is inserted into a structure like (61a), the conditions for afterwards inserting "there" are destroyed. Thus, none of (62) are generable (McCawleyishly speaking). On the other hand, various sentences with "there" can be generated from (61a) so long as "every" insertion is avoided—e.g.,

(63) There are not any poets not in debt
There are not any poets who are not singers
(?)It's not that there are poets not in debt

I myself think this is absurd—*not* because it wouldn't work to avoid grammatically sanctioning some unwanted strings such as (62), but rather because "Every" *does not mean* what "Not-some-not" *means*. The line between *logic* (in its simplest elements, of course) and *grammar* is being moved by such a proposal. Aristotelianly speaking, there is no way particular quantity can serve as the basis for merely defining universal quantity. Both are *real quantities*!

Now by analogy with the argument that particular and universal are real quantities, I argue that "predominant" and "common" are real quantities too. Thus, it is not a matter of (natural) language, but a matter of logic (via propositional equivalence) that statements like "Most S are P" (non-generic "most") and "Not many S are not P" are related. So, for rather more general and abstract reasons than merely avoiding "there" insertion in English for certain sentences, it is ill-advised to propose reducing the logical distinction between predominant quantity (what "almost-all" and "most" can easily express) and common quantity (what "many" can easily express) via proposing that the *meaning* of expressions for the predominant quantity are a function of the *meaning* of expressions for the common quantity (in an appropriate structure containing negations).

Now I can imagine that there might be a number of replies from McCawley to my objection, on any of very many details I have briefly sketched about his analyses and proposals—on quantifier phrase structure, various lowering transformations, orderings of transformations, particular lexical insertions as well as lexical insertion in general, his predicate "large" (which I have *largely* ignored), relative clauses, etc., etc. However, I won't speculate on any of these and consider only one possible reply—the one I myself would consider the most interesting. McCawley ought to acknowledge, admit, and adopt the distinctions between (i) sentence meaning and proposition expressed and (ii) propositional equivalence and propositional identity that I have been urging. Then he ought to say that what I consider absurd—viz., the generation of "every" (via lexical insertion) from "not-some-not" structures (say, (61b) from (61a))—is not at all absurd (just alarming) and is an additional proposal he ought to make. Granted, he could go on, you (Peterson) think that merely blocking "there" insertion is a small, local matter of linguistic interest probably only pertaining to English (and maybe a few other languages—but not of relevance for linguistic universals), *still* this is the kind of empirical consideration (even about merely contingent realities of one or a few natural languages) which nevertheless can have relevance for the supposedly *a priori* inquiry into logical phenomena. But how could there *be* such—*empirically* motivated data and hypotheses on *contingent* natural language facts which nevertheless is of real significance for *a priori* logical inquiry (I might rejoin)? For *a priori* inquiry concerns (by definition) non-contingent facts which are not determined empirically. Doesn't it? Well, that is just the question, McCawley might say in conclusion. For either (i) the nature of such *a priori* inquiry (such as in logic and mathematics) is not so completely unaffected by supposedly empirical and contingent realities as is usually thought, or (ii) basic inquiry into logic is *not* so purely *a priori* and concerned only with necessary and universal truths as had been thought, or (iii) epistemologists and metaphysicians don't know so very much about what the *a priori*/empirical distinction really is (nor how it applies to our knowledge in the sciences and mathematics—cf. Kripke 1979 and Putnam 1975) as is usually presumed. (Or, perhaps all of the above.) Finally, McCawley can add in parting, you (Peterson) have already suggested there are legitimate, empirically obtained (possibly on contingencies) features of reasoning which might well constitute substantial inputs (data, facts, hypotheses, generalizations, etc.) into the allegedly purely *a priori* inquiry of logic (cf. Peterson 1986, 1989).

With such a reply I cannot of course, quarrel too much.[20] Still—*my* parting shot—I am not convinced that this isolated problem about "there" insertion for English-like natural languages (within a framework of linguistic investigation that many would consider totally anachronistic today) really is so well-understood and accounted for that such a very fundamental topic as the number of basic (prefractional) logical quantities should be reduced.[21]

Notes

1 For additional explanation of the conception of proposition in question here, see Peterson 1980 and 1995b, and Prior 1976. Concerning the relation of propositions to facts and events, see Peterson 1997b.

2 I sketched the basic idea of the traditional syllogism in the Introduction above. For a more detailed discussion, see Bird 1964. For the needed background discussion of intermediate quantifiers in English, see Chapter I.

3 Take any natural language, L, and determine whether each of the 105 valid syllogistic patterns can be fairly unequivocally expressed in L—and whether validity is preserved through translation. Failure to preserve validity won't necessarily (to my lights, won't at all) provide evidence that either reasoning itself is different for L-speakers or that not all genuine inferences can be expressed in L. It will probably mean adequate translation has not been achieved (e.g., search further for the right quantifier). For further information (relevant to discovering semantic universals on this topic), determine whether for each such translated inference in L there are also translations of typical English *paraphrases* of the inferences expressed in English—for example, paraphrases due to using "Few" in English (which need not be used to express any of the inferences in English). Now even if all the syllogisms expressed in English find adequate translations in L (some may think this is too much to hope for), still not all the English paraphrases will be so easy to translate, will they? (For every L?)

4 The second and third assumption are crucial to seeing the advantages of the 5-quantity syllogistic over McCawley's analysis (discussed below in the next section), that wherein he reduces "many" and "much" to (in part) the predicate "large" (applicable to a relevant set or ensemble). McCawley's analysis permits continual shifting of reference classes and prohibits the necessary linkings between predominant and common quantifiers—thereby undermining the development of the logic of intermediate quantifiers.

5 Cf. McCawley 1981a, pp. 50, 133, 190.

6 But there *is* a difference, some will say. "I didn't buy some book(s)" can be used to directly express the proposition that there is (exists) a book (or there exist some books) which I did not buy. Fine, but that is because "I didn't buy some book(s)" is ambiguous between narrow and wide scope negation. (Narrow scope synonymous with "There are some books I didn't buy", and wide scope synonymous with "(?)It's not that I bought some book(s)".) I was thinking of sentence (18) with *wide* scope negation. In fact, to get the reading of it with narrow scope negation requires, it seems to me for English, at least a little extra stress on "some". (This phenomenon of stress on English quantifiers causing negation-scope changes is important *vis à vis logical* inquiry carried on in English. The traditional example is "All that glitters is not gold" pronounced with Shakespearean intonation.)

7 Vendler 1967 doesn't recognize the use of "any" I am emphasizing (as negative polarity item meaning what "some" does). This is a small surprise, since Vendler doesn't seem to be an any-rule fan either. It might appear that much of my analysis is based upon Linebarger (1981) and/or other authors mentioned therein (those arguing against what Linebarger calls the "A-theory"—which is tantamount to the aforementioned "any-rule"). Actually, my analysis is not derived from Linebarger (or other such authors), even though it is quite compatible. It was devised in preparation of Peterson 1981b. Further, it is couched in terms of a view of proposition individuation (fine-grained, distinct from sentence meanings) which Linebarger and other supporters of the "E-theory" do not explicitly acknowledge (and may well be hostile to).

8 If there is more than one quantifier after the negation, the situation is confusing for both me and the any-rule fan. Consider:

(a) I didn't give any test to some student
(b) I didn't give any test to every student

For me, (a) is ambiguous. The reading I prefer is (al), that with the last quantifier in (a) having wide scope (what I suggested above in note 6 would require a little stress on "some"), but (a2) is also possible:

(al) $(\exists y\text{: Student } y){\sim}(\exists x\text{: Test } x)(\text{I gave } x \text{ to } y)$
(a2) ${\sim}(\exists x\text{: Test } x)(\exists y\text{: Student } y)(\text{I gave } x \text{ to } y)$

An any-rule fan will (applying his rule mechanically) say that (a) is:

(a3) $(\forall x\text{: Test } x){\sim}(\exists y\text{: Student } y)(\text{I gave } x \text{ to } y)$

Now this is okay, logically speaking since (a3) is logically equivalent to (a2)—my non-preferred reading. However, can the any-rule fan get something equivalent to what I prefer, (al)? Yes, viz.:

(a4) $(\exists y\text{: Student } y)(\forall x\text{: Test } x){\sim}(\text{I gave } x \text{ to } y)$

To get this, he must restrict the any-rule to the effect that "any" takes wider scope than a negation in the same context, but not necessarily wider scope than every other quantifier there.

Now look at (b). I prefer (b2) as the reading (following the surface order of quantifiers *and* negation), but (bl) *is* a possible reading (and (bl) is closely analogous to the reading, (al), I preferred for (a)):

(bl) (∀y: Student y)~(∃x: Test x)(I gave x to y)
(b2) ~(∃x: Test x)(∀y: Student y)(I gave x to y)

Can the any-rule fan get either one? Mechanical application of his rule (it seems to me) yields:

(b3) (∀x: Test x)(∀y: Student y)~(I gave x to y)

But (b3), though equivalent to (bl), would also represent

(c) I didn't give any test to any student

for the any-rule fan—which causes a *loss* of contrast of (c) with (b) with respect to "any"/"every". As I see it, this would *force* the any-rule fan to invent another application of his rule, so that applied to (b) it would yield

(b4) (∀x: Test x)~(∀y: Student y)(I gave x to y)

Granted that (b4) is equivalent to (b2)—where (b2) is *my* preference for (b), but it looks like (b4) was coerced or *ad hoc* (and that the any-rule is failing since we got to (b4) by noting that we need a contrast with (c)). I think this state of affairs shows that the any-rule can't stand application in more complicated cases without *ad hoc* corrections that are guided by my approach (wherein "any" with "not" means "some", *and* surface order of expressions for quantifiers and negation dictates the usual logical order of quantifiers and negation in logical form—though variations of order are sometimes possible (e.g., (al) for (a))). I also think that no any-rule fan will be persuaded by such discussion, since the cases are so complicated (not really *very* complicated though) that intuitions are very shaky or fail (i.e., it's hard to decide whether (b4) is a fair application of the any-rule to (b)). Too bad.

9 "Every book was not seen by me" is Shakespeareanly ambiguous (like "All that glitters is not gold" is). Thus, it may be used to express (16)', but also to express (17)'.

10 By "explanation" here I do not mean to refer to anything very lofty in semantics or logic; it is a low level explanation—perhaps really just alternative means of description of the data, pointed in an explanatory direction.

11 Many observers seem to think that contrariety between propositions is a function of underlying contrariety between terms. This is false. Propositional contrariety is basic; cf. Peterson 1995b.

12 In all the tree-structure diagrams and most of the logical form representations below I have tried to follow the notations and conventions found in McCawley 1981a and 1981b. McCawley's discussion of "there" insertion in 1981a is very

brief. So, I have leaned on 1981b to understand it. For one thing, McCawley is nowhere absolutely specific about what it is for a clause to be "immediately above" another one. His discussion is best interpreted as indicating that in (31), for example, "x are beneath contempt" is *lower* than the Q-phrase "E (some) singers x" and that the latter is "*immediately* above" the former. This just seems false diagrammatically speaking, but the only other apparent possibility is that he is speaking of "E (some)" as being "immediately above" the clause "singer x" (and that I am not inserting "there" in the right place). However, this alternative interpretation won't work in the explanation he is offering (as I shall point out below), so I don't think it is a genuine possibility, Another point is that I am also following McCawley's and other linguists' (and even many philosophers'; e.g., Quine's) semantic judgments on quantifiers—for example, that (29) is ambiguous with respect to existential quantifer scope while (30) is not. My own judgments are more liberal; e.g., that (30) as well as "There are some singers Bertrand thinks are beneath contempt" are equally ambiguous quantifier-scope-wise (and that surface order of various expressions for quantifiers is less coercive in assigning interpretations than is usually thought). However, for the sake of smoother discussion herein, I will suppress my liberalities.

13 In many of the diagrams below, I will represent the quantifier expressed by "many" and the "not-many-not" structures by putting the English word "many" alongside the usual existential quantifier symbol "∃". This is *not* McCawley's practice. Thus, it might appear that I have diverged so far from McCawley's notations (which I claimed to be adopting) as to make it very unclear whether I am discussing his position on "there"-insertion at all. This is only an appearance. McCawley's position on the *meaning* of "many" is that it is consists of the existential quantifier plus a sub-clause—usually represented by "Large(x)"—within the (restricted-quantification) quantifier phrase. One way to look at my (not unMcCawleyish) notational variation is to conceive of it as the result of lexical insertion on an underlying structure, one which replaces a longer structure with a shorter one—paralleling, as McCawley once suggested, "kill" replacing a "cause to die" structure and, in the present context, his replacing "most" in a "not-many-not" structure. In sum, I myself have (so to speak) "lexically inserted" (b) sorts of structures for McCawley's (a) sorts:

(a) Q[∃ S[S...S[Large(x)]]] (b) Q[[Many ∃] S[S...]]

where (i) "Many" is used as a technical symbol for a quantifier expressing the so-called "common" quantity (in 5-quantity syllogistic) and (ii) the attached "∃" is a mere reminder of its association with existential quantification (for motives like McCawley's). (Maybe the "∃" in (b) should be moved to the position of a subscript to "Many".)

14 This is the sense of "most" I expressed in Section 2 above (and in Chapter 2 above and Peterson 1985a) by using "almost-all". McCawley does not use "almost-all", but just "most" (as I did in Peterson 1979a). However, it is clear that he is not using "most" in the sense of just "more than half", but in the narrow sense; cf. p. 427, McCawley 1981a. Incidentally, I have a reply to those readers who think McCawley's analyses (and my revisions or complaints below) are of little interest today because of the alleged refutation of generative semantics (which framework McCawley's entire discussion seems to be within)—and/or its rejection by so many theorists in linguistics today. As far as I can see, nothing McCawley proposes (or I criticize or suggest) is absolutely dependent on accepting the generative semantics framework. For the relationships and patterns (between and among grammatical constituents and structures and logical forms and elements) that McCawley is discussing will still remain if generative semantics is completely rejected. Therefore, if an interpretive approach to semantics is associated with recent government and binding theory, then there will be in the latter (G&B syntax + interpretive semantics) *correlates* of McCawley's quantifier-lowering for example. Quantifier lowering (in McCawley) will have a correlate which is either (i) a "raising" transformational rule in the LF component (deriving LF's from S-structures), or (ii) an interpretive rule in the semantic component to derive a semantic representation (SR) with the quantifier appropriately "raised" or positioned, or (iii) a rule for producing correct quantifier-structure for *propositional* forms (when the SR does not achieve appropriate quantifier placement since it is left to a part of the theory which produces representations of propositional form—where the latter are conceived to be distinct from SRs). Similarly, "there" insertion (or its lack) will doubtless correlate in G&B+semantics theory with a "there" deletion (or *non*-interpretation) rule in either (i) the LF component, or (ii) the semantic component, or (if it is needed) (iii) the propositional form component (if proposition representations are distinct from both SRs and LFs), As far as I can see, every syntactic, semantic, and/or pragmatic phenomenon and issue addressed herein will have its correlate within G&B+semantics theory. Put another way, none of the issues (e.g., McCawley's analysis, my criticisms) is crucial with respect to arguing for *or* against (a McCawleyish) generative semantics. The issues will have to be addressed in every contemporary framework (Montague, lexical-functionalist, etc,) as well.

15 In saying this, I ignore part of McCawley's theory; i.e., (39) is a simplification of McCawley's complete proposal. My objections will be much easier to make about the simplification, and they carry over completely (I hereby stipulate) to McCawley's full analysis. McCawley's further theory of "many", "much", and "most" incorporates lexical insertions from underlying forms containing terms

for sets (his term "M") and so-called "ensembles" (also, denoted by "M"). (Ensembles are apparently what H. Cartwright called "quantities" in an approach that McCawley could have profitted from if he had noticed it; cf. Cartwright 1970.) I myself do not think that these further elements of his theory (what I leave out in my simplification) are very promising or (even) plausible. I hope a more plausible and natural approach (than McCawley's with sets and ensembles, and "Large" as in Note 13 above) will eventually result from taking the Aristotelian approach I introduce herein more seriously (for "many", "much", and "most").

16 McCawley's manuever with underlying forms for pseudo-relatives causes him a certain semantic problem. For on the one hand, the most basic structures underlying, for example, "Some singer is in debt", "There is some singer in debt", and "There is some singer who is in debt" are the same—viz., (35). They all have the same logical form (which I take it here means the same thing as saying that, on a certain reading and use of each, they all can be used to express exactly one and the same proposition). One way to represent this is to claim (as I. and I think McCawley, would) that this common logical/propositional form can be represented (in a slightly different notation from (35)) as

(a) $(\exists x\text{: Singer}(x))(\text{In-debt}(x))$

(a first-order predicate calculus formula in restricted-quantification format), However, the upshot of McCawley's first unnamed transformation in the derivation which ends in a near-surface structure for the pseudo-relative version "There is a singer who is in debt" is to transform a structure like (a) into one like (b):

(b) $(\exists x)(\text{ Singer }(x)\ \&\ \text{In-debt }(x)$

McCawley is explicit about this (cf. p. 116, 1981b, where he refers to the (b)-sort as a "pure existential sentence—though "&" is inexplicably omitted). Now the problem with this is that the pseudo-relative sentence "There is a/some singer who is in debt" has *two* logical forms—first (a). and then (b)—where the other sentences supposedly synonymous and co-expressive (proposition-wise) with it only have one (viz., (a)). I believe McCawley really meant what he said about pseudo-relatives, so that the best solution to this problem is to say that the *genuine* logical form of "There is some singer who is in debt" is (b)— and *not* (a). But then what should we say about the very close semantic relation between all three of these sentences? I think we must (in trying to defend McCawley) say that they are *not* all synonymous and co-expressive (proposition-wise). Rather, "Some singer is in debt" and "There is some singer in debt" are synonymous and can be used to express exactly one and the same proposition, *But* "There is some singer who is in debt" expresses (typically) a proposition that is (albeit very tightly) logically equivalent to the former proposition (not identical to it). (The lack of identity of proposition serves as the basis for saying there is a very slight meaning difference between the sentences. What *is* the very slight meaning difference? Well, for one thing it is revealed in the relations to other *uses* of the same relative clauses—pseudo-restricted, and non-restricted—which occasion detectable semantic variations of exactly the sort McCawley discussed, Especially, see pp. 114-115, On these two pages McCawley considers examples with "many" instead of just "some". With "many" his point shows more clearly. If you substitute "some" for "many" in his (25a and b), pp. 114, and in the associated discussion, the semantic differences become very difficult to see ("delicate", as I have sometimes said). My conclusion is that they *are* there, however, for the "some" sentences—if only by analogy with the "many" sentences.)

Now I do not expect McCawley to agree at once to what I say is a legitimate problem here (the two, vs. one, logical forms, even though they are equivalent), and so he need not agree that I have hit upon a McCawleyish solution. For the problem depends on making the very same distinction between propositional identity and logical equivalence that is my overall concern (in criticizing McCawley) herein. However, iIf he were persuaded by my overall point herein, then he would have to return to address the problem I raise in this note. In the end, I think he must *drop* the unnamed transformation as a transformation altogether and just admit that (a) and (b) are distinct deeper syntactic (or semantic) structures for two semantically distinct sorts of sentences which are very nearly synonymous and propositionally co-expressive; i.e., there is *no* transformational relation between (a) and (b).

17 Would I (in a McCawleyish mood) propose that "few" (≠ "a few") be introduced by lexical insertion on a "not-many" structure? If so, then "There are few S who are P/Prep P" (e.g., "There are few singers who are poets", . "There are few singers beneath contempt") will be blocked, since "Few" insertion will erase the "E" associated with "Many" (thereby blocking "there" insertion). However, "There are few..." sentences are grammatical. The McCawleyish solution to this problem is to let "there" insertion apply before "few" insertion, when both are optional. Thus,

S_0 [NOT S_1[Q[Many-∃ S]] S_2]]
=> (by "there" insertion)
S_0[NOT S_1[Q[Many-∃ S] S_2[...there...]]]
=> (by "few" insertion)
S_1[Q[Few S] S_2[...there...]
=> (by Q-lowering)
S_2[There are few...]

Both "there" insertion and "few" insertion are optional so that sentences like "There are not many singers in debt" and "Few singers are in debt" are derivable. *Then* notice that derivation of "There are *no* singers beneath contempt" can be exactly similar (replacing "some" for "many" above), where (say) the lexical insertion of "No" in a "Not a/some/one" structure occurs before "there"-insertion. But if "No" is not inserted, then "some" is replaced by "any" (or even "a"), either before or after "there" insertion.

18 "doesn't want" in (56c), "doesn't believe" in (56d), and "doesn't believe" in (57b) each create a similar kind of ambiguity—that between wide-scope and narrow-scope negation (e.g., (57c): Not(John wants (Mary sings)) vs. (John wants not(Mary sings)). For all three of these cases, I interpret the negation scope as *narrow* in order to make the pairs in (56c and d) and (57b) synonymous.

19 This passage suggests that McCawley is *not* inclined to make a distinction between propositional identity and propositional equivalence—that he takes the equivalence "p and (q and p)" and "p and q" (i.e., of instances of these forms) as evidence for their identity. On the other hand, maybe McCawley is inclined to agree with me—since he does avoid saying that all contradictions are identical (since equivalent); cf. p. xiii (a conclusion I, of course, would also advance). Perhaps the only reason he says "p and (q and p)" and "p and q" are identical is that (in addition to their logical equivalence) they have exactly the same propositional constituents and one is simply repeated—redundantly. 'Myself, I would not even permit this small liberality (permitting "p" and "p and p" to be propositionally identical). For the proposition "p and (q and p)" has a *doubly* conjunctive form (one conjunct is itself a conjunction) and the second proposition "p and q" does not. Incidentally, an interesting sort of case to ponder with respect to which list—(56) or (57)—two logically equivalent sentences should appear on is the identity sentence; for example:

"Tully = Cicero" *vis à vis* "Cicero = Tully"
"The US president = Ronald Reagan" *vis à vis*
"Ronald Reagan = The US president"
where "=" here is merely an abbreviation for
"is (the same person/thing as)"

A very easy thing to propose is that both of the above pairs are synonymous pairs (each pair consists, that is, of two synonymous sentences). But look at the question more carefully. The first has the logical form (at bottom):

(i) $a = b$

Now is any proposition with this form 'identical (over and above logical equivalence) with one that has the form

(ii) b = a

Why not? Well, some mathematical analyses contain the claim that *identity* is a *symmetric relation*. Not all relations are symmetric (e.g., being the parent of), but identity is. To merely *state* this fact for identity requires saying that p(i) is equivalent to p(ii). But one must *say* that significantly (if attributing symmetry to identity is significant). And if (i) and (ii) express one and the same proposition, then "p(i) is equivalent to p(ii)" is true because (simply) every proposition is logically equivalent to *itself*. I myself don't think attributing symmetry to identity is that trivial. So, I must hold that p(i) and p(ii) express different propositions (i.e., for a concrete example, p("Tully = Cicero") is a different proposition from p("Cicero = Tully")). Thus, such identity sentence pairs appear on (57)! (The only alternative to this conclusion would be to say that the so-called symmetry of identity is a truth about language or notation, not about a pure extra-linguistic relation. I would disagree with this tack. It seems to me that the symmetry of identity is a fact that is just as independent of language and notations as the Pythagorean Theorem is—that both are facts (truths) of pure mathematics.

[20] In addition to the heresies on logic in Peterson 1986 and 1989, I have also argued in Peterson 1984 that linguistics is irretrievably entangled in philosophy (viz., in epistemology). The results herein add further support to this thesis (as does Jackendoff's 1983 analysis: Jackendoff should adopt and utilize the Aristotelian view on quantifiers I have outlined herein, cf. his pp. 75 and 207).

[21] This chapter is based on earlier ms. circulated by the Indiana University Linguistics Club Publications, May 1988. That version was a revised and expanded version of Peterson 1981b. I am very grateful to Robert Carnes for his improvement of my understanding about nearly all of the matters herein. I am also grateful to James McCawley for useful comments and especially for calling McCawley 1981b to my attention. Many times in recent years Tom McKay has made various complaints and criticisms to me about what I say about quantifiers. I am very grateful for these reactions, which have nearly always been stimulating and eventually fruitful.

4 Complexly Fractionated Quantifiers

What if we add modifiers to the intermediate and fractional quantifiers?[1] In on way of looking at them, the modifier "more than" is already included. Since "More than half (of the) S" *means* what "Most (of the) S" does, on one good sense of "most", perhaps "almost-all (of the) S" *means* what "Much more than half (of the) S" does. Then, maybe each intermediate quantifier is the result of modifying a fractional. No, this is false. And the reasoning is misleading.[2]

"Much more than" is actually a *complex* (rather than a simple) iteration of quantifiers. Simply iterated quantifiers are like "Half of 30% of S". Even though this can be interpreted as "Half" applying to "30%" first, to get "15%", so that the resolution of this iteration is "15% of S", it doesn't have to be applied that way. Rather, we can just as well apply "30%" to the Ss and then apply "Half" to whatever the result is; i.e., the scopes can be "Half(30%(S...))..." as well as "(Half-30%(S...))...". Quantifiers like "50% more than half the S" cannot, however, be analyzed either way. For "50%" *must apply first* to "More than" and then the result of that applied to "half" (or to "half of S"). For "50% *of* more than half the Ss" *does not mean the same thing* that "50% more than half the Ss" does! For example, let there be 100 Ss. Half of them would be 50. So, 50% *more* than half would be half of half more—viz., 75% of them. 50% *of* more than half of them, however, is different and less precise. 52 Ss is more than half of them, and 50% of those would be 26. So, "50% of more than half the Ss" (when there are 100 Ss) could be only 26 Ss. This is *not* a possible interpretation of "*50% more* than half the Ss" (for 100 Ss). So, I will call genuine modifiers of fractions like "more than" *with* prefixed modifers like "50%" (as vs. "50% *of*") *complex* iterations of quantifiers—where *simple* iterations contain no modifers that can't be fractions themselves or can't be interpreted to be quantifiers applying to results of prior quantifiers (right-to-left). So, "Much more than", paralleling "50% more than", is *complexly* iterated.

To describe and explain an *algebra* which will be adequate for analyzing all intermediate (and related) syllogisms in which *complexly* fractionated quantifiers occur, I will first give some background and then introduce the crucial algebraic representations via an example. (I give no extension of Carnes' rules or Venn Diagrams, as in Chapter 2, to apply to these new syllogisms.) After that, I will state the general forms for algebraic representation and describe how to use them with some more examples. I conclude with some remarks on evaluation.

Here is the complex square of opposition for the 5-quantity syllogistic, with algebraic equivalences for each categorical stated below each form:

(1) 5-Quantity Squares of Opposition

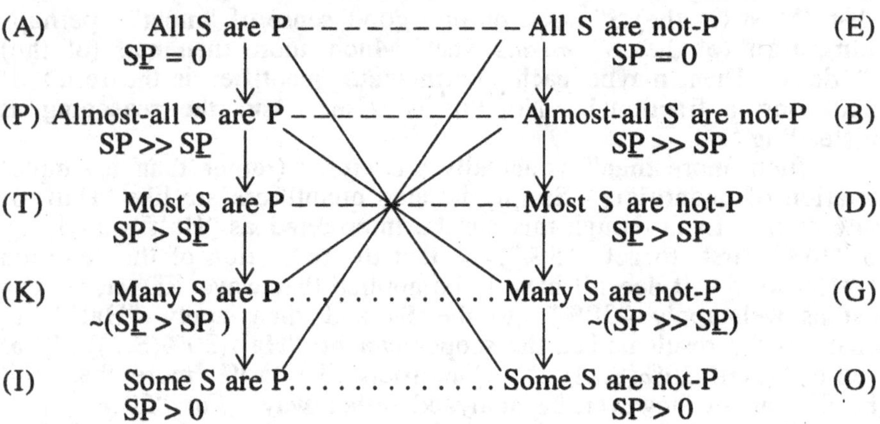

where arrows represent entailment (sub-alternation), dashes connect contraries, dots connect sub-contraries, and diagonal lines connect contradictories (notational conventions adhered to above and below)

Each of the algebraic formulae in (1) is interpreted as a. statement about quantities in and/or sizes of the sub-classes mentioned. Thus, "$SP = 0$" is read the "The size of SP (or quantity of Ss that are Ps) is zero (or none)" and "$SP \gg S\underline{P}$" is read "The size of SP greatly exceeds the size of $S\underline{P}$" or "The quantity of Ss that are P's greatly exceeds the quantity of S's that are not-Ps".

Following the practice of Chapter 2, I will often refer to the sub-classes (sub-portions) in question with names read off the following Venn Diagram (in saying something about their relative sizes):

(2)

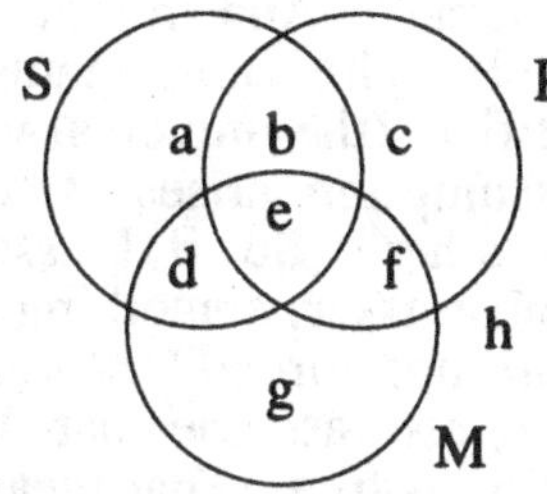

For example, instead of writing "$S\underline{P} > SP$" (read "the quantity of Ss that are not-Ps exceeds the quantity of Ss that are Ps"), I may write "$a + d > b + e$" (read "the quantity of a and d together exceeds the quantity of b and e together").

To further expand this background, consider the first of the "higher" quantities (the sixth) to be added to the 5-quantity syllogistic—viz., "half", as in "Half the S are P". This is added to the system by replacing the center line in (1) (the contrary T and D forms) with the following square of opposition:

(3) (T) Most S are P ------------ Most S are not-P (D)
($SP > S\underline{P}$) ↓ ↓ ($S\underline{P} > SP$)

(F) Half S are P . . . . Half S are not-P (V)
($SP \geq S\underline{P}$) ($S\underline{P} \geq SP$)

Many assumptions and provisos are in effect in understanding and using these squares and formulae (for complete discussion of which see Chapters 1 and 2 above and Peterson 1985a). Two assumptions are *very* important—the "liberal" interpretation of each quantifier, and the presupposition of a constant reference class. Each categorical proposition with intermediate quantifiers—such as those in (1) and (3)—must be interpreted in such a way that the quantifier carries with it a tacit "or more" rider. For example, "Many S are P" is understood as if it were "Many, or more, S are P" and "Half the S are not P" is understood as if it werc "Half, or more, S are not P". If this is *not* done, then the entailments down the rows in (1) and (3) do not hold (which will lead to failure of contrariety and sub-contrariety relations as well; cf. Peterson 1995b). But dropping these entailments would be departing from Aristotelian practice; i.e., even in Aristotle's square of opposition, AEIO in (1), the particular quantifier must be read or understood as if it was followed by an "or more" rider. "All S are P" entails "Some S are P" (not only because of presumption of existential import of the subject of the universal but) because "some" is understood to be "some *or more*". For if it weren't so interpreted, it would have to mean "only some". And in that case the universal to particular entailment would fail. This same manner of interpretation carries over to all other quantifiers (the universal vacuously).

The second important assumption arises as follows. (P) and (G) forms in (1) contradict each other. So, if I assert "almost-all U.S. soldiers are abroad", then I must assert something logically equivalent to "Not many U.S. soldiers are not abroad". Assume that there are 1 million U.S. soldiers. Further, also assume that 900,000 of them *are* abroad, so that my first assertion is true. That means that "Many U.S. soldiers are *not* abroad" is false and that "Not many U.S. soldiers are not abroad" is true. But is this right? 100,000 soldiers (the *rest of* the soldiers) is *a lot of* soldiers, isn't it? It's a lot more than I have ever seen, for example. But if so, then "Many soldiers are not abroad" is true (rather than the required false)—since 100,000 *are many*. Then the relevant square of opposition breaks down, since there are cases of the forms "Almost-all S are P" and "Many S are not P" *where both* are true (and they were supposed to contradict). The solution to this problem is a special requirement of "no switching reference classes" (first proposed in Peterson, 1979a, pp. 166-167). The alleged counter-example to (1) only works because reference classes have been switched—e.g., in saying "Almost-all S are P" ("S" = "U.S. soldiers", "P" = "abroad"), the reference class is *all* the soldiers (viz., I million). If we stick to that reference class, then "Not many S are not P" is false. For 100,000 soldiers is *not many* when compared to 1 million (for it's only one-tenth of them). It is only by switching reference classes (say, to all I have ever seen) that 100,000 seemed to be a lot of (or many) soldiers. Compared to 1 million, it's not.

Here is an algebraic proof of a 6-quantity syllogistic form, viz., AFK-1 (taken from Appendix II of Peterson 1985a, where also see the analogous proof of ESO-4). The proof is by *reductio ad absurdum*. (Proofs of invalidity are by counter-example.)

(4) AFK-I Proof

All M are P	(1) $d = 0$ and $g = 0$	premise
1/2 the S are M:	(2) $d + e \geq a + b$	premise
~(Many S are P):	(3) $\sim\sim(a + d \gg b + e)$	denial of concl'n
	(4) $a \geq b + e$	from (1) and (3)
	(5) $a + b \gg b + e$	from (4) (Peterson 1985a has a mis-print in this line)
	(6) $a + b \gg e$	from (5)
	(7) $\sim(a + b > d + e)$	from (2)
	(8) $\sim(a + b > e)$	from (1) and (7)
contradiction	(9) $a + b > e$	from (6)

To apply this kind of proof to *syllogisms* with complex quantifiers (e.g., those of Thompson 1986), consider first an example with just one fraction quantifier—viz., "1/4", as in "1/4 of the M are not P". Here are the major categoricals organized in squares of opposition with appropriate algebraic formulae stated directly beneath each categorical form:

(5) 'Quarter' Squares

Much more than 1/4 of the S are P ---- Much more than 3/4 of the S are not-P
$3(SP) \gg S\underline{P}$ — $S\underline{P} \gg 3(SP)$

More than 1/4 of the S are P --- More than 3/4 of the S are not-P
$3(SP) > S\underline{P}$ — $S\underline{P} > 3(SP)$

1/4 of the S are P . . . . . . 3/4 of the S are not-P
$3(SP) \geq S\underline{P}$ — $S\underline{P} \geq 3(SP)$

Almost 1/4 of the S are P . . . . Almost 3/4 of the S are not-P
$\sim(S\underline{P} \gg 3(SP))$ — $\sim(3(SP) \gg S\underline{P})$

Review of (1) and (3) above will reveal how two ideas are intimately combined to produce the oppositions of (5)—viz., the linking definitions of "Much more" and "Almost" (paralleling the connections of P-forms to G-forms and B-forms to K-forms) *and* the treatment of fractions implied by (3). On the latter point, compare (3) with (6) and (7):

(6) More than 2/3 of the S are P--- More than 2/3 of the S are not-P
$SP > 2(S\underline{P})$ — $SP > 2(S\underline{P})$

1/3 of the S are P . . . . . 1/3 of the S are not-P
$2(S\underline{P}) \geq SP$ — $2(S\underline{P}) \geq SP$

(7) More than (n–m)/n of the S are P ---- More than (n–m)/n of the S are not-P
$m(SP) > (n-m)(S\underline{P})$ — $m(S\underline{P}) > (n-m)(SP)$

m/n of the S are P . . . . . . m/n of the S are not-P
$(n-m)(SP) \geq m(S\underline{P})$ — $(n-m)(S\underline{P}) \geq m(SP)$

(for m and n, $n \geq 2m$: when $2m > n$, the contrary and subcontrary relations switch and the implications reverse direction)

Now notice that (5), though similar, does not follow the pattern of (3), (6) and (7) *exactly*. In particular, notice that the middle square of opposition in (5) is *not* an instance of (7). Rather, the middle of (5) can be viewed as derived from an instance of (7) by rotating 90° the matrix of fractions of an instance where "m/n" is "1/4" (while leaving the remainder of the square as is). Interestingly, this rotation preserves all the Aristotelian relations (contradiction, contrariety, subalternation). Rotation of the fraction matrix shows very clearly in comparing (6) to (12) below. (12) is the rotated form of (6).

(5) includes the quantifiers: "More than", "Much more than", "Almost", and unmodified fractions like "1/4". Since it is assumed, as mentioned above for the 5-quantity and higher-quantity syllogism, that each quantifier phrase carries the tacit rider "or more", a simple fractionally quantified form like "1/4 of the S are P" is *also* understood as "1/4 or more of the S are P". Thus, "1/4 of the S are P" does *not* mean *"exactly* 1/4 of the S are P". Quantifiers of the form "exactly m/n" can be easily defined, however—as follows:

(8) "Exactly m/n of the S are P" =df. "(m/n of the S are P) & ((n–m)/n S are not-P)"
i.e., $m(SP) = (n-m)(S\underline{P})$ if & only if $(m(SP) \geq (n-m)(S\underline{P}))$ & $((n-m)(S\underline{P}) \geq m(SP)))$

What about the modifiers (of quantifiers) "less than" and "or less"? "Less than m/n" is defined as follows:

(9)"Less than m/n of the S are P" =df. "Not(m/n of the S are P)"
$m(S\underline{P}) > (n-m)(SP)$ $\qquad$ $\sim((n-m)(SP) \geq m(S\underline{P}))$

The right hand side of (9) is equivalent via (7) to "More than (n–m)/n of the S are not-P" (= "$m(S\underline{P}) > (n-m)(SP)$"), and so is the left-hand side of (9). "Or less" only comes in as a tacit rider with genuine "Less than" statements as just defined. (So, "or more" and "or less" play opposite roles, the former very pervasive and the latter nearly non-existent.)

The only really interesting aspect of (5) is the proposal that the corresponding "Much more than" and "Almost" forms contradict. Indeed, the "almost" forms are represented algebraically as simply denials of corresponding "much more...not" forms (and "almost...not" as denials of "much more" forms)—where the modified fractions are adjusted appropriately (as exemplified in (5)). Perhaps some convincing is in order. Consider the *denial* of

(10) Many more than 1/4 of the sailors are males

If the denial of (10) is true, it is *not* the case that many more than 1/4 of the sailors are male.[3] Alternatively expressed, *not* many more than 1/4 of the sailors are males. But if that is so, then *not* many less than 3/4 of the sailors are not-males. But *not*-many-less than 3/4 is *almost* 3/4, isn't it? Well, if it's not exactly the same, it is damned close. It's so close that I propose identifying them. And note that without such an identification logical troubles about relating "Almost m/n" statements to "Much more than m/n" statements are bound to arise.[4]

Exactly what I am saying about these denials and equivalences can be easily misunderstood here. So, I will clarify what I take the denial of (10) to *be*.[5] I do *not* take the denial of (10) to be the proposition expressed when (10.1) is uttered (with the stresses pronounced as indicated by italics):

(10.1) Not *many* more than 1/4 of the sailors are males

Rather, I take the genuine denial of (10) to be what would be ordinarily expressed with a use of (10.2), a proposition containing widescope negation as represented in (10.3):

(10.2) *Not* many more than 1/4 of the sailors are males

(10.3) ~(Many more than 1/4 of the sailors are males)

Although the differing stresses of (10.1) and (10.2) are not perfect disambiguators (as analogous stresses do seem to be perfect in contrasting "*All* that glitters *is* not gold" with "All that glitters is *not* gold"), still they are pretty good; i.e., (10.2) makes it pretty clear that full-sentence denial (wide-scope negation) is what is expressed.

(10.1) can easily be misapprehended as what I intend to be logically equivalent to (10.4):

(10.4) Almost 3/4 of the sailors are not males

But it is (10.2) that is logically equivalent to (10.4), instantiating part of (5). In (10.1), then, something else is expressed.

I claim that the most straightforward use of (10.1) would be to assert that it is not *many* more than 1/4 of the sailors who are male, even though it *is* still more than 1/4. In short, the "not" modifies "many" in (10.1) (logical-grammar-wise) and it is not a full-sentence modifier.[6] In this usage it *is* implied that "more than 1/4 of the sailors are males" is true. (To repeat: asserting (10.1) is like saying "'Many more' is *not* the quantity more than 1/4 of the S which are

M"—where "S" = "sailors" and "M" = "Males".) This implication is *not* contained in asserting the full-sentence denial of (10)—e.g., as represented in (10.3).

So, there *is* a use of "Not many more than 1/4 of the sailors are male" wherein (10.5) is implied and another use of it where (10.5) is *not* implied:

(10.5) Many more than 1/4 of the sailors are males

The full-sentence denial of (10)—i.e., (10.3), as typically expressed by (10.2)—does *not* imply (10.5), but (10.1) *does*. Thus, (10.1) and (10.3) cannot be logically equivalent. To see this in another way, consider whether (10.4) *could* entail (10.1). (10.2) is, of course, entailed by (10.4), since the two are logically equivalent (or so I propose and defend herein). *But* there is a situation in which (10.4) is true, but (10.1) is false. This is when (10.4) is true because the following is true:

(10.6) 3/4 of the sailors are not males

(10.6) entails (10.4)—mainly due to the liberal interpretation of quantifiers mentioned above (the "or more" rider). This is represented in (5) in the right hand column. But when (10.6) is true, then (10.7) is false:

(10.7) More than 1/4 of the sailors are males

(This is a very unobjectionable incompatibility also drawn from (5).) When (10.7) is false, then (10.1) is false too (since (10.1) entails (10.7)). So, we have here a case where (10.4) is true *and* (10.1) is false. So, (10.4) does *not* entail (10.1). So, (10.1) cannot be the denial of (10) which is relevant to being a case of a part of (5)—that wherein "Almost 3/4 of the S are not M" is said (i) to contradict "Many more than 1/4 of the S are M" and (ii) to be logically equivalent to "Not many more than 1/4 of the S are M".

The general form for the relations between "Much more than m/n", "More than m/n", "m/n", and "almost m/n" categoricals (so-called) can be easily extracted from the example pursued in (5). Simply generalize the fractions, to get:

(11) "Much more" Squares

Much more than x/y of the S-are P ---- Much more than u/v of the S are not-P
$(y-x)(SP) \gg x(S\underline{P})$ | $(v-u)(S\underline{P}) \gg u(SP)$

More than x/y of the S are P ---- More than u/v of the S are not-P
$(y-x)(SP) > x(S\underline{P})$ | $(v-u)(S\underline{P}) > u(SP)$

x/y of the S are P . . . . . . u/v/ of the S are not-P
$(y-x)(SP) \geq x(S\underline{P})$ | $(v-u)(S\underline{P}) \geq u(SP)$

Almost x/y, of the S are P. . . . Almost u/v of the S are not-P
$\sim((v-u)(S\underline{P}) \gg u(SP)$ | $\sim((y-x)(SP) \gg x(S\underline{P}))$

where if x/y = m/n, then u/v = (n–m)/n, and if u/v ≠ m/n, then x/y ≠ (n–m)/n, and m and n are integers m/n ≥ 1/2.

(11) only holds for n > m > 0; i.e., n/n is *not* taken to be "all" and "0/n" is not taken to be "none". For when such values are permitted the bottom two rows collapse left-to-right.[7]

(5) and (11) strike me as *less* Aristotelian than (3) and (6)—though, of course, both have all the right components (contradictories, contraries, sub-contraries, and subalternations).[8] An interesting feature of rotated squares–say, (12) below compared to (6)–is that their sub-contraries are "closer" in the sense that they can (apparently) only be true under one condition–e.g., in (12) that *precisely* 1/3 S are P, so that *precisely* 2/3 S are not-P. The sub-contraries of (6) are more loosely connected. For there, are lots of conditions under which 1/3 *or more* S are P *and* 1/3 *or more S* are not-P.

(12) More than 1/3 S are P ----- More than 2/3 S are not-P
$2(SP) > S\underline{P}$ | $S\underline{P} > 2(SP)$

1/3 S are P . . . . 2/3 S are not-P
$2(SP) \geq S\underline{P}$ | $S\underline{P} \geq 2(SP)$

With algebraic representations dictated by (1) and (11), any syllogistic form that has one or more of its quantifiers replaced by a percentage, or by an intermediate quantifier, or by a complexly iterated percentage quantifier (such as the "much-more-than" and "almost" forms of (11)) can be completely represented in algebraic formulae. Then if the algebraic representations of its premises together with the algebraic representation of the denial of its conclusion produces a contradiction, the form is valid. On the other hand, if there is an instantiation of the algebraic representations of the premise which also makes an algebraic representation of the conclusion false, then the form is invalid. (From here on, I will drop the phrase "algebraic representation of" and just speak of premises and conclusions of an argument form, tacitly presupposing the categoricals to be represented algebraically.) Here are some examples.

(13) Validity Proof

All M are P	$M\underline{P} = 0$:	(1) $d = 0$ & $g = 0$	premise
<u>1/4 S are M</u>	$3(SM) \geq S\underline{M}$:	(2) $3(d + e) \geq a + b$	premise
1/4 S are P	$3(SP) \geq S\underline{P}$:	(3) $a + d > 3(b + e)$	denial of concl.
		(4) $3e \geq a + b$	from 1 & 2
		(5) $a > 3(b + e)$	from 1 & 3
		(6) $a > 3b + 3e$	from 5
		(7) $a > 3e$	from 6
		(8) $\sim(3e \geq a)$	from 7
	contradiction	(9) $3e \geq a$	from 4

(14) Invalidity Proof

All M are P	$M\underline{P} = 0$:	$d=0$ & $g=0$	true		$d = g = 0$
<u>1/4 S are M</u>	$3(SM) \geq S\underline{M}$:	$3(d + e) \geq a + b$	true	when	$a = 12$
1/2 S are P	$SP \geq S\underline{P}$:	$(b + e) \geq (a + d)$	false		$b = 2$, $e = 6$

(13) and (14) are routine, as inspections of Venn Diagrams of them will reveal. But (15) and (16) are more interesting. Although (15) is predictably valid, simple replacement of "All" in (15) with "95%" produces an invalidity, (16).

(15) Validity Proof

All M are P	$MP = 0$:	(1) $d = 0$ & $g = 0$	premise
<u>More than 1/3 S are M</u>	$2(SM) > S\underline{M}$:	(2) $2(d + e) > a + b$	premise
Almost 14% S are P	$\sim(7SP >> 43SP)$:	(3) $7(a + d) >> 43(b + e)$	denial of conclusion
(14% = 7/50)		(4) $2e > a + b$	from 1 & 2
		(5) $7a >> 43b+43e$	from 1 & 3
		(6) $7a >> 43e$	from 5
		(7) $a >> 43/7e$	from 6
		(8) $a >> 6e$	from 7

	(9) $a > 2e$	from 8
contradiction	(10) $2e > a$	from 4

(16) Invalidity Proof

95% M are P . . . . $MP \geq 19(M\underline{P})$:	$(e + J) \geq 19(d + g)$	true
<u>More than 1/3 S are M</u> . $2(S\underline{M}) > SM$:	$2(d + e) > (a + b)$	true
Almost 14% S are P. $\sim(7SP >> 43SP)$:	$\sim(7(a + d) >> 43(b + e))$	false

when $b = c = g = 0$; $a = 60, e = 1$; $d = 40, f = 959$

(Since 700 *is* much greater than 43!)

A more extreme example of the same thing occurs for the argument form in (17). The proof that the form[9] is invalid is (18).

(17) Many more than 97% of M are P
<u>42% of *S* are M</u>
So, 42% of *S* are P

(18) Invalidity Proof

Many more than 97% M are P . . $3(MP) >> 97(M\underline{P})$:	$3(e + f) >> 97(d + g)$	true
<u>42% S are M</u> . . . . $29(SM) \geq 21(S\underline{M})$:	$29(d + e) \geq 21(a + b)$	true
42% S are P . . . . $29(SP) \geq 21(S\underline{P})$:	$29(b + e) \geq 21(a + d)$	false

when $b = c = g = 0, e = 2$; $a = 58, d = 40$; $f = 91{,}958$

If someone objects by saying these values don't necessarily make the first premise true since (for one thing) for "x >> y" to be true "$x \geq y^2$" should be, then simply replace the value of f in (18) so that f = 5,018,134. If we substitute "All" for "Many more than 98%" in (17)—analogous to moving from (16) to (15)—we obtain a valid syllogism. Perhaps the move from the valid (15) to the invalid (16) did *not* seem odd. However, here we have *only* the difference "All" and "Many(much) more than 97%". It might appear first (to untutored intuitions) that many or much more than 97% is sufficiently different from merely 97% or more-than-97% to be as close to 100% (i.e., all) as you like—especially where "as close as you like" is cashed out as meaning preserves validity in all the same kinds of arguments (i.e., "much more than 97%" is just as powerful as "all" logically speaking). But the validity of (17) with "All" substituted for "Much more than 97%" in contrast to (17)'s invalidity proves such appearances to be wrong. (And see below about "reflective equilibrium".) Here is the proof of (17) when the substitution is made:

(19) Validity Proof

All M are P	$M\underline{P} = 0$:	(1) $d = 0$ & $g = 0$	premise
<u>42% S are M</u> .	$29(SM) \geq 21(S\underline{M})$:	(2) $29(d + e) \geq 21(a + b)$	premise
42% S are P . . .	$29(SP) \geq 21(S\underline{P})$:	(3) $21(a + d) > 29(b + e)$	den. con.
		(4) $29e \geq 21a + 21b$	from 1 & 2
		(5) $29a > 29b + 29e$	from 1 & 3
		(6) $29e \geq 21a$	from 4
	contradiction	(7) $21a > 29e$	from 5

A more interesting example is (20), which is the argument form (15) of Carnes & Peterson (1991):

(20)	Many more than 29% of M are not-P . . .	$71(M\underline{P}) >> 29(MP)$
	<u>Almost 70% of M are S</u>	$\sim(7(M\underline{S}) >> 3(MS))$
	Some S are not-P	$S\underline{P} > 0$

Here is a not quite successful proof of its validity (which some may think is intuitively obvious):

(21)	(1) $71(d + g) >> 29(e + f)$	premise
	(2) $\sim(7(g + f) >> 3(d + e))$	premise
	(3) $a = 0$ & $d = 0$	denial of conclusion
	(4) $71g >> 29e + 29f$	from 1 & 3
	(5) $\sim((7g + 7f) >> 3e)$	from 2 & 3
	(6) $\sim(7g >> 3e)$	from 5
contradiction?	(7) $71g >> 29e$	from 4

The problem with this proof is the supposed contradiction. If it's a genuine contradiction, it's certainly not obvious it is. Someone might think that the difference between "70g >> 30e" and line 7 is so small that line 7 can be interpreted to *be* (or be equivalent to) "70g >> 30e"—since, for one thing, ">>" is *not* a precise relationship. So, interpretive latitude is permitted. This would be fallacious reasoning. For there are two possibilities, that " >> " is a precisely definable relation with sharp boundaries or that it is not. If it is precisely defined—e.g., "x >> y" if & only if "$x \geq y^2$" (a strong requirement)—then it is clearly possible that "71g >> 29e" is true but "70g >> 30e" is false (so the interpretation of the former to be equivalent to the latter would be false and the proof in (21) would be illicit). But also if ">>" is *not* precisely definable but there are clear cases of it and clear cases of its not applying, then there would be a "gray" area in between positive and negative cases wherein the applicability would be indeterminate (i.e., no clear sense for some values of x and y to "x >> y" being true or false). But then how are we to tell whether the difference between "71g >> 29e" and "70g >> 30e" is between two clear cases or between a clear one and a "gray" area case, or between two "gray" area cases? In short, we cannot tell, except for some values of g and e together with a description of what the less-than-precise criterion of ">>" *is.* But this means that "70g > 30e" cannot be substituted *in general* for "71g >> 29e". So, even here (with ">>" defined with an indeterminate "gray" area in between positive and negative instances), (21) is *not* a general proof.[10]

I conclude, at this point, that there have to be counter-examples to (20)—assignments of quantities to the subclasses which make the premises of (20) true and its conclusion false. Seeking such an assignment is equivalent to seeking an assignment of quantities for g and e in lines 6 and 7 of (21) which makes them both true. (That is, such an assignment will make the premises of (20) true and its conclusion false.) So, discover some.

For the first attempt at such assignments, presume that "x >> *y*" is true if and only if "$x \geq y^2$" is true (the strong requirement, which many might think is required for any use of ">>"). Applying this to line 7, "71g >> 29e", yields "$71g \geq (29e)^2$" for which quantities of g and e must be assigned that are compatible with line 6, "~(7g >> 3e)". There are two cases: "$71g = (29e)^2$" and "$71g > (29e)^2$". For the first case, this interpretation of line 7 implies that $g = (29e)^2/71$" is true. When we use this truth to support the substitution for "g" in "~(7g >> 3e)", we obtain "$(((7-29^2)/(3\cdot 71))e^2$ >> e)". But the latter statement can't be true for any values of e, since (i) the coefficient of "c^2" in it is greater than one which implies that "~(ne^2 >> e)" is true for some value of n such that n > 1, *and* (ii) the latter implies that "~(e^2 >> e)" is true, *and* (iii) this cannot be true (by the definition of ">>" adopted)—i.e., "e^2 >> e" is provably *true.* So, no counter-examples on this first alternative are going to be found. (Moreover, assuming the strong requirement for ">>", this case provides the contradiction needed to make (21) succeed—presuming that the second case does not provide a counter-instance, which it does not.)

The second case is when we assume "$71g > (29e)^2$" (for "x >> *y*" defined as "$x \geq y^2$"). This assumption immediately produces "$g > (29e)^2/71$" as a basis for substituting in "~(7g >> 3e)" (to seek some range for which values for e can be proposed with consequent values for g). But look at the challenge here. We want to make "~(7g >> 3e)" true—i.e., to make "(7g >> 3e)" false. But the *best* chance we have of making "(7g >> 3e)" false is to make 7g as small as possible (i.e., alternatives which make 7g larger than we need won't increase the chances that "(7g >> 3e)" is false). To make 7g as small as possible make g as close in value to $(29e)^2/71$ as you can—since "g > $(29e)^2/71$" is true. But notice that we have already proved that if it were so close as to be identical a contradiction results (and there is no possibility of proposing consistent values for e and g). This was the first case above. *Increasing* the values of g will *not* improve the possibility "(7g > 3e)" being false. So, there *won't be* any values of g greater than $(29e)^2/71$ which make "(7g >> 3e)" false. So, there won't be any consistent values for e and g on this case. So, for *both* cases when "x >> y" is defined as "x = y^2", *no* counter-examples (cases making the premises of (20) true and its conclusion false) will arise. So, (20) *is* valid on this strong requirement for ">>".

But maybe strength is the culprit. Select a weak requirement for ">>". Then perhaps consistent counter-examples will be discovered and (20) proved invalid. Consider, first, what I myself take to be *too* weak a requirement—viz., that "x >> *y*" if and only if "x >, 2y". That is, twice the size sufficient for being-very-much-greater-than produces, perhaps, counter-examples to (20). This seems to work. For example, let g = 58 and e = 71. Then "7lg >> 29e" is true because 71x58 = 2x29x71 and "~(7g >> 3e)" is true because (7x58 < 2x3x71). So, we can assign a = b = d = f = 0, g = 58, and e = 71 and thereby show that these values make the premises of (20) true and its conclusion false. Of course, *given* how I am interpreting (20)—via (11)—*and* the assumption that x >> *y* if and only if *x* ≥ 2y, we *do* have the counter-example. But shouldn't we (at least) recheck this counter-example *vis-à-vis* the English of (20)—to wit:

(22) Many more than 29% M are not-P. . . true because 45% are
Almost 70% of M are S . . . . true because 55% are
So, Some S are not-P. . . . . false because all S are P

(These truth conditions are calculated as follows: Given the assignment above, there are 129 Ms of which 58 are not-P, which is 44.96%, and 71 of them are Ss, which is 55%.) Okay? I think not. In particular, it seems to me—and this is a very strong intuition—that 55% is definitely not enough to be almost-70%, which is what this assignment gives for truth conditions for the second premise. I conclude that what this shows is that the weak requirement for ">>" is, therefore, *too* weak. For it produces a truth condition (in the purported counter-example) which cannot be accepted (at least by me). So, we do *not*, by my lights, have a counter-example to (20).

This means, I submit, that we must search elsewhere for a counter-example. But where? A very strong requirement for ">>" won't yield a counter-example (on pain of contradiction) and a very weak one won't (on pain of violating ground-level intuitions). Could something in between, then? I believe the answer is most certainly "no", but to confirm that, consider a slightly less objectionable weak candidate for ">>". Let "x >> y" be defined as "x ≥ 3y". Here is an assignment that satisfies this criterion: a = b = c = d = f = 0, e = 71, and g = 87. For then "71(d + g) >> 29(e + f)" (the first premise) is true because 71x87 >> 29x71 (because 71x87 ≥ 3x29x71), *and* "~(7(g + J) >> 3(d + e))" (the second premise) is true because 7x87 is *not* very much greater than 3x71 (because it is not the case that 7x87 ≥ 3x3x71). And the conclusion is false because a = d = 0. But now recheck this assignment with the argument form stated in English:

(23) Many more than 29% M are not-P . . . . true because 55% are
<u>Almost 70% of M are S</u> . . . . . . true because 45% are (or 44.9%)
So, Some S are not-P . . . . false because all S are P

But this is worse! The trouble, again, is with the second premise. 45% is simply *not* enough, by my lights, to be almost-70%. In fact, what is offered in the second premise (for this counter-example) is *less* plausible than what was offered in (22)—via the unacceptably weak criterion for ">>". I conclude, confidently now, that no criterion in between the weakest and the strongest for ">>" is going to provide an acceptable counter-example *and*, since there are no other routes to acceptable counter-examples, that there are *not acceptable counter-examples* to (20). Finally, then, (20) must be adjudged valid—even though the *direct* proof of validity in (21) *fails*. For we have proved (with a kind of mathematical induction) that there aren't going to be any counter-examples to it.

This total argument for the validity of (20) shows, I believe, the fruitfulness of my approach. It leads to the convincing—doubly convincing *because* complicated—argument for the validity of (20), a validity that maybe only a few people will think is intuitively required. (For example, R. Carnes thought it was intuitively valid and I myself did not.)

This example shows a general feature of non-intuitive (or not-obviously-intuitive) argument forms (syllogistic forms with complexly fractionated quantifiers). This is that the troubles with not-obviously-intuitive argument forms come down in the end to certain embedded (or implied) immediate inferences. For (20), these were, first, whether 55% of M being S is sufficient for the truth of "Almost 70% of *M* are S" and, second, whether 45% of M being S is sufficient for the same truth. I judge that obviously and intuitively each of these is not sufficient—i.e., neither entailment holds. But what if the example were even more troublesome? What if it was *not* obvious (not immediately intuitively true) that such an inference were valid or invalid? What then? Will my approach help? Yes. Here are some examples of immediate inferences where it is *not* at all obvious (or intuitively true) that the inferences are valid:

(24) More than 9/20 of the S are P; so, 1/2 the S are P
(25) Much more than 9/20 of the S are P; so, Almost 1/2 the S are P
(26) More than 9/20 of the S are P; so, Almost 1/2 the S are P
(27) Much more than 9/20 of the S are P; so, 1/2 the S are P

The algebraic method will show—perhaps surprising to some investigator—that although (24) is invalid, (25)-(27) are valid. (My immediate intuitions were that (24) was invalid and that it was not obvious that the rest were valid.) (24) is proved invalid as follows:

(28)

More than 9/20 S are P . .	$11(SP) \geq 9(S\underline{P})$:	true	if $SP = 9$, and
1/2 the S are P	$SP \gg SP$:	false	$S\underline{P} = 10$

Of the three forms in (25)-(27), perhaps (25) seems the closest to being obviously valid (and such that we would have to reject the theory which deems it invalid). Here's the proof:

(29)

Much more than 9/20 S are P:	(1) $11(SP) \gg 9(S\underline{P})$ . .	premise
Almost 1/2 the S are P:	(2) $S\underline{P} \gg SP$	denial of concl.
	(3) $11/19(SP) \gg S\underline{P}$ . .	from 1
	(4) $11/19(SP) \gg SP$ . .	from 2 & 3
	(5) $11 \gg 9$.	from 4
contradiction	(6) $\sim(11 \gg 9)$	arith. fact

But this proof assumes that it is an arithmetic fact that 11 is *not* verv much greater than 9. Is that true? It *seems* to me to be true. Certainly if we accept the weak requirement for ">>" mentioned above (weaker-than-which it seems not plausible to consider) of " x >> y" if and only if "x ≥ 2y", then we can derive a flat contradiction from (1)-(6) of (29)—e.g., that 11 is and is not less than 18. On the other hand, it would be more elegant not to have to use *any* such potentially objectionable requirement. I see no way *not* to in a proof of validity like (29). Further, examination of possible counter-examples also utilizes such a requirement (postulate or definition concerning ">>"). Could there be any counter-example to (29)? To obtain one we need values of SP and S$\underline{P}$ which make "11(SP) >> 9(S$\underline{P}$)" true and "~(S$\underline{P}$ > SP)" false (the premise and conclusion of (29)). To assign such values, either "SP ≥ S$\underline{P}$" is true or "S$\underline{P}$ > SP" is true. But for SP ≥ S$\underline{P}$, the premise and conclusion are both true. So, only the possibilities where S$\underline{P}$ > SP could produce counter-examples. But if SP > 1119(SP), a contradiction with the premise results. So, S$\underline{P}$ ≤ 11/19(SP). So, S$\underline{P}$ is larger than SP (but no more than 2/9th larger). But these conditions cannot make the conclusion false (equivalent to making "S$\underline{P}$ >> SP" true).

So, either way, the proof of (25)—which, remember, seems close to being an obvious validity—requires that an assumption about ">>" be made explicit (e.g., that "11 >> 9" is false), perhaps not a totally convincing result. (I myself am satisfied with it.)

Although (25) is close to being obviously valid (and has a fairly satisfying proof), (26) is weaker and so might be expected to have a more troubling proof (if any at all). It turns out to be (almost) the *same* proof:

(30)

More than 9/20 S are P:	(1) 11(SP) > 9(S$\underline{P}$)	premise
Almost 1/2 the S are P:	(2) S$\underline{P}$ >> SP.	denial of concl.
	(3) 11/19(SP) > S$\underline{P}$	from 1
	(4) 11/19(SP) >> SP	from 2 & 3
	(5) 11 >> 9	from 4
contradiction	(6) ~(11 > 9).	arith. fact

And, then, all the same things said about (29) apply to (30); i.e., the proof of (26)'s validity is at least as convincing as the proof of (25)'s. In fact, now a subtlety can be mentioned that improves the proof of (25). In deriving line 4 of (29), it was simply assumed that if "x >> y" and "y >> z" were true, then "x >> z" is true. But such merely simple transitivity for ">>" might be objected to (given the connotations of "*very* much greater than"). If we were to adopt the postulate "if x >> y and y >> z, then x >>>> z", then the application of it within (29) would produce the following *replacement* for line 5: 11 >>>> 9.[11] And certainly *that* contradicts arithmetic fact on any (no matter how weak) criterion for ">>", doesn't it?

Perhaps it will now be no surprise that the proof of (27) also looks very similar to those for (25) and (26).

(31)

Much more than 9/20 S are P: (1) $11(SP) >> 9(S\underline{P})$. . . . premise
1/2 the S are P: (2) $\sim(SP >> S\underline{P})$ . . . . denial concl.
(3) $S\underline{P} > SP$. . . . . from 2
(4) $11/19(SP) >> S\underline{P}$ . . . . from 1
(5) $11/19(SP) >> SP$ . . . . from 3 & 4
(6) $11 >> 9$. . . . . from 5
(7) $\sim(11 >> 9)$ . . . . arith. fact

Finally proving that (27) is valid while (24) is provably invalid is a very convincing result, it seems to me. For though one could always have a little bit more than 9/20th of a quantity and still be short of 1/2 of it, still to have *much* (i.e., a lot) more than 9/20ths of a quantity is simply enough to be 1/2 (or more) of it. Interestingly, the same thing does *not* happen at the "near to all (= 100%)" end of the spectrum of fractional quantities—as revealed in the discussion of (18) above. For if "Many more than 97% M are P" entailed "All M are P" in parallel to (27)—then (18) would be valid. For "All M are P; 42% S are M; so, 42% S are P" is valid, a fact which can be noticed via simple application of Venn Diagrams prior to anything presented herein. But since (18) is demonstrably invalid, so is

(32) Much more than 97% M are P; so, All M are P

To make the premise "$3(MP) >> 97(M\underline{P})$" true and the conclusion "$M\underline{P} = 0$" false, simply let $M\underline{P} = 1$ and $MP = 3137$ (which satisfies even the strict requirement of "$x >> y$" if and only if "$x \geq y^2$").

It might have appeared above that I frequently was arguing that intuitions about the validity and invalidity of such argument forms—especially as revealed in contemplating typical expressions of them in English—could over-rule a result established by the algebraic methods I have introduced. For example, the intuition that 55% is *in*sufficient for almost-70% in (22) above. Although I believe it is conceivable that there are some algebraic methods or other which must be modified because they violate too *intuitively* obviously valid inferences—such as Barbara, or the P-K immediate inference of the 5-quantity syllogism—this is *not* the case with the methods herein. For the case in question, here is a proof of its invalidity

(33)

55% S are P
. . . . 11/20 S are P: $9(SP) \geq 11(S\underline{P})$ . . . . true
Almost-70% S are P
. . . Almost 7/10 S are P: $\sim(7(S\underline{P}) >> 3(SP))$ . . false

if $SP = 11$ and $S\underline{P} = 9$

The falsity of the conclusion of (33), for these values, however, is equivalent to the truth of "63 >> 33". But this truth requires that a weaker criterion for "x >> y" than "x ≥ 2y" be adopted (i.e., it must be possible that (x >> y & x < 2y)—say, "x >> y" if and only if "2x ≥ 3y"). Increasing the value for S$\underline{P}$ or decreasing it for SP leads to either no counter-examples or even further weakening of the criterion for ">>". Also, if "x >> y" is defined as "x ≥ 2y", then a proof that (33) *is valid* can be constructed. That is, contrary to my own intuitions, *another* way of looking at (33) produces a proof of it!

So, do I over-rule the methods (the theory?) here for the sake of my own intuitions? No. I claim we have, rather, a new result! (This result is even more interesting than that one above about the *lack of* parallel—which some might have expected (intuitively?)—between (27) and (32).) For it comes down to how weak can ">>" be defined *versus* the (perhaps undesirable) validity of 55%-so-almost-70%.[12] If we *do* require that "x >> y" be defined as at least as strong as "x ≥ 2y", then an *un*intuitive (to me, anyway) inference is valid. If we permit a weaker definition (criterion, requirement) for "x >> y", then the intuitively invalid inference is provably invalid. This is a clash of expectations (for me), since I had hoped that a stronger criterion for ">>" was compatible with a "closeness" of inference for "almost". (By "closeness" here I mean the following: when two inferences of the forms "X% S are P/so, almost-Y% S are P" *and* "W% S are P/so, almost-Y% S are P" are compared, if W < X < Y, then X% is *closer to* almost-Y% than W% is.) However, strength of ">>" criterion varies *inversely* with closeness of inference to "almost". I would have hoped for strength and closeness to vary directly (non-inversely). But such a hope or expectation is definitely *not* an intuition (of mine) violated.

Finally, I conclude with an answer to an important to-be-expected objection. Someone might claim that the algebraic methods I have introduced constitute rules which correctly label a form valid *if* it is valid by some independent test (completeness) and which correctly label a form valid *only if* it is valid by some independent test (soundness). I respond that this is *not* what I have done. The reason I have not done this (or should not be interpreted as having done so) is that there is *no independent test* for validity of these forms. Quite the contrary, the algebraic method is a means for formulating determinations of validity and invalidity for these kinds of argument forms, determinations which can be used to decide whether some *other* means of specifying validity is sound and complete—but for which there is *no* further means for determining their adequacy. Take any argument form determined to be valid above. Is it really valid? That is the wrong question. The right question is does some proposed system of rules for dividing these forms into valids and invalids dictate that the form in question is valid. For if it does not, then that system of rules is incomplete. (Contrariwise, if it does predict it to be valid, then part of the question of the soundness of the rules is answered, since a predicted-to-be-valid form is valid.) In short, the algebraic approach provides a *semantics* which must be *used* for testing any system of rules which supposedly marks off the valid inferences (of this type) from the invalid ones. (So, if some extension of some system of "generalized" quantifiers for first-order predicate logic is proposed to encompass these kinds of inferences, the semantics for evaluating the extension is herein introduced.)

But if the algebraic method is semantic (and *not* subject to independent validation), then how are we to *evaluate* it? Does it do all the right things (completeness) and is everything it does actually right (soundness)? I submit that the right way to ponder this is with the concept of "reflective equilibrium" (from Goodman, 1965, p. 64; much mentioned recently, cf. Rawls, 1971; Cohen, 1981; Goldman, 1986, and Resnick, 1985). I have offered a *theory* (or the outlines for one) for the semantics for certain argument forms (those syllogistic-like forms with complexly fractionated quantifiers in addition to Aristotelian and intermediate quantifiers). The theory is motivated by data that are certain intuitions about clear cases—both clear cases of validity and clear cases of invalidity.[13] To be successful the theory must apply to all of these clear cases. And to be fruitful (i.e., non-trivial), it must help us decide at least some of the unclear cases. The degree to which it does not apply to clear cases is the degree to which it is clearly unsuccessful. But no such theory is perfect, or should be expected to be. There will be at least a few cases where the theory will *not* agree with what intuitions say is clear. (Of course, if there are a lot of these cases, we will drop the theory as being out-in-left-field, or even off-the-wall.) The "equilibrium" that is to be sought is between the fruitfulness of the theory (such as how much it helps with old and new unclear cases), on the one hand, and the counter-intuitive results on the other. A large amount of fruitfulness can easily offset a few counter-intuitive results. But no amount of fruitfulness can balance a lot of counter-intuitive results.[14] I judge that the algebraic methods I have introduced provide a moderately highly evaluated semantic theory in that the counter-intuitive results are quite small, even if fruitfulness is still fairly open. And I predict that its fruitfulness will be increasingly revealed in future inquiry, so that eventually it will be easily seen to be high.[15]

Notes

1 Chapter 4 is a revision of Peterson 1991a.

2 Thompson reasoned this way, and his account (1986) of syllogistic-like arguments containing simple and complex percentages did not work. His rules for testing validity of his syllogisms were unsound and incomplete, and they did not non-trivially "include" the 5-quantity syllogistic (developed by Carnes and myself) as he claims. (Cf. Carnes & Peterson 1991.) Since Thompson's validity rules for what *he* calls "statistical syllogisms" were flawed, new rules were needed to replace them. Whether such rules can be found or not, the need to search for them can be deflected by obtaining an algebra which can be used to determine validity and invalidity. The algebra introduced herein for this purpose is an *extension* of that developed for the 5-quantity and "higher"-quantity syllogistics—an extension already put to use on Finch's "proportional syllogisms" (Finch 1957; see Section 5.4 of Chapter 2 above, or Peterson 1993a, for how to extend the algebra to Finch's system, thereby obviating the need to use his difficult rules to demonstrate validity and invalidity). The simplest form of percentage quantifiers that Thompson used were *un*modified percentages. They replaced the traditional quantifiers in categorical statements; e.g., "59% of the S are (not) P". He then added modifiers to such percentages—viz., "more than", "less than", "exactly", "almost", "or more" and "or less" as in "More than 95% of the S are (not) P" and "25% or less of the S are M". Finally, he added a modifier to some of these modifiers—viz., "much" (added to , "more than" and "less than" to get "much more than" and "much less than"). (In many places he writes "many" where he should, for grammatical reasons, write "much".) Thompson falsely assumes that occurrences of "much" and "almost", as he uses them, are simply uses of the 5-quantity predominant and common quantifiers "much" and "almost-all".

3 Note that "many" is used because "sailor" is a count noun. If "soup" and "is milky" were substituted for "sailors" and "are males", "much" would be appropriate.

4 This is part of what happened to Thompson's (1986) system when he *failed* to relate the value for "σ" assigned in one premise (e.g., one with "almost") *clearly* to the value for "σ" assigned in another premise (e.g., one with "Much more"); cf. Section 11 of Carnes & Peterson 1991.

5 I am grateful to an anonymous reviewer raising this problem. Its nature (and my solution) is continuous with the level and kind of logical analysis of natural language I am centrally interested in—continuous, that is, with the analysis of "few", "a few", "many", "most", etc. I have given in Peterson 1979a, 1985a, 1988 (all included in Chapters 1-3 above) and with my attention to scope problems and further Aristotelian-like assumptions.

6 If I were to pursue this Montaguishly, I would continue by saying that the difference between (10.1) and (10.2) is a difference which depends on taking "not" in (10.2) to be a sentence modifier (the sentence modification of negating

a whole sentence), and taking "not" in (10.1) to be a modifier of a modifier: i.e.. "not" *qua* non-sentence-modifier modifies the quantifier-modifier-modifier "many"—where "many" (a quantifier-modifier-modifier) modifies the quantifier-modifier "more than" (the modifier of the quantifier "1/4").

So:
(i) not-(many)(more than)(1/4 S) =
(ii) (not-many)(more than)(1/4 S) =
(iii) (not-*many*-more-than)(1/4 S) =
(iv) (not-*many*-more-than-1/4 S

Thus, the "not" of (10.1) is a modifier of a quantifier-modifier modifier. Another such modifier (in English) is "very". Of course, "not" (like "very") has several logical-grammatical roles to play. Playing the role of quantifier-modifier-modifier-modifier is simply quite distinct from playing the role of sentence-modifier, as it does in (10.2). Finally, the fact that (10.1) entails "More than 1/4 of the S are M" would be acknowledged bv stipulating that the derived operator-modifier "not-much", represented at level (ii) above, is like a positive predicate modifier which entails its de-modified form—parallel to "x runs slowly" entailing "x runs" and "x is a tired man" entailing "x is a man". (For a closely related discussion of "quantifier negation", see pp. 169-172 of Peterson, 1979a. For analogous examples and analyses, see Peterson 1993b.) One *philosophical* challenge to be eventually produced from these kinds of complexities about "not" and negation will be the challenge of presenting one single and coherent epistemological-and-metaphysical account of what negativity is (e.g., *is* there one single concept of generic negativity that can be plausibly proposed given the great disparity between ordinary sentence-modifier negation and extraordinary quantifier-modifier-modifier-modifier negation?).

7 When m = n, it is a plausible proposal that m/n = n/n = all. Similarly, when m = 0, then m/n = 0/n = none. But then the squares almost [*sic*] collapse left-to-right. Especially, the bottom two rows of (11), in that "All (n/n) S are P" is equivalent to "No (0/n) S are not-P" and "Almost all (n/n) S are P" is equivalent to "Almost no (0/n) S are not-P" (= "Few S are not-P"). The top two rows don't appear so obviously to collapse (left-to-right), however. Still, they don't make perfectly clear logical sense (e.g., "(Much) more than all" doesn't).

8 Now, however, it can be seen *why* Thompson's three squares of oppositions (1986, pp. 98-99) are not notational variations on (11) at all. For none of them have rotated fractions (or percentages). Also, an initial virtue of (11–compared to Thompson's three squares (with the peculiarity of his third one)–is that there are *no* reversals due to fraction size (as with Thompson's percentages above and below 50%).

9 This form was used in Carnes & Peterson 1991 to show that the system of Thompson 1986 was unsound (since he falsely claimed (17) valid). The proof in (18) is from Carnes & Peterson 1991.

10 There is another problem about ">>" which may slow or prohibit understanding of its features—especially *vis à vis* "almost". For, it will be said, the fundamental *vagueness* about how much is "a lot" (or "much", or "many") and

how much more is "much (many) more" will permanently cloud these issues—preventing any definite answers of the type I have been proposing and pursuing. I have answered challenges of this kind before in explicating the logic of the intermediate quantifiers. In general, the logic of "few", "many", and "most" *can* be precisely described (and is itself as precise as any "logic" of anything can be). The general answer to vagueness challenges (e.g., "how few are just 'few'?", etc.) is that the relationships between roles and uses of these quantifiers—e.g., that "Few S are P" does mean what "Not many S are P" means (as argued in Chapter 3 above) and that "Not many S are P" is logically equivalent, exactly, to "almost-all S are not P"—give us precise logical characteristics. And that is all that could reasonably be wanted in a logical analysis. (By realizing this—being undaunted by charges of debilitating vagueness—some unusual, even surprising, discoveries have eventuated; e.g., that Aristotle's ideas on logic are not only not wrong, but fruitful—the syllogistiç is extendible!) Here is a way the vagueness challenge can arise concerning ">>":

> "Consider the argument '$11 billion >> $9 billion /so, 11 >> 9'. It is *in*valid, since (by any of the weak-to-strong criteria discussed herein) the conclusion is false but the premise is true. But assuming such arguments are valid is crucial to formal and informal reasonings herein. And the reason this kind of mistake is introduced (resulting in overall incoherence) is the inherent and irremediable vagueness of terms such as 'much', 'many', and 'many more'."

(I am grateful to the anonymous reviewer for Peterson 1991a for the ideas behind this objection. I have, however, paraphrased and expanded his criticism.) My answer to this is to apply the moral of the example analyzed in Peterson 1979a (pp. 166-167) and summarized above (at least twice)—the alleged counter-example to "Almost-all soldiers are abroad" entailing "Not many soldiers are not abroad" when there were a total of 1 million soldiers of which 900 thousand were abroad. The right answer is to claim that reference classes have been switched. So, a necessary requirement to insure overall soundness of the intermediate, 5-quantity syllogistic is no switching of reference classes (i.e., to classes with different sizes) in any inference. The moral of that discovery applies exactly to the alleged invalidity of "$11 billion >> $9 billion /so, 11 >> 9". The reason this might appear invalid is that $2 billion (the difference involved in the premise) may seem like a lot of money to you and me. (Recall the recent D.C. ironicism: "A billion here and a billion there and pretty soon you're talking about real money.") However, that would be violating the obvious (even if not perfectly explicit) reference class that is relevant to the premise—viz., $9 billion! Compared to that sum, $2 billion is *not* much (since it is only two-ninths of it). (Two-ninths of something is not "a lot" of it, though of course it is "some".) So, contrary to the allegation above, the premise "$11 billion >>

$9 billion" is *not* true, but false. So, this counter-example (allegedly due to vagueness) does not survive to be a challenge to my reasonings herein about ">>"—especially *vis à vis* "almost". (R. Carnes has asked me: "Do we take 'many S are P' to mean 'there are lots of things that are both S and P', or do we mean 'the Ss that are P are many when compared to all the Ss there are'?" I answered: "The latter, of course.")

11 Suddenly, I have introduced ">>>>". In case it's not perfectly obvious what it is, I stipulate that ">>>>" is a relation like ">>", but (i) ">>>>" stands to ">>" as ">>" stands to ">" and (ii) it represents English relational expressions like "very very much greater than". I don't use it again.

12 To defend my intuition that 45% of M being S is simply *in*sufficient for almost-70% of M being S, for (23) above, requires that "x >> y" *not* be defined as strictly as "$x \geq y^2$". To me, this means we have a good theoretical argument (if not a proof) that such a strong requirement for ">>" cannot be adopted. For the price is that 45% of a quantity is such-and-so entails almost-70%—which is just too flagrant a violation of the meaning and/or use of "almost" in English.

13 Is this *empirical* data, so that this is an empirical theory? If not, since *inter alia* this kind of inquiry is traditionally regarded as *a priori*, then what is it *exactly* that makes this kind of theory evaluation (via reflective equilibrium) non-empirical, while other kids are empirical?

14 Counter-intuitive results are *not* just cases of theory with superficial intuitions (say, the theory confirming Carnes' intuitions that (20) was valid vs. disconfirming mine that it was invalid). Rather, the more interesting ones are the complicated cases like (i) the *dis*analogy of (27) and (32) and (ii) the *in*compatibility of strong ">>" criterion and "closeness" of "almost" inferences.

15 I am grateful to Robert Carnes for many stimulating discussions on the issues and the examples in this chapter. Also, I am grateful for earlier useful comments and criticisms on these topics from Ernest W. Adams.

5 Distribution and Proportion[1]

My aim in this chapter is to defend the Aristotelian concept of distribution by expanding Robert Carnes' application of it (cf. Carnes & Peterson 1991, Chapter 2 above and Peterson & Carnes 1983). In Section 1, I apply distribution to k-quantity "fractional" syllogistic systems. In Section 2, I consider unrestricted "proportional" syllogisms and sorites. Proportional systems with an infinite number of quantities are described in Section 3.[2] Finally, in Section 4, I show how the new understanding of distribution survives Geach's criticisms.

1. Fractional Syllogisms

If we add "Most" and "Half" statements to the traditional categoricals, we obtain eight basic forms:

(1)

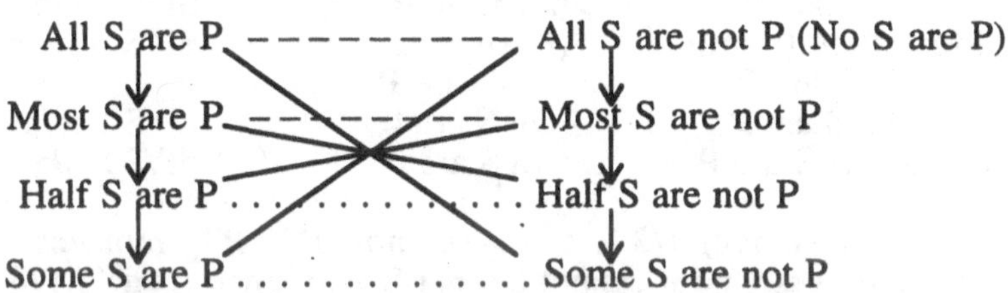

> where dashes connect contraries, dots connect sub-contraries, straight lines connect contradictories, arrows indicate sub-alternation, and each form is interpreted as possessing a tacit "or more" rider attached to the quantifier-phrase.

With eight such forms, it is a 4-quantity rather than a 2-quantity syllogistic system—one with 2048 syllogistic forms and 72 valid forms (cf. p. 354, Peterson 1985a). This 4-quantity syllogistic system is *not* simply the 5-quantity system of Chapter 2 above, with one of the quantities removed. Rather, the system based on (1) results from removing two of the quantities from the 5-quantity system ("almost-all", "few" and "many") and then adding the new quantity ("half").

The syllogistic system of "fractional" quantities (cf. Chapter 2 and Peterson 1985a) is most easily introduced as a generalization of this 4-quantity system:

(2)

All S are P. – – – – All S are not P

More than (n–m)/n S are P – – – More than (n–m)/n S are not P

m/n S are P. . . . . m/n S are not P

Some S are P . . . . . Some S are not P

where $1/2 \geq m/n > 0$.

The number of quantities of a particular fractional syllogistic system will depend on how many different (non-reducible) fractions m/n (all equal to or less than 1/2) are introduced: $q = 2f + 2$, for "q" quantities and "f" different fractions in reduced forms.[3]

The basic idea in Carnes' application of the traditional rules to the 5-quantity syllogism can be developed for the fractional syllogistic. First, the categorical forms are understood as follows:

(3)

English	*Schematized*	*Algebraic Interpretation*
All S are P	>n/n S are P	$SP/S \geq n/n$
More than (n–m)/n S are P	>(n—m)/n S are P	$SP/S > (n-m)/n$
m/n S are P	>m/n S are P	$SP/S \geq m/n$
Some S are P	>O/n S are P	$SP/S > 0/n$

where (as above) $1/2 \geq m/n > 0$, "not P"/"$\underline{P}$" replaces " P " for negatives, and it cannot be that $S = 0$ since then "SP/S" is undefined.

In the algebraic formulae, read "SP/S" as "the ratio of the quantity of Ss that are Ps (or S that are P) to the quantity of Ss (or S)". The traditional form "All S is P" is given an algebraic interpretation wherein it is true if and only if the ratio of Ss that are Ps to the Ss is equal to or greater than 1. Since no ratio will be considered that is greater than 1 (for you cannot have 8 out of 7 Ss for example), $SP/S = 1$. However, stating the ratio for the truth of "All S is P" as $SP/S \geq 1$ is required by the demand that its denial be equivalent to "Some S is not P"—viz., $S\underline{P}/S > 0/n$. The truth-condition $SP/S = n/n$ is proved equivalent to $SP = 0$ via use of $S = S\underline{P} + SP$. Universal forms entail corresponding particulars, since existential import is assumed.

Here are my extensions of Carnes' application of the traditional rules.

(5) Validity Rules for Fractional Syllogisms

Distribution

R1: The sum of the DIs (distribution indices) of the middle terms exceeds 1 *(is* >1).

R2: No term bears a larger DI in the conclusion than it bears in the premises.

Quality

R3: At least one premise must be affirmative.

R4: The conclusion is negative if and only if one of the premises is.

Quantity (dispensable)

R5: At least one premise must have a quantity of majority ("most") or higher (i.e., subject-term DI must be ">1/2" or higher).

R6: If any premise is non-universal, then the conclusion must have a quantity (DI) that is less than or equal to that premise.

where the Distribution Indices (DIs) are as follows:

≥x/x	for subjects of universals and predicates of negatives, where "x" is a non-zero whole numeral (i.e., DI ≥ 1)
Qx/y	for subjects of fractional forms, where "Q" = ">" or "≥" and "x" and "y" are non-zero whole numerals;
>0/x	for subjects of particulars and predicates of affirmatives, where "x" is any non-zero whole numeral (i.e., DI > O).

and where DIs are "summed" as follows
DI(Qx/y) + DI(Ru/v) *is* (Q + R)(x/y + u/v) where "Q" and "R" are each one of ">" and "≥" and > + > = ≥ > + ≥ = ≥ and ≥ + ≥ = ≥.

and where Qx/y *exceeds* Ru/v if and only if
either (1) x/y > u/v
or (2) "Q" = ">" and "R" ="≥" when x/y =u/v.

Every valid syllogism is such that the algebraic formulae for the premises together with the formula for the denial of the conclusion are inconsistent. When a syllogism is invalid a counter-example can be formed (premises true and conclusion false). Failed attempts to demonstrate validity supply reduced formulae for hypothesizing counterexamples. The following assumptions, definitions, and axioms are adopted for the algebraic manipulations:

(6) (a) Existential Import: X > 0, for every *term* X (e.g., S, P, M) in a categorical
(b) Ratios: (x)(y)~(x/y > 1); e.g. "7/8 S" is interpreted as 7 out of the 8 Ss (or 7/8 of the amount of S). "≥9/8 S" has *no* interpretation (since "9 out of the 8 Ss" is incoherent), although "9/9 S" means 9 out of the 9 (i.e., *all)* of the Ss.
(c) "x ≠ 0" =df. "~(x = 0)" =df. "x > 0"
(d) Axioms: (x)~(O > x) . . . . non-negativity
(x)~(x > x) . . . . anti-reflexivity.

The following are some k-quantity fractional syllogisms (for finite k) illustrating (a) how RI-R6 distinguish valid from invalid syllogistic forms[4] and (b) how algebraic proofs confirm valid cases and provide counter-examples (via failed proofs) for invalid cases. Any proof of the soundness of RI-R6 must show that every form they deem valid possesses an algebraic proof and any proof of the completeness rules must show that every form which possesses an algebraic proof is deemed valid by RI-R6.

(7) All M are P
≥1/8 S are M
Some S are P

(a form analogous to AKI-1, p. 350, Peterson 1985a)
Satisfies RI-R6. Dls of middle term are "summed" to obtain: ≥1 + >0 *is* >1. DI of each of S and P in conclusion does not exceed their occurrences in the premises (DI(P3)>O and DI(Pl)>O, where DI(S3)>O which does not exceed DI(S2) ≥ 1/8).

Proof (via RAA)
1. d+g = 0 . . . . premise All M are P
2. (d+e)/(a+b+d+e) ≥ 1/8 . . . . premise ≥1/8 S are M
3. b + e = 0 . . . . denial of (Some S are P)
4. 8(d + e) ≥ (a + b)+(d + e). . . . . from 2
5. 7(d + e) ≥ (a + b) . . . . from 4
6. 7e ≥ a + b. . . . . from I and 5
7. (a + b + d + e) > 0 . . . . axiom: S > 0
8. a > 0. . . . . from 1, 3, and 7
9. 0 ≥ a. . . . . from 3 and 6
10. a = 0 . . . . from axiom and 9
a contradiction (QED).

To read the proof (and others like it below) the following Venn Diagram is used.

(8)

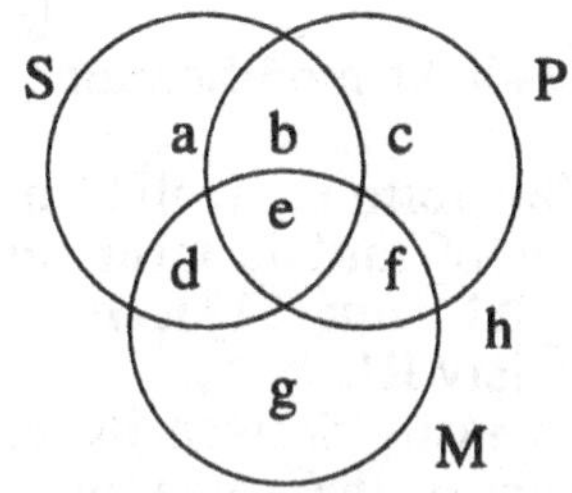

(9) No M are P (a form analogous to EPB-1, *ibid.)*
<u>>3/4 S are M</u>
>3/4 S are not P

Satisfies R1-R6. DIs of middle terms terms are summed: ≥1 + >0 *is* >1. DI(P3) is same as DI(P1), viz., ≥1; and DI(S3) is the same as DI(S2), viz., >3/4.

Proof by *reductio ad absurdum* is analogous to (7).

If we modify (9) by replacing the minor premise with "≥3/4 S are M", then R2 would be violated (confirmed invalid via counter-example d = 3, b = 1, and a = 0). Such a modification departs from the fractional syllogisms defined in (2), but will be exploited below.

(10) All M are P (a form analogous to APP-1, *ibid.)*
<u>>3/4 S are M</u>
>5/6 S are P

This form is invalid, since R2 is violated. Middle term DIs do sum to >1, but DI(S) in conclusion is larger than the DI(S) in minor premise.

By attempting an algebraic proof, the following formulae can be derived:

$5a \geq e \qquad e > 3(a + b)$

To fit these formulae, the following values can be hypothesized:

$a = 3 \qquad b = 1 \qquad e = 13$

which together with d = g = 0 make premises true and conclusion false.

(11) >1/2 M are P (analogous to TTI-3, *ibid.)*
≥1/2 M are S
Some S are P This for is valid, satisfying R1-R6.
Proof (by *reductio)* is analogous to (7).

(12) ≥1/2 M are P (a slight modification of (11))
≥/2 M are S
Some S are P This form is invalid, for R1 is violated. DIs of middle term sum as: ≥1/2 + ≥1/2 = ≥1. But ≥1 is not large enough to satisfy RI.

A counter-example is easily derived by examining the proof in (11). It would appear the same or (12) except that all occurrences of “>” would be replaced with “≥”.

(13) All P are M (analogous to AEG-4, p. 354, *ibid.*)
No M are S
≥1/8 S are not P This form is valid since RI-R6 are satisfied. Middle terms' DIs sum to >1, and DIs of conclusion terms do not exceed occurrences in premises (e.g., ≥1/8 does not exceed ≥1).

Proof need *not* be by *reductio* to SP/S ≥ 1/8 via 8(a + d) > (a + d) + (b + e).

(14) All P are M (modification of (13))
≥1/8 M are not S
No S are P This form is *in*valid, of course. The sum of the middle term DIs is *not* >1 (but >1/8), so R1 is violated (though R2 is not since the DIs for the terms in the conclusion are ≥1, the same DIs they have in the premises).

Counter-example: For 24 Ms, distributed as d = 1, e = 2, g = 10, and f = 11 (to make the minor premise true) and b + c = 0 (to make the major premise true), the conclusion (requiring b + e = 0) is false since e = 2.

(15) >1/8 M are not P (analogous to GPO-3, *ibid.* and cf. (11) and (12) above)
≥7/8 M are S
Some S is not P This form is valid since RI-R6 are satisfied. Middle term DIs sum to >1, and DIs of conclusion terms do not exceed occurrences in premises.

Proof by *reductio* analogous to (7).

(16) All M are P (almost similar to AKK-1, *ibid.)*

$\underline{\geq 1/3 \text{ S are M}}$

$>1/3$ S are P

This form is *in*valid since R2 is violated; i.e., DI(S3) is $>1/3$, which exceeds DI(S2), which is only $\geq 1/3$. (Sum middle DIs is >1.)

Counter-example: Let there be 3 Ss distributed as a = 2, e = 1, and b = 0, where d = 0 due to the major premise. Then though the minor premise is true (1/3 or more S are M because exactly 1/3 are), the conclusion is false since it is not the case that more than 1/3 the S are P.

2. Proportional Syllogisms

Since we can expand the 5-quantity syllogism to fractional quantifiers, we ought to consider whether the fractional syllogistic can be expanded to encompass, for example, (i) more quantifiers, (ii) arguments with more than two premises and three terms, and (iii) relations. If *all* of these extensions were successful, then a new approach to the foundations of mathematics may arise in a quantifier-theory of numerically relevant intermediate quantifiers (wherein a particular number is not identified with a set, but rather with the *meaning* of one of the quantitative adjectives). I merely *begin* the envisioned expansion in this chapter, not reaching relations (but see Chapter 6).

First, it is extremely simple to include the inverse of ">" and "≥". The following square is *not* proposed for new *categoricals, even* though all its relations are *true*:

(17) $<$m/n S are P------ $<$m/n S are not P

↓ ╳ ↓

≤(n—m)/n S are P . . . . ≤(n—m)/n S are not P.

Rather, introduce all propositions expressing "$<$" and "≤" *by definitions*. The *un*defined elements in the definitions are the basic categoricals with "$>$" and "≥" so that the defined forms are *not* categoricals (and remain just defined forms, or "non-basic categoricals" if you like):

(18) "Qy/x S are P" =df. "Q'(x—y)/x S are neg-P"

where
if "Q" is "<", then Q' is ">"; if "Q" is "≥", then Q' is "≥";
if "are P" contains no negative element, then "neg-P" is "not P"; but
if "are P" contains "not" (is "are not B"), then "neg-P" is simply "B".

Also, an '*affirmatizing*' of traditional universal-negatives is required:

(19) "No S are P" (i.e., ≥0/n S are P) =df.
"All S are neg-P" (i.e., ≥n/n S are neg-P),

where "neg-P" is defined as in (18). (See note 13 below for a defense of (19).) Finally, the customary interrelations will be frequently used in discussion and proofs below (and have already been used above):

(20) "x > y" = "~(x ≤ y)" = "~(y ≥ x)" = "y < x", and
"~(x > y)" = "(x ≤ y)" = "(y ≥ x)" = "~(y < x)".

Another way to grasp the point of (18) is via "rotated" squares, such as (5) and (11) of Chapter 4 above. Here is a particular rotated square (matrix of embedded ratios "rotated" 90° from previous patterns in fractional squares):

(21) >1/4 S are P - - - - - - - >3/4 S are not P
↓ ✕ ↓
≥1/4 S are P. . . . . ≥ 3/4 S are not P.

(21) supports the equivalence of "~(>1/4 S are P)" with "≥ 3/4 S are not P". However, if we looked at the denial of ">1/4 S are P" as a denial of the ">" relation, then we might be inclined to say that "≤1/4 S are P" is equivalent to "~(>1/4 S are P)". But *then* "≤1/4 S are P" is equivalent to "≥ 3/4 S are not P" via (18).

To add more quantifiers to the restricted set of fractional systems, define k-quantity *proportional* systems as follows:[5]

(22) A k-quantity *proportional* syllogistic system is a system wherein each well-formed syllogistic form contains three categorical propositions, three terms (one, the middle term), two premises, and a number of quantities k (two of which are the traditional universal

and particular) such that the "intermediate" quantities (i.e., non-universal and non-particular) are distinct ratios (between zero and one) modified with "more than" or "or more".

This definition makes any k-quantity proportional system (for finite k) distinct from a similar k-quantity *fractional* system by permitting quantifiers with ratios x/y, where 1/2 > x/y, to be prefixed with " > " *and* those such that x/y > 1/2 to be prefixed with "≥". However, it does not permit the quantities expressed by "(less than) x/y (or less)"; i.e., all propositions are to be reduced (no "less") and "affirmatized" via (18) and (19). There will be the following *kinds* of categorical propositions in any k-quantity proportional system (1 > x/y > 0):

(23)	*English*	*Schematic form*
	All S are (not) P	≥ x/x S are (not) P
	More than xly S are (not) P	> x/y S are (not) P
	x/y or more S are (not) P	≥ x/y S are (not) P
	Some S are (not) P	> 0/x S are (not) P.

The number of well-formed syllogistic forms, s, in any k-quantity *proportional* system will be discovered with the same formula used for fractional systems—i.e., $s = 32k^3$, for k the number of quantities. Also, for the number of ratios, r, contained in the intermediate quantifiers: $s = 256(r + 1)^3$, since $k = 2r + 2$. Fractional systems produce patterns of valid forms that are direct expansions of those for the 5-quantity system (e.g., in (6) of Peterson 1985a). Consequently, the number of valid forms, v, for any k-quantity fractional system can be calculated: $v = 3k^2 + 6k$. So far the best that can be said for k-quantity proportional systems is that the number of valid forms, v', for any k-quantity proportional system won't be less than the number of valid forms for a similar fractional system (value of k the same). So, $v' \geq 3k^2 + 6k$. But *will* it be more? Comparing a proportional system to a fractional one it is generated from may raise doubts. For example, take the 6-quantity fractional system with the quantifiers ALL, >3/4, >1/2, ≥1/2, ≥1/4, and SOME will have 6912 syllogistic argument forms of which 144 will be valid. If we add to this system the quantifiers ≥ 3/4 and >1/4, then we have an 8-quantity system with 16,384 argument forms. So, what if these two small additions produced exactly the same proportion *[sic]* of valid forms as the 6-quantity system—and no more? Would that be such a low number—viz., 240 (vs. the previous 144)? Maybe the very same formula holds: $v = 3k^2 + 6k$ (= $12r^2 + 36r + 24$, for r = number of ratios, here 3).

Now, how do we modify the rules of (5) for determining validity of k-quantity fractional syllogisms so they can be used for *proportional* syllogisms? The answer, happily, is that no modification is required. *The rules for determining validity of proportional syllogisms are identical to those for determining validity of fractional syllogisms*—viz., those in (5)! I won't prove this herein, but only illustrate it.

Illustrations are easily produced by simply inspecting examples used above. In (7), if the minor premise quantifier is changed to ">1/8", then the form is still valid for the same reasons. In the proof substitute ">" for "≥". Further, if *any* intermediate quantifier of the form Qx/y (for "Q" = ">" or "≥" and any ratio "x > y", 1 > x/y > 0) is substituted for the quantifier in the minor premise of (7), the form is still valid. Similarly, for (9). Replace both occurrences of ">" with "≥". Then the rules are satisfied identically, and the algebraic proof would appear the same except for interchange of ">" and "≥". No combination of replacements of "≥" for ">" in (10) will make it valid. On the other hand, if we switch the minor premise and the conclusion (so "P" is middle term), the form is valid no matter what combination of ">" and "≥" are substituted in the two intermediate quantifiers.

If we change the quantifier in the conclusion of (13) above to ">1/8 S are not P", then the form is still valid (via the rules of (5)) and the algebraic proof will be the same—except one line shorter. Similarly, (14) is still invalid if a similar change of intermediate quantifier is made—replacing "≥1/8" with ">1/8". To prove it, use the same counter-example as for (14) but change d = 1 to d = 2.

Notice that (15) is *not* a well-formed fractional syllogism! For since the ratio in the quantifier of the major premise is 1/8, its degree should be "≥" (not ">" as it is in (15)). Similarly, since the ratio in the quantifier of the minor premise is 7/8, its degree should be ">" (not "≥"). So, (15) should *not* have been listed as an illustration of a fractional syllogism (say, one of a 9-quantity fractional system). But now we can see exactly what it is, a valid *proportional* syllogism. Finally, notice that the invalid (16) (also *not* a well-formed fractional syllogism) would *be* a valid proportional if the quantifiers of the i-minor premise and the conclusion were interchanged.

The following reduction test is proposed to extend the methods of the proportional syllogistic to arguments with *more* than two premises (and one middle term).

(24) A sorites (or syllogistic-like form with more than two premises and one middle term) is valid *if* either
(1) the conclusion follows validly from two of its premises *or*
(2) from two of the premises a proposition follows validly which when added to the other premises permit step (1) to be satisfied, *or*
(3) from two of the premises a proposition follows validly which when added to the previous premises permit step (i—1) to be satisfied—for i = 3, 4, 5, etc. as required to produce a series of valid forms (polysyllogism) wherein the conclusion of the last is the conclusion of the original argument form.

The standard example is a Barbara-sort of sorites such as "All A are B, All B are C, All C are D, All D are E, All E are F / thus, All A are F"—wherein the intermediaries required to show that a valid polysyllogism can be generated are "All A are C, All A are D, and All A are E". This procedure, of course, gives us only a sufficient (not a necessary) condition for validity of more-than-two-premises "syllogisms".

By using (18), additional kinds of premises and conclusions can be included. Also, premises and conclusions can be allowed which begin with negatives—such as "Not all S are P", "Not more than 1/2 S are not P", "Not 3/22 or less S are P", etc. However, just as each proposition with a "less" quantifier in it must be replaced with one without it (i.e., reduced via (18)), so each externally negated proposition must be replaced with an equivalent proposition which is a categorical. Simply use the relevant squares of oppositions in (1), (2), (17), and (21).

Before considering propositions which have proportional quantifiers in the *predicate* (Finch 1957), consider the quantifier type "=x/y", in English *"exactly* x/y". Why can't we also have "=1/8" ("exactly one-eighth") and "=3/4" ("exactly three-quarters") as quantifiers? If forms containing "=" quantifiers are simply added to the basic categoricals of (23) above, then their occurrences *totally disrupts* the use of the rules in (5) (though *not* the use of the algebraic semantics of the proofs)! Some argument forms like those discussed above remain valid when "=" quantifiers replace the proportional quantifiers ">x/y" and "≥x/y". For example, replacing "≥1/8" in (7) above with "=1/8" preserves validity. And replacing "≥" in (11) with "=" preserves validity and "=" for both "≥" in (12) preserves *in*validity. On the other hand, the valid (9) becomes invalid if one or the other or both of the ">" in it are replaced with "=". The only way (apparently) to obtain a valid modification of (9) with "=" is to replace ">" in the minor premise with "=" and ">" in the conclusion with "≥". But in all these modifications of (9), the rules of (5) would deem the forms to be valid (with appropriate emendations in (5) so that DIs about phrases with "=" in them can be calculated).

The reason that "=" quantifiers added to proportional categoricals raise havoc is that they are complex forms *vis à vis* the basic categoricals; e.g., "=3/4 S are P" is equivalent to "≥ 3/4 S are P *and* ≤ 3/4 S are P"—or better, to "≥ 3/4 S are P *and* ≥1/4 S are not P". So, when the "=" quantifier appears in a conclusion, we have *two* conclusions and to be valid two forms must be valid. And when a proportional statement containing "=" in its quantifier occurs as a premise, two separate premises are really involved. In general:

(25) "=x/y S are P" = df.
"(≥ x/y S are P) & (≥(y—x)/y S are not P)"

To analyze any apparently well-formed proportional syllogism containing an "=", first replace the "=" quantified proposition with its equivalent form via (25). If the replacement occurred in the conclusion, the form is valid if and only if the two argument forms (the same premises in each and one conjunct for the conclusion of the first and the other for the conclusion of the second) are both valid. Analogously, an argument form is valid if it contains an " = " quantified proposition in the premises if and only if it is replaced by two separate propositions—each of which is one conjunct obtained by applying (24)—and the resulting sorites is valid.

Finally, consider quantifiers in the predicate. Finch (1957) analyzes categorical-like propositions containing two quantifiers, such as "At most 3/4 of the P are at least 1/2 of the M"[6]—which I call "Finch propositions". Finch propositions are reducible to two (or a conjunction of) singly quantified categorical-like propositions—e.g.,

(26) At most 3/4 of the P are at least 1/2 of the M <=> (At most 3/4 of the P are M) *and* (At least 1/2 of the M are P).

Finch does not consider the same kind of examples with negated copulas, such as "More than 3/4 of the S *are not* 9/10 or more of the Ps". The correct reduction makes both conjuncts negative categoricals (perhaps a surprise); e.g.,

(27) More than 3/4 of the S are not 9/10 or more of the P
<=> (More than 3/4 of the S are non-P) *and* (9 / I 0
or more of the Ps are non-S).

That (26) and (27) are correct rests, at bottom, on *empirical* evidence about the meanings and uses of the component English sentences in (26) and (27).

Consider, for example, the first proposition in (26), "At most 3/4 of the P are at least 1/2 of the M", with respect to a Venn Diagram. Let "x" represent the one or more individuals in the $P\underline{M}$ region (i.e., that are P but not M), let "y" represent the individuals (one or more) in the PM region (that are P and M), and "w" represents the individuals in the $\underline{P}M$ region.

(28)

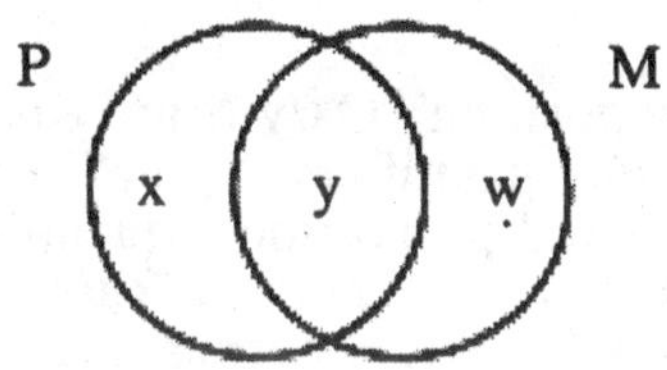

The statement in (26) refers, to begin with, to at most 3/4 of the Ps. Are those Ps, the x ones or the y ones? It seems to me that the meaning of the whole sentence is such that they have to be the y ones in (27), for the rest of the sentence identifies these Ps (the at most 3/4) with a certain quantity of Ms. So they have to be in the PM overlap in (28) *and* the relation between the x individuals and the y individuals is that 3 times the number of x equals or exceeds the number of y—i.e., $3\#x \geq \#y$. Now these Ps, the y, are said by the statement to be identical to a certain quantity of Ms—to *be* the very same objects (not to be merely equal in number). So, the "is" of identity which seems to be involved in the first statements in (26) and (27) is not used to identify two quantities (as arises with "exactly", "precisely", and insidc the proportional quantifier phrases). So, they must be in the overlap with the M region in (28). But the statement says more—viz., that these particular Ps are not just some Ms or other, but that they are identical to at least half the Ms. So, where 'w' are the Ms which are not also Ps, the relationship between the y individuals (those Ms) and the w ones must be that $\#y > \#w$. In sum, we have *two* facts resulting from Venn Diagram analysis of (26)—that $3\#x > \#y$, and $\#y > \#w$. But the former fact is expressible in English by "At most 3/4 of the P are M" and the latter by "At least 1/2 of the M are P".[7]

(27) is analyzed similarly, but is more surprising—due to the negatives. Examination of (27) via a Venn Diagram helps again. The first statement of (27) says that more 3/4 of the Ss are *not identical to* a certain quantity of the Ps. So, those Ss have to be the x individuals in the diagram in (28) (no Ps are among them). Further 9/10 or more of the Ps are *not identical to* those Ss just mentioned. So, two facts result: #x > 3#y (since the ratio of *x* to y is more than 3 to one); and #w > 9#y (since the ratio of w to y is 9 to one or more). But these two facts are the same ones expressed in English by the two conjuncts of the right hand side of (27). Again, this is an empirical proposal, made with the help of a Venn Diagram representation of what the sentences mean. The least I would claim is that the two statements (one a conjunction) are logically equivalent.

It seems clear to me that these kinds of examples can be generalized:

(29) For any Finch proposition "Qx/y S are Ru/v P" or "Qx/y S are not Ru/v P" with quantifiers "Qx/y" and "Ru/v" ranging over basic and derived proportional quantifiers,
Qx/y S are Ru/v P = (Qx/y S are P & Ru/v P are S), *and*
Qx/y S are not Ru/v P = (Qx/y S are P & Ru/v P are

Here is one of Finch's "syllogism-analogues":

(30) At most 4/7 P are at most 2/3 not-M
At least 3/5 S are precisely 7/8 M
so, At most 1//3 S are P.

To analyze (with a k-quantity proportional system) any syllogism-analogue or sorites-analogue in which a Finch proposition occurs requires *replacing* the Finch proposition as follows:

(31) (i) If the Finch proposition occurs in the premises, replace it with the two propositions which are the conjuncts of the conjunction equivalent to it (so the overall argument form is "reduced" by increasing its premises); and
(ii) If the Finch proposition occurs in the conclusion, replace the whole argument with two forms each with the same premises but one with a conclusion which is one conjunct of the equivalent proportional conjunction and the other with a conclusion that is the other conjunct.

Then an argument-form containing a Finch-proposition which is otherwise a well-formed syllogism or sorites of the k-quantity proportional syllogistic is valid if and only if (i) the 'reduced' argument (Finch proposition was in the premises) is valid and/or (ii) the two new arguments are each valid (Finch proposition in the conclusion).

To evaluate (30), then, replace it with[8]

(30)'

At most 4/7 P are not-M
At most 2/3 not-M are P
At least 3/5 S are M
<u>Precisely 7/8 M are S</u>
so, At most 1/3 S are P

Schematically, (30)' is

(32)

Derived Qs	*Basic Qs*
1. $\leq 4/7$ P are not M	1. $\geq 3/7$ P are M
2. $\leq 2/3$ not M are P	2. $\geq 1/3$ not-M are not P
3. $\geq 3/5$ S are M	3. $\geq 3/5$ S are M
4. $=7/8$ M are S	4. $\geq 7/8$ M are S
———————	5. $\geq$<u>1/8 M</u> are not S
6. $\leq 1/3$ S are P	6. $\geq 2/3$ S are not P

Here is a counter-example, making the premises and denial of conclusion of (32) all true:

(33)

1. $4(e + f) \geq 3(b + c)$
2. $2(a + h) \geq b + c$
3. $2(d + e) \geq 3(a + b)$ ——premises
4. $d + e \geq 7(g + f)$
5. $7(g + f) \geq d + e$
6. $2(b + e) > a + d$ . . . *denial* of conclusion

$a = c = d = f = 0;\ b = g = h = 1;\ e = 7$

So, (30) is invalid. Which of rules R1-R6 does (30) violate, however?

To answer this question, we must first determine what the rules R1-R6 of (5) are supposed to apply to. For they do not apply directly to a sorites, but rather to each syllogism of the series of syllogisms which need to be evaluated in order to decide whether the sorites they are generated from is valid. To obtain a series of candidate syllogism from the right hand side of (32), or from lines 1-5 of (33), one must first select a pair of propositions which will validly entail an intermediary that might, by repeating the process, lead to the desired conclusion. However, these premises are not typical of what sorites are classically envisioned to be, where the number of premises is the same as the number of middle terms. For some pairs selected from these five premises are not coherent or sensible candidates to start with (e.g., 1 and 2, or any pair of 3-5). Rather, the first premise must be paired with one of 3-5, then the second paired with each of 3-5, to see if any one path through 1-5 can produce 6, the conclusion. Here is a useful diagram of the alternatives:

(34)

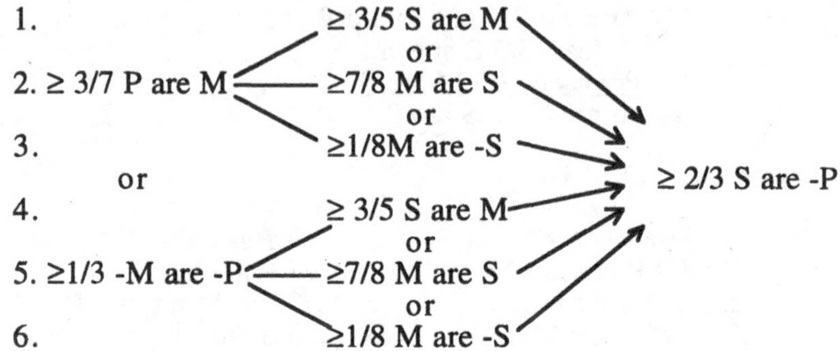

None of these inferences, paths 1-6 on (34), should be valid according to rules R1-R6.

Alternate 1 of (34) violates R1. Similarly, alternatives 2 and 3. Alternative 5 violates R2, since DI(S3) exceeds DI(S2). Alternatives 4-6 may well seem very problematic. For the first premise contains a negated subject term—something *not* permitted in the classical syllogism, and for which no allowances in the intermediate systems have been provided. In alternative 5 the issue can be avoided since the rule violated, R2, does not concern the negated subject of the major premise. So, we are left with only alternatives 4 and 6 as problematic. If we ignore the negativity of the subject term in the major premise, we will be led to think that R1 is *not* satisfied in 6. However, R5 is also violated by the same reasoning. I do *not* favor this approach; i.e., we can't just ignore the negativity. The best way to dispose of 6 is to say that it violates R4. I favor the speculation that essentially negated (with ineliminable negation) subject terms with intermediate quantifiers be taken to be fully distributed exactly like negated terms in the classical predicate position. Thus, the DI for the subject term of the major premise of alternatives 4-6 in (34) *is* ≥1. That means R1 *is* satisfied for alternatives 4-6 (since the sum of the middle term DIs is >1). So, we are only left with alternative 4 as problematic.

Concerning alternative 4, we know it *is* invalid since the counterexample in (33) confirms its invalidity. Re-inspection of 4 suggests that R2 is violated, for DI(S3) exceeds DI(S2). This does resolve the problems with (34) and show the applicability of the rules to (30) and (32). But it is not a good solution. For we can imagine another inference just like alternative 4 but with the ratio in the conclusion changed from 2/3 to 1/3. Then the new inference would not violate R2. Nor would it seem to violate any other of R1-R6. Yet, it ought to, since it's invalid—as shown by the following counterexample (exactly the same one used in (33), by the way):

(35) 1/3 -M are -P . . . . $2(a + h) \geq b + c$
$\geq$ 3/5 S are M . . . . $2(d + e) \geq 3(a + b)$
so, $\geq$1/3 S are -P . . . . $2(a + d) \geq b + e$
where premises true and conclusion false, if
$a = c = d = 0$, $h = b = 1$, and $e = 7$.

But in (35) R2 is *not* violated. DI(S3) does not exceed DI(S2). So, what is violated by (35) of rules R1-R6?

If we are to permit negated subject terms in the proportional syllogistic, then we have a definite problem with R1-R6. We might regard this as a 'syntactic' problem. Semantically, we know that (35) is invalid—i.e., via the algebraic semantics. But the 'syntactic' rules R1-R6 say it is valid. So, R1-R6 are 'unsound'. My conclusion is that rules R1-R6 simply cannot handle negated subject terms. Just as the traditional rules cannot).[9] So, rather than enter a revision of them, I propose that a qualification be added to their statement in (5): they do not apply to syllogisms with negated subject terms.

3. Infinite Proportionals

Throughout above, I have spoken of many *separate* fractional and proportional syllogistic systems. Each one has some finite number of quantities, k, which result from what the intermediate quantities are for the system—e.g., a 4-quantity system derived from (1) in which only two fractional quantities are added or an 8-quantity system with the proportional quantities based on the ratios 3/4, 1/2, 1/4 (each combining with ">" and "≥"). The latter system would not be identical to another 8-quantity system—viz., one which is a *fractional* system containing ">6/7", ">5/7", ">4/7". "≥3/7" "≥2/7", "≥1/7". *Now*, however, we can envision combining such systems to obtain higher quantity systems. Combining the two just mentioned would produce a 14-quantity system containing varieties of "fourths" and "sevenths". So, let's combine them all for all values of embedded ratios "x/y", where 1 > x/y > 0. Since there are an infinite number (denumerably) of them, the combination will have an infinite number of quantities, well-formed arguments, and valid ones. Call this ultimate *proportional* syllogistic system the infinite-quantity—or "i-quantity"—syllogistic system. All the same rules, R1-R6, apply as does the algebraic semantics!

Isn't the i-quantity proportional syllogistic what we were thinking of all along—in short, utilizing all the finite, genuine ratios? (Irrationals are *not* included. Lines 2-4, p. 289, Peterson 1991a, are a joke.) There can, then, exist an infinite number of quantities added to the classic syllogistic which sets the stage for a quantifier-theoretic approach to mathematics. But this quantifier-theoretic approach need *not* be reduced to some species of relational-quantifiers or restricted quantifiers in the predicate calculus. It is an *Aristotelean* theory of quantifiers based on propositional quantity.

The i-quantity system appears to be equivalent to Johnson's (1994) syllogistic with "fractional quantifiers". (Also, see Johnson 1991.) In the i-quantity system "<", "≤", and "=" are introduced by definitions (18) and (25), even though in Johnson's system they are basic. And sorites in the i-quantity system are evaluated by reduction to polysyllogisms via (24), rather than directly as in Johnson's system. Still, Johnson's necessary and sufficient conditions for validity ought to determine the same syllogisms and sorites to be valid that the rules R1-R6 do for the i-quantity system. I think of Johnson's theorems as material for proving the soundness and completeness of R1-R6 i-quantity-wise. These rules are, of course, (a) sound if each form they deem valid is such that its premises together with the denial of its conclusion is inconsistent and (b) complete if each form which is such that its premises are inconsistent with the denial of its conclusion is deemed valid by them. *Proving* soundness and completeness may be easier with Johnson's Theorems 1 and 4. Briefly, R1-R6 for i-quantity syllogistic are sound, if every valid inference form (valid according to R1-R6) has a T-form—where each of the five T-forms (listed in Johnson's Theorem 1) is a different set of inconsistent proposition-types (each such generable from premises and denials-of-conclusions of valid forms). Similarly, using Theorem 4, R1-R6 for i-quantity syllogistic is *complete* if every i-quantity inference form that does have a T-form is deemed valid via R1-R6. Justification for this use of Johnson's theorems rests in the obviously semantic nature of his characterization of T-forms.[10]

It is not surprising to hold that an i-quantity syllogism or sorites should be considered valid if and only if its premises are inconsistent with the denial of its conclusion—the idea behind Johnson's Theorem 1 and which was central above. However, it *is* surprising to learn that no other types of inconsistencies will (or ought to) be generated from valid i-quantity syllogisms and sorites than just the five types Johnson listed. So, does every valid i-quantity syllogism or sorites have a Johnson T-form and is every inference-form that does have a T-form valid (according to R1-R6)? Yes—though I leave the proof as an exercise for the reader.[11]

4. Distribution Explained

Geach's objections to distribution ought to apply to this Aristotelian account of rational proportions. For Geach, there are two concepts (or two aspects) of distribution—the formal (perhaps "syntactic"), and the semantic. Formally, distribution is simply a property (call it the "D-factor") which subjects of universals and predicates of negatives have. Although Geach's best known, and most discussed, criticisms concern distribution semantically speaking, he does criticize the formal concept (1960). He says that "by the doctrine of distribution the inversion will be valid *only if* ... the predicate term of q is not distributed unless that of p is" (1972, p. 63), where "an inversion is an inference from a categorical p to a categorical q such that (i) p and q have the same predicate term, but the subject terms of p and q are contradictory; [and] (ii) the quality of p is opposite to the quality of q"(*ibid.*). I agree with Geach that this rule does not work and that adjustments from some others (Keynes and Lukasiewicz) are not convincing. *My* solution to this criticism is to find the culprit elsewhere. Geach blames distribution. I blame negative subjects. We have seen above at the end of Section 11 that negative subjects lead to troubles with R1-R6. The same kind of troubles occur in allowing negative subjects in the traditional syllogism. So, prohibit negative subjects in genuine traditional categoricals, where only genuine categoricals occur in well-formed syllogisms (256) and in the valid ones (24). The traditional rules do not necessarily work for validating inferences outside the syllogism.[12]

The *semantic* concept of distribution is that a term "T" with respect to its occurrence in a proposition "B" is distributed if and only if "B" says something (or implies something) about *all* of the Ts. The weaker way of expressing this is the easiest to defend—viz., "T" is distributed in "B" if and only if "B" *entails* a proposition about all of the Ts. I understand this to mean that the entailed proposition has the form "All (each, every) T are(is) .....", where "....." is filled in with some appropriate continuation. Then, in "All S are P", "S" is distributed because "All S are P" is about all the Ss (entails itself); in "No S are P", each term is distributed because "All S are not P" and "All P are not S" are both entailed; and in "Some

S are not P", "P" is distributed because "All P are-not (are distinct from) some S" is entailed by "Some S are not P".

Geach objects very plausibly (1956). For if the truth of "All P is not some S" (entailed from the 0-form) shows that "P" is distributed semantically, then a closely analogous thing can be done for *both* terms of the I-form. "Each S is either a P or is distinct from some P" *and* "Each P is either an S or is distinct from some S" can both be validly inferred from "Some S is P". So, the semantic test fails. For neither term of the I-form categorical *can* be distributed traditionally.

I conclude that Geach *has* shown that a very typical statement of the semantic concept of distribution is faulty. In particular, it is too broad, permitting terms to be distributed which can't be (by the formal criterion). In light of the advancements herein, I offer a new defense of a semantic concept of distribution. I propose that the *kind* of semantic explication Geach has formulated and criticized is the wrong kind.

First of all, R1 and R2 *replace* the two traditional rules. R1-R2 concern *relative* quantities. A term's being distributed or not is replaced in R1-R2 with a term's being more, or less, distributed than some other term in the same context. Distribution is *not*, then, about all the members of the class designated, *but* is about *how much or many* of something you have got. In "More than 3/4 of the S are P", the term "S" has a distribution property which is a function of its *quantity* as expressed by its non-traditional quantifier "more-than-3/4". At first, it seems that the distribution value just concerns the proportion of the term in question. But this is not true, for the value "more-than-3/4" for "More than 3/4 the S are P", for example, concerns the relation of the ratio "3/4" to the ratio of S-*that-are*-P to all the Ss; i.e., the *semantic* character of the distributedness of "S" is expressed in the *whole* algebraic formula. So, "P" *is* involved. Yet, the quantity of Ps that there are, or are referred to or designated via the proposition, might seem *not* to be involved. "More than 3/4 of the S are P" is true if 9 out of 10 of the S are P—whether there are 9 P or 90 P (or an infinite number, a topic Johnson attends to but I ignore). But for 9 out of 10 S to *be* P, there must be at least 9 Ps! So, the quantity of Ps there are *is* involved.

Crucial to using the rules R1-R2 are decisions concerned with summing distribution indices and judging relative size. Distribution indices, DIs, might have been taken to just be formal notations. But now we can consider what they really are—they are quantities of concrete things. "More-than-3/4 of the musicians (M)" refers to (semantically!) a certain *proportion* of the musicians. So, distribution is certainly semantically characterizable. Distribution concerns what the distribution indices *are* (viz., proportions) and what in a statement refers to these indices. So, distribution *is* proportion!!!

What happens, then, to the traditional notion of distributed vs. *un*distributed? Well, it is not now a question of whether a term is distributed or not, but of what the distribution index *is*—which is some ratio between 0 and 1, with various modifiers. Every distribution level is a genuine level of distributedness. (Is the old "undistributed" now the minimal level of distribution? Or, is it the non-maximal? Does it matter?)

This still leaves something hanging—viz., the distribution indices assigned to terms which do *not* have an explicit modifier expressing relative quantity. This is also the problem of distribution of predicate terms in basic categoricals, for *every* subject term in the i-quantity syllogistic has an explicit distribution-index-referring component as its explicit quantity-expressing modifier.[13] *But* predicates of negatives are stipulated as referring to ≥n/n, and predicates of affirmatives are stipulated as referring to >0/n (similar to stipulations in the traditional syllogistic).

First, the predicate of the E-form categorical is legitimately assumed to have the distribution index "≥n/n" because the same term when it appears in the logically equivalent *converted* form acquires an explicit expression for the maximal distribution level (≥n/n). For example, in "No singers are musicians" the term "singers" has the maximal distribution index because the compact quantifier "No" in the quantifier-phrase "No singer" *does* express universality in English.[14] Alternatively, in "All singers are not musicians", the term "singers" has maximal distributedness because "all" very plainly refers to as large a proportion of the singers as there could be. In either way of looking at the E-form, it is validly convertible. Converting either form, the previous predicate term acquires an explicit quantity indicator. I conclude this is a good reason to hold that in its original position the predicate *tacitly* referred to ≥n/n. The same kind of argument holds for predicates of particular affirmatives, but there it is minimal rather than maximal distribution level that is in question.[15]

But there is no similar account for the O-form. And *why* are the predicates of all *intermediate* negative categoricals said to have the DI of "≥n/n" and the predicates of *intermediate* affirmatives said to have DI of ">0/n"? The reasons these claims are not pure stipulations might be difficult to see prior to considering *Finch's* extensions of categoricals.

I defined "Finch proposition" above in Section 11, and gave analyses of affirmative and negative forms in (29). Now I introduce the idea of "hamiltoning" a propositional form. A basic or non-basic categorical proposition (extended to include intermediate categoricals with all types of proportionals) has only one quantifier phrase in it, in subject position. A Finch proposition is similar to a categorical, but the predicate in it has an explicit quantifier. I shall call the process of adding an explicit quantifier to the predicate term in a categorical proposition a "hamiltoning" of it, where *only* the explicit quantifier is added which produces a proposition logically equivalent to its pre-hamiltoned form *and* exactly the same terms in the same positions remain (a term does *not* become negated in the process).[16] In the cases which are negative categoricals, the hamiltoned proposition retains the negated copula. (Also, the E-form that appears as "No S are P" is replaced *before* hamiltoning with "All S are *not* P"; cf. note 14.) Here are some pairs of unhamiltoned and hamiltoned propositions:

(36)	Most S are P;	Most S are some of the P
	More-than-2/3 S are P;	More-than-2/3 S are some of the P
	1/8-or-more S are not P;	1/8-or-more S are not all of the P.

Here is the traditional square of opposition with each hamiltoned form appearing below the standard representation:[17]

(37)	A: Every S is P Every S is some P	E: Each S is *not P* Each S is not each P.
	I: Some S is P Some S is some P	0: Some S is not P Some S is not each P.

Now I will *use* hamiltoned forms of the traditional categoricals in the basic test for distribution-level of predicates, as follows:

(38) (i) First, "hamilton" the categorical so that a logically equivalent categorical is obtained, one with exactly the same number of terms as the original form;
(ii) Second, take the explicit quantifier of the predicate in the hamiltoned form to refer to the DIs used above—i.e., "each", "all", or "every" refers to the DI ≥ n/n and "some" or "at least one" refers to the DI > 0/n.

Applying this to the traditional negatives, the distribution index for the predicate terms—"P" in the right-hand column of (37)—will be ≥n/n. In sum, the distribution-levels of the predicates of each categorical are determined by the DIs of each predicate in the hamiltoned transformation of the form (and see last three sentences of note 18 below).

This method also applies to all of the forms containing proportional quantity. But before discussing this, consider the following objection. Reducing a Finch proposition via substituting the right-hand sides of (instances of) the equivalences in (29) for the left-hand sides might be thought to be something which should apply to a hamiltoned proposition (since a hamiltoned one *looks* like a Finch proposition, both having two quantifiers and two terms). But this is a mistake. A hamiltoned proposition is simply not a Finch proposition. Thus, deFinching via (29) does not apply to the hamiltoned transforms of the basic four categoricals. (DeFinching reveals a compound nature for Finch propositions, not something genuine hamiltoneds possess.)

I have only argued that the predicates in negative categoricals have maximal DIs and the predicates in affirmative categoricals have minimal DIs for the four traditional categoricals. *Should* this carry over to all the basic proportional categoricals? Yes, for two good reasons. First, any such basic categorical is "in between", logically speaking, two traditional categoricals in such a way that the corresponding universal entails it and it entails the corresponding particular. So, shouldn't the predicate of the "in between" proposition have the same distribution level that it has in the entailing and entailed propositions? For example:

(39) All S are P $\longrightarrow$ > 3/4 S are P $\longrightarrow$ Some S are P
No S are P $\longrightarrow$ Half S are not P $\longrightarrow$ Some S are not P.

Since "P" in the first *proportional* form in (39) occurs "between" (entailment-wise) two forms in which it is minimally distributed (first row), I conclude "P" is minimally distributed in ">3/4 S are P". Similarly, for the same term being maximally distributed in "Half the S are not P".

Second, the reasoning for "P" being maximally distributed in "Some S is not P" (justification via hamiltoned forms) applies to *every* form "Qm/n S are not P" ("Q" is ">" or "≥" and 1 > m/n > 0). For example,

(40) (>3/4 S are not P) $\longleftrightarrow$ (>3/4 S are not each P),

where the right-hand side is the hamiltoned version of the left. On the right side, "P" has the distribution indicator "each" which designates maximal distribution, ≥n/n. This applies repeatedly for every basic negative categorical with a proportional quantifier.

Similarly, for all affirmative proportionals. Each of their hamiltoned forms will reveal that their predicates have minimal distribution, >0/n.[18]

But now we can ask: What if a proposition occurs in an inference to be evaluated by the i-quantity rules, R1-R6, which is one of the hamiltoned forms in (39)? Obviously, wherever such a hamiltoned form occurs it must be replaced, for the sake of evaluating the inference, by an acceptable categorical—the result of applying the *inverse of* the hamilton function.

One problem remains—*mixed* forms, with the "is" of identity but with one *traditional* quantifier and one *proportional* quantifier. It is no surprise that their analysis is mixed as well. The affirmative variations all succumb to treatment as genuine Finch propositions (e.g., (41)), but the negatives do not. For neither of (42) are true.

(41) (>2/3 S are all P) ⟷ (>2/3 S are P) & (all P are S)
(All P are >2/3 S) ⟷ (All P are S) & (≥ 2/3 S are P)
(>2/3 S are some P) ⟷ (>2/3 S are P) & (some P are S)
(Some P are >2/3 S) ⟷ (Some P are S) & (>2/3 S are P).

(42) (>2/3 S are not some P) ⟷ (>2/3 S are non-P & Some P are non-S)
(>2/3 S are not each P) ⟷ (>2/3 S are non-P & Each P is non-S).

So, perhaps the negative mixed cases need *un*hamiltoning rather than *de*Finching. The first thing to notice, on this hypothesis, is that mixed cases with the traditional quantifier in the subject cannot plausibly be unhamiltoned (since proportions would disappear). So, to *try* unhamiltoning these, invert the forms where necessary. Secondly, there is no alternative to dropping the traditional quantifier from the grammatical predicate. For the left-hand sides of (42), for example, unhamiltoning produces:

(43) >2/3 S are not P.

This *is* reasonable when the quantifier dropped is universal (paralleling negative categoricals which had been hamiltoned). An example reveals the problem with negative mixed cases with *particular* quantity. Consider:

(44) More than 2/3 of the singers (S) are not all the pianists (P).
(45) More than 2/3 of the singers are not some of the pianists.
(46) More than 2/3 of the S are not some particular P (at least one).

Even though (44) can be equivalently expressed by (43), this is plausible for only some uses of (45). Reading "some" in (45) as "a" or "any", it is synonymous with (44). But (45) can be read as (46). (44) and (43) each entail the existence of Ss that are non-P. (46) *permits* the non-existence of S that are non-P. For example, if all and only S are P, but they are sub-divided into two groups of 21 and 9 (say, 9 Ms and 21 non-Ms), then (46) is true. For more than 2/3 (21 of 30) of the Ss are *distinct* from some particular P (viz., any one of the 9 Ms). But this reading is incompatible with the (43) reading of (45).

So, the i-quantity syllogistic can be extended to cover the occurrences of propositions that are mixed cases by unhamiltoning them if the traditional quantifier is universal and if the quantifier is particular on one reading of the sentence. On the other reading, (46), it might be hoped that deFinching applies. It doesn't. To try it, wide-scope of the particular quantifier must be recognized (cf. note 18) so the product of deFinching is:

(47) Some P are not S & >2/3 S are not P

But this can't be right, since each conjunct is incompatible with the truth conditions for (46) just given. So, there *is* one reading of negative mixed forms with particular quantity which simply cannot be transformed into forms the i-quantity syllogistic can accept.[19]

The fact that negative particular mixed forms do not always permit equivalent unhamiltoning (nor deFinching) does *not* disprove anything I have said about the i-quantity syllogistic. It only shows that empirical facts of English syntax and meaning are in control. The limits of logical analysis of English or any other natural language can be reached. However, these limits have been pushed back considerably with regard to analyzing sentences containing quantifiers expressing rational proportions in English—whether you take Johnson's formalistic (meta-theoretical) approach or my own (with Carnes') Aristotelian approach. And if you are particularly interested in the *empirical semantics* of natural language quantifiers, my advice is that you adopt the Aristotelian approach.[20]

Notes

1 Peterson 1995a was an earlier version of this chapter.

2 Johnson 1994 motivated me to try to give an Aristotelian alternative to his excellent extensions, which I return to in Section 3.

3 The "middle-quantifiers"—cf. Sections 5.2, 5.3, and note 17 of Chapter 2 above and Peterson 1985a, p. 354—should not be included in a purely fractional syllogistic. I use "fractional" in a narrower sense than Johnson does.

4 The k-quantity fractional syllogistic was introduced in Peterson and Carnes ms. and later appeared in Peterson 1985a; cf. Section 5.2 of Chapter 2 above. What is new here is the formulation and application of R1-R6.

5 I use the term "proportional" to acknowledge Finch (1957), about which cf. Peterson 1993a (drawn from Chapter 2 above).

6 He does not, however, consider doubly quantified propositions containing relations—such as "Half the students failed 3/4 of the tests". For how to begin to include such propositions, see Chapter 6 (not available when Peterson 1995a was published).

7 I have not *proved* this, since the English meanings are crucial. I hold that the reason the two sides of (26) are logically equivalent is that their meanings are identical. However, I don't need to *defend* this synonymy for anything in this chapter.

8 This analysis is drawn from (15)-(18) of Peterson 1993a (and Section 5.4 of Chapter 2 above).

9 Many syllogistic forms with negative subjects can be shown valid via appropriate replacements. For example, in "All non-M are P, All M are non-S, so All non-P are non-S", replace the first premise with its contrapositive and then replace "non-P" with "S" and "non-S" with "P" and a case of Barbara is obtained. But using such replacements does not amount to extending R1-R6 to negative subjects, but rather shows how to obtain substitute forms to which R1-R6 can apply. As far as I can tell, no such replacements for intermediate/ proportional categoricals with negative subjects exist. For one thing, the traditional immediate inference rules of obversion, conversion, and contraposition do *not* apply to intermediate/proportional categoricals (even though some immediate inferences for intermediates are valid—e.g., inferences read off various squares and reductions via (18)). I admire Williamson's (1971) treatment of negative terms. Although his techniques can save R1-R6 for traditional forms with negated subjects, I do not see how to apply them to intermediates/proportionals.

10 I speak of inference forms having T-forms. This is briefer than Johnson puts it. He says, for an inference-form "X, so y" ("X" premises and "y" conclusion), that {X, y*} is the set of premises and denial of conclusion. When this set is ordered in a certain way (as a "chain"), it may satisfy one of the five T-forms of Johnson's Theorem 1. Only five patterns of inconsistent <X, y*> satisfies one of the five T-forms. I say "X, so y" itself satisfies a T-form when its associated chain, <X, y*>, does.

11 Such a reader should note the following. What if there *is* some kind of evidence or argument for (a) a form being valid according to R1-R6, (b) the form not having, a T-form, and (c) the form still having premises and denial-of-

conclusion inconsistent? If such an example turns up, it might be as much evidence against Johnson's proofs as against the soundness of R1-R6 i-quantity-wise. Similarly, with respect to completeness, though in the reverse. Rather than finding too easy a *dis*proof of soundness, we might find too easy a proof of completeness. *And*, a further question: Do Johnson's natural deduction rules of inference (expansions of Smiley 1973) generate all and only the same deductions (valid inference forms) that R1-R6 do in the i-quantity system? The answer should be "yes", and understanding why it is ought to be revealing for R1-R6. (And, are Finch forms assimilable to Johnson's fractional syllogistic? Or could an example like (32) be a counter-example to Johnson's Theorem 1, as it appears to be to R1-R6?)

12 Williamson (1971) finds the culprit in distribution applied to universal-to-particular immediate inferences. Sommers (1975, 1982) has a quite different concept of distribution, which Englebretsen (1979, p. 117) uses on this example via treating it as an enthymeme (omitted premise "Some non-P are non-P").

13 "More than 3/4 of the musicians" is a quantifier *phrase*. "More than 3/4" is its quantity-expressing component, a *modifier* (logico-grammatically) of its component *term*, "musician "More than 3/4" refers to the distribution index >3/4. And "all" and the tacit universal-quantity component of "no" refer to the distribution index ≥n/n.

14 This is the usual account. I prefer another one—that "No S are P" is a direct expression of denial of the I-form, a contracted form of "Not any S are P", where the latter is the grammatical expression in English for explicit denial of the I-form. "Not some S are P" is not grammatical in English, even though "Not all S are P" is. But you *say* the former grammatically by replacing "some" with "any". ("Any" after "not" in English often *means* what "some" ordinarily does.) So, "No S is P" is an explicit denial of the categorical "Some S is P", just the way "Not all S are P" is an explicit denial of "All S are P". So, "No S are P"—contrary to the entire tradition in the history of logic *and* to current practice!!—is not a good candidate for expressing the E-form categorical. It is just as bad as saying, "Not all S are P" *is* the 0-form categorical. So, what *is* the E-form categorical? Simply "All S are *not* P". Emphasis is required in English so that the E-form won't be confused with the similar form pronounced with Shakespearean intonation, "*All* S *are* not P" (an alternative expression for the denial of the A-form). For more discussion, see Chapter 3 above.

15 There may be a Geach-like objection that distribution must be used to justify the validity of these inferences (about converted forms), so this test for distribution is circular. I reply that conversion is otherwise valid for E- and I-forms, via the algebraic semantics.

16 Finch's idea of quantifiers in the predicate is not new. Sir William Hamilton made the most of such quantifiers, leading to the controversy between him and De Morgan. P. Heath sums it up: "Bentham was the first writer in English to quantify the predicate, Hamilton the first to make any extensive use of it, and De

Morgan the first to grasp what it was all about. Since the result of [De Morgan's] investigation was to expose the hollowness of the claims that had been made for it, the dispute over priority has ceased, in any case, to be a matter of serious concern." (De Morgan 1966, p. xxiv). I have not herein been influenced by Hamilton or De Morgan (or Bentham either). Rather, I wonder whether looking at distribution and the syllogism as I propose might be used to cast new light on that debate. (Here's a start: only four of Hamilton & De Morgan's eight basic propositions are hamiltoned. The other four are what I would call "compounds", inequivalent to any traditional categorical. And all Finch propositions are similar to the compound "Some S are not some P" which De Morgan (mistakenly, as I see it) said has "no ordinary use" and "no denial".) (Also, see "Hamilton's Cube" in Chapter 6.)

17 I alternate "every", "each", and singular copula with "all" and plural copula to increase plausibility. Also, in negative Finch and hamiltoneds, it can be useful to replace "is/are not" with "is/are distinct from".

18 It is instructive to imagine the right side of (40) formalized as "$(>3/4Sx)[(\forall Py)[x \neq y]]$" just as "$(\exists Sx)[(\forall Py)[x \neq y]]$" is a restricted-quantifier notation for "Some S is not P" *after* hamiltoning. With this speculation, I can clear up a possible misunderstanding. Even though the "=" of predicate logic notation is appropriate for formalizing the "is" of identity mentioned above, still that does *not* mean an exchange of quantifier-positions in the notation corresponds to inversion in the English forms. (I refer to ordinary mathematical inversion, of functions and relations, *not* what Geach mentioned, as quoted above in Section 4.) This is important for the hamiltoned O-form. In English, it is "Some S is not each P". Schematizing the English yields "$>0/n$ S is-not $\geq n/n$ P". Both the English and the schematization are invertible yielding "Each P is not some S" and "$\geq n/n$ P is not $>0/n$ S". (An ambiguity arises with the inverted English. The side of it I am pursuing is where it is synonymous with "Each P is not some one (or more) particular S", *not* with "Each P is not any S" which is equivalent to "Each P is not S".) But the two forms of English and the two schematizations both have *exactly one* representation in predicate logic notation—e.g., "$(\exists Sx)[(\forall Py)[x \neq y]]$". So, quantifier scopes are not necessarily, nor usually, reversed via inversion in the English and schematizations. This may help to explain why I should *not* be understood to be advancing entailment-distribution vs. Geach; e.g., that the O-form entails, but is not entailed by, "Each P is such that some S is distinct from it", formalized "$(\forall Py)[(\exists Sx)[x \neq y]]$". I am *not* considering any variant of the argument wherein an entailed statement is found with predicate term transferred to grammatical subject. The relevant predicates "P" in negative categoricals, on my view, have the maximal distribution level *simply* because their explicitly present quantifier in *hamiltoned* forms designate that level!

[19] Actually, the merely apparent hamiltoneds which I call 'compounds' in Note 16 are also not covered. Something akin to deFinching them seems needed—but is only necessary, not sufficient, for affirmatives and is mistaken for negatives.

[20] I am grateful to Fred Johnson as I explained in note 2 and elsewhere above. As always on this topic, I have been importantly aided by Robert Carnes. Also, I have profited from Joel I. Friedman (via unpublished remarks; but cf. Friedman 1994) and from the anonymous reviewer of the original version of this chapter (for several important corrections and additions).

6 Reasonings About Relations[1]

The most efficient, accurate, and fruitful way to communicate reasonings is in natural languages. Use of formal systems, mathematical notations (in which all substantive advanced science appears to be expressed), new artificial languages, projected post-space-age "information-highway" networks, etc. are not improvements over natural language communication. My aim below is *not* to argue for or defend this thesis of natural language communicational superiority. Rather, I will just introduce one way to understand it further—a way which also contributes to showing how "natural language can be viewed as a Knowledge Representation system with its own representation and inferential machinery" (cf. AAAI program description associated with Peterson 1996).

The proper way to approach the question of how human reasoning is expressed and communicated in natural languages is *not* via contemporary applications of formal systems (first and/or higher order predicate caculii) or any analogous artificial language (from APL to PASCAL), but rather with *Aristotle's* syllogistic approach to logic. [And knowledge representation systems will significantly profit from adopting the Aristotelian approach. For example, it will illuminate and expand the complexity of denial and negation of expressible inferences as introduced by Iwanska (1993). Iwanska's eleven targets for logical negation (in eleven syntactic categories) will find a deeper explanation through the Aristotelian approach (though showing this is not part of my aims herein.)] For the Aristotelian concept of logical forms expressible in ordinary language statements (and strings of them in reasonings) is *directly* relatable to the surface grammatical forms found in many natural languages. It is easy to see that many *English* forms are completely amenable to Aristotelian analysis (as shown below). But remember that the syllogistic was not designed that way, but for Greek (and, through later developements, Latin). I *conjecture* (again, not a topic for explanation or defense herein) that Aristotelian analysis is as easy in (for and about) any natural language as it is in English, Greek, or Latin (or in French, German, or Spanish).

The basic syllogistic system is a method for analyzing the correctness of certain simple reasonings ("arguments") in which exactly three so-called "terms" are crucial, where each term is easily associatable with certain NPs and VPs in surface sentential structure. The idea is that the simplest kind of "move" of reasoning is to *conclude* a connection between two terms via two separate propositions—where the connection can be one of four types: all-are; none-are; some-are; and some-are-not. The kind of reasoning considered by Aristotle is the forging of a link between two terms (concepts, kinds, classifications, or categorizations of things) by finding some one thing each term can be separately linked *to* (the third, *middle* term). The form of the links are the again the four styles just mentioned for the conclusion: all-are; none-are; some-are; and some-are-not. One natural way to *represent* this forging of a link (that type of reasoning) is the traditional formal syllogism wherein there are two "premises" (each being one of the propositions linking one of the conclusion terms to the crucial middle term) and the aimed-for (single) conclusion—as follows:

Premise 1	All Some	P are (not) M M are (not) P
Premise 2	All Some	S are (not) M M are (not) S
Conclusion	All Some	S are (not) P

"Every" and "each" can be substituted for "all", with correlated adjustments of noun-verb number—when the term (S, P, or M position) that "all" is modifying is a *count*-term (i.e., expressible with a count noun). Also, sometimes nothing at all can be used for either "all" or "some"; e.g., "Whales are mammals" (i.e., all are) and "Elephants aggravate farmers" (i.e., some do). (Also, I simplify tradition by substituting throughout "All-not" forms for "No" forms; cf. Chapter 3 above.)

The Aristotelian rules of quality and distribution (rules of quantity being superfluous) are sound and complete methods for filtering out the 24 correct reasonings (valid syllogisms) from the 256 logical possibilities of Aristotelian syllogistic reasonings. Existential import of each term is adopted. That is, a presupposition of expressing a purely syllogistic reasoning is that some instance (at least one) of each of the terms (e.g., some singers for the term "singers") exist, where the presupposition relation is not a logical relation between propositions, but rather a 3-place relation between presupposer, proposition affirmed (or denied) and fact presupposed. Thus, when a presupposition of an assertion (or series of such in an expressed reasoning) is false, no proposition at all is asserted or expressed—often contrary to obvious appearances. An interesting detail is that some mass terms (the concrete ones, expressed via non-count nouns in English) also must have "instances" whose nature was not clear until H. Cartwright (1970) explained how they are "quantities" (in *her* sense of "quantities").

Now it has been often been concluded, and is still widely believed, that the narrow "straitjacket" of forms that the syllogistic system provides is not of much utility, practically or theoretically. Most expressed reasoning are just not of that form, and since so few forms (of a fairly small number, 256, of candidates) are valid, it seems very unlikely that the syllogistic methods can be of much use in describing and explaining all the reasonings expressible in natural languages. For one thing, as was long ago urged, syllogisms apparently can't even begin to handle *relations*—which predicate calculus (formal system) methods excel at. I disagree—though I admit that until recently not much had been done to show the utility of syllogistic methods for relations (with the almost lone exception of Sommers 1982). (Another reason for the low expectations of syllogistic methods was the *philosophical* confusion about relations—cf. Peterson 1990.)

The way in which the syllogism could actually be considered fundamental reasoning-wise is not often remembered; viz., that complex and complicated reasonings (about any subject matter whatever) can be broken down into syllogistic steps—each of which could be a valid syllogism. Two models illustrate what is at issue here—the "polysyllogism" (wherein several intermediate premises are produced via applying the syllogistic rules to appropriate premises of any many-premised argument and the final step produces a valid conclusion)—polysyllogisms with the intermediate conclusions unexpressed being "sorites"—and the "enthymeme" (where new premises needed to produce a valid syllogism must be hypothesized and added to given ones). Of course, there ought to be many other manners of extending the basic syllogistic system for analyzing complicated reasonings (in addition to polysyllogisms and enthymemes), *if* Aristotle is right—that the syllogism is the foundation of human logical reasoning.

Recent developments (Sommers, Englebretsen) have shown that the basic Aristotelian methods *can* be extended to relations. My own variation on how to extend the syllogism to relations is based on my applications of syllogistic methods of the 2-quantity (i.e., traditional universal and particular) system of Aristotle, first, to three more "intermediate" quantities, then, to finite numbers of additional intermediate quantities and, finally, to an *infinite* number of quantities (cf. Chapter 5 above).

Basic to the Aristotelian approach is the breaking down of negation and denial into two fundamental types—that labeled "contradictory" and that labeled "contrary" (and "sub-contrary") on the traditional square of opposition. This distinction is repeatedly exploited by all the developments presented above and below. The fruitfulness of it can be further demonstrated by noticing how it applies to Iwanska's "qualitative scales" (1993, p. 487). For example, consider the love-hate scale *re*conceived Aristotelianly as follows:

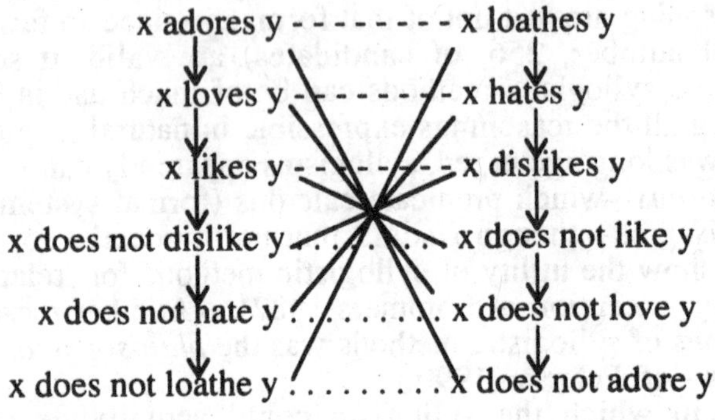

(where straight lines connect contradictories, dashes connect contraries, dots connect subcontraries, and arrows represent entailments). Making use of such negating characteristics for this kind of qualitative scale will, of course, depend on developing an Aristotelian account of relations (since the love-hate scale is relational), which is my main topic below. Adjective and adverb modifiers succumb similarly. For example (in sum),

x is a tall man —>* x is not a short (anti-tall) man
x ran slowly —>* x didn't run fast (anti-slow)
x is a very tall man —>* x is not a barely (anti-very) tall man
(where "—>*" =df. "entails but is not entailed by" and "anti-Ø" is one disambiguation of not-Ø"). See Chapter 4 above for typical complications due to embeddings.

Syllogistic systems just like the 5-quantity system for as "high" a number of intermediate quantities as you like can be constructed (Peterson & Carnes 1983 and Peterson 1985). Also, iterations of such quantifiers—such as expressed by "almost-all of 3/4" and "most of 1/2"—can be accommodated (Chapter 4 above). And some rivals turn out to be *unsound and incomplete*; cf. Carnes & Peterson 1991.

The *infinite-quantity* (iQ) syllogistic (Chapter 5 above; also Johnson 1994) is modeled on the traditional 2-quantity and the higher-quantity fractional systems. The intermediate quantities in iQ are *rational fractions* (<1) that are *intermediate proportions* between universal and particular. Categorical form is “Q S are(not) P”, where “Q” = “>1” (“every”), “>m/n” (integers n>m), “>m/n”, or “>0” (“some”).

(1) iQ square of opposition (schema for n>2m):

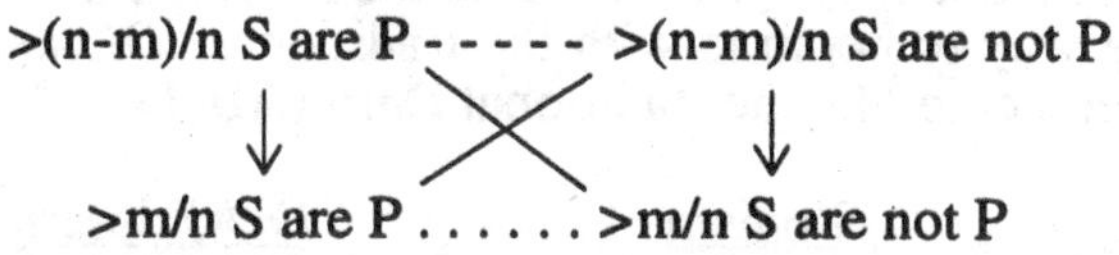

For “most”, “few”, and “many”, cf. Peterson 1979, 1985. When 2m>n, the schema flips, so that “≥n/n S are P” (=“All S are P”) is contrary (i.e., ---) to “≥n/n S are not-P” (=“All S are not-P”).

An argument form of iQ is valid if filtered by the following rules—extensions of the classical ones which I produced (Peterson 1995c) by revising (only slightly) R. Carnes' extensions of Aristotelian rules in Peterson & Carnes 1983 (and Chapter 2 above).

(2) Rules for iQ Syllogistic

Distribution

Rule 1: Sum of distribution indices (DIs) of middle terms is >1.
Rule 2: No DI of conclusion term > DI of same term in premises.

Quality

Rule 3: At least one premise is affirmative.
Rule 4: Conclusion is negative if and only if one premise is.

where DI(T) = explicit quantity of subject T; DI(T)= ≥1 for predicate Ts of negatives, DI(T)= >0 for predicate Ts of affirmatives; and DI(T_i + DI(T_k)=(G_i +G_k)(m_i/n_i + m_k/n_k) for “G” = “>“ or “≥” (when (>+>)= >, (>+≥)= >, and (≥+≥)= ≥) and G_im/n > G_ku/v iff m/n > u/v or G_i is > and G_k is ≥ when m/n = u/v).

Now to *relations*. The challenge today of extending Aristotle's methods (thus revealing how it can be the foundation for explaining all logically correct reasonings) is *not* just supplying suitable methods for formulating relational propositions for syllogistic (or syllogistic-like) analysis in reasonings in which they occur, but rather doing that for an extension of syllogistic to all possible intermediate quantities. In sum, we want to be able to easily represent reasonings containing all possible kinds of quantifiers. A very good start at this is achieved in the iQ syllogistic—a single syllogistic system with an infinite number of intermediate quantities (the rational fractions). (And further additions to quantifier-expressions were addressed above in Chapters 4 and 5.) So, I propose that an ambitious attempt at adding relations to syllogistic systems will add them not to the traditional 2-quantity system (or to any other finite-quantity system), but to the iQ system.

The way to begin is with the traditional "*Dictum de Omni*" (DDO). Consider a case like the traditional Darii (AII-1)

	syllogism	DDO description
(P1	All M are P	"is P" is said of *every* M
(P2)	Some S are M	.certain Ss are Ms
so,	Some S are P	so, "is P" can be said of those Ss

The idea is that what "is said" of each one of some kind—of the Ms in premise 1 (P1)—can be applied to any particular cases—the Ss that are Ms in P2. Here is my own reinterpretation (or reworking) of DDO, utilizing classical distribution (D), where "being-distributed" =df. "+D", and "not-being-distributed" = df. "–D". (Remember the new explication of distribution, in Chapter 5 above, where it is identified with quantificational *proportion*.)

(3) DDO^P . . . . . an interpretation of DDO:

	+D PRED	
(Darii-1)	All M [are P]	.the *source* premise (i.e., M must be +D)
	–D	
	Some S are M	the *target* premise (i.e., M must be –D)

To generate the valid conclusion, carry out these 3 steps:

1. *SUB*stitute PRED of the *source* for M in the *target* (where M must be –D),
   which => Some S are [are P]
2. *GRAM*maticalize the result of *SUB*,
   which => Some S are T [wh are P]
3. *RED*uce the result of *GRAM*,
   which => Some S are P

where: (i) *Q-order of source predicate is preserved* through SUB; and
(ii) If both premises have Ms that are +D, replace

one with something it entails that contains M which is –D.

VALIDITY:

V1. Any form generated by DDO^P is valid.

V2. Any form Y is valid, if it is exactly like a valid form X except that Y's conclusion is entailed by (or distinct but equivalent to) X's conclusion.

V3. Any form Y is valid, if it is exactly like a valid form X except that one premise of Y only entails (or is distinct but equivalent to) one of X's premises.

Since Q-order *must* be preserved, some results of SUB will have PRED first. For example, consider

Baroco(AOO-2): All P are M
Some S are not-M
so, Some S are not-P

Here the source is P2, because M is +D in it—i.e., P2 says something about *all* the M. (Although P1 says something about *all* the P, P is not the middle term and so not a candidate for a basis of substitution.) So, SUB is on P1, the target—which produces (with source predicate in SUB-product remaining in square brackets):

[Some S are not] All P are--

If the PRED "Some S are not--" (seemingly, a *new* variety of Aristotelian VP-predicate) were simply placed in the position "M" holds in P1, the result would be "All P are [what] some S are not" wherein quantifier-order of *source* ("some" first) is violated. And "All P are not (some) S" does not validly follow from Baroco's premises (since, for one thing, it violates the traditional second rule of quantity).

Then GRAM and RED produce

[Some S are not T] wh all P are

and Some S are not P.

GRAM may seem superfluous, but it will become crucial when DDO^P is extended to relational statements. Also, recognizing GRAM assists in relating syllogistic forms to surface forms of English (and with appropriate adjustments within GRAM, of other natural languages). In GRAM notice that the "T+wh" is crossing the source predicate right-hand bracket here, but crossing the left-hand bracket in (5) above, because of different position of source predicate—due to the need to retain quantifier-order of source. Further motives for GRAM appear below.

Why does REDuce produce such a result? Understanding the interplay of these components with elements of Hamilton's "Cube of Opposition" has been very helpful to me. For example, the RED step on Baroco above is easier to understand if the particular negative is remembered to be equivalent to "Some S ≠ all P", as Hamilton would have it. Here is (what *I* call) Hamilton's Cube of Oppositions (for why it's called a *"cube"*, see Peterson 1995b):

(4) Hamilton's Cube (i.e., 3 related squares)

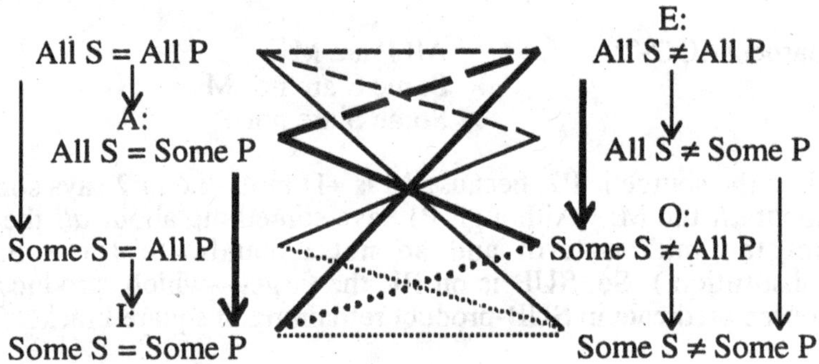

In sum, schematically: if All=All, not(All≠All); if All=All, not(All≠Some); if All=Some, not(All≠All).

To clarify DDO^P, and prepare for its applications and extensions below, it is helpful to look at a re-analysis of Baroco, wherein the *Hamiltoned* versions of each propositions are used:

Baroco(AOO-2) Hamiltoned: All P = some M
Some S ≠ all M /so, Some S ≠ all P
SUB on P1 => [Some S ≠] All P = some--
then GRAM => [Some S ≠ T] wh All P = some
then RED => Some S ≠ All P

Notice that if Q-order of the source predicate—"[Some S ≠]"—were not maintained (making "Some S" the grammatical predicate), then the SUB-result would read "All P = Some T[wh Some S ≠]" and the GRAM and

RED steps would produce "All P ≠ Some S". Then, *de*-Hamiltoning it together with its *de*Hamiltoned premises would be:

All P are M
<u>Some S are not M</u>
All P are not S (i.e., No P are S)

And this result, as mentioned above, violates the traditional second "rule of quantity" that if any premise is non-universal, then the conclusion is non-universal (about which see R6 of (5) in Chapter 5 above). By extending DDO to relations and multiple quantifier forms, we see that maintaining Q-order is evidently another way of maintaining the second rule of quantity.

Concerning some other forms: Celarent(1) is like Darii, but Celaront(1) requires V2 above. Festino(2) requires V3 (on P1 producing "All M are not P"). Fesapo(4) requires (ii) (on P2 producing "Some M are S"), V3 (on P1 producing "All P are not-M"), and V2 (from "Some which are not P are S").

DDO^I is DDO^P extended to iQ syllogisms. First, DDO^I *is* DDO^P, where every *intermediate* quantity (IQ)—e.g., ">3/4"—is treated as "some" (= ">0") is treated by DDO^P. So, consider every IQ *less* than "≥1" (i.e., "Gm/n", for n > m, "G" = ">" or "≥") to be -D (undistributed). Then, all forms in Figures 1, 2, and 4 for k-quantity systems (finite k; e.g., 5-quantity with 105 valids) succumb to DDO^P. But not *Figure 3!!*

In *Figure 3*, there are many valid forms where no M is +D (i.e., has DI ≥ 1). However, valid Figure 3 forms satisfy Rule 1 (sum of DI's of Ms > 1). So, at least one M must have DI of ">m/n" (2m > n). *So*, let the highest DI of an M (where Rule 1 *is* satisfied) play the role of being +D, and replace the IQ of M in the other premise with ">0" ("some") (which it entails). Then, the +D premise (one with highest DI of M) is the *source* for DDO^I and the other premise is the *target*.

(5) IQ examples for Figure 3:

```
                 -D                   -D
A. ≥>3/8 of the M are not P . . so, >0 M are not P      target
                 +D     PRED
   >3/4 of the M [are S] . . . (M with highest DI => +D) source
   ______________________              (similar to GPO-3)
                        PRED
   SUB=>          >0 [are S] are not P
   GRAM=>         Some T [wh are S] are not P
   RED=>     so,  Some S are not P
```

```
                          +D      PRED
B. TTI-3 (5Q)         Most M [are P] . . . . . selected source
                              -D
                      Most M are S . . . . . . so, Some M are S
                      ______________
SUB=>                 Some [are P] are S
  GRAM=>              Some T[wh are P] are S
  RED=>               Some P are S
                  so, Some S are P      (via V2)
```

I claim (conjecture) that DDO^{I} applies to iQ (infinite-quantity) syllogistic, as well as to every kQ syllogistic system (for finite k).

Now to DDO*, which is what I baptize DDO^{I} when it is extended to syllogistic-like arguments wherein one or more IQ-categoricals is replaced by a "basic relational categorical" (hereafter a "BRC"). (I have been especially inspired here by Sommers 1982 and Englebretsen 1992, though I depart from both.) BRC forms are either simple or complex:

(6) BRC Form:

Simple: Q_i T_i (are) R (to) Q_j T_j e.g., Every boy loves >3/4 of the girls;

Complex (n-level, here n=2):

Q_i T_i [wh (are)R(to) Q_k T_k] (are) R (to) Q_j T_j [wh Q_l T_l (are)R(to)]

e.g. , Every singer who loves some poet hates every musician some critic knows.

BRC forms are generated by the following PS-grammar:

(7) BRC Grammar (here only "—>" represents grammatical PS rule)

S —> NP VP	VP—> V NP (PP)
NP—> QT	VP—> NP V (PP)
T—> (T) S*	V—> V NP (for n-place R, n>2)
S* —> wh VP	PP—> PrepNP [ignored herein]

T—> S, P, M, singer, poet, girl, picture, snow, etc.;
V—> R, R', R'', is, loves, hates, saw, touched, found, etc.

The *terms* in syllogisms containing BRC forms are *atomic* (the simple Ts of G(BRC)) and *molecular*—e.g., forms like (T)(wh every T is R to), and VPs. Note that relations themselves ("R"s above) are not terms even though they relate terms and play various roles in molecular terms.

The adjustments required to turn DDO^{I} into DDO* are revealed in the following examples:

(8) DDO* EXAMPLES

                    +D   PRED
Hamiltoned Darii: Every M [is some P] . . . . source
("=", a relation)   -D
                    Some S is some M . . . . target

SUB=>   Some S is some [is some P]
GRAM=>   Some S is some T[wh is some P]
RED=>   so, Some S is (=) some P

Look at the same form with "drew" and "saw" replacing "=":

                    +D   PRED
                    Every M [drew some P] . . . . . . source
                                -D
                    Some S saw some M . . . . target

SUB=>   Some S saw some [drew some P]
GRAM=>   Some S saw some T[wh drew some P]
RED=>   so, Some S saw some -one/-M who drew some P

(9) Q-order example:

Some girl loves every boy. So, Each boy, some girl loves.

as in "(SOME-Gx)[(EACH-By) x loves y]" entails
but is not entailed by "(EACH-By)[(SOME-Gx) x loves y]"

An *enthymeme* (!)   -D . . . . . . a VP M-term
               Some G [each B loves] . . . . target
                    PRED   +D . . VP M-term
          [Each B loves] each(one) [each B loves] . . . source
SUB=>   [Each B loves] (Some G---) . . . . (PRED is first to maintain Q-order source predicate)
GRAM=>   [Each B loves T] wh some girl (is)
RED=>   Each B loves some girl

It is important to realize that the suppressed premise is the BRC

(Each B) loves (each one that (each boy loves)) . . .
form: Q B is R to (Q T (wh Q B are R to))

For then the required +D term (due to its quantifier "Each one that") has the needed source predicate "[(each B) loves--]" which is SUBed into the target (with Q of source predicate first). If the source were taken to be the product of a certain grammatical transformation,

"Each one that (each boy loves) each boy loves" =>
"Each boy loves, each one that each boy loves"
(parallel to "Each Athenian is a Greek" => "A Greek, each Athenian is" or "A Greek is each Athenian"),

then the *un*transformed version would appear to be available as a source (or even be the proper source). But that form does not have the needed Q first predicate—since it is

+D
"Each one that (each boy loves) [each boy loves]".

(But see the discussion in (II) at the end below.) Further, using the latter in SUB would only produce

"Some G each B loves"

which is what P1 already is. (The question of some suppressed analytic premise *possibly* leading to violation of the traditional second rule of quantity must eventually be faced. See the related comments in (I) below.)

In both (9) and (10), the suppressed premise is analytic and/or logically (trivially) true, but in (9) it is a source and in (10) it is a target!

(10) *"Heads of Horses"* Syllogisms:

Easy case . . . All horses are animals. So, all heads of horses are heads of animals.

i.e., an enthymeme: +D PRED
All horses [are animals] . . . . *source*
-D
All T[wh is-head-of some horse] is-head-of some horse
. . . . *target* (suppressed)

SUB => All T[wh is-head-of some horse) is-head-of
some [are animals]
GRAM => All T[wh is-head-of some horse] is-head-of
some T[wh are animals]
RED => so, All heads of horses are heads of some animals

Harder case . . . Almost-all horses eat some apples.
So, all heads of almost-all horses are heads of something
that eat apples [...heads of some apple eaters]

Enthymeme again: +D? PRED
Almost-all H [eat some apples] . . . . source
+D?
All heads of almost-all H are heads of almost-all H . . . . target

Like Figure 3 (discussed in (5) above) , first adjust second (suppressed) premise:

-D
=> All heads of almost-all H are heads of *some* H

then:

SUB=> All heads of almost-all H are heads of some [eat some apples]
(Q-order is maintained because "some apples" of source predicate is grammatical *object*—and so "last".)
GRAM=> All heads of almost-all H are heads of some T[wh eats some apples]
RED=> so, All heads of almost-all H are heads of something which eats apples [some apple eaters]

The challenge of applying DDO* to all BRCs requires specifying +D (i.e., distributedness, D-value) for all varieties of Ts (terms)—simple and molecular, at any level of embedding. For potential targets and sources for DDO* are M-terms (simple and molecular); i.e., targets contain Ms that are -D and sources Ms that are +D. For an *embedded* term T, its D-value is a function of the Q which immediately precedes it (commands it, grammatically)—for the most part. The question concerns structures like:

(QQ) Q_iT_i [wh + R + Q_j T_j]...e.g., some M who swallowed each S
Q_i T_i [wh + Q_jT_j + R]...e.g., every M which some P chased

For *non*-embedded T (and for T *initially* in some BRC structure),

(DV-1) If QT is "every(>1) T", D-value of T is +D
If QT is "some(>0) T", D-value of T is -D

If QT is "Gm/n T" ("G"=">" or "≥", n>m), D-value of T is -D (derives entirely from above material)

Does the nature (D-value) of the "higher" T—i.e., T_i with respect to T_j in (QQ)—over-ride the D-value for the "lower" term, T_j? Yes, and no. For T_i and T_j of (QQ),

(DV-2) (a) if T_i is -D and T_j is +D, then T_j remains +D (still a source), and

(b) if T_i is -D and T_j is -D, then T_j remains -D.

However,

(c) if T_i is +D and T_j is -D, then T_j *changes* to +D (a source!)

(d) if T_i is +D and T_j is +D, then T_j *changes* to -D (but retain Q_j, since if part of target, it remains)

Here are some relational syllogisms illustrating (a)-(d)—where (a) and (b) are valid and (c) and (d) cases are as marked:

(a) Some G who loves each B is F
Each M is B
so, [Some G who loves--is F] Each M-- . . . . .via SUB
so, [Some G who loves T is F] wh T each M is . . . . . .via GRAM
so, Some G who loves each M is F . . . . .via RED
(Since the source predicate has "Some G" in grammatical subject, i.e., first, it cannot be placed after "Each M" via SUB.)

(b) Some G who loves some B is H
All B are M
so, Some G who loves some M is H

(c1) Each G who loves some B is H
Some B is M
Each G who loves some M is H . . . . INVALID

(c2) Each G who loves some B is H . . . B is +D via DV-2 (so, middle
Each B is M distributed twice and there is no target)
so, Each G who loves some M is H . . . . INVALID

(c3) Each G who loves some B is H
Each M is B . . . . cf. P2 of (c2)
so, Each G who loves something each M is is H . . . . . VALID

(d1) Each G who loves each B is H . . . . . . (so, "B" is no source)
<u>Some B is M</u>
so, Each G who loves some M is H . . . . INVALID

(d2) Each G who loves each B is H (so, "B" is a target)
<u>Each B is M</u>
so, Each G who loves each M is H . . . . VALID

(d3) Each G who loves each B is H . . . . .B is -D via DV-2 (so,
<u>Each M is B</u> middle is undistributed!)
so, Each G who loves each M is H . . . . INVALID

(a) and (b) are straightforward, illustrating applications of DDO* that were to be expected. However, each of the (c) and (d) examples are unexpectedly surprising and intriguing. On first viewing (c1), prior to the introduction and discussion of (QQ) above, the reason it would be thought to be invalid would be that there is no source for "B" (the middle term) in it. Since both occurrences of "B" are seemingly undistributed (have the quantifier-proportion of "some"), no proper link can be found to derive the conclusion (which is confirmed by applying the predicate calculus). This turns out to be the wrong diagnosis when we go on to (c2)-(d3). Again, on *first* viewing, (c2) can appear to be *valid*. For P2 of it says something about *all* the Bs and what's said (that each is M) is simply substituted in the conclusion. But (c2) is *in*valid, as confirmed by the predicate calculus. And, (c3) looks *in*valid, though predicate calculus testing shows it to be *valid*.

DV-2 explains (c2) and (c3), though not quite (c1). For in (c3), P1 becomes a source, since "B" in its P1 is *changed* to +D by DV-2. And "B" in P2 of (c3) is -D, so that P2 is a target. Thus, the derivation of (c3)'s conclusions is as follows:

(c3) Each G who loves some B is H
<u>Each M is B</u>
SU B=> [Each G who loves some--is H] Each M is--
GRAM=> [Each G who loves some T is H]wh Each M is
RED=> Each G who loves something(-one) which each M is is H

A very interesting aspect of this example is that the product of RED, (c3)'s conclusion is not equivalent to another conclusion which might be thought be the desired one—viz., "Each G who loves some M is H", which is validly derived via the predicate calculus. Is this a defect—that DDO* does not produce what the predicate calculus does? Well, first notice that this predicate-calculus-conclusion entails, but is not entailed by, (c3)'s conclusion (although E-import(!) on "M" is required in the derivation). (E-import is never a drawback on this Aristotelian approach, but a characteristic virtue.) Rather than a flaw of DDO*, I conclude that a subtlety has been unearthed. For (c3)'s conclusion is also valid in the predicate calculus. Thus, "Each G who loves some M is H" is an intermediate conclusion in the predicate calculus derivation of what DDO* produces.

DV-2 also explains the *in*validity of (c2). For with "B" in P1 of (c2) changing to +D, we see that (c2) has *only* sources for "B" and no targets (since "B" in P2 is also a source). So, DDO* does not apply to generate (c2)'s conclusion.

So, why is (c1) invalid? Doesn't it *appear* to be valid? And doesn't DDO* generate its conclusion—as follows?

(c1)	Each G who loves some B is H
	<u>Some B is M</u>
SUB=>	[Each G who loves some--is H]Some--is M
GRAM=>	[Each G who loves some T is H]wh is M
RED=>	Each G who loves some M is H . . . . so, VALID?

Some adjustment or restriction to DV-2 is obviously needed, since (c1) *is not valid* (especially as confirmed by the predicate calculus). The first thing to realize is that (c1) violates the second rule of quantity (no universal conclusion validly follows if one premise is non-universal). In many other cases above, attention to Q-order produced satisfaction of the rule. But here, surprisingly, it does not. In fact, enforcing Q-order produces invalidity. Although I think a more sophisticated resolution of this problem will eventually be discovered, for now I can re-institute officially the supposedly dispensable second rule of quantity (an inelegant stopgap, I admit).

The (d) cases are more satisfying. (d1) does not have the problems that (c1) does. If we ignore restriction (d) of DV-2, then it would appear that P1 in (d1) is a source for "B" and P2 its target. Then preserving Q-order of source predicate would generate the conclusion. But (d1) is invalid (e.g., via predicate calculus). So, restriction (d) *is* required. "B"s D-value in P1 changes to -D. Then we have no source and SUB can't apply (as it shouldn't).

It is interesting to note that (d2) and (d3) have conclusions that reverse the pattern of (c2) and (c3). That is, with the B+M order of P2 in (d2), the form is valid, whereas that order of P2 in (c2) produces invalidity. And with the M+B order of P2 in (d3), the form is invalid, whereas that order of P2 in (c3) produces validity.

Also, "higher" predicate (T_is) D-values are not affected by "lower" predicate (T_js) D-value. For example, (d4) and (d5) are both valid:

(d4) Each G who loves each B is H
Some G is P
SUB => Some [who loves each B is H] is P
GRAM => Some T [wh if it loves each B is H] is P
RED => Someone who if she loves each B is H is P
(where GRAM is assisted by interpolating exportation)

(d5) Each G who loves some B is H
Some G is P
Some one who if she loves some B is H is P

Of course, (d6) is invalid, since it contains no target:

(d6) Each G who loves each B is H
Each G is P
Each P who loves each B is H

Further, (e1) and (e2) are valid, so "G" in their P1s is unaffected by "lower" (i.e., "B"s) D-value:

(e1) Some G who loves each B is H
Each G is P
so, Some P who loves each B is H

(e2) Some G who loves some B is H
Each G is P
so, Some P who loves some B is H

Here are four considerations important to solving the problems raised by (c1):

(I) Notice that *some* non-universal proposition ought to be deducible from (c1)'s premises. Here is one such inference (confirmable by the predicate calculus):

(c1.1) Each G who loves some B is H
Some B is M
so, Some M is such that each G who loves it is H . . . . . VALID!

(c1) is invalid even though it satisfies DDO* and DV-2, whereas (c1.1) is valid even though it *violates* Q-order in applying SUB. Since satisfying the second rule of quantity is often achieved by enforcing Q-order of source predicate, the second rule is obviously intimately involved in DDO*. Perhaps a further refinement to DDO* will result from specifying the condition under which Q-order should be violated (preserving validity), such as when applying it violates the second rule of quantity *and* an appropriate universal+particular to particular extended (valid) syllogism can be generated.

(II) Q-order retention can be confusing. (f1) is a very straightforward result of DDO*, but (f2) is deceptive.

(f1) Each A [loves each B]
Some A is C
so, Someone who loves each B is C

(f2) Each A [each B loves]
Some A is C
SUB=> [Each B loves]Some--is C
GRAM=>[Each B loves T]wh is some C
RED=> Each B loves some (-thing which is some) C

For (f1) is valid and (f2) is *not*! (Try these forms with "B"="Belgian", "A"="Alsatian", and "C"="cheerful". The difference between these two inferences is in P1. In (f1) Alsatians love Belgians, and in (f2) Belgians love Alsatians.) *One* way we know that (f2) is invalid is via the second rule of quantity (a universal can't be inferred from a universal and non-universal). However, it is not difficult to see what is going *wrong* with the application of DDO* in (f2). It appears that "each B" is logically first in the source predicate of P1, but that is due to unwarranted restriction of logical order to just the source predicate itself. The logical order required by SUB is order (e.g., widest quantifier-scope) in regard to the *whole* of the source premise in P1. In that whole premise, "each A" is first (widest scope), and "each B" is embedded in the grammatical predicate (VP). So, though "first" within the source predicate (VP), "each B" is not "first" in the whole source. Rather, it is directly analogous to an object-of-the-verb quantifier phrase—as in the sentence "Each A is loved by each B" (a sentence synonymous, by some lights, with P1). Thus, SUB in (f2) is wrongly applied. The source does not have a "quantifier-first" form, but only an embedded one. The correct application of DDO*, then, to the premises of (f2) is:

(f3) Each A [(each B loves]
Some A is C
SUB=> Some [(that) each B loves] is C
GRAM=> Some T[wh each B loves] is C
RED=> Someone who each B loves is C

And (f3) satisfies, thereby (and without explicit attention), the second rule of quantity.

(III) The following two inferences appear very similar, but the first (g1) is valid and the second (g2) is not—contrary, in both cases perhaps, to first appearances. (Try "B" = "Barbarian", "G" = "Greek", and "A" ="Athenian")

(g1) Socrates saw each B who loves some G
Each A is G
so, Socrates saw each B who loves something(-one) each A is
(Parallel to (c3) vs. (c2) above, it is a misleading appearance that the obverse of P2 here is required for validity!)

(g2) Each B loves some G
Each A is G
so, Each B loves some A

Perhaps, (g2) appears at first to *be* invalid, but after noting its embedding in (g1) *and* the validity of (g1), it would be re-assessed as valid. But that's wrong. (g2) remains invalid. For SUB won't apply to (g2), since "G" is -D in both premises (and "some G" in P1 is not a (QQ) case). But SUB does apply in P1 of (g1) because "G" there changes to +D and is, thereby, source. And, as was mentioned for (c3) above, there is an intermediate conclusion in the associated predicate calculus derivation—viz., "Socrates saw each B who loves some A" which properly entails (via E-import on "A") (g1)'s conclusion, "Socrates saw each B who loves something (-one) which each A is". More importantly, (g1)'s parallel to (c3) suggests that embedded (QQ) cases will function logically the samc no matter what their argument position (grammatical subject, grammatical object, or other).

(IV) It is important to realize that there are further contrasts like (g1) vs. (g2). For example, although (in predicate calculus)

(h1) "Each G who loves some B is H" entails
(with E-import on "B"), but is not entailed by,
"Each G who loves something which each B is is H"

still the unembedded form is the opposite:

(h2) "Each G loves something which each B is" entails
(with E-import on "B"), but is not entailed by,
"Each G loves some M"

Then, some observers will find it soothing to say that the D-value reversals in DV-2 are simply the result of this (h1)-(h2) difference together, perhaps, with the equivalences from the predicate calculus:

$$(x)((\exists y)Rxy \longrightarrow \emptyset) \longleftrightarrow (x)(y)(Rxy \longrightarrow \emptyset)$$

Fine! But this seems only to apply to (c) cases, not the (d) cases. What is similarly soothing to say about them? Finally, notice that the (h1)-(h2) contrast can be carried even further ("=>*" = "entails (often via E-import) & is not entailed by"):

(h1.1) "Each G who loves some B is H"
=>* "Each G who loves each B is H"
=>* "Each G who loves something which each B is is H"

(h2.1) "Each G loves something which each B is"
=>* "Each G loves each B"
=>* "Each G loves some B"

And (h2.1) ought to be expected from the Hamilton Cube discussed above! (Such immediate inferences have a syllogistic explanation via enthymemes. The suppressed premise in (h2) is "Each thing which is each B is is B". The suppressed premise in (h1) is "Each G who loves something which each B is is a G who loves some B". Each of these suppressed premises are analytic or logical truths, provable in predicate calculus with E-import on "B".)

Obviously, refinement of DDO* is needed. It appears to me that Q-order requirements *vis à vis* the second rule of quantity is the locus of the problems with (c1) and (c1.1), about which I judge cautious optimism to be warranted given all the other successes with DV-2 in (d1)-(g2).

So, the present challenges for further research on it include the following:

A. Do iterations (repeated embeddings) satisfy these apparent restrictions —and/or raise no new difficulties—for DDO* (concerning candidates for sources and targets)?

B. Do IQs, and/or iQ syllogistic forms, in BRC "syllogisms" disconfirm DDO* as so far described?

C. Do embedded terms due to n-place relations, n>2 (via PS-Grammar of (9) above) raise any new problems for applying DDO*? (It is promising that (g1) shows that rudimentary application of DV-2 to grammatical objects is satisfactory.)

D. Do VP-modifiers (presumably adverbial phrases, not included in PSG of (9) above, introducing further clauses with atomic and molecular terms) succumb to these techniques (refinements of DDO*)? (E.g., "Each athlete ran slower than some race horse trotted.")

E. Do clausal NPs (not included in PSG of (9) above) succumb to these techniques? (E.g., "The man who saw Mary realized that all the bottles were empty" vs. "The man who saw Mary leave realized that all the bottles were empty" and "The man who hoped that Mary left realized that all the bottles were empty.")

Note

1 I am particularly grateful to George Englebretsen for drawing my attention to an important mistake in earlier versions of this chapter. Also helpful was additional discussion with Englebretsen, Joel Friedman, and Fred Johnson on the Round Table on Recent Developments in Syllogistic Logic, 20th World Philosophy Congress, Boston, August 13, 1998.

Bibliography

Angell, Richard B. *Reasoning and Logic*. Appleton-Century-Crofts, 1964.

Barwise, John and Cooper, Robin. "Generalized Quantifiers and Natural Language." *Linguistics and Philosophy*, 1981, *4*, 159-219.

Bird, Otto. *Syllogistic and its Extensions*. Prentice Hall, 1964.

Brown, Mark. "Generalized Quantifiers and the Square of Opposition." *Notre Dame Journal of Formal Logic*, 1984, *25*(4), 303-322.

Carnes, Robert D. and Peterson, Philip L. "Intermediate Quantifiers *Versus* Percentages." *Notre Dame Journal of Formal Logic*, 1991, *32*(2), 294-306.

Cartwright, Helen. "Quantities." *Philosophical Review*, 1970, *69*, 25-45.

____________. "Some Remarks About Mass Nouns and Plurals." Abstract in *Journal of Philosophy*, *69*(19), 1972, p. 680.

Cohen, L. J. "Can Human Irrationality be Experimentally Demonstrated." *Behavioral & Brain Sciences*, 1981, *4*, 317-370.

Copi, Irving. *Introduction to Logic*. Macmillan, Editions 1-9, 1953-1994.

De Morgan, Augustus. (P. Heath, ed.) *On the Syllogism*. Yale University Press, 1966.

Englebretsen, George. "Notes on the New Syllogistic." *Logique et Analyse*, 1979, *85-86*, 111-120.

____________. "Linear Diagrams for Syllogistic (with Relationals)." *Notre Dame Journal of Formal Logic*, 1992. *33*(1), 37-69.

____________. *Something to Reckon With*. University of Ottawa Press, 1996.

Finch, Henry A. "Validity Rules for Proportionally Quantified Syllogisms." *Philosophy of Science*, 1957, *24*(1), 1-18.

Friedman, Joel. "Towards an Adequate Definition of Distribution for First-Order Logic." *Journal of Philosophical Logic*, 1994, .

Geach, Peter T. "The Doctrine of Distribution." *Mind*, 1956, *65*, 67-74.

____________. "Distribution: A Last Word." *Philosophical Review*, 1960, *59*, 396-398. (Also in Geach 1972.)

____________. *Reference and Generality*. Cornell University Press, 1962.

____________. *Logic Matters*. Blackwell, 1972.

____________. *Reason and Argument*. University of California Press, 1976. (Chapter 13.)

Goldman, Alvin. *Epistemology and Cognition*. Harvard University Press, 1986.

Goodman. Nelson. *Fact, Fiction, and Forecast*. (Second Edition) Bobbs-Merrill, 1965.

Iwanska, Lucja. "Logical Reasoning in Natural Language: It is All about Knowledge." *Minds and Machines*, 1993, *3*(4), 475-510.

Jackendoff, Ray. *Semantics and Cognition*. MIT Press, 1983.

Johnson, Fred. "Syllogisms with Fractional Quantifiers." *Journal of Philosophical Logic*, 1994, *23*, 401-422.

____________. "Three-Membered Domains for Aristotle's Syllogistic." *Studia Logica*, 1991, *50*(2), 181-187.

Keynes, John Neville. *Formal Logic*. Macmillan, 1887.

Kripke, Saul. *Naming and Necessity*. Harvard University Press, 1979.

Lemon, E. J. *Beginning Logic*. Thomas Nelson, 1965.

Linebarger, M. "Polarity *Any* as an Existential Quantifier." *Papers from the 16th Regional Meeting of the Chicago Linguistic Society*, 1980, *16*, 211-219.

Lukasiewicz, Jan. *Aristotle's Syllogistic*. Oxford, 1957.

McCawley, James. *Everything that Linguists Have Always Wanted to Know About Logic*. University of Chicago Press, 1981a.

____________. "The Syntax and Semantics of English Relative Clauses." *Lingua*, 1981b, *53*, 99-149.

Peterson, Philip L. *Concepts and Language*. Mouton 1973.

____________. "On the Logic of 'Few', 'Many', and 'Most'." *Notre Dame Journal of Formal Logic*, 1979a, *20*, 155-179.

____________. "On Representing Event Reference." In *Presupposition* (C. K. Oh and D. Dinneen, eds.). Volume 11 of *Syntax and Semantics*. Academic Press, 1979b.

____________. "Philosophy of Language." *Social Research*, 1980(-81), *47*, (4), 155-179.

____________. "What Causes Effects?" *Philosophical Studies*, 1981a, 39, 107-139.

____________. "Intermediate Quantifiers." Read to the Annual Meeting of the Linguistic Society of America, New York, N.Y., December 28, 1981b.

____________. "Real Syllogisms Permit Five Quantities." Read to the 17th World Philosophy Congress, Montreal, August 25, 1983a.

____________. "Numerical Quantifiers and the Syllogism." Read to the 7th International Congress on Logic, Methodology, and the Philosophy of Science, Salzberg, July 14, 1983b.

____________. "Semantic Indeterminacy and Scientific Underdetermina-tion." *Philosophy of Science*, 1984, *51*, 464-487.

____________. "Higher Quantity Syllogisms." *Notre Dame Journal of Formal Logic*, 1985a, *26*(4), 348-360.

____________. "Event." (with Kashi Wali) *Linguistic Analysis*, 1985b, *15*(1) 3-18.

____________. "Intermediate Quantifiers and the Syllogism." Read to the Institut fuer Philosophie, Universitaet Salzburg, July 3, 1985c.

____________. "Real Logic in Philosophy." *The Monist*, 1986, *69*(2), 236-263.

__________. "Syllogistic Logic and the Grammar of Some English Quantifiers." Indiana University Linguistics Club Publications, May 1988.

__________. "Logic Knowledge." *The Monist*, 1989, *72*(1), 78-116.

__________. Critical Notice of *An Essay on Facts* (by K. R. Olson). *Philosophy and Phenomenological Research*, 1990, *50*(3), 610-615.

__________. "Complexly Fractionated Syllogistic Quantifiers." *Journal of Philosophical Logic*, 1991a, *20*, 287-313.

__________. "What is Empirical in Mathematics?" *Philosophia Mathematica*, 1991b, *6*(1), 91-109

__________. "Intermediate Quantifiers for Finch's Proportions." *Notre Dame Journal of Formal Logic*, 1993a, *34*(1), 140-149.

__________. "Logical Negation in English?" *Logique et Analyse*, 1993b, *141-2*, 121-134.

__________. "Distribution and Proportion." *Journal of Philosophical Logic*, 1995a, *24*, 1-33.

__________. "Contraries and the Cubes and Disks of Opposition." *Metaphilosophy*, 1995b, *26*(1), 107-137.

__________. "Are Some *Propositions* Empirically Necessary?" *Philosophy and Phenomenological Research*, 1995c, *55*(2), 251-277.

__________. "Basic Relational Infinite-Quantity Syllogisms." Section 5: Philosophical Logic. 10th International Congress of Logic, Methodology, and the Philosophy of Science, August 19-25, 1995, Florence, Italy. 5 pm Tuesday, Room A1, Palazzo Degli Affari, August 22, 1995d.

__________. "How to Use Aristotelian Logic to Formalize Reasonings." Proceedings of the AAAI-96 Symposium on *Knowledge Representations Systems Based on Natural Language*, Massachusetts Institute of Technology, November 9-11, 1996a, pp. 106-119.

__________. "Singular (Non-)Existence Propositions." *Acta Analytica*, 1996b, *15*, 45-65.

__________. *Fact Proposition Event*. Kluwer (Studies in Linguistics and Philosophy, Number 66), 1997a.

__________. "Kripke on Reference and Mind." *Cogito*, 1997b, *11*(3), 183-191.

__________. "Human Reasonings about Relations." Presented at the Round Table On Recent Developments in Syllogistic Logic, 20th World Philosophy Congress, Boston, Massachusetts, August 13, 1998.

Peterson, Philip L. and Carnes, Robert D. "Syllogistic Systems with Five or More Quantities." Read to the Annual Meetings of the Association for Symbolic Logic, January 7, 1983. (Abstract: *Journal of Symbolic Logic*, 1984, *49*(2), 680.)

Prior, A. N. *The Doctrine of Propositions and Terms*. University of Massachusetts Press, 1976.

Putnam, Hilary. "The Meaning of 'Meaning'." In K. Gunderson (ed.) *Language, Mind, and Knowledge.* Minnesota Studies in the Philosophy of Science, VII. University of Minnesota Press, 1975.

Rawls, John. *A Theory of Justice.* Harvard University Press, 1971.

Rescher, N. and Gallagher, N. "Venn Diagrams for Plurative Syllogisms." *Philosophical Studies*, 1965, *16*(4), 49-55.

Resnick, Michael D. "Logic: Normative or Descriptive? The Ethics of Belief or a Branch of Psychology?" *Philosophy of Science,* 1985, *52*, 221-238.

Smiley, T. J. "What is a Syllogism?" *Journal of Philosophical Logic,* 1973, *2*, 130-154.

Sommers, Fred. "Distribution Matters." *Mind,* 1975, *84*(333), 27-46.

___________. *The Logic of Natural Language.* Clarendon Press, 1982.

Strawson, Peter F. *Introduction to Logical Theory.* Metheun, 1957.

Thom, Paul. *The Syllogism.* Philosophia Verlag, 1981.

Thompson, Bruce E. "Syllogisms Using 'Few', 'Many', and 'Most'." *Notre Dame Journal of Formal Logic*, 1982, *23*, 75-84.

___________. "Syllogisms with Statistical Quantifiers." *Notre Dame Journal of Formal Logic*, 1986, *27*(1), 93-103.

Vendler, Z. *Linguistics in Philosophy.* Cornell University Press, 1967.

Williamson, C. "Traditional Logic as a Logic of Distribution Values." *Logique et Analyse,* 1971, *56*, 729-746.

Index